· J O U R N E Y ·

· T H R O U G H ·

· J U D A I S M ·

The Best of KEEPING POSTED

edited by

A L A N D . B E N N E T T

UAHC Press
New York, New York

To Florence
with love and esteem

Library of Congress Cataloging-in-Publication Data
Journey through Judaism: the best of Keeping posted/ [compiled] by Alan D. Bennett
p. cm.
Includes bibliographical references and index.
Summary: A collection of readings selected to enhance the new directions of
Reform Jewish education covering such areas as "The Jew and the Law,"
"Of Jews and Languages," and "A Jew Congregates with Other Jews."
ISBN 0-8074-0311-3: $12.00
1. Judaism. 2. Jews–Civilization. 3. Reform Judaism–United States.
[1. Reform Judaism. 2. Judaism.] I. Bennett, Alan D. II. Keeping posted (New York)
BM42.J68 1991
296.8'346–dc20   √ 90-19938
CIP
AC
This book is printed on recycled paper

DESIGNED BY JACK JAGET

▪ CONTENTS ▪

Preface v

Introduction vii

▪ PREFACE ▪

I've had a love affair with *Keeping Posted* magazine for over twenty years. It began in 1967 when Edith Samuel ז״ל invited me to write the teacher's guide for what was then a monthly magazine of Jewish news. Edith was a stern editor who offered, along with a friendship that lasted to her death, the bonus of delightful hours with her husband, Maurice Samuel ז״ל. By 1970, after fifteen years, *Keeping Posted* had served its historic purpose as a news magazine for Jewish teenagers. Edith proposed instead a publication to bring Jewish issues to teen and adult audiences and to present those discussions in a high quality format. The teacher's guide evolved into a leader's guide, in recognition that use of the new journal would not be limited to Jewish classrooms.

Edith will be long remembered for her pioneer work with *Keeping Posted*; her innovative approaches to adult Jewish learning; her charm, wit, and editing skills. I am grateful for having worked by her side.

God provides for people in wonderful ways. The void left by Edith's untimely death was soon filled by Aron Hirt-Manheimer. Quietly, competently, he began to build on his predecessor's legacy and soon carried *Keeping Posted* to new heights. Under his skillful management and editorship, *Keeping Posted* has built a remarkable library, encompassing nearly every aspect of Jewish belief, history, practice, culture, and literature. Within and outside the Reform movement, Jewish educators and lay leaders looked to *Keeping Posted* for lively, readable, accurate, and informative issues for school and other study programs.

This volume presents the best of *Keeping Posted* in a way that will enhance the new directions of Reform Jewish education as exemplified in the William and Frances Schuster Curriculum. The ten chapters here mirror the ten "Goals of Reform Jewish Education," which were created by the Joint Commission on Jewish Education. Each chapter contains six or more readings, each of which explores a dimension of the chapter's theme. I have prefaced each chapter with an essay on the general topic and each reading with a brief introduction and discussion questions.

In dedicating this work to my wife, Florence, I do more than acknowledge her support and encouragement for over four decades of marriage and family. This is also my way of thanking her for her patience when the closed study door so often proclaimed, "Silence. *Keeping Posted* at work."

A.D.B.
Beachwood, Ohio
5750

▪ INTRODUCTION ▪

Judaism is the oldest religion in the Western world. That's an important achievement, but no special claim derives from it. While age and tradition are important, they are, for Judaism, instrumental values. Pharaoh learned that from Jacob who, despite his greatly advanced age, considered his years to have been few and hard (Gen. 47:9). The measure of a year's worth is what has been accomplished in it. Survival and ancestry must serve a purpose or they have no meaning. The Jewish purpose is simply stated: to serve God.

How does the Jew serve God? How shall we know what God wants us to do? Those are not mere speculations in theology or idle questions of belief. Were that the case, they would attract scant attention in most Jewish quarters. But, because Judaism emphasizes deed over creed, such inquiries strike to the core of the religion. They compel us to define the balance between knowing and doing. The tradition is enlightening: learning in order to practice, Rabbi Ishmael taught, leads to learning, teaching, observance, and practice (*Pirke Avot* 4:6). Learning, too, is instrumental. Fulfilling God's commands requires knowing what they are and how to carry them out. But they must be carried out.

Judaism is a developmental religion, still evolving after almost 4,000 years. Like the evolution of species, the evolution of Judaism has gone forward in twists and turns, producing new branches and twigs. Twice it has put forth branches so different they became separate religions. First Christianity and then Islam followed their own directions and patterns of growth. But, to push the metaphor, the original trunk, Judaism, deeply rooted in the covenant with God and the history of the Jewish people, stood strong and solid. Buffeted by cruel and cutting winds, hacked by relentless foes, troubled by internal tension, Judaism yet holds fast; it remains dynamic, adaptive, growing.

Challenges of modernity present new problems for Jews, new opportunities to seek profound answers in Jewish perspectives. Not all Jews search along the same paths. Jewish identity does not mean the same thing to all Jews. Response to mitzvah, God's commandments, is not identical for all Jews. Jews differ about *halachah*, Jewish law. To some Jews, other Jews are lesser Jews. To some Jews, other Jews are unreasonable Jews. Nevertheless, except for the furthest fringes of the Jewish corpus, all Jews identify with one another, care about one another, and call upon the same God to protect and sustain God's holy people. More unites than separates the segments of the Jewish people.

This volume explores aspects of the unity of the Jewish people from a liberal/progressive Jewish outlook. Yet, it does not explicate "the" liberal Jewish view. There are many points of view within the Reform as, indeed, within the Orthodox and Conservative Jewish communities. The readings, therefore, may not always concur, nor should they. As a whole, these readings provide a large picture of Reform Judaism's responses to crucial questions. What does it mean to be a Jew? How does a Jew demonstrate faith in God, acceptance of Jewish values, and fealty to the Jewish people? How does the Jew express loyalty to the synagogue and other institutions of Judaism? How does the Jew respond to the demand to be God's partner in fulfilling the world, repairing its flaws, leading it to a better tomorrow? How does the Jew assure that a next Jewish generation will carry on the Jewish task, which is always just short of completion? How does the Jew unite with Jews of ages past and future to satisfy God's expectation that Jews will be a realm of priests, a holy nation, a light unto the nations of the world? Chauvinism? Perhaps. But a chauvinism that makes great, often sacrificial demands, that seeks no reward, that is content to bear witness to God's justice in an unjust world, to God's compassion in an indifferent world, to God's promise that things will be better in a world where many are bereft of hope. These are suffocating burdens, not vehicles for self-adulation.

Reform Judaism's goals for Jewish education provide the framework for this volume. They suggest how a Reform Jew might participate in the religious journey Abraham began when, responding to God's command, he departed Ur of the Chaldees for a land God promised to show him. The adventure is hardly over, but the mileposts are many. Today's Jew, like yesterday's, is guided by covenant (*berit*), commandment (*mitzvah*), prayer (*tefilah*), righteousness, (*tzedek*), and a host of other values. The legacy illumines the path and strengthens the traveler, but first it has to be learned. For that task, this volume is a starting place.

To return to the tree-metaphor–Rabbi Eleazar ben Azariah taught that one whose wisdom exceeds one's deeds is like a shallow-rooted tree with many branches; it is easily overturned. One whose deeds exceed one's wisdom is deeply rooted but with few branches; it cannot be moved (*Pirke Avot* 3:22). Being a Jew means living Jewishness daily, alone and in the company of other Jews. Being a Jew denies passivity, affirms activism. To be a Jew means to uphold Jewish values: pursuing justice, choosing good over evil, using God-given talents to nurture and protect God's universe and all it contains. Jewish ritual, ceremony, and observance remind the Jew of these obligations and reinforce the resolve to be a Jew in the fullest sense. Overwhelming? Maybe. Jewish wisdom provides balance: Rabbi Tarphon taught that while you are not required to complete the task, neither may you desist from it altogether (*Pirke Avot* 2:21). The Jew is required to be a Jew.

I

A JEW IS NEVER ALONE

JEWS AFFIRM IDENTITY BY BINDING THEMSELVES, BY WORD AND DEED, TO OTHER JEWS. Jews come in all sizes, shapes, and colors. Jews are farmers, doctors, philanthropists, and paupers. Jews are baby-boomers and Gray Panthers. Jews have straight hair, kinky hair, curly hair, and hair in every color you'd expect to find anywhere. Jews wear small hats, black hats, and no hats. In short, it's hard to tell a Jew from anyone else in the world simply by face, clothing, or size. Yet Jews do recognize one another. Non-Jews can identify a Jew. How can that be?

Jews are recognizable because, as a group, Jews display identifying characteristics. Jewish practices and beliefs, for example, make us different from any other group. In addition, Jews identify with other Jews because of shared values and acknowledged kinship, without which Judaism could not survive. Even when all alone, a Jew feels the company of other Jews and relies on their protection, acceptance, and love.

This chapter will introduce you to some components of Jewish identity and identification. The readings will invite you to consider elements of your Jewishness, and will suggest ways to become more aware of yourself as a member of the Jewish people. You will be asked to think about when and why Jewish identity became a matter of some concern to Jews and how Jews chose to respond to new and difficult questions about themselves as Jews. You will consider how parentage determines Jewish identity and how a non-Jew might become a Jew and vice versa. You will probe whether Judaism is or has been a missionary or proselytizing movement and whether it should be. You will learn about the special circumstances of Jewish identity in the State of Israel and why new questions there are challenging all sides in a growing conflict. You'll look into a new twist in Christian efforts to bring Jews to Christianity: the false assertion that you can be both a Jew and a Christian. You will evaluate options for preserving Jewish identity and protecting against the forces for assimilation. You will reflect on whether Jewish identity is a private matter or whether being Jewish requires visible, public evidence of commitment.

▪ Who Is a Jew? ▪

There are many ways to define "Jew." Each element of the definition is necessary, like "nation," "parentage," and "religion," for example, but no one by itself is sufficient. It's like trying to define baseball as a game in which a ball is hit with a stick. Without other information you might just as easily be talking about golf.

The following reading describes some of the factors that help to define "Jew" and hence to describe Jewish identity. Think about how each element contributes to the total picture. The characteristics are of ancient origin. Does that make them more, or less, important for Jewish identity today? Explain. What's the role of *halachah*, Jewish law, in determining Jewish identity? That's a controversial issue that will appear again in various readings in this chapter. You will also encounter the idea of *haskalah*, enlightenment. Explain how *haskalah* contributed to assimilation. What else was responsible for assimilation? How did assimilation create new and unexpected threats to Jewish identity? Is assimilation still a serious Jewish concern? Explain. If it is, what can you do about it?

▪ Who Is a Jew? BY RAPHAEL PATAI ▪

According to Webster's Dictionary, a Jew is "a person whose religion is Judaism." Is this definition adequate? There can, of course, be no question that it covers the overwhelming majority of Jews. But, still, it is too narrow. The same objection can be raised to other frequently heard definitions, such as a Jew is a member of the Jewish people or a person born of Jewish parents. None of these definitions comprises *all* individuals who are Jews. Who, then, is a Jew? The answer requires a glance at history.

The question of Jewish identity first arose after the nineteenth-century emancipation of the Jews in Western and Central Europe and the spread of the *Haskalah*, the Jewish Enlightenment. As some Jews became alienated from Judaism and attempted to join the gentile majority culturally and in some cases religiously, Jewish identity became a problem.

Prior to that time Jewish self-identification was not an issue. In biblical times the Hebrews derived their identity from the tradition that they were the descendants of Abraham, Isaac, and Jacob, and heirs to the religion that went back to the revelation on Mount Sinai. To dwell in the Land of Israel was an integral part of the Hebrew identity, and as long as one lived in the Land one remained a member of the Hebrew people. Only by going abroad did one lose one's share in "the inheritance of God" (1 Sam. 26:19), that is, one's identification with the Hebrew religion and people.

In Biblical Israel

The foreigner who came to settle in the Land of Israel was absorbed into the Hebrew community. Internally distinctions were made by tribal affiliation, especially between the Kohens (the priestly descendants of Aaron), the Levites (who served them), and the common people, the Israelites. Descent was reckoned patrilineally, which meant that every person belonged to the tribe of his or her father. The mother's ethnic origin was disregarded. When a Hebrew man married a non-Hebrew woman–as did the sons of Jacob, Moses, Boaz (the great-grandfather of David), and others–his children were considered Hebrews.

The biblical Hebrews designated themselves as *Ivrim* (Hebrews) in relation to other peoples. Abraham was called both "Aramaean" (Deut. 26:5) and "Hebrew" (Gen. 14:13), and the prophet Jonah, when asked by his gentile shipmates to identify himself, answered, "I am an *Ivri*, and I fear the God of heaven...." (Jonah 1:9).

Threefold Identifying Badge

Once the descendants of the Hebrews began to live in the Diaspora, they were called, and called themselves, *Yehudim*, "Jews" (Esth. 2:5). During the biblical period the Hebrew language was called both *Yehudit* (2 Kings 18:26), "Jewish," and *sefat Kena'an* (Isa. 19:18), "the language of Canaan." Throughout this period, the identity of the Hebrews, whether called *Ivrim, Yehudim, B'nai Yisrael, Yisrael,* or by one of the tribal designations, was never in doubt. The Hebrew religion, the Hebrew peoplehood, and the Hebrew language were the threefold identifying badge and the threefold barrier separating the Hebrews from the Gentiles.

Geographical Unity Lost

With the Babylonian Exile, traditionally counted from the destruction of Jerusalem in 586 B.C.E., this situation began to change. Geographical unity was lost. Moreover, in the countries of the ever-widening Diaspora, although the Jews (as they were by that time called) still constituted closed ethnic and religious groups, they adopted the languages of their gentile environments and retained Hebrew only as the ritual tongue. Though they were deprived of their linguistic unity (even the Bible had subsequently to be translated into Aramaic, Greek, Arabic, and other languages for Jews ignorant of Hebrew), their Jewish identity remained clear-cut because of the undiminished power of the Jewish religion and the Jewish historical, ethnic, and cultural tradition. One has only to read a passage in Philo or Josephus to sense the extent to which these Greek-writing, Hellenized Jews were committed to the cause and suffused with the spirit of Judaism. The same observation can be made about the Jews in all countries of the Diaspora until the Enlightenment. Whether they spoke and wrote Greek, Latin, Arabic, Persian, or Yiddish, whether they were politicians or philosophers, mystics or physicians, merchants or bankers, peddlers or beggars, their total commitment to Judaism, their essential Jewishness, was never in doubt, either in the eyes of their gentile compatriots or in their own. As late as the nineteenth century, East European Jews, who constituted the overwhelming majority of the Jewish people, differed from the non-Jews of their countries in religion, traditions, behavior, language, dress, values, and outlook on life and the world. The question of whether one was a Jew or not simply could not arise.

In relation to this reality the *halachic* (Jewish legal) definition of who is a Jew—a person either born to a Jewish mother or formally converted— had little practical significance. The first part of this rule was invoked in cases in which a Jewish woman was raped by a Gentile (as happened during pogroms). Any child born of such a union was considered a Jew. As for conversion, the low status and frequent victimization of the Jews until their emancipation made conversion to Judaism a highly unattractive proposition, even in countries where it was not a capital offense to do so, as it was in Muslim lands.

Almost Impossible to Leave Judaism

This situation, which obtained for some twenty-five centuries, also meant that it was almost impossible for a Jew to leave Judaism. True, both the Christian and the Muslim environments welcomed Jewish converts and indeed put considerable pressure to bear on the Jews to adopt their faiths. But for Jews to leave their ancestral religion meant to break with their family and the whole social and communal environment in which they had grown up and of which they were a part and a product. And even in rare cases when Jews denied their Judaism, they became in the eyes of Jewish law not Christians or Muslims but sinful Jews. They could become renegades but remained Jews.

This solid, unbreachable framework of Jewish identity began to crack once the *Haskalah* spread among the Jews. For many "enlighteners" the culture of the Gentiles, particularly in Germany, France, and England, appeared more attractive than traditional Talmud-based Judaism. The more enchanted enlightened Jews became with gentile culture, the more indifferent they became toward Judaism, including its religion and values. Many members of the newly emerging Jewish intelligentsia converted to Christianity; many more, though they refrained from that ultimate step, nevertheless turned their backs on their Jewish heritage. The ideal preached by the leaders of the *Haskalah*, to become equally at home in Jewish and in secular culture, remained beyond the

A Jew Is Never Alone

reach of most "modern" Jews in the early post-Enlightenment decades.

It was in connection with, and among, the Jewish apostates, semi-apostates, and assimilators that the question of who is a Jew arose. They themselves were plagued by the ambiguity of their position. Jews who had nothing to do with their parental religion and community or had themselves converted–were they still Jews? Did the attitude of converts toward Judaism affect these Jews' identity? This last question is relevant because quite a few among the converts became notorious Jew-haters (Karl Marx is a case in point). Others retained a sympathy for and appreciation of the Jewish people and even idealized it from the distance they put between it and themselves (Heine and Disraeli come to mind). Common to both types was the inability to sever entirely their emotional ties to the Jewish people.

Jewishness Vs. Israeliness

Assimilation, with the problems it creates for both individual Jews and the Jewish community, is a Diaspora phenomenon. Its precondition is a social environment in which Jews live as a minority in the midst of a gentile majority, possessed of an attractive culture. Hence in Israel, where the Jews are the majority, Jewish assimilation away from Judaism does not exist. This, however, does not mean that Israel is not vexed by the question of who is a Jew.

Jewishness in Israel is, in fact, quite a problem because of a number of factors. One is that among most Israeli Jews (including also the young generation of those who hail from Muslim countries) the traditional Jewish religious consciousness has been replaced by a new Israeli self-awareness in which not religion but nationhood–country, language, and culture–play the central role. It was on account of this phenomenon that, some years ago, the state educational authorities felt the need to introduce courses on "Jewish consciousness" into the school curriculum. Still, most Israeli Jews feel religion does not have to be part of their "Israeliness."

Another factor is the rigorous position of the Israeli rabbinate. In the political constellation of Israel, the Orthodox rabbinate, with the help of its close allies, the religious parties, has been able to gain control of all official religious functions and to have the power of decision in the question of who is a Jew, which in Israel is a vital national and political issue. The Israeli Law of Return, the first law promulgated upon the establishment of the state, provides that every Jew has the right to settle in Israel and automatically become a citizen. In this connection the status of converts to Judaism and of traditional but exotic Jewish communities, such as that of Ethiopian Jews, became a stumbling block. The rabbinate, which does not recognize the validity of conversions carried out by Conservative and Reform rabbis, has attempted to bar such converts from invoking the Law of Return. The problem has created much tension between the Israeli Orthodox and the American Conservative and Reform Jews.

As against this a compromise solution has been worked out for the question of the Jewish identity of the black Jews of Ethiopia. For centuries they had been cut off from contact with the Jewish mainstream and did not know, let alone observe, the talmudic elaboration of the *halachah*. The Israeli rabbinate raised no objection when, in 1984, thousands of starving and homeless Ethiopian Jews were airlifted to Israel; but it demanded that, if one of them wanted to marry, he or she had to undergo a symbolic conversion ritual. The public outcry that followed over this exclusion from the Jewish community of a tribe that for centuries had preserved its own form of Jewish religion and identification, accompanied as it was by public demonstrations, ultimately induced the rabbinate to modify its position.

The foregoing brief review should make it clear that Jewish identity has two separate but interlocking aspects. To be a Jew one must define oneself as a Jew, but also be so defined by others. The "others" can include individuals in one's immediate social environment, the community at large, official communal institutions (such as the rabbinate), or even the gentile society. Only if the self-definition coincides with the definition by these others can one be considered an undoubted Jew.

Jewishness, Rich and Poor

Jewishness, moreover, can range from rich to poor. If the Jewishness of a person comprises religion, ethnicity, tradition, culture, and values, it is a rich Jewishness. To the extent that one or more of these elements are lacking or possessed only to a minor degree Jewishness is impoverished. Still, as a minimum definition of a Jew, I would offer this:

A Jew is a person who is the adherent of Jewish religion, and/or the offspring of Jewish parents, or, at least, considers himself or herself a Jew and is so considered by others.

▪ Is Judaism a Missionary Faith? ▪

This reading draws from Jewish sources to demonstrate that Judaism was a proselytizing faith from the very beginning. Moreover, converts to Judaism and to the Jewish people were, from the start, accepted as full Jews. Some converts even made important contributions to the Jewish people.

History illustrates that Jewish identity need not rest on parentage. The beauties of the Jewish religion are available to anyone who chooses them. Nevertheless, many Jews find it hard to accept converts as "true" Jews, or to think of Judaism as a faith that embraces non-Jews. Why? Should Judaism again be an active missionizing religion? Explain. Judaism teaches that *Adonai* is the God of all humanity. Why, then, should it matter which religion a person follows? Why does it make a difference whether a Jew marries a Jew or someone of another religion? Compare conversion procedures in biblical and talmudic times with practices today. Describe Reform-Orthodox-Conservative differences in the procedures for conversion. What are the common elements? What components of Jewish identity are found in conversion procedures?

▪ Is Judaism a Missionary Faith?

BY BERNARD J. BAMBERGER ▪

Does Judaism seek converts? Is it a missionary religion?

Many Jews answer "No!"–and they are quite proud about it. But they are mistaken. For many centuries, Judaism was an active missionary faith. If we today seek out new adherents to Judaism, we are not introducing some new and alien practice. We are returning to a classic Jewish position that can be documented from the Bible and the Talmud.

God of the World

What we now call Judaism began as the religion of a group of tribes and later of the nation established by those tribes. The God of the Israelites was no mere national deity, but the Creator of the world and the Ruler of all nations. And so, during the biblical period, we find the beginnings of an outreach to other peoples to bring them into the covenant Israel had made with its God. The prophet Zechariah (8:23) foresees the day when those of every tongue will grasp Jews by the corner of their garment and say: "Let us go with you, for we have heard that God is with you." This was not just a dream. Another prophet speaks directly to foreigners "who have attached themselves to God," assuring them they will be an integral part of God's people.

[Those who] minister to [God]. . .
To love the name of the [Almighty],
To be God's servants–
All who keep the Sabbath and do not profane it,
And who hold fast to My covenant–
I will bring them to My sacred mount
And let them rejoice in My house of prayer.
Their burnt offerings and sacrifices
Shall be welcome on My altar;
For My house shall be called
A house of prayer for all peoples.

–Isaiah 56:6-7

Ruth of Moab, of heathen birth, who said to Naomi, "Your people shall be my people, and your God my God," became the ancestor of King David. The Moabites were not only heathens; they were traditional enemies of the Israelites. Yet Ruth, Moabite-born, was accepted, loved, and honored by the Jewish people. Indeed, Abraham himself was not born a Jew. In Jewish tradition he came to be regarded as the first convert to the true faith and its first missionary.

The Talmudic Era

The Bible does not tell of any formalities by which non-Jews "attached themselves to God." In the days of the Second Temple, however, a regular procedure of conversion was devised. This was all the more necessary because the number of converts was increasing rapidly. The victories of the Maccabees generated a wave of enthusiasm among Jews; their religious zeal was carried over to many sympathetic gentiles in the Land of Israel and throughout the Mediterranean world. It has been estimated that at the beginning of the Christian era ten percent of the population of the Roman Empire–roughly four million souls–was Jewish. Even if this estimate is high,

there was, beyond doubt, a vast increase in Jewish population at the time–an increase that must have been caused by an influx of converts.

The Hebrew word *ger* occurs frequently in the Bible to denote a foreigner residing in the Land of Israel. In talmudic literature the word *ger* has come to mean a convert to Judaism. The law of the Talmud fixed the procedure of conversion. Candidates had to be warned of the hardships they would have to endure–those coming from the hostility of outsiders, and those resulting from the strict demands of the Torah. But they were not expected to master all the requirements of Judaism in advance. They were to be "pushed away with the left hand and drawn near with the right"–that is, discouraged a little but not too much.

A male convert had to submit to circumcision; after the wound had healed, he received a ritual bath. When he emerged from the bath, he was regarded as a Jew in every respect. A woman had to undergo the ritual bath as the one decisive act. Converts were regarded as "newborn." Their previous family ties were considered to be broken, as their lives as members of the Jewish community began.

We have a large body of information about converts in the first century before the Christian era and for about five hundred years thereafter. One of the leaders of the revolt against Rome in the year 66 was Simon bar Giora (that is, Simon the "son of the convert"). Early in the Christian era the royal family of Adiabene in upper Mesopotamia adopted Judaism. So far as we know, Judaism never employed professional missionaries. Individual Jews were enthusiastic and knowledgeable in telling others about the beliefs and practices of their faith. We still have some Jewish propaganda literature written in Greek, the language spoken everywhere in the eastern Mediterranean world.

After Christianity became the state religion of the Roman Empire under Constantine the Great (early in the fourth century), Jews were forbidden to seek or even to accept converts. But the repressive law was not immediately obeyed. We know this from a series of edicts issued over a period of time, which made the penalty for violation increasingly severe. Later, when Islam conquered the Near East in the seventh century, Muslim rulers also forbade Jews to continue their conversionist efforts.

The Harsh Middle Ages

Under Christian or Muslim rule Jews were very often offered attractive inducements—all sorts of financial, political, and social advantages—to convert to the ruling faith. Converts to Judaism, on the other hand, had much to lose, even their lives. No doubt the number of those who left Judaism exceeded the number of those who embraced it. Yet conversions to Judaism continued in virtually every country and every century. The converts included some people of importance in the Catholic Church. We possess a pathetic letter from a French community of the eleventh century, appealing for funds to support the widow of a martyred rabbi and stressing that the woman had left the wealthy Christian family of her birth to "enter under the wings of God's presence." This is only one of many such documents that still exist on the subject of converts. Perhaps the most famous case of conversion in Jewish history occurred about the year 740, when the pagan king of the Khazars and many of his nobles adopted Judaism. This Jewish kingdom (located in what is now southeastern Russia) practiced toleration to Muslims and Christians. It continued to exist for several centuries before it was finally destroyed by a coalition of Russians and Byzantines.

Changing Attitudes

Even though Jews were prohibited from carrying on open missionary activity during the Middle Ages, they welcomed converts whenever they could. The record of evidence previously sketched could not have come about by accident. The Jews of the time must have looked upon the task of winning converts as good and as important. As a matter of fact, several medieval rabbis said so in so many words: It is a mitzvah to seek converts. One declared that this mitzvah followed naturally from the principle "You shall love your neighbor as yourself."

But beginning about 1600, there seems to have been a change of attitude among rabbis and among the rank and file of the Jewish community. They now became reluctant to accept converts and went far beyond the talmudic rule in discouraging them. The reasons are not entirely clear. This negative attitude, strangely enough, appeared at a time when persecutions of Jews were beginning to ease. This negative attitude persisted even after the French and American revolutions started a process of emancipation and citizenship for Jews in certain countries of the Western world. In the nineteenth century a number of Jews were baptized for the sake of personal advancement. Disgust at their behavior may have led loyal Jews to assume that *all* conversions were insincere.

Revival of Missionary Spirit

In recent years we have seen evidence of a different spirit, more in keeping with older Jewish tradition and with the universal outlook of Judaism. This different spirit—an easing of the four-hundred-year-old negative attitude—has arisen in part because of practical considerations. With the disappearance of the Jewish ghetto, marriages between people of Jewish and gentile birth have become more frequent. In many such cases, the non-Jewish party is willing, and even eager, to embrace the Jewish faith. Although traditional law questioned conversions under such circumstances (fearing that they were prompted more by convenience than by sincere religious intent), rabbinic authorities have usually been willing to accept these candidates; and the results have generally justified this "stretching" of the law. Many of the converted spouses have displayed an intense loyalty to Judaism and have played a constructive role in the Jewish community.

In the past few years a growing number of Jewish leaders, most notably within the Reform movement, have been arguing that it is not enough to give a decent and cordial reception to those who approach us of their own accord. We should take a more positive approach, by bringing the message of Judaism to others and by publicizing that we welcome those who want to join us. Although controversial, this more tolerant posture is likely to gain ground in the years to come.

▪ Patrilineal Descent ▪

The previous reading showed that conversion may substitute for parentage as a necessary condition for Jewishness. In the following selection the question of parentage is considered from another perspective: parentage counts, but it should not matter which of the parents is Jewish. The idea is known as patrilineal descent as opposed to the traditional view that one's religion follows only the line of one's mother, or matrilineal descent. It's a new idea on the Jewish identity agenda, new in modern times, at least. Note its precedent in biblical and later times. Patrilineal descent was met by some opposition in liberal Jewish quarters, and by furious antagonism from Orthodox Jews, when first put forth in the early 1980s. Although the public debate has diminished, the Orthodox animus has not. It is a central issue in Israeli politics, where Orthodox parties seek to amend the Law of Return.

Why do some Jews decry the idea that you are Jewish regardless of which parent is a Jew? Should Reform stand by its decision? Explain. In the following reading, which of the three reasons for patrilineal descent seems most important to you? Explain. The reading asserts that parentage, whether mother or father, is not sufficient to define a Jew. What more is required? Do you agree? Explain.

▪ Patrilineal Descent   BY ALEXANDER M. SCHINDLER ▪

Several years ago you proposed that children born of a Jewish father and a non-Jewish mother should be considered Jewish if raised as Jews. Traditionally only children born of a Jewish mother are considered Jewish. Why did you feel it necessary to propose that we adopt patrilineal descent in defining who is a Jew?

I raised the patrilineal descent issue for three reasons. To begin with, I felt it was in keeping with our fundamental Reform principle of making no distinction between the rights of men and women in religious life. To consider a mother as a valid transmitter of Judaism while denying that role to a father was a gross violation of the principle of equality. We want women to have an equal status with men in religious practice and we want fathers to have equal status with mothers in determining the identity of their children.

The second reason concerns the high rate of intermarriage, often involving Jewish men marrying non-Jewish women. Some of these marriages, unfortunately, end in divorce. In such instances I believe the Jewish father has the right to determine the Jewishness of his child, so I have proposed a rabbinical ruling guaranteeing that right. Barring such an official declaration on our part, civil divorce courts have based custody decisions on the traditional definition of Jewishness, ruling that the mother can determine the religious identity of the child. Thus, in many cases, children who had been raised as Jews during the marriage were raised as Christians after the divorce.

The third reason concerns the tens of thousands of children who have Jewish fathers and non-Jewish mothers. The traditional definition of Jewishness made them feel less than Jewish, perhaps even inferior. This problem was driven home to me immediately after patrilineal descent was adopted by the Central Conference of American Rabbis, the Reform rabbinical organization. A young rabbi approached me and said, "This is the happiest day of my life!" I asked "Why?" He said, "You see, my mother is not Jewish, and until this day I had a sense of lacking full authenticity and legitimacy. Today I feel fully a Jew." Now, if it had been possible for a rabbi to feel not fully Jewish before the CCAR declaration, how much more so for the children of similar circumstance. This third reason, above all others, led me to assert this principle.

Was patrilineal descent your idea?

While I insisted on the CCAR resolution, I am not the first rabbi to assert the principle. Patrilineal descent has been the prevailing practice of Reform virtually since our movement's founding. Most Reform Jews consider a child of a Jewish father and a non-Jewish mother to be Jewish–provided that the child goes to religious school and is either confirmed or becomes a Bar or Bat Mitzvah. Historically no further conversion was ever demanded.

Is there any historical justification for asserting patrilineal descent?

I don't believe that the matrilineal principle always held sway. The genealogical tables of the Torah are overwhelmingly patrilineal. In matters of inheritance, the paternal line alone was followed. Solomon married many non-Jewish wives and the child of one of them, Rehoboam, succeeded him to the throne. Moses married Zipporah, the daughter of a Midianite priest, yet her children by him were considered Jews. Joseph married Asenath, the daughter of a

Priest of On, and the children of their union were reckoned as Jews. Indeed, unto this day when Jewish male children are blessed, the father says, may you be like Joseph's sons Ephraim and Manasseh–even though their maternal grandfather was a priest who worshiped the sun in the heathen shrine at Heliopolis near Cairo. In rabbinic literature we see evidence of the patrilineal tradition as well. We invoke God of our fathers in prayer. We are summoned to the Torah by our father's name. We are reminded that we live by *Zechut avot*, the merit of our fathers.

Perhaps most significantly, both the Torah and rabbinic law hold the male line absolutely dominant in matters affecting the priesthood. Whether one is a Cohen or a Levi depends upon the father's priestly claim. If the father is good enough to bequeath priestly status, why isn't he good enough to bequeath Jewishness?

Yet, the rest of the Jewish community still abides by the principle of matrilineal descent. Doesn't the CCAR declaration portend a split in the Jewish world?

If every kind of a change portends a split in the Jewish world, then there will never be any change. Every step along the way, Reform risked a split, but the Jewish world remained whole, and I think it will continue to in this case.

From a strictly *halachic* point of view, some of the decisions that Reform made in the past were infinitely more radical than is this patrilineal decision. Moreover, it isn't a departure in practice–it is merely a departure in law. When, for instance, over a hundred years ago, Reform ruled that we would not require a *get*, a religious divorce, *halachically* we consigned generations of young people to *mamzerut*, to bastardy. (Without a *get*, a civil divorce is not considered valid in Jewish law; therefore, the children of a second marriage are considered illegitimate by the Orthodox religious court.) Now, that is an irremedial step *halachically*; not so the acceptance of the paternal line, which from an Orthodox standpoint is subject to remedy through conversion. The greatest danger comes from the extreme religious right within Orthodoxy, which,

A Jew Is Never Alone

because of its inherent weakness, has become very intolerant. It is my hope, however, that the moderate voices within Orthodoxy will prevail, and religious pluralism will thrive.

Is being born to a Jewish father sufficient for declaring oneself a Jew?

No. The Reform decision is in many ways more stringent than is the Orthodox position. The matrilineal approach to the definition of Jewishness is limited to genealogy; that is, anyone born of a Jewish mother is Jewish. But Reform adds Jewish involvement, leading a Jewish life. In our view, Jewishness is *presumed* through Jewish descent but *confirmed* only through Jewish deeds. The purely genealogical definition can result in absurd situations. Nikita Khrushchev's grandchild, for example, is considered Jewish *halachically* because the Soviet leader's son married a Jewish woman. This grandchild probably isn't even aware that he is Jewish. Indeed, being raised in the highest levels of the Communist hierarchy, he is assuredly anti-Jewish and anti-Israel. Now take the case of David Ben-Gurion's grandchild. The grandson of Israel's first prime minister came to visit me in New York and said, "The rabbinate in Israel doesn't consider me Jewish." Why? Because his mother was converted to Judaism by a Reform rabbi. (The Israeli rabbinate does not accept the validity of Reform conversions.) And yet, this grandchild of Ben-Gurion is most affirmatively Jewish. He fought in the Lebanese War. He told me that if, God forbid, he had been killed in action, the Israeli rabbinate would not have allowed him to be buried in a military cemetery or to have a religious funeral. So the strictly genealogical approach of the Orthodox can expose us to dreadful anomalies. Therefore, in our real-world practice of Judaism we have struck a real-world definition of who is a Jew. In the Reform view Jewish identity is established by "acts of identification with the Jewish people" and by "the performance of *mitzvot.*" Jewishness must be expressed in concrete ways through an active involvement in Jewish life and the willingness to share the fate of the Jewish people. Such is the intent of our historic decision on patrilineal descent.

▪ Becoming a Jew ▪

Previous readings considered aspects of parentage as components of one's Jewish identity. The following personal odyssey examines how Jewish actions are related to Jewish identity. The author discovered that marrying a Jew, making a personal commitment to Judaism, raising her children as Jews did not make her a Jew. Compare that conclusion with the closing argument in the previous reading and with the last reading of this chapter. Further, the author describes her anguish as she came to realize that Jewish identity is not a sometime thing. Why not? Later in the chapter we will explore further the idea that you can be a Jew or a Christian but never both.

Why was the author's conversion to Judaism a painful experience for her? Why was it necessary for her to convert? What might you have done in those circumstances? Explain. Today many marriages include a non-Jewish partner. How can the Jewish community, through the synagogue, help that partner achieve a stable identity? How can the synagogue help the family achieve religious stability?

▪ Becoming a Jew   BY NANCY KLEIMAN ▪

I had never dated any Jewish men. In fact, growing up in a small town in America, I had known only six Jews during my school years. I met fewer still when I entered the convent and later as a VISTA volunteer in the desert prairie of Wyoming. All that changed when I took a teaching job at a private Connecticut school and fell in love with a fellow teacher–a Jew.

Our infatuation was soon to sober. I remember returning from our first visit to my folks, elated that they had been so impressed with the fine young man I had brought home. On the long drive back I announced to Ed that we were getting married. He smiled with approval and consent. Then he dropped the bomb: "Nancy, our children must be Jewish."

"What do you mean Jewish? I'm a Catholic! You're a Jew! Our kids will be both!" Our little ship had hit an iceberg. Silence blanketed our joy, and we froze in our thoughts to assess the damage.

What compromise could we possibly agree upon that would begin to resolve this seeming impasse? Could we go forward while going our separate religious ways without creating a wedge in our relationship? Or could we find a commonality that would not discredit either's religious identity? Such questions sharpened when we tried to project how their ramifications might affect our future family life and children. And as we shared our feelings about each other and the issues that divided us, we both sensed we would sink if a mutual commitment were not made.

Conversion was out of the question–how could Ed ask me to become Jewish any more than I could ask him to embrace an alien set of beliefs? Although I had rejected a monastic lifestyle, spirituality was vital to me and had been expressed from childhood in the religious language of Roman Catholicism. For Ed to turn his back on a 4,000-year heritage would have been an affront

to the very core of his identity!

As we continued our drive we agreed on nothing more than to begin to talk about these issues. And talk we did! Through tears, through laughter, together, alone, with friends, with family, we talked. We talked until we made a comfortable agreement: I committed myself to creating a Jewish home as long as I felt respected and supported in practicing my Catholic faith privately, and Ed promised to take the lead in guiding that goal. Although we could not predict what future religious conflicts we might face, we felt our love and communication skills were strong enough to deal with such unknowns.

Those unknowns gradually unfolded at various stages of our relationship–our first Christmas/Chanukah season, Passover/Easter, a death in the family, a wedding. Later we dealt with the *bris* and *mikveh* of our two sons, their consecration into the religious school, and their first innocent announcement at the family seder: "This is our special holiday, but not Mommy's." Only this latter statement, however, warned of the most painful question that eventually caught me off guard–a question not of the children's confusion or the logistics of interfaith sharing–but rather, a question of my own identity.

My initial commitment toward Judaism in the context of my marriage freed me to enter a process–a freedom not without risk. For, though I paid the price of suspending a very central theological point–that of the divinity of Jesus–I did so to concentrate on finding the commonality between our two great traditions. What I did not bargain for was my becoming vulnerable to change! For a dozen years I was a bridge on which I walked back and forth freely between these two communities, eventually becoming so familiar with both that I became as fluent in the religious language of Judaism as I had been in my Roman Catholicism. But a bridge merely connects. By definition, it goes nowhere. And for me to continue an honest spiritual journey required that I pass through one of the thresholds before which I stood.

More Than a Spiritual Journey

But this was more than a spiritual journey! The emotional me cried out not only "Where do I belong?" but "Where do I want to belong?" I had to face the fact that three of the people I love most—my husband and sons—belonged to a community separate from the one to which I had always identified. Thus what my intermarriage eventually required of me was to evaluate my adult response to the course of my life.

I learned, first, that I had grown away from my childhood formation of understanding the divine through the vehicle of Christianity and had become more comfortable with the liberal Judaism that shaped my husband's religious identity. This process was so gradual that the force of its realization shocked me like a death, and I needed to grieve and mourn this childhood loss.

Secondly, I had become a part of a people. Even though I had entered this community through the love of one Jew, I had given birth to two others and made lasting friendships and ties with countless other Jews. This community was as much a part of me as I had become of it, and I realized I was deciding whether or not I could cross the line that separated "outsider" from "one of us." I decided to cross the line.

An Essential Statement of Belonging

Was there a difference between my being a Jew and my commitment to Judaism for so many years as the non-Jewish wife? Was conversion merely a formalization of what was already there? What was unique about the conversion itself that made me Jewish? To answer these questions I had to ask others: Had marrying a Jew made me Jewish? No. Had committing myself so deeply to Judaism for my marriage made me Jewish? No. Did shaping the Jewish identities of my children make me Jewish? No. What, then, made the difference? Conversion. What once seemed imposing and threatening now became an essential statement of belonging. Like my marriage vows, this public acknowledgment reflected my desire to take on a new identity, to choose another name, to change my status as friend to partner and thus begin a relationship with a community of others committed to the same ideals, struggles, and hopes.

As the first anniversary of my conversion approaches, I ask myself if I can detect or measure any change in myself. Having lived for years as a non-Jew in a Jewish environment, I can report no fireworks or fanfares. Nevertheless, in subtle ways, my life is different. I no longer look first to Ed before expressing an opinion on Jewish matters. He is no longer the only parent who represents to our children an "authentic" source of their Jewish identity. I enjoy the equality this brings to our marriage. But perhaps on a deeper level I recognize that my conversion to Judaism marks an adult change that expresses one of the noblest of human abilities—the ability to choose and share responsibility for one's own destiny.

▪ The Jewish Identity Crisis ▪

Israel presents special problems for the idea of Jewish identity. That's because religion and nationalism, joint aspects of Jewish identity, assume a different coloration in Israel, where political concerns of the nation intersect with the personal lives of its citizens. Because it is a Jewish state, Israel's laws deal with Jewish matters. Who a Jew is becomes a legal issue, not only a question of Jewish self-identity. Important Knesset debates and Israeli Supreme Court cases have tested, in a series of "Who Is a Jew?" debates, crucial components of Jewish identity. *Halachah* has been equally tested. Jewish identity is an arena in which Orthodox-Liberal confrontations and tensions are often violently displayed in Israel.

The Law of Return is the focus of the conflict that rips at the fabric of the nation and tries its Jewish spirit. Should Liberal Jews accept Orthodox interpretations of the Law of Return for the sake of harmony in the beleaguered Jewish nation? Explain. Orthodoxy has not relented in its efforts to amend the law. How would the Orthodox version affect Reform and Conservative rabbis outside of Israel? How would such a new definition of "Jew" affect the character of the Jewish state? How would the Orthodox definition affect the Jewish identity of those who adopted Judaism in Reform and Conservative settings?

Because this issue is so closely linked to changing Israeli politics, determine the latest status of the Law of Return before you read the following.

▪ The Jewish Identity Crisis   BY RICHARD G. HIRSCH ▪

In modern democracies, where freedom of worship is a basic right, a person's religious identity is not a factor in determining citizenship status. In the United States the principle of separation of church and state prohibits the state from intervening in any matter concerning religion. Therefore, no American law would ever permit, let alone require, government action to define Jewish identity. Indeed, the United States census does not even permit a question about religion.

In only one modern democracy, Israel, is Jewish identity an issue for state discussion. Israel was established as a Jewish state and recognized as such by the United Nations. In July 1950 the new Jewish state enacted one of its first laws—the Law of Return, which states that, upon arriving on Israeli soil, a Jew is entitled to the rights of full citizenship if he or she so chooses. On the other hand, for a non-Jew citizenship is not automatic but requires a process of naturalization similar to that in the United States. Related to the Law of Return is the 1949 Law of Population Registration, which requires every inhabitant of Israel over sixteen years old to carry an identity card noting nationality, religion, and citizenship.

The adoption of these two laws generated controversy within Israel, and between Israel and the Diaspora. Initially, each individual upon regis-

tration decided how to define himself or herself. In accord with this simple practice Minister of Interior Israel Bar Yehuda issued a directive in 1958 stating, "Any person declaring in good faith that he is a Jew shall be registered as a Jew and no additional proof shall be required." Regarding children, the directive stated, "If both parents declare that the child is Jewish, the declaration shall be regarded as though it were the legal declaration of the child itself." The Bar Yehuda directive provoked the first major controversy over "Who is a Jew?" The National Religious Party, speaking on behalf of the Orthodox chief rabbinate, contended that the minister of interior's action was contrary to *halachah*, which defines a Jew as a person whose mother is Jewish or who has converted to Judaism. In protest, the National Religious Party resigned from the coalition government.

Prime Minister David Ben-Gurion established a special ministerial committee to attempt to resolve disputes over registration. At the same time, recognizing that the issue was of intense concern to Diaspora Jewry, Ben-Gurion sent a letter to forty-five of the greatest scholars in the Jewish world, requesting their counsel as to how to deal with the problem. Significantly, more than half the recipients of the prime minister's letter lived in the Diaspora, an implicit recognition that Jews outside Israel have a voice and a stake in actions taken by israel affecting the personal status of Jews outside Israel's borders. While the responses to Ben-Gurion's questions varied considerably, the vast majority were opposed to separating Jewish national identity from Jewish religion. The government decided, therefore, that it was premature to pass legislation on the subject and issued directives that were not at variance with *halachah*.

The Brother Daniel Case

In 1958 the "Who is a Jew?" issue erupted once again in the famous Brother Daniel case. Brother Daniel, a Carmelite monk living in a monastery on Mount Carmel in Haifa, petitioned the Israel High Court of Justice to become a citizen of Israel according to the Law of Return. Brother Daniel had been born in Poland in 1922 to Jewish parents named Rufeisen, and at his circumcision was given the first name Oswald. He was raised and educated as a Jew in every respect and was active in a Zionist youth movement in preparation for immigrating to Israel. During World War II he escaped a Nazi prison and evaded recapture by using forged documents certifying that he was a German Christian. Exploiting his Christian identity, he joined the anti-Nazi underground and saved many Jews by warning them of German extermination plans. In fleeing the Nazis, he entered a Christian convent in 1942 and there converted to Christianity. Following the war, he became a monk and entered the Carmelite order, knowing they had a monastery in Palestine. He had never forsaken his aspiration to live in the Land of Israel.

Brother Daniel applied for Israeli citizenship in 1958 under the Law of Return, arguing that, according to Jewish law, a person born a Jew always remains a Jew. His lawyer cited the talmudic dictum: "A Jew, even if he or she has sinned, remains a Jew" (*Sanhedrin* 44a) and contended that even the most Orthodox Jew could not deny that Brother Daniel was a Jew. The Israeli High Court of Justice ruled that the term "Jew" in the Law of Return "has a secular mean-

ing. As it is understood by the ordinary plain and simple Jew . . . a Jew who has become a Christian is not called a Jew." In refusing to accept the *halachic* definition of Jew, the High Court thus gave "Jew" a national definition, reflecting "the healthy instinct of the Jewish people and its thirst for survival."

The Shalit Case

Another landmark decision of Israel's High Court led to the first legislative amendment to the Law of Return. A lieutenant commander in the Israeli navy, Benjamin Shalit, born in Israel, married a non-Jewish woman in Scotland. After the marriage they settled in Israel, where Shalit's wife became a naturalized citizen. Though Mrs. Shalit never converted to Judaism, the Shalits reared their two children like other Israeli children, inculcating in them loyalty to the Jewish people and homeland. When Commander Shalit filled out the questionnaire for the Population Registry for his firstborn child, in the space for nationality he entered the word "Jewish" and left the space for religion blank. The registrar of the Ministry of Interior struck out the entry for nationality and in the space for religion he wrote, "Father Jewish, mother non-Jewish." When the second child was born, Commander Shalit did not fill in the spaces for religion or nationality. In the second instance the registrar wrote in the space for nationality "Father Jewish, mother non-Jewish." In the space for religion he wrote "not registered."

Shalit petitioned the High Court of Justice, demanding that the nationality of his children be registered as Jews and, since both he and his wife regarded themselves as atheists, that in the space for religion the children be registered as of no religion. Initially, the High Court, understanding the explosive character of the issue, recommended to the government that it abrogate the law requiring citizens to enter their nationality and suggested that only two questions be asked: citizenship and religion. But the government, concerned about the internal security problems vis-à-vis Arab citizens of Israel, rejected the Court's recommendation. The Court had no choice but to render a judgment. On January 23, 1970, in a historic decision and by a five-to-four majority, the Court ruled that the registrar had to register the children as Jewish by nationality, even though their mother was not Jewish.

Law of Return Amended

The decision caused a furor in Orthodox circles. Once again the National Religious Party threatened to withdraw from the coalition government. Prime Minister Golda Meir was besieged by demands to pass legislation nullifying the decision. Even many non-Orthodox Jews feared the decision would be interpreted as sanctioning intermarriage in Israel and abroad. The country, at the time, was engaged in the war of attrition with Egypt, and a broad coalition government of national unity had been established. Concerned about the stability of the government and the unity of the Jewish people, Prime Minister Golda Meir moved quickly to work out a compromise. After a historic debate in the Knesset, an amendment to the Law of Return was enacted on March 10, 1970, which for the first time accepted the definition of the term "Jew" as "a person born to a Jewish mother or who has converted to Judaism and is not a member of another religion." The last phrase was to assure that people like Brother Daniel could not be considered as Jews for the purposes of the Law of Return.

During the course of the debate some of the Orthodox leaders had suggested that the words "according to *halachah*" be inserted after the words "converted to Judaism." Their proposed addition was intended to disqualify recognition of conversions performed by non-Orthodox rabbis outside of Israel. (Since the established Orthodox rabbinate has been given a monopoly in Israel, conversions performed in Israel are registered only if they are performed under Orthodox auspices.) But the Knesset refused to insert the words "according to *halachah*" because it was understood that the majority of conversions outside Israel are performed by Reform and Conservative rabbis. Neither the Knesset nor the government wanted to pass judgment on the religious practices of the major non-Orthodox Diaspora movements abroad, nor did they want to jeopardize the close and interdependent relationship of the Diaspora and Israel. Furthermore, they were keen to keep the gates of Israel open to all potential immigrants, including converts and the progeny of converts of all branches of Judaism.

It was thought that the amendment to the Law of Return would settle once and for all the legal issue of "Who is a Jew?" In effect, the Orthodox view had prevailed against those who preferred a more secular, liberal, nationalistic definition of the term "Jew." However, the State of Israel was to have no respite from the issue. Some Orthodox elements have kept up a steady barrage against the alleged peril of Reform and Conservative conversions. Ever since 1970, the issue of "Who is a Jew?" has come to the fore *after* every national election. Why *after* the election and not *before* the election? Because no political party has ever won a majority in the Israeli elections for the Knesset. In order to form a government, the party with the largest plurality needs to seek the support of the smaller parties. In almost every case the easiest potential coalition partners are the religious parties. Recognizing that the major party blocs are willing to compromise to gain their support, the religious parties make demands far beyond what their electoral strength would warrant. High on their agenda of demands has been amending the Law of Return. But, despite the heavy political pressures exercised by Orthodox Jewry in Israel and abroad, the Knesset has to this date continued to reject all efforts to amend the legislation.

No political body has the right or the capacity to impose a political solution in the area of religious practices. The Knesset has no jurisdiction over Diaspora Jewry and cannot affect the practice of religious movements abroad. The religious differences between Orthodox, Reform, and Conservative Judaism should be reconciled by religious leaders in dialogues based on mutual respect and recognition of a shared Jewish destiny.

If Israel is not a society where all Jews feel at home, then Israel will not remain the spiritual home for all Jews. What is at stake in the "Who is a Jew?" issue is no less than the very character of the Jewish state and its relationship to the Diaspora. Through this struggle Reform Jews are helping to maintain Israel as an open and pluralistic society, one with which all Jews can proudly identify.

▪ From Pontiac to Jerusalem ▪

This is the story of a journey by a young man who thought he was Jewish, discovered that he wasn't in any real sense, and began a search for what being Jewish is all about. The author's long trek from Michigan to Jerusalem might be yours. How is your Jewish life like his? How different? Are your present experiences preparing you for a Jewish life? Explain.

It was by accident—and in Jerusalem—that the author discovered how shallow his Jewish life had been. It was in Jerusalem that he was able to do something to bring meaning to his Jewish identity. Can that be accomplished only in Jerusalem? Is there a way, in North America, to follow a similar path? Explain. Describe the kind of Jewish life you'd like to have. Will it include the same level of Jewish activities and practices the author describes? A higher level? A lower? How do you understand the idea that the North American Jewish community is in a holding pattern? Do you think that should be changed? Explain. What can you do to change it?

▪ From Pontiac to Jerusalem ▪ BY ZE'EV CHAFETS

When I was a kid, Judaism was an extracurricular activity, a part of my weekly schedule like music lessons, basketball practice, or Wednesday night dances at school. I went to Sunday school but didn't learn much, and I knew I wasn't expected to learn much. I knew the difference between Sunday school and "real school." The first was more or less a social activity; the second, the one my parents took seriously, was my real business.

Eventually I joined the temple youth group; became president of the state federation, MSTY; and later was elected president of NFTY. I had a great time in youth group, made some lifelong friends, and attended countless conclaves, workshops, creative services, Saturday night socials, and teary friendship circles. I learned the words (but not the meaning) of a dozen Hebrew prayers and folk songs, heard innumerable lectures on the Jewish social responsibility to solve most of the world's problems, and, on one memorable occasion at NFTY camp in Warwick, I even took part in a workshop to rewrite the *Pirke Avot*, the talmudic "Sayings of the Fathers," without, unfortunately, knowing anything about the Talmud or the people who wrote the original sayings. Judaism, my Judaism, was a good thing to do on the weekends or during summer vacation.

No Jewish Obligations

Best of all, it wasn't too Jewish. For every Hebrew song we sang there were three by Buddy Holly; for every workshop on Israel there were a dozen on nuclear disarmament or civil rights.

Because we had no Jewish obligations and no Jewish skills were required of us, I thought of Judaism as just another facet of liberal America. Our only responsibility was to be moral, to practice the golden rule, to be, in short, good people.

I liked MSTY so much, I thought about becoming a rabbi. Not, as a college friend later put it, a "Jewish" rabbi, more like a community leader. I would march for civil rights, eat shrimp cocktails at brotherhood-week banquets, and play softball with teenagers at idyllic summer camps.

A Jewish Disneyland

To get a head start on Hebrew, which I knew the Hebrew Union College required, I took a year off from the University of Michigan and enrolled as a junior-year-abroad student at the Hebrew University in Jerusalem.

That year was the most humiliating and astonishing one of my life. I arrived in Jerusalem considering myself almost abnormally Jewish–NFTY, Hebrew classes, and even rabbinical ambition–but within three days I realized I was hardly Jewish at all. I met Arabs who spoke Hebrew better than I did. When I visited a yeshiva for the first time I had to ask about the difference between the Talmud and the Torah. I was shown famous biblical sites I had never heard of, listened to debates about Jewish issues I hadn't known existed. I went to a synagogue–the kind my grandparents had prayed in before they came to America–and I didn't know how to act or what to do. And, perhaps most humiliating of all, I met Jewish boys my age who were giving years of their lives to defend the country that I, in an offhand way, had come to visit as if it were a Jewish Disneyland.

During that year I realized I did not know how to act and live Jewishly. I knew Christmas and Easter songs and would have felt perfectly at home in a Baptist church; read Shakespeare and Hemingway; knew the dates of American history. But in a Jewish context–Jewish language, geography, history, literature–I was wholly lost, as ignorant as a tourist in some exotic land.

Luckily there was an antidote for my ignorance. Hebrew could be learned, and so could Jewish history. I spent hundreds of hours exploring Jerusalem, and I read like a madman the Bible, folktales, Jewish history, Sholem Aleichem–anything with clues about what being Jewish was all about.

Gradually I began to live a Jewish lifestyle. I became conscious of the rules of *kashrut*, since most restaurants served either dairy or meat. I had Saturday off instead of Sunday and *Tishah Be'av* and *Tu Bishvat*, which I could never keep straight, were real holidays in Israel. So were *Sukot* and *Shavuot*, *Simchat Torah* and *Purim*.

Uncool Jewish Kids

Before that year I would have divided Jewish history into three parts: the Bible, two thousand years of kvetching, and the golden age of NFTY. I thought of anything too Jewish as uncool, even wimpy, like the little kids in yarmulkes and thick glasses I used to see peering out the window of the United Hebrew School bus. In Israel I found out that there was nothing embarrassing about being Jewish and that there had been more than a little self-hatred in my attitude toward those "uncool" Jewish kids.

As the year went along I began to wonder what strange process had taken some Hebrews from Palestine, buffeted them around the world for two millennia, washed them up on the shores of the U.S. in 1915, and brought them to Pontiac, Michigan, where I had been born one year before the foundation of the new Jewish state. I realized that Israel offered me not only a chance to recapture my roots and to live a Jewish life but an opportunity to be a part of one of the most dramatic events of modern history. Despite logic, despite Hitler, a new Jewish state had arisen. It was still an infant, still in need of protection, still new enough so that every person counted. The idea of recreating a Hebrew culture, wringing justice and meaning out of the bitter history of a hundred generations, was overpowering. It made the Judaism I had been taught seem one-dimensional and irrelevant, and the issues on my liberal American agenda–free school lunches, demonstrations against the war in Vietnam, letters to the editor about world disarmament–seem fleeting and unreal. The idea of being born a Jew in the most exciting generation in two thousand years made the idea of going back to the great American Jewish middle class seem unimaginative and dull.

That was seventeen years ago, seventeen years since I became a full-time Jew. I rarely think of myself as Jewish anymore, any more than an Englishman thinks of himself as English; I simply am a Jew. I speak a Jewish language, live a Jewish lifestyle, have Jerusalem-born children who regard Christianity in about the same way I used to think about Buddhism. I have discarded some religious customs–regular synagogue attendance and *kashrut,* for instance–and have kept others. In either case I make my choices knowing that regardless of what I do or don't do, my Jewish identity is assured by the context in which I live. Being Jewish is no longer a burden, a duty, or a puzzling appendix to my life. Everything I do is, in a sense, "Jewish."

A Holding Pattern

There was a time when I believed that every American Jew ought to come to Israel. I still believe it, but I don't think it will happen. Judaism is not a supplement to America; it is a competitor, a total civilization, with its own land, customs, language, and destiny. The effort to turn it into one of the "three great Western religions" trivializes it. The American Jewish community is in a holding pattern, trying desperately to keep in the fold young people who have only a marginal Jewish identity so that they in turn can keep their not-so-Jewish children in the fold twenty years from now.

The Jewish experience has to mean more than that. The Bible and the prophets, the Diaspora and Hitler, the rebirth of the State of Israel, have to mean more than friendship circles and universal ethics and temple softball leagues.

It is startling for an American kid to realize he is the inheritor of an ancient tradition. The Zionist experience has always been for the few, the imaginative, the romantic–those who, for some peculiar reason, have been born with Jewish hearts. They are the ones who respond to the great adventure of Israel; and they are the ones whose lives can be transformed by the chance to recapture the Jewish past, live in the Jewish present, and build the Jewish future.

▪ The Roots of Jewish Self-Hatred ▪

Like a thunderbolt, emancipation struck European Jewry some two hundred years ago. Jews have never been the same. This selection explains that Jewish identity was not on anybody's agenda until Europe's Jews, finding medieval shackles suddenly released, encountered new freedoms, including the right to be like other people. The price of freedom, Jews discovered, was extremely high. We are still paying for it. Assimilation and self-hatred are part of the cost.

How can you recognize Jewish self-hatred? Is "Jewish humor" an example? "JAP"? Assimilation? Explain your answers. The author says that Jewish self-hatred is a psychological disorder. Explain what he means. Self-hatred is the antithesis of positive Jewish identity. How does Jewish knowledge affect either? The author sees Jewish education and a strong Jewish home as the cure for and prevention of self-hatred. How can these remedies be available to all Jews in the modern, emancipated Jewish world? Are they sufficient remedy? Explain.

■ The Roots of Jewish Self-Hatred

BY RAPHAEL PATAI ■

The phenomenon of ethnic self-hate has been studied among many minority groups, including blacks, French Canadians, the Irish, and the Jews. For almost two thousand years the Jews were the classical example of a persecuted, low-status minority wherever they lived. Few have noted, though, that the Jews did not develop self-hatred until their emancipation in late eighteenth-century Europe. Jews such as the historian Josephus Flavius in imperial Rome, the philosopher-codifier-physician Maimonides in Muslim Egypt, and Don Joseph Nasi in the court of the Turkish caliph all lived in alien societies but also remained convinced of the superiority of their own people, its religion and tradition.

However persecuted and downtrodden they were, Jews regarded themselves as the chosen people, as the only true servants of God, and as keepers of the commandments. This deep-down certainty protected them from certain feelings of inferiority, especially self-hate.

With the onset of the Enlightenment and Emancipation, Jewish tradition was no longer a source of certainty. The Jews of the Enlightenment wanted to participate in European culture, including the language, clothes, manners, and values of the country in which they lived. They assumed—for the first time in Jewish history—that gentile culture was superior to their own Jewish customs. The Enlighteners never preached conversion to Christianity; quite to the contrary, Moses Mendelssohn (1729-1786), the founder of Jewish Enlightenment, wrote, "Adapt yourselves to the mores and the constitution of the country into which you have been placed but also cling steadfastly to the religion of your ancestors." Still, many Jews converted to Christianity. Others, unwilling to sever all ties with Judaism, tried to discard the traits that made them recognizably Jewish.

Jews Imitate Neighbors

Try as they did to imitate the ways of their gentile neighbors, those Jews were still regarded as inferior. But despite this rejection by non-Jews, they continued to identify emotionally with the ideal image of the gentile, and began to adopt much of the gentiles' often negative view of the Jews. Even among the most outstanding Jewish thinkers and scholars of the Enlightenment era, we find two German figures who criticized their fellow Jews harshly. Mendelssohn, one of the greatest philosophers of the age, considered Yiddish "a tongue of buffoons... corrupt... from which a reader capable of elegant speech [read: German] must recoil in disgust." A century later the great Jewish historian Heinrich Graetz (1817-1891) spoke of the Jewish "race deformity," labeled the study of Talmud "perverse," the Jewish mind "blunted," and the Yiddish language a "hateful jargon."

In France, the birthplace of the Enlightenment, Jewish self-hatred took a similar course. While blaming Jewish faults on gentile oppression, socially advanced French Jews also began to accept the French gentile stereotype of the Jews. These Jews came to regard their own people as physically and morally decadent, hypocritical, and cowardly, a people manifesting all the vices of oppressed and deprived "races."

The image of the Jew as parasite was another damaging anti-Jewish stereotype. In the nineteenth century, "parasitism" became a code word for the Jewish character, and by the twentieth century the allegation that the Jews were parasites had become commonplace in the anti-Semitic literature of England and America. Worse, many self-hating Jewish leaders and writers adopted this concept and characterized Jewish life as parasitical. For example, certain Zionists spoke of Jewish parasitism in the Diaspora and contrasted it to the productive life of the Jewish working people in Palestine.

"Good" and "Bad" Jews

The differentiation between Diaspora parasitism and a life of productivity in Palestine-Israel was but one expression of Jewish self-hate. By dividing the Jewish people into two parts, "good" and "bad," one could identify with the former while directing one's hatred at the latter. In an earlier example, nineteenth-century West European Jewish leaders and authors claimed that "good" Jews were well advanced on the road of assimilation, while "bad" Jews remained bound to their East European traditions. Those Jews who differed from the gentile majority were considered as "other" and therefore could serve as targets of hatred. By following this path, Jewish self-haters no longer recognized their feelings for what they were–namely manifestations of a pathological self-hatred–but masked them as hatred of *other* Jews, a group to which they themselves did not belong.

Suicide and Self-Hatred

Jewish self-hatred exacted a heavy toll. For centuries, despite humiliation, persecution, and suffering, tradition-bound Jewry was almost immune to suicide. (Only during the Middle Ages, to avoid baptism, did Jews commit mass suicide.) However, after the Enlightenment, in the new gentile environment of which they desperately wanted to become a part, in some places suicide rates among Jews were twice or even three times as high as among gentiles.

The psychological mechanism that produces self-hatred among Jews and members of other minorities has been explained by Kurt Lewin (1896-1947), the famous German-American psychologist. The low-status minority group desires a share of the respect and rewards enjoyed by the higher-status majority. This creates in some the desire to leave the low-status group and become part of the higher-status majority. When the way to accomplishing this is blocked, frustration results and gives rise to aggression. The aggression cannot be directed against its logical target, the majority, which is powerful and still remains the ideal. Therefore the aggression is directed against one's own group, and, ultimately, against one's self. In extreme cases, feelings of inferiority can turn into self-hatred and result in serious maladjustment.

Cure and Prevention

Having diagnosed Jewish self-hate as a psychological disorder, we should face the question of its cure and prevention. A case history can point the way to the cure. Bernard Lazare (1865-1903), an outstanding French Jewish literary critic who in his early years suffered from an acute case of Judeophobia, described the East European Jews in traditional anti-Semitic caricature: coarse, dirty, pillaging, contemptible, lepers, rotten. As for the assimilated French Jews, he advocated that they "lose themselves in the mass of the French nation," and thus "disappear totally." At the age of twenty-seven Lazare began working on a book on anti-Semitism, and, in the course of that work, as he became better acquainted with Jewish history and Judaism in general, his attitude changed from negative to positive. He then recognized Jewish "national consciousness" and even "national pride" and discovered that all Jews had "received the impress or the national genius [of Judaism], acting through heredity and early training." From that time on Lazare became a fearless champion of the Jewish cause, a fighter against anti-Semitism, and a leader of French Zionism.

This and other case histories teach us that Jewish knowledge can be a remedy for Jewish self-hate. If one can induce Jewish self-haters to study Jewish religion and history, chances are that the more they learn, the more they will appreciate Judaism.

Childhood is the best time to apply this preventive medicine. Children who receive an adequate Jewish education and grow up in a home atmosphere in which they develop a positive Jewish identification and Jewish values usually benefit from lifelong protection against the infection of Jewish self-hate and the maladjustments that can result from it.

▪ Myths and Realities ▪

Jewish identity can be fragile. That's especially true because, as you saw in reading the Chafets piece, the state of Jewish learning in many Jewish schools is inadequate. Minimal Jewish knowledge leads to weak defenses against the many threats to Jewish affirmation. Serious threats from seemingly logical and deceptively well-intentioned Christian missionaries are a constant challenge to Jewish identity and survival.

Missionary promises to help you find yourself in a loving community are seductive. They are also too often successful because young Jews don't have the weapons to resist the verbal and philosophical onslaughts. With Jewish identities already weakened, wanting to gain acceptance into the "other," "larger" culture, and unprepared to evaluate the missionary pitch to accept Jesus, many Jews succumb to the appeal to "remain Jewish and find fulfillment in Jesus." How can you counter the missionary appeal? Do the missionaries offer anything not already available within Judaism? Explain.

The following reading offers realities that puncture some of the missionary myths. What makes them myths? Why should you be wary of them?

▪ Myths and Realities BY ANNETTE DAUM ▪

MYTH: Jewish prophets foretold the coming of Jesus as the Messiah.

REALITY: There is no mention of Jesus as the Messiah in Hebrew Scriptures. Most Christian and Jewish biblical scholars agree that such "proof" is based on quotations that are mistranslated, misunderstood, and/or taken out of context. For example, Isaiah 7:14 is often mistranslated as "Behold, a *virgin* shall conceive and bear a son" to indicate that Jesus is the expected Messiah. But the Hebrew word *almah* means young woman, not virgin. Furthermore, the verse refers to events that took place in antiquity, not events to come. Many scholars believe the Gospel accounts of Jesus, written long after his death, were tailored to fit earlier biblical descriptions of the Messiah. Historically, the term "messiah" has had different meanings for Jews and Christians. Orthodox Jews await a human being, a leader like Moses, to rescue them from oppression, lead them back to the Promised Land, and usher in an era of peace and justice

on earth–expectations that have remained unfulfilled to this day. Reform Judaism does not anticipate the coming of a personal messiah but works for the coming of a "Messianic Age," an age of peace and justice.

MYTH: Missionaries proselytize Jews because of their love of Israel and the Jewish people.

REALITY: Fundamentalist Protestant missionaries aggressively proselytize Jews today, not only to offer the salvation they believe comes through Christ alone, but because of a theological conviction that Jews must make *aliyah* (settle in Israel) and accept Jesus as a precondition of Christ's second coming. Israel, they believe, must be strong and survive until that time, when an apocalyptic battle between the forces of good and evil will erupt, bringing enormous destruction in its wake and spelling the end of Israel, Judaism, and the Jewish people.

MYTH: Belief in Jesus makes one a completed Jew.

REALITY: Fundamentalists believe that the new covenant through Christ supersedes the Jewish covenant at Sinai. This theological one-upmanship denigrates the validity of Judaism, implying that God deserted the Jews, that Christians are the new chosen people, and that Christianity, therefore, "fulfills" Judaism, reducing Judaism and the Jewish people to second-class status. Hebrew-Christian missionaries use the term "complete" to obscure the fact that Jews who accept Jesus are converts to Christianity. Most Christian theologians reject these as anachronistic beliefs that, over the centuries, led to the persecution and forced conversions of the Jews.

MYTH: It is possible to be both Jewish and Christian.

REALITY: Missionaries take advantage of a technicality in Jewish law, adopted during a period of forced conversions, to make it easier for Jews to return to Judaism. Born Jews remain Jews, technically, even if they convert to another religion. They are, however, regarded as apostate Jews who, having deserted Judaism, are not generally entitled to the right of marriage by a rabbi within the Jewish community, to burial in a Jewish cemetery, or to membership in a synagogue.

MYTH: Atonement requires a blood sacrifice.

REALITY: Missionaries frequently refer to biblical verses (such as Leviticus 17:11) that speak of the blood of animal sacrifice as an act of atonement to buttress their argument that Jesus died for the sins of humankind. Other types of sacrifices, however, such as flour and incense, are also mentioned in Hebrew Scriptures. Sacrifice alone is not sufficient for atonement in Judaism. The prophets often denounced sacrificial offerings alone as insufficient without repentance and righteous behavior. In Judaism, atonement is the responsibility of the individual and is achieved through *teshuvah* (repentance), *tefilah* (prayer), and *tzedakah* (righteous acts). The story of the *Akedah* (the binding of Isaac) in Genesis is regarded in Jewish tradition as a dramatic rejection of human sacrifice. Fundamentalist Protestants believe that people do not have the power to atone for their sins, that atonement can only be achieved through belief in Jesus Christ, who sacrificed himself for the sins of humanity.

MYTH: Messianic Judaism is merely another branch of Judaism and Hebrew-Christianity just another way to be Jewish.

REALITY: Missionaries quote derogatory remarks made by each branch of Judaism about the other, claiming the disagreements and diversity within Judaism as justification for the addition of "Messianic Judaism" and/or "Hebrew-Christianity" as other ways to be Jewish. Within Jewish diversity, however, there is general agreement on central precepts that bind Reform, Reconstructionist, Conservative, and Orthodox Judaism together: the Messiah has not yet come; God is an indivisible unity, without body; only Hebrew Scriptures are sacred for Jews; God made an eternal covenant with the Jewish people at Sinai; people must atone for their own sins; and Judaism is a complete faith.

MYTH: Jews are only an ethnic group, not adherents of a common religious tradition.

REALITY: Missionaries redefine Jews as an *ethnic* group like the Germans, Greeks, Italians, or Irish, who may be of common national origin and heritage but are religiously diverse. Applied to Jews, this definition robs us of the uniqueness as well as the essence of our heritage as a dispersed people who share a common religious tradition–Judaism. Destroying the tie that binds us would effectively destroy both Judaism and the unity of the Jewish people.

▪ Origins of Our Symbols ▪

A symbol is a sign that has acquired deep meaning, stimulates feelings, and is valued enough to lead to action. For example, the American flag is a sign for the United

States. Its symbolic meaning, however, conveys ideas like democracy, freedom, equality, and justice. Soldiers have died to hoist the symbol high. In the same way, a wine goblet is a sign for drinking; but a *Kiddush* cup is a symbol that embodies and conveys Jewish ideas and feelings about blessing, Creation, the Exodus from Egypt, and bonds between Jews across generations.

In what ways are Jewish symbols important components of Jewish identity? Could they be so without leading to Jewish actions? Explain. Which of the items in the following essay has symbolic meaning for you? Explain. Why are the other items outside your own symbolic value thinking? How does the presence or absence of Jewish symbols around you, and their use or nonuse by you, affect your Jewish identity? Explain. Jewish symbols, like all symbols, derive their power from public acceptance. That's one reason Jews seek the company of other Jews—to use symbols together in customary ways. Why else do Jews seek one another?

▪ Origins of Our Symbols

BY BERNARD M. ZLOTOWITZ ▪

The origin of most Jewish symbols is shrouded in mystery. Scholars agree, however, that Jewish symbols and customs derive from the cultures in which Jews lived.

The Star of David

The Star of David (*Magen David* [literally: shield of David]), for example, is identified in Western nations exclusively with the Jews, but Muslims regard it as a traditional decorative design. When the Ottoman Sultan Suleiman I (1494-1566) erected the wall around Jerusalem, he put the six-pointed star on the North Wall as one of many designs. In Morocco this popular North African symbol appears on their ten-franc coin.

Dating back to antiquity, the six-pointed star appeared on a column in the Capernaum Synagogue (on the western shore of the Sea of Galilee) of the third century C.E. Some scholars date its first appearance well before that to the second century B.C.E. According to one theory, when the Jews fought the Greeks they adopted the delta, the Greek letter "D," because it stood for David, Israel's great warrior king who brought peace to all Israel and expanded its borders. Then they imposed an inverted delta over

the first, representing the Messiah, a descendant of King David, who would bring eternal peace to Israel. The symbol resulting from the two triangles, a symbol of the past combined with a symbol of the future, was an expression of the warriors' belief that David and his descendants would protect them.

In all probability, however, the symbol was merely a geometric design that was adopted by the Jewish people. Nowhere in rabbinic literature is the *Magen David* mentioned. In fact, it did not come into general use as a Jewish symbol until the nineteenth century when it began to appear on tombstones and synagogues. It was adopted in 1897 by the World Zionist Congress at Basle, Switzerland, as an identifying symbol for Jews.

The Menorah

The *menorah*, on the other hand, is more easily traceable as a Jewish symbol. We first read about this seven-branched candelabrum in the Torah when Bezalel, the great biblical artisan, is commissioned to design one for the Tabernacle, the portable sanctuary in the Sinai wilderness. This *menorah* was placed between ten others that Hiram made for Solomon's Temple in Jerusalem. In the Second Temple there was only one *menorah*, which was destroyed by the Syrian King Antiochus, who reigned from 175 to 164 B.C.E. It was later replaced by Judah Maccabee. This *menorah* is depicted on the Arch of Titus in Rome, which was built to commemorate the Roman destruction of the Second Temple.

The belief that the lights of the *menorah* stand for the planets or the seven eyes of God wandering over the earth may account for its becoming the symbol adopted by the State of Israel in its wish to be a "light unto the nations." Some scholars have agreed that symbolically the *menorah* represents the six days of creation, with the center light representing the Sabbath.

Josephus, the Jewish historian of the first century, claims that in the Jerusalem Temple only the center lamp burned continuously. It was called the *ner hama'aravi* (the western lamp), which in the Book of Samuel was called *ner Elohim* (the lamp of God). When the Temple was destroyed, the rabbis decreed that in remembrance of the center lamp, the synagogue should have a *ner tamid*, a perpetual lamp burning before the ark. Following the destruction of the Temple, the rabbis forbade the use of the seven-branched *menorah* in the synagogue so that it would not be confused with the *menorah* of the Jerusalem Temple, a practice followed today by Orthodox and a number of Conservative congregations but rarely by Reform.

The shape of the *menorah* suggests a tree. In antiquity its symbolic use was probably influenced by the cosmic tree of the Sumerians, which was the symbol of life and light. But even though in the remote past the *menorah* may have been borrowed from another culture, it is an authentic Jewish symbol, representing for over two millennia the ideals of Judaism–the giving of light and life.

The Mezuzah

Hardly a Jewish home is without its *mezuzah* on the front doorpost. The Bible enjoins us to write the *Shema* "on the doorposts of your house and your gates" (Deuteronomy 6:9). Within the *mezuzah* is a parchment scroll inscribed with the words from Deuteronomy 6:4-9 and 11:13-21 (not the Ten Commandments as some people believe), written in twenty-two lines by a scribe in the same manner in which a Torah scroll is written. The parchment is then rolled up and put into a wooden, metal, or plastic box and affixed in a slanted vertical position on the right side of the door as you enter. (Rashi claimed it should be vertical, but his grandson Rabbenu Tam claimed it should be in a horizontal position. Thus, the slanted compromise was reached.) On the other side of the parchment the word *Shaddai* (Almighty) is inscribed and can be seen through an opening in the container. The rabbis attached great importance to the *mezuzah* as a physical reminder of the Jews' responsibility to fulfill God's commandments.

Some Jews believe the *mezuzah* can ward off evil spirits. So pervasive was the belief of the potency of the *mezuzah* that, according to an apocryphal account, during the Middle Ages Christians bought them to put on their doorposts to ward off the Black Plague.

Other peoples share this practice of placing the deity's name or a quote from a sacred text on the entrance to their homes as a means of protecting them from harm. Muslims put the name of Allah, a verse of the Koran, or something similarly sacred, over their doors. The ancient Egyptians observed a similar custom. It is hard to say which group borrowed from whom.

Tzitzit

Just as the *mezuzah* is a reminder to walk in the right path, so *tzitzit* serve to "remember all the commandments of God and do them..." (Numbers 15:39). How do the *tzitzit* serve as reminders of all the commandments? Here we have to revert to *gematria*. The numerical value of *tzitzit* is 600. But there are 613 commandments. The difference is made up by the eight threads and five knots. Originally one of the threads (fringes) was blue "because this color resembles the sea, the sea resembles the sky, and the sky resembles the throne of glory" (*Menachot* 43b). But this was discontinued because the process of getting the proper shading of blue was lost and the rabbis forbade its use. So the blue was introduced as stripes in the *talit*, which later inspired the blue and white colors of the Jewish flag.

The Talit

The Bible requires that men wear fringes on four-cornered garments. When this type of garment went out of style, the wearing of *tzitzit* was endangered. So a special four-cornered garment was introduced to allow observance of this *mitzvah*. Worn under a shirt at all times, this garment is called a *talit katan* (a miniature *talit*) or *arba kanfot* (four-cornered garment), not to be confused with the *talit*.

The large *talit* originated as a distinctive garb for the rabbi, much as an academic robe identifies a scholar. In time the lay leaders took a fancy to it and eventually the rest of the male population began to wear it at worship services. In Eastern Europe only married men wore it, enabling the women to know which men were eligible. Today Orthodox Jewish males over thirteen years of age wear the *talit* as a sign of adulthood. So important is the *talit* to Orthodox Jews that it is a gift generally bought by grandparents for the Bar Mitzvah and by in-laws for the groom. An Orthodox Jew is buried in a *talit*. Among Reform Jews the wearing of a *talit* is optional, though very few choose this option. But Reform rabbis often wear a *talit*-like garment called an *atorah* over their rabbinic robes.

The *talit* certainly is a distinctive Jewish symbol. Why it captured the imagination of the Jew remains as mysterious as the adoption of *tefilin* as a unique Jewish symbol.

Tefilin

Archeologists discovered *tefilin* in the Bar Kochba caves, which makes their use at least two thousand years old. Orthodox and Conservative males are required to put on *tefilin* (leather boxes with straps for head and arm containing parchment scrolls of selected biblical passages) once they reach the age of thirteen years and one day. Though the requirement of wearing *tefilin* is ascribed to four biblical passages, this *mitzvah* is derived from the commandment "and

you shall tie them for a sign upon your hand and they shall be for frontlets [or memorials] between your eyes" (Deuteronomy 6:8). However, whether this really means *tefilin* as we know it today is a matter of dispute. One scholar has suggested that "[the memorials] between the eyes" meant the placing of ashes upon the forehead as a sign that one had brought an offering to the Temple.

The Kipah

Another practice shrouded in mystery is the wearing of a head covering, or *kipah*, a custom that was not enshrined as law until the sixteenth century, when Joseph Karo declared in the *Shulchan Aruch* that a man is not permitted to walk four cubits (about seventy-two inches) with head uncovered.

In biblical times bareheadedness among men was customary. The stories of Samson (Judges 13-16) and of Absalom (2 Samuel 14:26) speak of their hair as a crown of glory, indicating that their heads were uncovered. The priests covered their heads as a sign of dignity, and the High Priest wore a golden diadem on his miter inscribed with the words "Holy unto the Lord."

The wearing of a head covering during worship might have been influenced by the practice of Roman priests, who offered sacrifices with covered heads. Muslims, too, worship with heads covered. The Talmud speaks of the desirability of covering one's head as a sign of fearing God. In one passage, Rabbi Huna, son of Rabbi Joshua, would not walk four cubits bareheaded, saying: "The *Shechinah* (Divine Presence) is above my head" (*Kiddushin* 31a).

According to the Talmud (*Berachot* 60b), the morning blessing, "Blessed art Thou, O Lord . . . who crownest Israel with beauty," was written to add sanctity to the act of covering the head. But the practice of wearing a head covering never fully gained acceptance in the talmudic period, remaining a status symbol and a sign that a man was married. When Rabbi Huna met the great scholar Rabbi Hamnuna, he was amazed that he was not married, as noted by the absence of any head covering (*Kiddushin* 29b).

A Jew Is Never Alone

Centuries passed before the head covering was accepted as a religious symbol. As late as the thirteenth century, it was not customary in France for Jews to cover their heads during worship; yet during the same period in Spain the opposite was true. But by the sixteenth century it became a Jewish law, capturing the imagination of the Jewish people and gaining universal Jewish acceptance. Elijah of Vilna (1720-1797), known as the Vilna Gaon, acknowledged that the practice is based on custom.

Reform Judaism in America (unlike Reform in Europe) adopted the practice of this country: to remove one's hat and stand bareheaded before persons of repute. Thus, Reform congregants worshiped God with heads uncovered as a sign of devotion and faith, respect and awe. Today, however, many Reform Jews wear head coverings in the synagogue as a way of affirming Jewish tradition.

II

THE JEW AND THE LAW

JEWS ACKNOWLEDGE THE COVENANT THROUGH TORAH STUDY AND OBSERVING MITZVOT. Visit Jews in any North American city; visit Jews anywhere in the world. Wherever you go, you'll find the Jews there doing much the same Jewish things. What individual Jews do may vary depending on whether they are Orthodox, Reform, or Conservative, whether they follow Sephardic or Ashkenazic traditions. What they do will depend also on their individual commitments to observance. But you will find enough similarity to recognize that you are among Jews. It's as if all Jews are following, with variation, the same script.

The script has a name and derives from an agreement, over three thousand years old, entered into by the Israelites at Mount Sinai. That unique event marked the creation of the Jewish people and bound them and all Jews since to *Adonai*, the one God. The agreement, which has been renewed over and over again, is called *berit* in Hebrew—literally, pact or treaty. It is frequently translated as covenant. The covenant is embodied in the ancient contract we call Torah, which, in its narrowest meaning, comprises the Five Books of Moses. In its wider usage, Torah implies all the interpretations, commentaries, and related literatures that elucidate the meanings of *Chumash*, the Five Books. Torah is sometimes translated as "law" because so much of Torah tells Jews what to do to fulfill God's expectations and demands. *Mitzvah* (plural, *mitzvot*) is the Hebrew term for "commandment." The *mitzvah* system, based on Torah, is uniquely Jewish; it sets Jews apart from all other people. It's the fine print of the *berit*. Not all Jews have the same understandings of *mitzvah* or of specific commandments; however, all Jews, even those who select from among the *mitzvot*, acknowledge God in their lives and seek ways, within the broad spectrum of Jewish practice, to worship *Adonai*.

In this chapter you will explore *berit*, Torah, and *mitzvah* and how they interact. You will be introduced to the profound historical context in which the three originated. You will consider the importance of Mishnah, the written form of the vast body of oral law that is derived from the written Torah. You will also be introduced to Talmud, the further development of the system of Jewish law.

Today's Jews differ in their views on the meaning and place of Jewish law in their lives. Some of the differences cannot be resolved; the similarities are not strong enough to balance the disagreements unless drastic changes occur in Jewish life. Well-entrenched ideologies will not easily accede to change, making the perpetuation of the movements, the streams of Judaism, inevitable. Is this diversity good for Jews and for Judaism? Explain.

▪ What Is the Covenant? ▪

The Hebrew word for contract, *berit* (Ashkenazic pronunciation, *beris*), is also the name of the circumcision ceremony. The ritual has acquired that name because it symbolizes the entry of a male Jew into the covenant, the pact our ancestors made with God. In fact, the Torah describes the circumcision ceremony as precisely that, the sign or token of the covenant (Genesis 17:1-14). As important as the ceremony is–and it is very important–it's the covenant itself that defines the relationship between God and the Jewish people. Induction into the midst of the Covenant People, the Jewish people, is not a matter of choice, nor is it a puberty rite in which the young man actively participates. Induction is a mandate on the parent.

The following essay discusses other covenants and other covenant signs. As you read, think about covenants–contracts–that are consummated daily between and among contracting parties. What are the tokens or signs of those contracts? What makes the *berit* a very special contract? Describe the unique interrelationship between God, People, and Land in this contract. Explain why a three-thousand-year-old agreement is still valid for Jews. Explain why the parent is commanded to impress on the son the symbol of the contract. Some Jews believe infant girls should also be inducted into the Jewish people with an appropriate ceremony. What do you think? Explain.

▪ What Is the Covenant?   BY SEYMOUR ROSSEL ▪

Being Jewish is a matter of both choice and chance. Most of us did not choose to be Jewish; we were born of a Jewish parent, raised in a Jewish home, given a Jewish education. Birth, it seems, is a matter of chance. But the practice of Judaism, our Jewish way of life, is a matter of individual choice–you have to choose, just as a convert chooses, to live as Jews. Generations ago, our people made a collective choice, turning them into the "Chosen People." As our tradition tells the story:

When God decided to give the Torah, none of the nations except Israel would receive it. . . . When God revealed the Divine Presence upon Mount Sinai, there was not a nation at whose doors God did not knock, but they would not accept the Torah and keep it. But when God came to Israel, they said, "We will keep it, and we will heed it."

[*Exod. R.* 27: 9; 24: 7]

"*Na'aseh venishma,*" "We will keep it, and we will heed it." With these words our ancestors made the choice to accept the teachings of the Torah, to keep its commandments. In return God gave us the gift of Torah and the Land of Israel. This agreement between God and the people of Israel the Bible calls a "covenant," or "berit".

The Rainbow Covenant

To understand what the Bible means by "covenant," it is necessary to go back in time to the first covenant, the *berit* made with Noah, just after the terrible flood.

Then God said to Noah and to his offspring along with him, "I am hereby establishing my covenant with you and with your descendants after you, and with every living thing. . . . I establish My covenant with you, that never again will all flesh be wiped out by the waters of the flood, and that there will not be another flood to destroy the earth." So God said: "This is the sign of the covenant.... I set My bow in the clouds.... And when I gather clouds over the earth, the bow will appear in the clouds. Then I will remember My covenant.... The bow shall be in the clouds, and I shall see it and remember the everlasting covenant between God and every living thing, all flesh that is on earth." Then God said to Noah, "This is the sign of the covenant that I have established between Me and all flesh on earth."

[Gen. 9:8-17]

Surely this is a covenant, for the word "*berit*" occurs many times here. Yet it is a strange agreement, for it seems that God had a definite part in it, promising never again to destroy the world by flood. But what part did the other party have? What obligations were demanded of Noah in return?

The rabbis of the Talmud discussed this question and decided that indeed Noah *did* agree to follow seven commandments given by God to all human beings. Any human who follows them, the rabbis said, is deserving of a place in the world to come–just as deserving as any Jew who follows the commandments of Torah.

These are the seven commandments Noah agreed to in the rainbow covenant:

1. Idols must not be worshiped.
2. One should never take a false oath using the name of God.
3. Courts of law must be established.
4. One shall not take the life of another person.
5. One must never commit the sin of incest.
6. One shall never steal.
7. The flesh of a living animal shall not be eaten.

This teaching, that anyone of any religion could be as good in God's eyes as any Jew, was unique. Most religions taught that their way was the *only* true way, that all who did not follow it were doomed. But the idea of a *berit* was so central to Judaism that the ancient rabbis reasoned there must be a *berit* for all human beings, Jewish and *non-Jewish*.

Abraham, the Covenant, and the Promised Land

The Torah next tells us of a *berit* between God and Abraham. In fact, there are two stories. In the first Abraham makes a sacrifice to God by cutting animals in half (this was an old and respected way to make a covenant, and the Bible often speaks of "cutting" a covenant).

And God said to him: "I am the Eternal who brought you out of Ur of the Chaldees, to give you this land to inherit." And he said, "O Almighty God, how shall I know that I shall inherit it?" Then God said to [Abraham]: "Know this for sure, that your descendants will live as strangers in a strange land, and they will be enslaved ... four hundred years. But I will judge the nation they serve, and afterward they will go forth with great possessions. And you shall go to your forebears in peace. You will be buried after reaching a good old age. And the fourth generation shall return to this place.... On that day God made a covenant with [Abraham]: "To your seed I give this land, from the river of Egypt up to the great river, the Euphrates."

[Gen. 15:7-18]

But, once again, this is a strange agreement. What is Abraham's part in it? It is clear that God promises the Land of Israel to Abraham's people forever, but in return for what?

The rabbis pointed to the verse that comes just before this covenant [Gen. 15:6], "And [Abraham] believed in God; and God counted it to him for righteousness." Even before the Torah was given at Mount Sinai, Abraham had a sort of "sneak preview." He knew, even then, that the Torah would be based on righteousness. Since God could count on Abraham to continue being righteous, that became the condition of the agreement.

God spells this out more clearly in the second story of the covenant with Abraham. This story begins with Abraham's duties:

And when Abram [Abraham's original name, later changed by God] was ninety years old and nine, the Eternal appeared to Abram, and said to him:

"I am God Almighty; walk before Me, and be whole-hearted. And I will make My covenant between Me and you. . . . I will establish My covenant between Me and you, and your descendants after you throughout their generations, as an everlasting covenant. . . . And I will give you and your descendants after you the land in which you have lived, the whole land of Canaan, as an everlasting possession, and I will be their God."

Then God said to Abraham: "And as for you, you shall keep My covenant, you and your descendants after you throughout their generations. This is My covenant. . . . Every male of your family shall be circumcised . . . and it shall be for a sign of the covenant between Me and you. . . ."

[Gen. 17:1-2; 7-10]

No wonder we call the ceremony of circumcision *berit milah,* "the covenant of circumcision." Like the rainbow, the sign of the circumcision is a sign of the everlasting covenant.

The Covenant with David

There is one further covenant in the Bible that bears directly upon the Land of Israel. This is the covenant with King David. Like the covenants with Noah and with Abraham, this covenant also binds God by a promise:

Thus says the Lord of hosts: "I took you from the sheepcote, from following the sheep, so that you might be a prince over My people, over Israel. And I have been with you wherever you have been, and have cut off all your enemies from before you; and I will make your name great, as the names of the greatest of those on earth. And I will choose a place for My people Israel, and will plant them, that they may dwell in their own place, and be disturbed no longer; neither shall the wicked peoples afflict them any more, as at the first, even from the day I commanded judges to be over My people Israel; and I will give you rest from all your enemies. . . . When your days are fulfilled, and you shall sleep with your forebears, I will set up your son after you . . . and I will establish his kingdom. He shall build a house for My name. . . . I will be to him like a parent, and he shall be to Me like a son; if he is wicked,

I will punish him . . . but My mercy shall not depart from him. . . . And your house and your kingdom shall be made sure for ever before you; your throne shall be established for ever."

[2 Sam. 7:8-16]

I have made a covenant with My chosen,
I have sworn unto David My servant:
Forever will I establish your children,
And erect your throne to all generations.

[Ps. 89:4-5]

Here, too, the sages pointed to David's great righteousness as the reason for God's promises. The agreement states that if David's son is wicked, he will be punished; but even if he is punished, the promise to David will still stand firm "forever."

And what is the promise? That the people of Israel will have their own land and be ruled by the line of King David. It was already clear which land that would be: David ruled over it. It was the same land that was promised to Abraham "forever." It was the Land of Israel. Here, just as the covenant promised, Solomon, David's son, would "build a house for My name," God's house, the Temple.

One thing, however, seems missing in this covenant. A sign. In the covenant with Noah, God gave the sign of the rainbow. In the covenant with Abraham, God gave the sign of circumcision. Even in the story of creation–since creation itself is a kind of covenant between God and all living things–God gave a sign: *Shabbat.*

You may be able to guess what sign God gave to David from the fact that David's throne was to be "established forever." What can that mean, since no ruler from the house of David seems to be sovereign now? The rabbis understood from this that the Messiah, who would rule over Israel and all humanity in the End of Days, would come from the house of David. So, the Messiah is the sign that was given in this covenant–the Messianic Age, a time to come when peace will dwell in the hearts of all, and all nations will give up war forever.

Is this a sign like all the others? Is it like *Shabbat,* like a rainbow, like circumcision? The rest of these we can see or we can honor through our obedience. But what of the sign of the Messiah, the sign of the age of peace? Look around. It is nowhere to be seen. Not in Israel today. Not in the rest of the world.

Yet it is as real as all the others. As Maimonides put it when he made faith in the Messiah one of the thirteen most important principles of Judaism, "I believe with perfect faith in the coming of the Messiah; and even though he may tarry, yet I shall wait daily for his coming."

So the Messiah and the time of peace the Messiah represents are already present in our world in a way. Like a seed that has been planted, the time of the Messiah is already in the world, growing. The Messiah is like a goal, even though we are not yet able to touch it, we see it as a signpost just ahead. As God promised, the "throne" of peace is established forever. It is up to us to reach it.

The Berit

Basically, a covenant, or *berit*, is an obligation concerning two parties. At times it is an obligation made by one party to reward the other–as in the cases of Noah, Abraham, and David, who all received God's covenant as a reward for their righteousness. In ancient times covenants were "cut" when an animal was divided, or sealed by an oath, or by a solemn meal in which both parties ate together.

The Land of Israel is tied up with this idea of a covenant made between God and human beings. The people of Israel is tied up with this idea of covenant, too. At Mount Sinai a very different kind of covenant was cut, a *berit* greater than any of the others in the Bible. Here, too, both the land and the people of Israel were joined together. And, because of this binding agreement, we are tied to the Land of Israel forever.

▪ The Living Law ▪

Many kinds of covenants were known in the ancient world. All are found in the biblical narrative. In promissory covenants, God gives something but makes no demands in return (e.g., Genesis 15:5-7; 2 Samuel 7:13-15). In the obligatory covenant, God will deliver on his promise if the people fulfill their part of the bargain (e.g., Deuteronomy 4:1, 7:12-15, 26:16-19, 28:1ff). Mediated covenants, as the name implies, are made through a third party but are no less valid or demanding (e.g., Exodus 24:3; Joshua 24:25-27; 2 Kings 11:17; Hosea 2:20). In a fourth type of covenant, God witnesses an agreement between people, thereby sanctifying the arrangement (e.g., Genesis 21:22-24; 31:22-48; 1 Samuel 18:3-5; 2 Samuel 3:17-21; 1 Kings 20:31-34; Malachi 2:13-14; Isaiah 28:14-15).

The following essay describes yet another kind of covenant, the kind made at Mount Sinai. In this covenant Jews were given no choice but to accept God's demands. However, and despite that stricture, some Jews did exercise choice: they built a calf of gold to worship and rejected God and Moses. The consequences were drastic. What are the consequences today of rejecting God and the covenant? We are asked to renew the covenant in many different ways. Why? Note again the extraordinary connection between the Jewish people and the Land of the Covenant. Why else is the Land of Israel so precious to Jews?

■ The Living Law   BY SEYMOUR ROSSEL ■

The covenant made at Mount Sinai was similar to those made between God and Noah, Abraham, and David. But it was also different, and the differences are important to us. The covenant made at Sinai was not an agreement between equals or a reward given freely by a powerful party to a deserving servant. It was, instead, an agreement of the kind usually made by a king to a weaker party. It was a suzerain–vassal or "kingship" covenant. In a sense God agreed to be the sovereign over Israel, so long as Israel would follow God's laws.

In a kingship covenant, the parties are far from being equal. The stronger party makes the rules, explains the history of its power to show why the weaker party should obey these rules, then tells what will happen if the rules are broken.

So it was at Mount Sinai. Tradition tells us that God even *forced* the people of Israel to accept the covenant. God, the rabbis say, held the mountain above the heads of the people and said: "If you will accept My Torah, well and good: if not, this place will be your grave" [*Shab.* 88a].

The Israelites had little choice. They could not negotiate, saying, "We'll accept the law not to steal but not the law stating that we must help any stranger." Or, "We'll agree to honor our parents, but we aren't particularly interested in this law about resting our animals on the Sabbath day." It was all or nothing. Choose the whole Torah with all its commandments or die.

The people stood at the foot of the mountain. There came "thunders and lightnings and a thick cloud upon the mount, and the voice of a horn exceedingly loud; and all the people that were in the camp trembled" [Exod. 19:16].

And God spoke all these words, saying: I am the Lord your God, who brought you out of the land of Egypt, out of the house of bondage.

[Exod. 20:1-2]

The Commandments

At once we have the clue that this is, indeed, a kingship covenant, for it begins with the history of God and the Israelites. It's a brief history about God's dealings with the people of Israel to that time. After we know just how powerful God is, we are told what God wants of us. In brief, God wants us to follow the Ten Commandments. There is a penalty for not following them, and God spells this out clearly in the next statement:

You shall have no other gods before Me. You shall not make for yourself a graven image, nor any manner of likeness . . . you shall not bow down to [idols] or serve them, for I the Lord your God am a jealous God, visiting the wickedness of the parents upon the children even to the third and fourth generations of them that hate me. . . .   [Exod. 20:3-5]

God adds, there is a reward, as well. God will show "mercy to the thousandth generation of them that love Me and keep My commandments" [Exod. 20:6].

If this reminds you of God's promise to King David, it is no accident. Covenants are contracts, after all. And, if you were to read the deed for a piece of land, and then read the deed for another piece of land, you should not be surprised to see much the same language in both. In fact, the very next commandment reminds us of the covenant with Noah, as we are told not to swear falsely, invoking God's name.

Then God commands us to keep the Sabbath again, for a historical reason: "For in six days God made heaven and earth, and sea, and all that is in them, and rested on the seventh day . . . [Exod. 20:11].

Enter the Land of Israel. God commands us to "Honor your father and your mother. . . ." If you do honor your parents, "your days may be long on the land the Eternal your God gives to you"

[Exod. 20:12]. You may wonder why this commandment was chosen to be related to the Land of Israel. There are many possible answers. God may be telling us something about freedom, for example.

The people who received the commandments were the children of slaves. When they thought of their fathers and mothers, they thought of slaves who were forced to work for Pharaoh. Now they were free. So there was immediately a generation gap. It would have been easy for a child then to respond to his or her parents by saying, "You don't have any idea what's best for me! You grew up in slavery; and you think like a slave. Let me alone. I know what it means to be free!" In truth, the person who really understands freedom is the one who remembers slavery. So, in one sense, God was saying "as long as you remember what it was like to be a slave, you will know just how precious is the gift of this land–your own land, a land in which you can live in freedom. But, if you forget slavery–that is, if you fail to honor your parents who understand the lessons of slavery–your days on the land are numbered."

This is just one possible explanation, however. You may have one of your own. God did not explain any further. The commandment is simple in its statement: honor your parents and you will possess the Land of Israel; stop honoring them, and the Land will be lost."

Those are the first five commandments. Five more follow:

6. You shall not murder.
7. You shall not commit adultery.
8. You shall not steal.
9. You shall not bear false witness against your neighbor.
10. You shall not covet your neighbor's house, your neighbor's wife, your neighbor's servants, your neighbor's animals, nor any thing that belongs to your neighbor.

The Ten Commandments are the basic terms of the agreement, the *berit* between God and the people of Israel. The rest of the *mitzvot* spell these ten out in greater detail, making them easier for us to understand, easier for us to follow.

The "Chosen People"

Just before giving the covenant to the people at Sinai, God made a promise that is really a part of the covenant:

If you will obey Me faithfully and keep My covenant, you shall be My treasured possession among all the peoples. Indeed, all the earth is Mine, but you shall be to Me a kingdom of priests and a holy people. [Exod. 19:5-6]

This is the great secret of being the "Chosen People." When we choose to keep the laws of the covenant, we become God's "treasured possession . . . a kingdom of priests and a holy people."

All that is left is to see how the people agreed to the *berit* that God placed before them. The Torah tells us:

And he, Moses, took the Book of the Covenant and read it aloud to the people, and they said, "All that God has commanded we will faithfully do." [Exod. 24:7]

The people of Israel took an oath. In effect, they swore to behave in ways of righteousness. They swore to live up to the models of Noah and Abraham, who had been rewarded by covenants in the past.

The Living Covenant

From that moment, the covenant became a way of life for our people, constantly being renewed. Joshua was the first to renew it.

[Joshua] wrote there on the stones a copy of the law of Moses. . . . There was not one word of all Moses commanded that Joshua did not read before the whole assembly of Israel. . . .
 [Josh. 8:32; 35]

King Josiah renewed it again in much the same way:

And the king went up to the house of God . . . and he read in their ears [to all the people] all the words of the Book of the Covenant, which was found in the house of God. And the king stood on the platform, and made a covenant before God . . . to keep God's commandments . . .

to confirm the words of this covenant that were written in this book; and all the people were witnesses to the covenant.

[2 Kings 23:2-3]

And, much later, Ezra brought the Torah scroll and read it and explained it to the people living in the Land of Israel.

. . . We make a firm covenant and write it and our princes, our Levites, and our priests set their seal to it. . . . And the rest of the people . . . entered into a curse, and into an oath, to walk in God's law, which was given by Moses the servant of God, and to observe and do all the commandments of God. . . .   [Neh. 10:1, 29-30]

Judaism and the Covenant

Today we renew the covenant on the High Holy Days, on *Sukot*, on Passover, and especially on *Shavuot*–the day on which we commemorate the *berit* made at Sinai. We renew it, too, when we keep *Shabbat*, which was commanded in the covenant. We speak of God's love through which Torah with its commandments was given to us, and we say the *Shema* prayer, promising to teach the covenant diligently to our children.

We renew the covenant when a child is born, when a male child is circumcised or a female child named. We renew the covenant each time there is a consecration, Bar or Bat Mitzvah, a confirmation, a wedding ceremony, and even as we mourn for those who have died.

And, whenever we renew the covenant, we recall the Land of Israel, the Promised Land given to the Chosen People. So long as Jews continue to choose the way of the covenant, the Promised Land remains part of our agreement with God. So long as Jews choose *not* to forget, we honor the covenant and prove ourselves worthy of possessing the Land of Israel.

The Covenant and You

You play a special and essential part in the covenant. And Jewish tradition knows it. For it is a Jewish belief that the *berit* at Mount Sinai was not just an agreement between God and the people who stood at the foot of the mountain, but between God and the people of Israel forever. Here is how it was explained by Moses in the Torah:

You are standing this day, all of you before the Almighty your God . . . that you should enter into the covenant of the Almighty your God–and into God's oath. . . . Neither with you alone do I make this covenant and oath; but with the one who stands here with us this day before the Almighty your God, and also with the one who is not here with us this day.   [Deut. 29:9ff]

And who is "the one who is not here with us this day"? You.

Each generation of Jewish parents chooses to teach its children the path of righteousness, the way of Torah; and all of the children choose to teach that same path to their children–and this has happened all the way through history, down to you.

Now it is your turn to choose. The covenant has already been made. For countless generations we have kept it and guarded it, and tried to live by it. But it is always up to you whether Judaism will survive. And it will survive only if you continue to make Jewish choices and make them more and more because they *are* Jewish and because Judaism is important to you. In other words, as long as you honor the agreement, the *berit*, between God and Israel.

Much depends on you–not the least our presence in the Land of Israel. That, too, is a matter of choice, not chance. As a state in the Middle East, Israel's future survival is by no means assured. In the midst of enemies that far outnumber it, even its fine army cannot protect it without the support of the Jews in the Diaspora. As far as our eyes can see into the future, this will always be true.

What, then, would happen to Israel if you choose *not* to renew the covenant?

The Gift

Once a family was given a great gift: a map showing the spot where a chest full of precious stones–rubies, emeralds, and diamonds–was buried. Though the family knew it was buried on their land, they could not read the map. So they spent their lifetimes guarding the map, making sure no one else would see it, while digging everywhere to find the treasure, but never finding it. All the time the answer was right there, if only they stopped digging long enough to learn how to read.

You are a part of something that special, the *berit*, the agreement that ties heaven to earth. Unfortunately, many Jews are a part of it and never know just how special it is! Like the family with the map, they hold it and guard it, without learning to read it. So they pass the treasure on from generation to generation without ever truly touching it. Many such people are good Jews: they live good and useful lives. Yet they understand little about their Judaism, and still less about their land. They hardly know what the covenant is, or why the Promised Land is theirs. To know, you must stop digging for a while and study.

Yet here is something wonderful indeed. For the study of the covenant is like the study of a treasure map. As you study, you move in the right direction. Each bit of knowledge brings you a step closer to the treasure itself. Because you are alive the covenant lives. All that remains is that you choose life, that you choose the covenant for yourself and for your children, too.

The Future

The Maccabiah, Israel's own Olympics, begin. Thousands of Israelis watch the parade of athletes. An Israeli dance festival is under way. Yemenites perform the dances of their heritage, and kibbutz dance groups show the many ways of doing the hora. Israeli soldiers at the front pause to pray. In Tel Aviv, an artisan raises a hammer to delicately strike the edge of a raw diamond. Harvesters sort the Jaffa oranges by sizes, saving the best to be sent to Spain, Italy, and the United States.

Israeli scientists and doctors study and teach. Students come from around the world to learn of their latest advances. In the midst of the desert, wheat grows, using just the small amounts of rainfall that come to the Negev. Off the coast of Eilat, saltwater is turned into fresh drinking water in a desalinization plant. The promise of enough water for everyone in the world lies in this kind of process, for the world is three-quarters ocean.

On the hour *Kol Yisrael*, "The Voice of Israel," the official Israeli radio station, broadcasts the news of the day. What has happened in the United Nations? What is the government doing? What's happening in the West Bank? Is the economy going to get better or will inflation just keep rising? Are Israel's neighbors planning new wars and conflicts or are they thinking at long last about peace? Will the next government be different? Have the Palestinian terrorists hijacked an airplane or assassinated more innocent people? Has the U.S. decided to ship badly needed new arms to Israel so that Israel can stay ahead of its enemies militarily? Has the Israeli soccer team won in the international soccer competition?

Loyalty

Scattered among the nations of the earth, Jews tune their television sets and radios to listen to the news. They feel a special surge of loyalty when the word "Israel" is spoken, or when Israel is in the headlines. They watch and listen with special care to what is happening in the Middle East. Many have visited Israel; some have studied there or lived there briefly; hundreds of thousands hope to visit Israel soon.

Standing Together

We who live outside of Israel have a great stake in what happens there. The people of Israel know that Jews must stand together. As the Talmud puts it, "Every Jew is responsible each for the other."

The State of Israel has caused a revolution in modern Jewish thinking. Jews have returned to the land, as farmers, as workers. Jews have built a society based on freedom and democracy. Jews have brought their own people home to safety in an ingathering of the exiles. And the Jews who did this, the Jews of Israel, have also begun to awaken to their Jewishness, to seek out what it can mean to them personally, politically, culturally.

Behind all this is the ancient covenant with its promise and its demand. The promise has, in many ways, been fulfilled: the Jewish people and the Jewish land are again free to live Jewishly. The demand of the covenant has yet to be fulfilled.

Holy People

The new goal of Israel and Jews who love Israel, wherever they may live, must be to shape a Jewish people on its own soil that will become a "light to the nations," that will finally be "a kingdom of priests and a holy people." So much depends on how these words are understood–on how you understand them, and what you make of them in your life and in your dealings with the State of Israel.

So much depends on this, in fact, that you are the only one who truly knows what the future of Israel may be. The world of the future will be the world you create.

There have always been Jews living in the Land of Israel. Through all the long years when the land was not in our hands, when we were not free, these Jews have waited for the people of Israel to come home again, for the ancient promises of the covenant to be fulfilled.

In a sense God was waiting, too.

In the midst of all this waiting our ideas have changed. We have changed. But some things have not changed. To be a holy nation, we must act righteously toward one another and toward the stranger. It was the same in the time of Noah, Abraham, Moses, and David. To be a kingdom of priests, we must look to a future of holiness, a future free of war and struggles against others. Governments may come and go–for the Jews this is only the natural way of things. But in the end there is One who must be made ruler over us all. So it was in the time of Joshua; so it is for us:

Thus said the Eternal, the God of Israel: . . . Then you crossed the Jordan and you came to Jericho . . . I sent a plague ahead of you, and it drove them out before you . . . not by your sword or your bow. I have given you a land for which you did not labor and towns which you did not build, and you have settled in them; you are enjoying vineyards and olive groves you did not plant.

Now, therefore, revere the Eternal and serve God with undivided loyalty. . . .   [Josh. 24:2, 11-14]

Whether you live in Israel or not, you are a part of it, just as it is a part of you. The covenant binds us. Israel is much more than just a nation in the Middle East.

You are Israel.

▪ The Making of the Hebrew Bible ▪

The Bible is an anthology. The parts may be studied and analyzed. At the same time, the Holy Scriptures is our people's source book, the font of Judaism, a seminal work for Western civilization. Moreover, the anthology's essential unity reflects God's unity and is the source of the unity of the Jewish people.

Torah, the basis for the Jewish law and religion, is arguably the most important part of the Bible. That does not mean that the other sections are unimportant. The entire Hebrew Bible is the legacy and biography of the Jewish people. All of the books are sacred or holy. The Jew and the law, religion and culture, are understood only in the context of the entire Bible account of Jewish experience, starting with the Torah and continuing through all of the remaining books.

The following reading explains how biblical books came to be written and canonized. It requires detective work to unravel the clues regarding when and how Scriptures became sacred. In many cases the clues are in the Bible or in contemporary texts. What were the criteria for admitting a book into Scriptures? How do we decide today whether a book is "worthy"? Why is our Bible the most translated and most published book ever written? What's your favorite biblical book? Why?

The Making of the Hebrew Bible

BY HARRY M. ORLINSKY

Some people have the strangest notions about the Hebrew Bible. They imagine it is one continuous book, all of it written down at the same time. Or they reckon that Moses brought it down from Sinai, *all* of it engraved on the two tablets. If you ask them how old it is, some will guess that it goes back to Abraham. Some will even tell you that the famous English translation issued by a group of British Church scholars in 1611 at the order of King James I of England was *written* or handed down from heaven by "Saint James"! King James, a thrifty Scot who commissioned the translation and then found ways to avoid paying the scholars their promised fees, was called many things but never a saint, with a big or little "s." The correct term for the translation he commanded is the "King James (or Authorized) Version."

Every informed Jew knows that the Hebrew Bible is not *one* book but a collection of twenty-four books. That is the number accepted by Jewish tradition, but, if you count the three two-part books (Samuel, Kings, and Chronicles) as six instead of three, and the twelve Minor Prophets as twelve books instead of one, and Ezra and Nehemiah as two instead of one, the total will be thirty-nine. These twenty-four (or thirty-nine) books are divided into three main sections known in Hebrew as *Torah* (the Law), *Nevi'im* (the Prophets), and *Ketuvim* (the Writings). The initial letters of these names form an acronym, *TaNaCH*, a term popularly used by Jews when they are referring to the entire Hebrew Bible.

Every informed Jew also knows that these

books were set down over a very long period of time–more than a thousand years. They were canonized–that is, recognized as Sacred Scriptures, writings that had been revealed or inspired by God–also over a long period stretching out over many centuries. The process of canonization took place in stages, section by section, from the time of Moses until after the collapse of the Bar Kochba revolt in the second century C.E.

The Torah

The first section of the Hebrew Bible, the Torah, is the oldest part. Well over a thousand years (from about the eighteenth century to the fifth century B.C.E.) passed by from the time the earliest portions came into being orally until most of it was written down. The material in it came to be regarded as binding upon the ancient Israelite community–and upon their descendants after them–in various stages, only a few of which are known to us. Exodus 24:3-7 describes one of those stages:

Moses went and repeated to all the people all the commands of God and all the rules; and all the people answered with one voice, saying, "All the things that the Almighty has commanded us we will do!" . . . Then he took the document of the covenant and read it aloud to [*literally, in the ears of*] the people. And they said, "All that the Eternal has spoken we will faithfully do!"

Scholars have generally designated this document (the Hebrew word *sefer* is traditionally translated as "book") the "Book of the Covenant." It is found in Exodus 20-23 and 34, and it deals with what we would today call civil and criminal legislation, ritual rules, and humanitarian prescriptions.

The expression "to read . . . in the ears of the people," sometimes followed by an expression of consent by the people, describes the biblical procedure of designating a document as official and binding, in other words, as divinely inspired or Sacred Scriptures.

The Hebrew Bible itself describes how the Torah section was formally declared Sacred Scripture in the days of Ezra and Nehemiah, fifth century B.C.E. Nehemiah 8 reports it:

All the people gathered as one . . . into the square in front of the Water Gate and asked Ezra the scribe to bring the document of the Torah of Moses. . . . Ezra the priest brought the Torah before the assembly . . . and read from it . . . from early morning until noon in the presence of the men and women. . . . Ezra then blessed the Creator, the great God, and all the people replied, "Amen, Amen!" . . .

The Prophets

No one knows the exact year the second major section of the Hebrew Bible came into being, but we do know it was sometime before 200 B.C.E. How do we come by this knowledge? By finding important clues in other books of that period.

For example, about 120 B.C.E., a man who identified himself as the grandson of Jesus son of Eleazar son of Sirach (the Aramaic form of Greek-Latin *Jesus* is *Jeshu'a* or *Yeshu'a*, and the Hebrew is *Joshua* or *Yehoshu'a*) gave us some very valuable information in the Prologue he wrote for his Greek translation of a book his grandfather had composed in Hebrew. That book is known as *The Wisdom of Ben Sira*, or by its Latin-Greek name *Ecclesiasticus*, and should not be confused with the biblical book called *Kohelet*, or *Ecclesiastes*. This is a part of what the grandson wrote:

Whereas many great teachings have been given

to us through the Law and the Prophets and the other [books] that followed them . . . my grandfather Jesus, after devoting himself especially to the reading of the Law and the Prophets and the other books of our ancestors . . .

Later on in the book itself, Ben Sira discusses in succession the Torah (he mentions biblical figures like Enoch, Noah, Abraham, Isaac, Jacob, Moses, and Aaron), Joshua, the Judges, Samuel, Kings (Nathan, David–including a reference to Psalms–Solomon, Rehoboam, Jeroboam, Elijah, Hezekiah, Josiah), Ezekiel, the twelve (Minor) Prophets, etc. In other words, during the lifetime of Ben Sira, the grandfather of the man who issued a Greek translation about 120 B.C.E., the Prophets were already linked together with the Torah.

Clues from Philo

This same linking together of the Prophets with the Torah was made by two other writers, Philo and Luke. Philo, the Jewish philosopher of Alexandria in the early first century, wrote a treatise "On the Contemplative Life," in which he deals with a Jewish sect of ascetic hermits called the Therapeutae. Philo notes in passing how they used to bring into their rooms for study only "the Laws and words [Oracles] prophesied by the Prophets and Psalms and the other Writings by which knowledge and piety may be increased. . . ."

Luke, an early Christian evangelist, put it this way in his writings that appear in the Christian Scriptures (Luke 24:44): "Then he [Jesus appearing among them after rising from the dead] said to them [his disciples], 'These are my words which I spoke to you, while I was still with you, that everything written about me in the Law of Moses and the Prophets and the Psalms must be fulfilled.'"

In both Philo and Luke, there is still no indication of a third section of the Hebrew Bible, although the book of Psalms and some other–unnamed–books are clearly regarded as belonging to the category of Sacred Books.

Even the noted Jewish historian Josephus, in

his work *Against Apion* written about 90 C.E., knows no third division by name. He wrote Book I, 37-40:

For we do not have myriads of books among us, disagreeing from and contradicting one another [as the Greeks have], but only twenty-two Books, which contain the records of all past time and are justly accredited. Of these, five are [the Books] of Moses ... the prophets who subsequent to Moses recorded the history of the events of their times in thirteen Books. The remaining four Books contain hymns to God and precepts for the conduct of human life. . . .

Josephus's twenty-two Books may have lacked Kohelet and Esther, but scholars are uncertain about this and on which thirteen Books constituted for him the section Prophets.

The Third Section

If we knew when the third section of the Hebrew Bible, the *Ketuvim*, came into being, we would all know when the Hebrew Bible came to be closed. Unfortunately, we have few clear-cut clues, and to make our task even more difficult, we know that there was some discussion about whether or not several books should be included as sacred.

There is reason to believe that at about the time of the destruction of the Second Temple (70 C.E.) or shortly afterward (about 90 C.E.), the two main Jewish scholarly groups in Judea, the Shammaites and the Hillelites, met and discussed which of the books commonly regarded as divinely inspired ought to be formally designated as Sacred Scripture, along with the Torah and the Prophets.

We have little doubt that by this time, even though they had never been formally declared to be sacred, certain books already were considered to be authoritative, holy, and sacred in the same degree as those in the two sections of the Bible that had been canonized earlier. The book of Psalms was associated with King David and had become part of the temple service. In the same way, Proverbs was associated with King Solomon, Job with the patriarchal period, Ruth

---

BOOKS OF THE HEBREW BIBLE (TANACH)

I. TORAH (Five Books of Moses) –Pentateuch

(1) Genesis
(2) Exodus
(3) Leviticus
(4) Numbers
(5) Deuteronomy

II. PROPHETS

A. Former Prophets

(6) Joshua
(7) Judges
(8) Samuel I and II
(9) Kings I and II

B. Latter Prophets

The Major Prophets

(10) Isaiah
(11) Jeremiah
(12) Ezekiel

(13) **The Minor Prophets**

Hosea	Nahum
Joel	Habakkuk
Amos	Zephaniah
Obadiah	Haggai
Jonah	Zechariah
Micah	Malachi

III. WRITINGS – Hagiographa

Wisdom Books

(14) Psalms
(15) Proverbs
(16) Job

Five Megillot–Scrolls

(17) Song of Songs–Canticles
(18) Ruth
(19) Lamentations
(20) Ecclesiastes–Kohelet
(21) Esther
(22) Daniel
(23) Ezra-Nehemiah
(24) Chronicles I and II

with the period of the Judges, Lamentations with the prophet Jeremiah and the destruction of the First Temple, and Daniel with the end of the Assyrian Empire (late seventeenth century B.C.E.), Ezra and Nehemiah with the restoration of Judah and the Temple and the authority of the Torah; and Chronicles with the books of Samuel and Kings in the canon. In other words they were considered to have been either parts of continuations of divinely inspired books or authors. At the same time there was nothing substantive in any of these books that would suggest they should be omitted from Scriptures.

Controversial Books

However, several other books ran into difficulties. The rabbis of the Talmud used the special phrase "defiles the hands" as the technical term for "was divinely inspired" or "was to be regarded as canonical and binding on all Israel forever." This is the way the Mishnah (*Yodayim* 3:5), the postbiblical work that is part of the Talmud, explains some of the debate regarding Song of Songs and Kohelet:

All the Holy Writings defile the hands. [The books of] Song of Songs and Kohelet defile the hands. Rabbi Judah said, "Song of Songs defiles the hands, but Kohelet was in dispute." Rabbi Jose said, "Kohelet does not defile the hands, and Song of Songs was in dispute."... But Rabbi Akiba said, "God forbid! No one in Israel disputed the fact that Song of Songs defiles the hands, for the entire world does not compare with the day that Song of Songs was given to Israel. All the [books of the] Writings are holy, but Song of Songs is the holiest of all. If there was a dispute, it was only about Kohelet...."

What was the reason for the dispute about Song of Songs? If you will read it, you will see immediately, for it is obvious. The book is a collection of love poems. In poetic and unsophisticated language, the physical and emotional qualities of the two lovers are described in some detail:

Ah, you are fair, my darling,
Ah, you are fair.

Your eyes are like doves
Behind your veil.
Your hair is like a flock of goats
Streaming down Mount Gilead,
Your teeth are like a flock of ewes
Climbing up from the washing pool ...
Your lips are like a crimson thread,
Your mouth is lovely ...
There is no blemish in you. (4:1-7)

On the surface of it the book could hardly have been expected to qualify as Holy Writ, as divinely inspired. Fortunately, Song of Songs was declared divinely inspired and accepted as part of Sacred Scripture. Two arguments decided the case: Its authorship was attributed to King Solomon (as Proverbs and Kohelet were also); and the rabbis interpreted Song of Songs as an allegory intended to show the lovers not as individuals but rather as God and Israel. The fact that the book was probably quite popular among the people at large did not hurt the case.

Problems with Kohelet

The tone of Kohelet explains the hesitancy of the rabbis. The tone is set in the very first verses:

Utter futility! ... All is futile!
What gain is there for a man
For all his toil under the sun?
One generation goes, another comes,
But the earth remains the same for ever.

Nature and humanity, indeed the whole universe, moves unceasingly and aimlessly in circles, with rhyme perhaps but with no reason. This theme is repeated elsewhere in the book in various ways, for example:

In my own futile life I have seen everything: sometimes a just person dies even though he was just, and sometimes a wicked person lives long even though he is wicked. Do not be over-just.... Do not be over-wicked.... (7:15-17)

Or compare:

That is the sad thing about all that goes on under

the sun: that the same fate befalls everyone. (9:3)

Consequently,

Go, eat your bread in gladness and drink your wine in joy. . . . Enjoy life with a woman you love all the days of your futile life . . . for there is no doing or thinking, no knowing or learning in Sheol where you are going. (9:7-10)

Or as Mehitabel the alley cat put it to Archy the cockroach in the classic by Don Marquis: "Wottahell, Archy, toujours gai!"

If, however, Kohelet succeeded in the end in acquiring the authority to "defile the hands," it was because the rabbis attributed the authorship to Solomon and added on an acceptable ending. This ending repeats the verse in Kohelet 12:13 for emphasis, apparently to offset the strong note of pessimism and futility in the book:

The sum of the matter, everything having been heard: Fear God and obey God's commandments. For this is the duty of all humankind.

The book of Esther was not canonized even when Song of Songs and Kohelet were. It is not mentioned specifically by anyone prior to the second century C.E. as being canonical. Indeed, it is the only book of the Hebrew Bible whose text is not represented even by a fragment of any of the Dead Sea Scrolls. Look at its content! The name of God is nowhere mentioned in Esther; it is not God who is petitioned for help against Haman and his evil crew. Rather, it is Esther and her sex appeal that bring deliverance to the Jews of Susa and the Persian satrapies–Esther, a Jewish girl who became the wife of a Gentile after winning a beauty contest! It is hardly the kind of story that is associated with divine inspiration. (By contrast, read the book of Judith, with a Jewish heroine who also saved her people but in quite a different way. But Judith was excluded from the Hebrew Bible and found a home in the books of the Apocrypha.)

Nevertheless, so popular was the story of Esther among the Jewish populace after the destruction of the Second Temple and the collapse of the Bar Kochba revolt that the book simply became part of the canon. This was probably in the second century C.E. At that point the *Ketuvim* section was finished, and the three main sections were preserved together. The canon of the Hebrew Bible has remained closed ever since.

There is an ancient Jewish saying, "Everything depends on luck, even the Holy Writings in the Temple." Had the third division been closed a century earlier or a century later, in all probability our Hebrew Bible would be different from what it is today.

▪ The Making of the Mishnah ▪

Every nation must have laws. They can be imposed by an absolute authority like a king or a dictator, or developed by and agreed to by all the people. Laws can also be imposed by God, as is the case with the Jewish people. God's laws, recorded in the Torah, became the constitution for the Jewish people and for the nation it created in *Eretz Yisrael*.

Laws change as circumstances change. Constitutions are amended. Constitutional laws require interpretation. That's true also for Torah laws. The interpretations, once recorded, gave rise to a vast literature. Its beginning is known as the Mishnah (from the Hebrew *shanah*, repeat) which, in turn, became the basis of yet another, larger, literature, the Talmud.

The reading that follows describes how Mishnah was created. Identify the twelve stages starting with *berit* and ending with Judah ha-Nasi. What modern events might be suitable for a contemporary Mishnah-like process? (Clue: Mishnah preserves the record of ways of life that have vanished or are threatened with extinction.) The Mishnah was the law book for the ancient Jewish nation. For Orthodox Jews it continues to be the law book. Should it be the law for the modern State of Israel as well? Explain. The prominence and affluence of the Babylonian Jewish community provided suitable conditions for creation of the Babylonian Talmud. Might any of today's Diaspora communities be able to produce a Talmud? Explain.

■ The Making of the Mishnah   BY EUGENE J. LIPMAN ■

The Mishnah is the first writing down of what Jewish tradition calls Torah *shebe'al peh,* Oral Torah. Next to the Torah, the Five Books of Moses, the Mishnah is the most significant book of Torah we have.

How did the Mishnah come about? Why is it so important? What does it have to do with Jews today?

Let's go back, a long way back. Our ancestors three thousand years ago became a people. The bond that brought them together was the covenant. They believed–and we still believe–that something happened at Mount Sinai that brought Israel as a collectivity, a people, into a unique relationship with God. They believed that God promised them to be with them and to care about them. They believed that they would inherit the land of their ancestors. And they believed that God transmitted Torah to them– Torah, meaning divine instructions, rules, laws of conduct, principles, insights into reality. At that historic moment of contracting the covenant, God told Israel what was expected of them as a people and as individuals. And they said: "*Na'aseh venishma*"–"We shall do and we shall hearken."

That covenant was renewed after the conquest of Canaan by Joshua and his generation. At Shechem Joshua demanded adherence to Torah as the basis of group existence. The people responded, "We shall serve Adonai our God, and we shall hearken to God's voice." (Joshua 24:24)

There is deep disagreement among Jews about the content of Torah at Joshua's time and for centuries thereafter. Orthodox Jews teach that the Torah, the Written Torah, the Five Books of Moses, already existed in Joshua's time, in the same form in which we have it. Non-Orthodox Jews generally do not believe that the words of the Written Torah were given "as is" at Sinai; instead, they believe those words, insights, instructions, and divine principles emerged gradually, over many hundreds of years, as our ancestors lived in the Land of Israel and tried to puzzle out the difficult problem of what God expected of them.

Not every generation was zealous in fulfilling the demands of Torah. Other ritual systems competed successfully with Torah. Other civil systems of law came along and made demands on Jews contrary to Torah. Other cultures challenged Torah. Prophets emerged, messengers of the Divine, who reminded the people of their failings. The effect of faithlessness, they thundered, had to be punishment, exile from the land.

That exile did in fact occur; indeed several exiles occurred, beginning in 722-721 B.C.E., when the northern kingdom of Israel was destroyed and its leaders exiled. By 587-586 B.C.E., Jerusalem had been conquered, Solomon's Temple had been destroyed, and the leaders of the kingdom of Judea were subjected to the same fate as their northern brothers and sisters–exile from the land. In this exile they were sent off to captivity in Babylonia.

"Constitution" for Jews

Much happened during the Babylonian exile. One of the fateful events was that the Torah, the Five Books of Moses, was set down in its completed form. When the exile ended, that collection of five books became the "constitution" of the Jewish people. Not only were its laws (traditionally, 613 of them) considered sacred, binding, and in force, but within it were the basic building blocks for a host of new legal decisions. Why new decisions?

The Torah, the Five Books of Moses, did not contain all the answers to *all* questions. Life in Palestine, like life in the whole of the civilized world at the time, was becoming more complex with each passing generation. Cities grew up. International trade spread. Greek culture was an important force in the eastern Mediterranean. Then Rome conquered the Land and the Roman legal system had to be encountered. New problems brought new cases and the need for new decisions. And the Torah did not have all the answers. It did not deal directly with all the cases that kept arising in the changing world, and certainly not with all the "what if" situations that the fertile minds of the Jews could think up. So elders and scribes and sages gradually created a body of Oral Torah–judgments in cases, answers to questions, solutions to "what if" situations.

THE MISHNAH
ITS ARRANGEMENT AND CONTENTS

THE MISHNAH
THE COLLECTION OF THE "ORAL LAW"

That is, the rabbinic commentaries, legal decisions, insights, and interpretations of the Torah by the *Tana'im* over several centuries, transmitted by word of mouth until the time of Rabbi Judah, head of the Sanhedrin, around 160 C.E. to 200 C.E. The huge collection was set down and arranged (codified) in *Shishah Sedarim*, or "Six Orders" (major sections). Each "Order" in turn is made up of a number of books, or "tractates." The language is Hebrew. The total number of tractates is 63.

First Order: ZERA'IM ("Seeds")

Of the eleven books in this order, all but the first deal with the laws of agriculture. The eleven are:

Berachot (blessings, prayer)
Peah (edge of the field)
Demai (doubtful crops)
Kilayim (diverse kinds)
Shevi'it (the seventh year)
Terumot (heave offerings)
Ma'aserot (tithes)
Ma'aser Sheni (second tithe)
Challah (dough offering)
Orlah (fruit of the trees)
Bikkurim (first fruits)

Second Order: "MO'ED" ("Festivals" or "Appointed Seasons")

Twelve books:
Shabbat (Sabbath)
Eruvin (Sabbath travel regulations)
Pesachim (Passover)
Shekalim (temple taxes)
Yoma (the day [of atonement])
Sukkah (booth)
Yom Tov or **Betzah** (egg)
Rosh Hashanah (new year observances)
Ta'anit (fast day[s])
Megillah (the scroll [of Esther])
Mo'ed Katan (mid-festival days)
Chagigah (festival sacrifice)

Third Order: "NASHIM" ("Women")

Seven books on the laws of marriage and divorce:
Yevamot (sisters-in-law)
Ketubot (marriage contracts)
Nedarim (vows)
Nazir (the Nazirite vow)
Sotah (the suspected adulteress)
Gittin (divorces)
Kiddushin (marriage)

Fourth Order: NEZIKIN ("Damages")

Of the ten books all but one deal with civil and criminal law. The ten are:
Bava Kamma (the first gate)

Bava Metzia (the middle gate)
Bava Batra (the last gate)
Sanhedrin (the high court)
Makkot (punishment by flogging)
Shevuot (oaths)
Eduyot (testimonies)
Avodah Zarah (idolatry)
Pirke Avot (sayings of the fathers)–does not relate to civil or criminal law
Horayot (erroneous decisions)

Fifth Order: KODASHIM ("Sacred Things")

Eleven books on the laws of sacrifice and the dietary laws:
Zevachim (animal sacrifices)
Menachot (flour offerings)
Chullin (unconsecrated animals)
Bechorot (firstborn)
Arachin (evaluations)
Temurah (exchanges of sacrificial cattle)
Keritot (divine punishment)
Me'ilah (inadvertent sacrilege)
Tamid (daily sacrifice)
Middot (measurements)
Kinnim (bird offerings)

Sixth Order: TOHOROT ("Purifications")

Twelve books:
Kelim (vessels)
Oholot (tents)
Nega'im (leprosy)
Parah (the red cow)
Tohorot (cleanliness)
Mikvaot (ritual baths)
Niddah (the menstruating woman)
Makshirin (prerequisites for non-kashrut)
Zavim (bodily discharges in illness)
Tevul Yom (post-immersion uncleanliness)
Yada'im (uncleanliness of hands)
Uktzin (stalks and ritual uncleanliness)

System of Courts

Local judgments and teachings were transmitted to the whole country and to the people by word of mouth. But they, too, were not sufficient. More order was essential; an institutional system was needed. A court structure emerged.

Eventually there was a Sanhedrin of seventy men plus a president, known as the *nasi*. It met in plenary session in the Temple area in Jerusalem. As a sacred court, it met in sacred precincts. But it also divided itself into courts of twenty-three judges to hear criminal cases around the country. Its members also rode circuit in courts of three. These courts heard and decided civil disputes. And these experts in Written and Oral Torah also held classes for the entire citizenry–on the Shabbat and also on Mondays and Thursdays, the market days of the people. In Jerusalem, the members of the Sanhedrin compared cases; they argued case law and legal theory and *agadah* (non-legal Torah). But they did not write down their decisions or discussions. They believed that everything that had to be written had already been set down by Moses, *the* legal expert, at Sinai. All else was Oral Torah.

Jerusalem was the spiritual and the legal capital of the Jewish world. Scholars came from distant lands to consult, and there was much correspondence between scholars in Jerusalem and Jews living elsewhere in the world. After the Romans destroyed the Temple in 70 C.E., the Sanhedrin moved first to Yavneh (a few miles south of today's Tel Aviv), then to Usha in Babylonia. After the ill-fated Bar Kochba revolt of 135 the Romans declared Jerusalem to be off limits to Jews. Large numbers of sages and students lived in Babylonia. By this time Torah was being studied in Yemen and Spain and the Rhineland of today's West Germany. But without some central place and organization, without some ordered structure, what would become of Torah?

Writing Down Oral Torah

Rabbi Akiba, who lived through the destruction in the year 70, wrote down some legal discussions and decisions. His student Rabbi Meir wrote more, in spite of the prohibition against writing down such discussions. (It was felt that some Jews might revere the new material over the Written Torah of Moses.) But the needs of the troubled times were pressing: It was essential, when Jews were being scattered outside the land and the Temple no longer existed, that some

The Jew and the Law

way be found to have authoritative, universally acceptable Jewish law, *halachah*–the way for Jews to go on fulfilling their covenant with God, and also to retain the wisdom and insights of the *agadah*, the nonlegal material created over the centuries by the scholars who had been interpreting the Torah. The old prohibition had to be overturned, but, at the same time, the decision to write down Oral Torah had to be justified–just as every aspect of Oral Torah had to be justified–by a passage in the Bible. The sages cited the following passage from Psalms 119:126 as their justification: "It is time to act for the Almighty, for they have violated Your teaching."

The need to have a uniform body of legal Torah became even more overwhelming after the failure of the Bar Kochba revolt. Under the leadership of Rabbi Judah, the Nasi of the Sanhedrin in the last third of the second century C.E., a full-fledged project to write down Oral Torah was undertaken. It concentrated on *halachah*. It was finished just about 200 C.E. The large work was arranged in six "orders" or "sections," and each section contained a number of "tractates," or books. Altogether, there are sixty-three books, or tractates, in the Mishnah.

The compilers of the Mishnah selected their material carefully. They used the work of Rabbi Akiba and of Akiba's student Rabbi Meir. (Rabbi Meir must have been very vital to them, for we are taught in the Talmud that any Mishnah passage not attributed to someone by name was the work of Rabbi Meir.) They discussed this precedent versus that, this decision versus that, this point of view versus that. They wanted to make sure their compilation was authoritative.

In a sense, the Mishnah was accepted as authoritative. Why "in a sense"? The very ones who compiled it were not content with it, for there had been schools of thought, different points of view and different approaches to Oral Torah. These were not to be forgotten by disciples of great teachers who themselves had become great teachers. So they continued to discuss and to teach, to argue and clarify, using both the material included in the Mishnah and what had been omitted.

Two "Completions"

Both in Palestine and in Babylonia, this process of discussing, teaching, arguing, and classifying continued to go on generation after generation. The text of the Mishnah was the basis for their continuing discussions. *Agadah* (nonlegal material) was included as well as *halachah*. Early in the fifth century C.E. a Palestinian version of these interpretations of the Mishnah was written down. Toward the end of the sixth century, a much longer Babylonian version was finished. The Mishnah plus either what is called the "Jerusalem Gemara" or the "Babylonian Gemara" is the Talmud. (*Gemara* means "completion.") The Talmud is the inexhaustible source of legal doctrine, wisdom, and insight that has been, and continues to be, after the Bible, the most important of our sacred texts.

Since 425 C.E. there has been no Sanhedrin of the whole Jewish people, no supreme legislative or judicial body. And yet Judaism lives and flourishes as a religious system based on law. All branches of Judaism are dependent on the great classic texts of our literature for structure and order. We have never cut loose from our roots. We have expanded, we have changed, we have created new ways and new concepts. But there is a direct line from the Bible to our latest efforts. In the Jewish legal sphere, in responding in action to God's commands to us as covenant partner, the Mishnah remains the core book.

▪ A Reform View of Jewish Law ▪

When Reform Judaism began, its leaders endeavored to justify it within the *halachah*. However, that strategy was soon abandoned. Instead, Reform declared that *halachic* rabbinic authority and its codes were obsolete. In place of *halachic* traditions early reformers emphasized biblical writings, particularly the words of the prophets, whose compelling messages of social justice were especially appealing. But, as the following reading demonstrates, Reform soon began to doubt the authority of much of biblical writings. Why?

Why are present Reform attitudes about ancient authority more lenient than earlier views? What does contemporary Reform think about the authority of *halachah*? What is God's role in *halachah* from the Reform point of view? Should Reform have its own *halachah*? Explain. Interpret the phrase "We (Reform Jews) live without a clear philosophy."

■ A Reform View of Jewish Law   BY SOLOMON B. FREEHOF ■

Were the first Reformers in Germany concerned with *halachah* in any way?

The first type of defense made on behalf of Reform was a *halachic* one. The greatest Orthodox rabbis of the time had published a book of responsa that set out to prove the changes in the worship made by the Reform temple in Hamburg were in willful violation of Jewish law. Since the indictment was *halachic*, the defense had to be *halachic* also; and so, the first writings of the Reformers were intended to show it is quite permissible under certain circumstances to change Jewish laws and customs.

Was this *halachic* defense abandoned?

Yes. It became immediately evident to the Reformers that no adjustment in Jewish services or ceremonies could be made as long as the authority of the Orthodox rabbinate remained unchallenged. If there was to be Reform, there was no other way than to renounce the authority of the old rabbinate. The Reform movement was, therefore, from its beginning, anti-rabbinical and hence adverse to the rabbinical literature, the Talmud, and the codes that were the sources of rabbinical authority. The early Reform movement became essentially biblical. Its leaders held proudly to the inspiration of Scriptures–or at least to the Ten Commandments revealed at Sinai–and of the inspired prophets.

The Reform movement was well served by this emphasized prophetism that also enabled it to exert a strong influence on the Jewish community. In an era of fading tradition, where multitudes were abandoning their faith, Reform saved thousands of deserters by giving them an acceptable ideal and proclaiming it Jewish.

Does the Reform movement still see itself as essentially biblical?

The Reform movement is no longer certain that it has found in prophetism a sure foundation for its Judaism. There is now a search in Reform national meetings for a revived relationship with the postbiblical legal literature.

The self-description of Reform as being solely biblical was simply not true. All of Reform Jewish life in all its observances was actually postbiblical in origin. None of the arrangements of worship, the hours of service, the text of the prayers, no matter how rewritten, were primarily biblical. The whole of Jewish liturgy is an achievement of postbiblical times. The religious calendar, though based on Scripture, was elaborated and defined in postbiblical times. Marriage ceremonies and burial rites were all postbiblical. The Bible was the source of ethical ideas, but the actual religious life was rabbinic. Whatever percentage of the total traditional legislation Reform Jews observe, it is mainly postbiblical in origin. Our life is inspired by the Bible but organized by the Talmud.

But doesn't Reform Judaism differentiate between the Bible as divinely revealed and the Talmud as human-made?

Soon after the founding of the Reform movement the Bible itself began to be viewed by scholars as a human book, depriving it of its special uniqueness. It was now not necessarily different in status from the confessedly human, argumentative talmudic literature. However, since God speaks in "the language of human beings," God may be speaking through both literatures. If hitherto God had been revealed through the writers of the Bible by the flame of the human conscience, then afterward God was revealed through the debating scholars of the Talmud by the light of human intellect; and it may well be that the intelligence is as worthy a vehicle of revelation as the conscience.

Also, perhaps the facts of our own progress as a Reform movement have affected our relationship to the older legal literature. In the early days of Reform we were fighting against an overmastering Jewish legal authority. We could not attain our independence without denying and defying that authority. But now we are strong and can afford to be much more tolerant of the authoritative past.

We find it easier to honor the learning and wisdom of the rabbis of the past than to imagine our bowing to the pronouncements of the Orthodox rabbis of the present. Our pioneers freed us from Orthodox control and we will do nothing now that might restore any authority to it. Having been freed from older customs, we have had an opportunity to become creative, to transform old ceremonies, to invent new ones. In the totality of Jewish religious life this inventive creativity of Jewish ceremonial observance may well be our true and specific function.

When legal questions come up, what should be the basis of the answers? Is the talmudic literature the legal authority for Reform Judaism?

It is difficult to make even a simple practical decision without having an attitude on the question of the authority of the *halachah.* Of this much we are sure–that whatever authority the *halachah* has for us, it is certainly only a selec-

tive authority. There are vast sections of law about which we are never questioned and on which we do not volunteer decisions. No question among the Reform responsa concerns the mixing of meat and milk, the selling of leaven to a Gentile before Passover, or the construction of the ritual bath. These observances have ceased among Reform Jews and among large numbers of other Jews. Nor do Reform rabbis feel the obligation to restore them. These observances are in the Talmud but they have no legal status for us.

In what sense, then, has the rabbinic literature any authority at all, if Reform Jews feel they have the right to pick and choose?

We obey many rabbinic customs and neglect many more. As long as we are thus selective we cannot believe rabbinic law is God's mandate. It is possible that by some future date our part of the tradition will grow first habitual, then legal, then authoritative. But it is not authoritative now and cannot and perhaps should not be.

The law is to us a human product. That does not mean that God is not somehow revealed in the "language of the children of humans." Perhaps God is, but God's self-revelation is not so perfect, nor so clear, nor so final, as to make the whole law God's sure commandment. To us the law is human, but nobly human, developed by devoted minds who dedicated their best efforts to answering the question "What doth the Lord require of thee?" Therefore we respect it and seek its guidance. Some of its provisions have faded from our lives. We do not regret that fact. But as to those laws that we do follow, we wish them to be in harmony with tradition.

Are we obligated to live by those laws that are still vital?

The law is authoritative enough to influence us, but not so completely so as to control us. The rabbinic law is our guidance but not our governance. Our concern is more with the people than with the legal system. Whenever possible, interpretations are developed that are feasible and conforming to the needs of life.

What kind of observances do Reform Jews tend to adopt?

If we would list those observances that we

adopt and then contrast them with those we do not, it would be noticed that we do not adopt, or are not likely to adopt, the ceremonial prohibitions, the restrictive negatives in the law, except, of course, those of direct moral impact. We increasingly accept folk commandments, *minhagim* [customs], that have emerged from the life of the people and are dear to the people. . . . It may well be that behind our readoption of such observances there is not so much theology as sociology. We are strengthening our folk feeling. Some of the greatest changes in Jewish ceremonial life did not come from some legal decision of a legal scholar but arose spontaneously, almost mysteriously, out of the mood of the Jewish people. No rabbi and no group of rabbis ever ordained the use of the *chupah* (marriage canopy), or the practice of *yahrzeit* (marking a close relative's death), or the synagogue ceremony of Bar or Bat Mitzvah. These observances, which carry such strong emotional appeal, arose anonymously among the people of Israel.

Which parts of the *halachah* are most objectionable to Reform Jews?

Above all, our objections to much of the law are protests of conscience. The laws that will never be acceptable to us are those concerning chiefly the status of the Jewish woman. Aside from all the special tragedies in the life of Jewish women with regard to marriage and divorce, the very concept of her inferior legal status tends to turn us against the legal tradition. Perhaps the grandest achievement of Reform Judaism is its liberation of the Jewish woman.

Do you foresee the creation of a "Reform *halachah*"?

It may develop. Worthy actions may grow into religious duties, and so our Reform code will develop *mitzvah* by *mitzvah*, as each action achieves its sanctity. Some of these may be new *mitzvot*, but most of them will be rediscoveries of actions our tradition has cherished. We will have to find out which elements in the Jewish traditional lifestyle we can truly accept as a mandate and which will remain merely custom and therefore changeable. . . .

Somewhere, somehow, our thinkers will find harmony between discipline and freedom, between loyalty and individuality. Such a philosophy will not be imposed. It will emerge. In the meantime we live without a clear philosophy.

▪ Conservative Judaism and Jewish Law ▪

Conservative Judaism accepts the validity of *halachah* and tries to harmonize ancient law with modern life. The process of accommodation takes place in a committee of twenty-five rabbis appointed by the president of the Rabbinical Assembly, the Conservative rabbinical organization. However, the local rabbi is free to accept or reject the published opinions of the committee, except rulings prohibiting an action and in which fewer than three members disagree. In this way, Conservative Judaism offers clear guidelines for *halachah* while assuring the authority of the rabbi.

The following reading suggests some conditions Conservative Jews believe may require changes in the traditional law. What rationale prompts Conservative Judaism to allow laws to change? Is the ability to change laws good for Judaism? Explain. Explain the phrase "embarrassments and barriers that have made observance of Jewish law so difficult."

After reading this article, consider which point of view best serves Judaism and the needs of the Jewish people today: *halachah* is unchanging and binding on all generations (Orthodox); *halachah* is obsolete and not binding (Reform); *halachah* is valid but requires change so as to apply to modern circumstances (Conservative). Explain your choice.

The Jew and the Law

■ Conservative Judaism and Jewish Law

BY SEYMOUR SIEGEL ■

Conservative Judaism is committed to *halachah*. It teaches that the ancient rules of the Jewish faith, which regulate everything from what you eat to how you pray, are an essential part of a Jew's obligations. This does not mean that all or most Conservative Jews observe the laws today. But for some it remains a guiding light for life in a constantly changing world.

Legal decisions in the Conservative movement are based on *precedent* and *interpretation*. There is a long history in Judaism of discussions concerning Jewish law. It begins with the Bible, continues through the Talmud, and is carried forward in the codes of Maimonides, Joseph Karo, and others. In addition there are collections of legal decisions known as *she'elot* (questions) and *teshuvot* (responsa).

In the Conservative movement legal questions are submitted to the Committee on Jewish Law and Standards. (For a description of this committee and its work, see "How Conservative Judaism's Law Committee Works.")

Whenever Conservative *poskim*, or decisors, are faced with a halachic question, they first search out the precedents that are relevant to the case at hand. The next step is to analyze the precedents as to their roots and basic assumptions. They then consider whether these assumptions can be accepted under present conditions. Sometimes the conclusions drawn by the decisors are at odds with those of the traditional authorities. This may be because many of the assumptions of the past cannot, in good conscience, be accepted today. Though conclusions may differ, the process is the same one that has characterized Jewish law interpretation from its beginning.

When do new conditions and developments require modifications of Jewish law according to the interpretation of Conservative Judaism?

Ethical Considerations

When the outcome of the precedent is immoral, as in the case of the *agunah*, the precedent may be changed. An *agunah* is a woman who is unable to obtain a divorce from her husband, either because his whereabouts are not known or because he refuses to grant her one. (In Jewish law, only the husband can initiate a *get*, a divorce.) As a remedy to this problem, the Conservative movement grants powers of annulment to rabbinical courts in cases when a husband refuses to give his wife a *get* after a civil divorce had taken place. Orthodox rabbis are still wrestling with the *agunah* problem. Reform rabbis solved such problems by recognizing the jurisdiction of civil courts to terminate a Jewish marriage.

Technological Advances

A precedent may be changed if it is based on outdated scientific knowledge. Technological advances in medicine, for example, make it possible to transplant organs from a dead body into a living person. But are transplants permissible by Jewish law? On the one hand, any mutilation of the dead body is considered a desecration. On the other hand, it can be argued that the principle of *pikuach nefesh* (the saving of a life) permits the transplant. But is a person dead when the heart continues to beat artificially (a condition necessary for a successful transplant) after the brain has died? A controversy arose among the Conservative *poskim* over the definition of death. The majority decided that death occurs when the brain stops functioning. Other questions affected by or resulting from technological advances include test-tube fertilization, abortion, and euthanasia (letting a terminally ill patient die).

Sociological Change

Conservative Judaism holds that precedents based on sociological attitudes that no longer apply may be changed. In recent years the issue of women's rights in the synagogue has been a major agenda item of the Committee on Jewish Law and Standards. Ancient practice ordained that men and women be separated in the synagogues because it was thought that men could not pray with full concentration when sitting near women. Apparently, in past eras, a woman's dignity was not diminished by sitting behind a *mechitzah* [partition]. But, in light of our modern conception of women as equal participants in society, separation of this kind is seen by many as being offensive. Thus, the Conservative movement holds that synagogues may have family pews instead of segregated seating. Orthodox synagogues do not normally accept this interpretation and generally continue the tradition of separate seating. In Reform synagogues, seating is mixed.

Several years ago the Committee on Jewish Law decided that women should be included in the *minyan* (the prayer quorum) and that they should be given *aliyot* to the Torah. Local congregations have the right to accept or reject these practices.

A much debated question within Conservative quarters today is whether or not women should be ordained as rabbis and cantors. (The Reform and Reconstructionist movements already have women rabbis.) While it is likely that the Committee on Jewish Law will approve the ordination of women rabbis (the issue of cantors is more complex legally), the faculty of the Jewish Theological Seminary has not yet voted to accept women in its rabbinical program. Questions related to the activity of women in Judaism are certain to be part of the agenda of Conservative decisors for a long time.

Needs of the Times

Sometimes the needs of the times require modifications in Jewish practice. The prohibition of driving a vehicle on the Sabbath and festivals is a case in point. This prohibition is based on the idea that a Jew should not kindle a fire or travel far from home on a rest day. Such rules are fine for Jews who live in urban areas with easy access to the synagogue, but they create hardships for those who live in suburban areas where distances are much greater. The Law Committee decided that a congregant who is unable to walk to synagogue on the Sabbath or festivals can drive, but only to and from the synagogue.

Orthodox rabbis believing that Jewish law cannot be altered, even if there seems to be good reason, generally regard Conservative interpretations as being too liberal. Conservative rabbis, in turn, regard Reform Judaism as too liberal. One could say that the Orthodox are strict-constructionists (of Jewish law), that the Reform are loose-constructionists, and that the Conservative take a position in between.

The Conservative movement has tried to remove the embarrassments and barriers that have made observance of Jewish law so difficult for so many modern Jews. However, to be effective interpreters of the law, our people's interest and commitment to Jewish law must be strengthened. For, in the final analysis, it is the Jewish people in their striving for a relationship with God and speaking through their spiritual leaders who determine Jewish law.

HOW THE CONSERVATIVE LAW COMMITTEE WORKS

1. Clarifying questions of Jewish law for the Conservative movement is the task of the Committee on Jewish Law and Standards. This committee is composed of twenty-five rabbis appointed by the president of the Rabbinical Assembly, the international organization of Conservative rabbis. They represent a cross section of the Conservative rabbinate in age, location, and ideology.

2. The legal process begins when the rabbi of a local congregation submits an inquiry to the committee. (The committee will accept questions only from a rabbi, an arm of the movement, or an academic institution.) The question is considered in light of what the traditional legal texts say and with regard to the present needs and

prevalent attitudes of the synagogues in the movement. Individual committee members write papers that are kept in its archive. A vote is taken. Sometimes all members agree and the decision is transmitted to the rabbi or organization that asked the question. Sometimes committee members disagree, resulting in two or more opinions. Conservative responsa are published in *Conservative Judaism* and in books as special collections.

3. The Conservative movement views the local rabbi as the *mara d'atra*, the religious authority in his congregation. He is considered to be the best informed as to the beliefs and practices of his community and is thought to know what is best for it. The local rabbi is free to follow the majority or minority opinion of the committee. He is also free to reject or ignore its opinions. Though most committee decisions are not binding on each rabbi, they do carry great moral weight and become official policy of the Conservative movement.

4. There is, however, one exception to the rule giving autonomy to the local rabbi. When the committee prohibits something, with fewer than three members disagreeing, each member of the Conservative rabbinate is obliged to follow the committee's ruling. One such decision concerns the issue of performing mixed marriages. The committee has prohibited local rabbis from officiating in a marriage between a Jew and a non-Jew. If any Conservative rabbi violates this rule, he is subject to expulsion from the Rabbinical Assembly.

5. Many questions are received by the committee each month. They deal with problems of *kashrut, avelut* (the laws of mourning), liturgy, synagogue practices, medical ethics, and other matters of Jewish concern. The committee also hopes to tackle some of the larger social issues, clarifying the position of Jewish law on capital punishment, busing for racial integration, and socialized medicine.

▪ The Mishnah in Our Daily Lives ▪

Mishnah provides the details for the Jewish practices derived from Torah laws. Many of our most familiar and widely practiced observances are discussed in the pages of Mishnah. Thus Jews in far-separated communities were bound to one another through the same source books, the same laws, and, ultimately, much the same customs. Those customs and law practices continue almost without change among traditional Jews today. Reform and Conservative Jews also, in some of their daily and seasonal Jewish activities, preserve and perpetuate ancestral practices.

The following reading presents examples of how the Mishnah elucidates a Torah law, elaborates on it, and defines how the law should be implemented. Why did the compilers of the Mishnah provide such detail and such explicit instructions for carrying out a law? Explain what impact Mishnaic writings had on the survival of Judaism. What impact does the Mishnah have today on Jewish survival? Explain.

▪ The Mishnah in Our Daily Lives

BY BERNARD M. ZLOTOWITZ ▪

How do we know that Jews are required to fast on Yom Kippur? Our Bible tells us merely that

"you shall afflict your souls." (Leviticus 23:27) *How* are we to "afflict" our souls? For the answer we have to go to the Mishnah.

How do we know the Four Questions to ask at the Passover seder? They are not in our Bible. To find them as they were originally set down, we have to go to the Mishnah.

The Bible tells us that on the Sabbath day, "you shall do no manner of servile work." What is "work," and what, in particular, is "servile work"? To find out, again we must go to the Mishnah.

From these examples it is clear that the Mishnah is the code of Jewish law that spells out details of many teachings that are stated generally, or perhaps unclearly, or perhaps not at all, in the Bible. The Jews of two thousand years ago knew from the Torah that Yom Kippur was a solemn day of atonement; but what did that mean in practical terms? What were they to do or not do; what were their households expected to do? The rabbis of the Mishnah compiled the best answers from sages and teachers, both living and dead, debated them, and set them down for the guidance of the Jewish people. In this sense the Mishnah is an encyclopedia of Jewish law, written down in sixty-three books.

But it is far more than a code of laws. For, within the individual books, and within the discussions that ordinary people might consider "technical" or "legal," there are deep insights into human nature and human psychology that apply in any age or time. One entire book of the Mishnah is not "legal" at all. It is a small book of moral teachings, called *Pirke Avot*, which can be translated as "Teachings" or "Sayings of the Fathers." Of all sixty-three books of the Mishnah, *Pirke Avot* has always been the most popular among Jews, the book that most Jews read and reread every Shabbat and teach their children. *Pirke Avot* has a great deal to tell us about proper behavior, about how we treat others, and about what people nowadays call "values."

Teaching Moral Values

Throughout our history as a people, the study of Torah—meaning the study of God's teachings for humankind—has always been a primary Jewish value. The ignorant person, that is, the person who does not know what God expects of him or her, cannot be a truly pious person. But many Jews, like many human beings, have a tendency to postpone what is good for them, to keep pushing off doing what they know they must do. *Pirke Avot* advises: "Set a fixed time for your study of the Torah." (1:15) The rabbis understood the necessity of acquiring a good habit; they also understood that such a habit frees a person from the anxiety of putting off a task, saying "I'll do it later." Rabbi Hillel anticipated that in *Pirke Avot* 2:5. "Do not say, 'When I have leisure, I will study.'" Hillel went on, "Perhaps you will have no leisure."

Along with study the rabbis valued work: "An excellent thing is the study of the Torah combined with some worldly occupation, for the labor demanded by them both makes sin to be forgotten." (*Pirke Avot* 2:2) Between working and studying, a person is too busy to get into trouble.

How do we act toward others? *Pirke Avot* 1:15 tells us: "Receive all with a cheerful countenance." In other passages, we learn: "Let the honor of others be as dear to you as your own"; "be careful not to put others to shame in public"; and "despise not anyone, and carp not at anything." Respect for others also extends to their possessions: "Let the property of others be as dear to you as your own." Suppose a Jew happens to transgress the teachings of the Torah. Does he (she) save up his (her) sins for next week or next Yom Kippur? *Pirke Avot* 2:15 counsels otherwise: "Repent one day before your death." But who knows the date of one's death? Repentance therefore must be immediate.

In this post-Watergate era, many citizens are skeptical about politicians and about undue intimacy with powerful government officials. This has been true in many countries throughout the history of civilization. The rabbis of the Mishnah lived at a time when Rome was the leading world power. In *Pirke Avot* 2:3, they summarized their wariness:

Be careful in your relations with the ruling power, for they bring no one near to them except for their own interests, seeming to be friends when it is to their advantage, but they stand not by one in the hour of one's need.

These moral and ethical teachings in *Pirke Avot* concern Jewish attitudes, behavior, and values in everyday personal life. In other books of the Mishnah, the rabbis set down the insights of Judaism regarding other aspects of life that we today consider "personal"–among them, family life; the relationships between husband and wife, parents and children; the obligations, duties, and responsibilities involved in a sound family life.

Implications of "Love"

"Love" in Mishnaic times was not colored by the romantic notions that were to appear much later in human history nor by the combination of romantic longing and sexual attraction that today very often is confused for "love." In Mishnaic times love was understood in terms of responsibility and obligation, and it was expressed through the care and concern of one person for another. A husband showed his love for his wife by personally caring and providing for her needs and by fulfilling his duties toward her as guaranteed by her *ketubah*, or marriage contract. He gave her shelter, food, and clothing. She showed her love by "grinding flour and baking bread and washing clothes and cooking food and giving suck to her child and making ready his bed and working in wool," as *Ketubot* 5:5 states. Later the sages who set down the Gemara expanded this conception of love (responsibility) by including respect and regard for the wife's opinion. In a charming maxim they said: "If the wife is short, bend down and hear her whisper"–that is, consult her. (*Bava Metzia* 59a) Respect for the feelings and wishes of the wife was paramount. Only on rare occasions could a husband impose his will on his wife. He was not free to move her around like a stick of furniture:

None may take forth [his wife against her will] from one town to another or from one city to another [in another country]; but within the same country he may take her forth with him from one town to another or from one city to another [even against her will], but not from a town to a city, and not from a city to a town. He may take her forth from a bad dwelling to a good one, but not from a good dwelling to a bad one. (*Ketubot* 3:10)

Responsibilities to Children

Love of parents took the form of honoring them, and there is no measure to honoring father and mother (*Peah* 1:1)–it is infinite. Love of parents for children was also understood in terms of obligations. The father was obliged to see that his son learned Torah. He was also obliged to see that he learned an honest craft:

A man should always teach his son a cleanly craft and let him pray to God to whom riches and possessions belong, for there is no craft wherein there is not both poverty and wealth, for poverty comes not from one's craft, nor riches from one's craft, but all is according to one's merit. . . ." (*Kiddushin* 4:14)

Later, in the Gemara, still another obligation was added: A father should also teach his son how to swim. (*Kiddushin* 29a) The love of a father for his children was thus expressed in very practical terms. A father had to make sure that they knew what was expected of them by their God and their community, that they knew how to support themselves by useful work, and that they knew how to preserve their lives.

The Jewish Festivals

The Jewish family as a unit shared (and shares) the life experiences of each of its members. In addition it celebrates major events in the lifecycle of the individual and the group, the group being the Jewish people. For the individual Jew and the Jewish people it is the Mishnah that establishes the "how" of celebrating the festivals.

Were it not for the Mishnah, we would not know that Rosh Hashanah is the day when we are judged. Leviticus 23:24 states merely that the first day of the seventh month (the month of Tishri) is to be a memorial proclaimed with the blast of horns. The Mishnah explains:

At four times in the year is the world judged: at Passover, through grain [meaning that God will determine the richness or scantness of the harvest]; at Shavuot, through the fruits of the tree [same reasoning]; on the New Year's Day [the first of Tishri] all that come into the world pass before God like flocks of sheep . . . [and God judges who shall live and who shall die]; and at the Feast [of Tabernacles] they are judged through water [how much rain will fall]. (*Rosh Hashanah* 1:2)

A few chapters later in the same book, we are told that all shofars–horns of animals–may be used to proclaim the solemn day except "that of a cow." Why not a cow? The incident of the Golden Calf was never forgotten!

The Mishnah spells out the unclear passage in Leviticus 23:27, "You shall afflict your souls" on Yom Kippur:

On the Day of Atonement, eating, drinking, washing, anointing, putting on sandals . . . are forbidden. (*Yoma* 8:1)

In the same chapter of the Mishnah we are taught some of the profound implications of Yom Kippur. On that day transgressions are forgiven between a person and God, "but, for transgressions that are between a person and others, the Day of Atonement effects atonement only if one has appeased the others." In other words Jews who have offended others must first go to those people and obtain forgiveness *before* they go to services and plead for God's forgiveness.

Passover

The ritual of the celebration of Passover is described in detail in the Mishnah: the drinking of the four cups of wine, the eating of bitter lettuce and *charoset*, the asking of the Four Questions. The Mishnah has preserved the original Four Questions, which differ only slightly from those we ask today. In the Mishnah they read:

Why is this night different from other nights? For on all other nights we eat leavened or unleavened bread, but this night all is unleavened; on all other nights we eat all kinds of vegetables,

but on this night bitter herbs; on all other nights we eat flesh roasted, stewed, or cooked, but this night all is roast; on all other nights we do not dip even once, but on this night twice. (*Pesachim* 10:4)

Since the destruction of the Temple in Jerusalem the question about meat has been set aside in favor of the question about leaning. It is the Mishnah, too, that also teaches us that any kind of fermented grain is forbidden during Passover.

The Shabbat

The Torah, in addition to prohibiting work, cites only one specific act that is forbidden on the Shabbat: kindling fire. (Exodus 35:3) The Sabbath laws–the do's and don'ts–are known to us only because of the Mishnah. The rabbis listed thirty-nine main classes of work that are forbidden on the Shabbat:

Sowing, ploughing, reaping, binding sheaves, threshing, winnowing, cleansing crops, grinding, sifting, kneading, baking, shearing wool, washing or beating or dyeing wool, spinning, weaving, making two loops, weaving two threads, separating two threads tying [a knot], loosening a knot, sewing two stitches, tearing in order to sew two stitches, hunting a gazelle, slaughtering or flaying or salting it or curing its skin, scraping it or cutting it up, writing two letters [of the alphabet], erasing in order to write two letters, building, puling down, putting out a fire, lighting a fire, striking a hammer, and taking out from a private domain [a home] to a public domain [for instance, the street]. (*Shabbat* 7:2)

The life of observant Jews was disciplined in such a way that every act they performed during their every waking hour was governed by rabbinic Mishnaic law, as a reminder that they were members of a people holy to God. The discipline was spelled out in meticulous detail. For example, the *Shema* for the evening prayer could be recited from the time the priests entered the Temple to eat their heave offering (the priests at the Temple did not "work" in the ordinary sense

The Jew and the Law

and were dependent upon the offerings of the people) until dawn. The *Shema* for the morning prayers may begin when one can distinguish between the blue threads and the white threads in the fringes of the prayer shawl (in other words, when there is sufficient daylight), and it can be recited until the third hour of the morning (around 9 A.M. in the summer and 10 A.M. in the winter), according to *Berachot* 1:1, 2.

The Mishnah prescribes the proper blessings over food:

What benediction do they say over fruits? Over the fruit of trees one says, "(Blessed art Thou . . .) who createst the fruit of the tree," except over wine, for over wine one says, ". . . who createst the fruit of the vine." Over the fruits of the earth one says, ". . . who createst the fruit of the ground," except over bread, for over bread one says, ". . . who bringest forth bread from the earth." And over vegetables one says, ". . . who createst the fruit of the ground"; ". . . who createst diverse kinds of herbs." (*Berachot* 6:1)

In this way the Mishnah set the standard for religious observances and practices.

At first glance it would seem the Mishnah is a code of law that imposes a very restrictive type of behavior. On the contrary, when it is studied and understood in proper perspective, the Mishnah prescribes standards of practice and behavior, and thus it was a unifying force that helped to shape Jewish life and to preserve Judaism.

The Mishnah has a built-in elasticity, a method allowing for reinterpretation by rabbis in later generations. (As a rough analogy, the United States Constitution also has a built-in method allowing for reinterpretation by the courts.)

Within the Mishnah one finds the elements of permanency and also of change. Indeed, the commentaries that follow the Mishnah–the Gemara produced in Palestine, and the Gemara produced in Babylonia, and the many commentaries that appeared in later centuries–show that the scholars were reinterpreting and changing practices as the circumstances of the life of our people changed. This process continues to this day.

EVOLUTION OF JEWISH LAW

THE TORAH

Torah shebichtav, the "Written Law." According to tradition, the Torah was given on Sinai to Moses, who transmitted it to Joshua, who transmitted it to the elders, who transmitted it to the prophets . . . and, eventually, it was transmitted to the Sanhedrin.

THE MISHNAH

Codification and collection of **Torah shebe'al peh**, "Oral Law," transmitted by word of mouth over generations. Compiled by Rabbi Judah and his court around 160-200 C.E. in Palestine.

THE TALMUD

THE JERUSALEM GEMARA
Compilation of the commentary on the MISHNAH by the Amora'im in Palestine, approx. end of fourth cent. Together with the Mishnah, this forms the JERUSALEM TALMUD.

THE BABYLONIAN GEMARA
Compilation of the commentary on the MISHNAH by scholars in the Babylonian academies, approx. end of fifth cent. This is much larger and more significant than the Jerusalem Gemara. Together with the Mishnah, this forms the BABYLONIAN TALMUD.

Comments and decisions of the **GEONIM**, sixth-tenth cents.

Commentaries by **RASHI**
(France, eleventh cent.)

Tosafot: Commentaries by descendants of Rashi
(France/Germany, twelfth-thirteenth cents.)

Mishneh Torah by **MAIMONIDES** ("The Rambam")
(Egypt, twelfth cent.)

Shulchan Aruch: Code by **JOSEPH KARO**
(Palestine, sixteenth cent.)

Other codes and commentaries

Responsa literature

III

THE LAND AND THE PEOPLE

JEWS AFFIRM THEIR ATTACHMENT TO THE LAND OF ISRAEL. All Jews, wherever they have lived or journeyed through over thirty mostly turbulent centuries, are unified by common historical experiences, a shared destiny, resolute faith in God's Oneness, Sacred Scripture, the Hebrew language, an unfailing sense of their uniqueness as a people, and, of seminal importance, allegiance to *Eretz Yisrael*, the ancestral land of the Jewish people. The patriarchs and matriarchs began their long journey into history from the ancient soil. Moses and Joshua led the God-intoxicated descendants of slaves to form a new nation in that Promised Land. There David established the holy city of Jerusalem as reality and symbol of the Jewish spirit. From that sacred place Solomon launched a magnificent Jewish empire.

Even when conflict and conquest forced the Jews from *Eretz Yisrael*, it continued to be uppermost in their yearnings, prayers, and rituals. Torn from the holy soil, Jews nevertheless observed agricultural holidays as if nothing had happened, as if they were still farmers in their Promised Land. Daily and seasonal prayers, institutionalized in prayer book and synagogue, corresponded to ceremonies and observances associated with the cultic rituals of the holy Temple in the holy city. Each Jewish home became a small sanctuary where Shabbat, holiday, and other observances preserved the symbols of Jewish attachment to the Land. Home and synagogue ritual items further reinforced the unsunderable connection between Jews and their sacred land, the land in which God commanded them to fulfill the *berit*, the covenant made at Sinai. That eternal link between the Jewish people and its Land received a new name in modern times. The longing to return to *Eretz Yisrael*–Jerusalem–Zion, a longing born by the waters of Babylon, was called Zionism by modern thinkers and activists. The fulfillment of one aspect of Zionism came with the establishment of the Third Jewish Commonwealth in 1948.

This chapter explores the age-old connection between the Jewish people and its ancient land. Considered as well in the present chapter is the centuries-old yearning for return to the Land as manifested by Zionism. You will also meet some of the early leaders of the Zionist enterprise and explore why they looked on Zionism as a natural continuation of the Jewish longing for return that began with the Babylonian Exile some 2,500 years ago. Finally, you will explore the specialness of the eternal Jewish bond with Jerusalem, which is at once reality in time and space and a metaphor for the unquenchable Jewish spirit.

▪ Faith, Land, and People ▪

The Jewish people in its Land was, from the very beginning, an integral aspect of the Jewish religion. That the Land and People require each other and actualize each other is part of the uniqueness of Judaism. Thus, for the Jews, salvation is framed in national, not personal or individual, terms. Although Jews believe God is involved with individuals, it does not stop there. For Jews, Jewish religion insists that the corporate body, the Jewish people in its Land, gives Jews their definition and their meaning. The Land-People relationship earns further sanctity: It is recorded in and is a major aspect of Bible writings. The prophets, for example, held continued presence in the Land to be conditional on fidelity to God's law. Again, Isaac, the first "sabra," the first Jew to be born in the Land, is commanded by God never to go down from, never to leave, the ancestral land.

The following explores the history of the Land and its meaning for the Jewish people. The holiness of the Land of Israel begins with the promise to Abraham. It never diminishes. Why? Redemption of Land, culture, and law comprises fulfillment of *mitzvot*. Explain. Zionism is described as more and other than a modern "liberation movement." Why? Explain the phrase "the conquest of the land was the ultimate step in their redemption."

▪ Faith, Land, and People   BY EMANUEL RACKMAN ▪

For a Zionist who is also committed to the religious heritage of the Jewish people, Zionism and Judaism are one. There can be Jewish secularists–and even non-Jews–who want to achieve Zionist goals. And there are God-fearing Jews who shun Zionist organizations and Zionist activity. But, from the point of view of our millennial ideology, it is impossible to disentangle the Jewish triad–faith, land, and people. A Judaism without the Zionist component is hyphenated, and the Land or State of Israel without Torah is simply unthinkable.

The brilliant Abraham Joshua Heschel made a similar point in another context. He referred to a problem ancient and medieval philosophers were wont to debate: Do the gods love the good because it is good, or is it good because the gods love it? Such a problem arises only when the gods and the good are regarded as two different entities and where it is taken for granted that the gods do not always act according to the highest standards of goodness and justice. However, for a Jew, such an inquiry is meaningless, as meaningless as to ask if a particular point within the circle is called the center because of its equidistance from the periphery, or if its equidistance from the periphery is due to its being the center. "The dichotomy of the holy and the good is alien to the spirit of the great prophets. To their thinking the righteousness of God is inseparable from God's being."

What is true of God's being and righteousness is true of Jews and their Zionism. Those who profess their faith is Judaism must, of necessity, be Zionists, unless they have opted to share only a part of the historic religion. Perhaps that is why some prefer to view Zionism as a political movement, while the designation "Judaism" is reserved for the Jewish religion. But if from the beginning–from the very emergence of the patriarch Abraham–faith, land, and people were one, then it is a distortion of history to separate them. We may give new names to organizations that want to achieve limited goals of the total heritage but, if the heritage itself encompasses God, soil, and nation, then Jews committed to the whole cannot distinguish between their Jewishness and their Zionism.

The Meaning of the Land

The Bible itself is the source for this premise. Judaism begins with God's promise of the Land to Abraham, who traversed the land's length and breadth. The promise was confirmed to Isaac, who never separated himself from its soil; and it meant home for Jacob all the time that he was in flight from Esau, as well as thereafter when he asked his sons in Egypt to bury him in the Cave of Machpelah in Hebron. Even for the Hebrews in bondage to Pharaoh, and for their children who were liberated, the conquest of the land was the ultimate step in their redemption. Their several covenants with God involved the law and the land for which, indeed, they constituted a people.

The covenants help us to understand why land was so important in the very foundation of the faith. For Abraham and his followers ultimate salvation always involved a group–a family, a clan, a tribe, a people, all humanity. Christians usually think more of the salvation of individuals than of collective redemption, while for Jews God's mandate is to be "a holy nation and a kingdom of priests." The mandate was addressed to a people. *The people* were to establish a just society. *The people* were to put an end to poverty. Not in heaven–but on earth. And to establish a model society, a people requires a tract of land. God had to give them a place in the sun where they might achieve the very purpose God ordained for them. And presumably God gave them a tiny area whose inhabitants had sunk to a very low state of morality and merited expulsion from it.

Martin Buber said it well. "What is decisive for us is not the promise of the Land, but the demand whose fulfillment is bound up with the Land. . . . Judaism is a way of life that cannot be realized by individuals in the sphere of their private existence, but only by a nation in the establishment of its society."

Land was not important in Christianity's mission to the world. Indeed, for Christianity, holiness was based on the negation of *this* world and Christians were preoccupied with their individual salvation in a world-to-come. For them the Land of Israel was holy only because of its role in the history of Jesus and the apostles. But for Jews the Land was holy not only because of history but also because of ultimate purpose–the future–the perfect society. And just as no one can fathom Judaism without God or Torah, so one cannot fathom it without reckoning with the Land–a special land, marked for a special purpose. That is why Judaism and Zionism are inseparable. Total Judaism without the Land is inconceivable. And the Land without Judaism has no purpose.

Attachment to the Land

The ancient Canaanites were not the only ones whose iniquity caused them to lose the Land. Twice in their history God had to punish the Jews for their sins and send them into exile. However, God had promised they would return to it, and they never forgot the promise. Moreover, they never abandoned title to the Land, and their claim to it is still valid by Roman and international law. In no period of their millennial exile was the Land ever without some of them–as if these few were commissioned to be the watchkeepers! Through the years all of them dreamed of the day when all the dispersed would be gathered home. Sometimes they only prayed for the fulfillment of the dream; at other times they tried to coerce God to hasten the event. A few even heroically undertook aliyah; on occasion they did it in organized groups. Their attachment to the Land was virtually umbilical.

That attachment found expression in prayer and study. In their liturgy the Jews described the joys associated with the service in the Temple of Jerusalem as such that they could not be replicated anywhere else in the world. On every Pentecost festival, they studied the tracts dealing with the ritual of the first fruits and dreamed of their own ascent to the holy city in the Messianic Era. (Indeed, the reenactment of this colorful ceremony was one of the first to be reinstituted in modern Israel by religious and secular Jews alike.)

Reading and rereading the Bible and the Talmud, they realized that, once God had chosen

The Land and the People

the Land for God's people and charged it with the divine holiness, it must have been granted a special role in the fulfillment of God's ultimate purpose for all humankind. For that reason, while idolatry, from Judaism's point of view, is a crime everywhere, it is especially heinous if practiced in Israel, and homicide and sexual improprieties are especially contaminating to its soil. Higher moral standards must prevail there–not only for purposes easily discernible now but also for the future hope of humanity. For it is there that the Messianic Age is to be heralded. On its mountains God will ultimately judge among the nations.

Nevertheless, there were always dissenters. With the advent of the period of the Enlightenment some tried to abandon attachment to the Land. And even in this century some have tried to substitute other areas for the Land mentioned in the covenants. But there could be no substantial alteration of the agreements consummated between God and God's people. In those covenants Judaism and Zionism were one, and all the trauma of exile only deepened the Jewish people's awareness of and commitment to God, their Land, and their Peoplehood.

Christians and Muslims always knew this. They never denied that what we were claiming had been vouchsafed unto us by sacred scriptures. The best they could do to challenge our contention was to create new theories to undermine our legal and moral stance. They argued that new situations, new phenomena, or new revelations must be taken into account. To this we never gave our assent, and we remained loyal to the inseparability of God, land, and people. We deemed any attempt to remove one of the three an attack on the whole–call it anti-Judaism or anti-Zionism. It was an attack on our faith and commitment as we saw them. And if a mockery is not to be made of religious freedom, then we are entitled to retain our religious commitment as we conceive of it and not as our enemies would have us conceive of it.

The Holiness of the Land

Why did God choose the Land of Israel for the Jewish people? The choice itself may have a bearing on the destiny of the People of Israel even as the Land itself was the site of so much of their memorable past.

It was a land flowing with milk and honey, rich in mineral resources, and so varied and beautiful in its terrain as to be a microcosm of the entire earth. But this can hardly account for its selection. We know many countries that are richer in resources and more beautiful in topography.

Perhaps the Land was chosen because people sought God on the mountain peaks of Jerusalem even before Abraham–in the schools of Shem and Eber. As the place where the quest for God was first begun, it was to remain the central shrine where the quest would continue for the illumination of all humankind. The Bible does suggest that the land of Canaan differed from Egypt insofar as farmers would have to look heavenward for their rain. Perhaps that does suggest that the land was to become the cradle of Western religions as searchers for God tried to transcend their attachment to earth.

Even more important may be that the Land lay between two great river civilizations–that of the Nile and that of the Tigris and Euphrates valleys. It was on the so-called "Great Road" between the empires that always warred with each other. Therefore it was influenced by the confluence of these civilizations and could in turn influence them. That became the mission of the Jewish people–to bring God and God's justice to the East and West of antiquity, and that mission is one that begs for renewal and fulfillment in our time.

Thus the holiness of the Land began with a promise to Abraham. It became the subject of repeated covenants. But it is also linked with God's ultimate purpose–for Jews and for all humankind. How we would want it to play a role in a larger world with continuously immanent conflicts between the free and the enslaved segments of the human race!

The Equation

My equating of Zionism with Judaism will undoubtedly offend many a Jewish atheist or agnostic. Do I deny them the right to regard themselves as Zionists, since they have no commitment to Judaism as a religion? Not at all. Indeed, the tradition regards them as Jewish even if they have rejected the whole—not to mention a part—of their birthright. Jews can reject God or land or both, but that does not change their identity and the nature of Judaism, and Zionism is not altered simply because some or other Jews are selective of the parts of the whole they want to espouse.

Unfortunately, we too often identify Zionism with one specific program or another for fulfillment of a limited objective. The attainment of a sovereign Jewish state is an objective of both Zionism and Judaism. So is the reclamation of the soil of Israel. So is the establishment of a just social and economic order—whether capitalistic or socialistic. So is the revival of the tongue of the prophets. For the religiously committed Jew these are also "*mitzvot*"—religious obligations either explicitly or implicitly mandated by God. Some of us have concentrated on one program while others have concentrated on another. But that does not detract from the fact that for almost four thousand years Judaism included a passionate attachment to the Land of Israel, an overwhelming sense of Jewish peoplehood, and the vision of a perfect world in which the Chosen People would be a model and a light unto the nations.

Because I feel so deeply about equating Judaism and Zionism, I often find fault with many contemporary spokespeople for Zionism who have themselves brought Zionism to its present crisis. They have simply de-Judaized Zionism, even as some Jews in the extremist Orthodox and Reform camps have de-Zionized Judaism.

It would have been much easier to convince most of our fellow Americans—especially those to whom the Bible is still sacred—that Arafat's plea for a secular democratic state in Israel is an attack on Judaism itself. However, we played directly into his hand by de-Judaizing Zionism, by divorcing it from its religious source and mate. When Jews themselves speak of Zionism as their "people's liberation movement," they are traitors to their past. As if Zionism were a nineteenth- or twentieth-century phenomenon comparable to the modern movements of Asians and Africans for freedom! Our liberation movement was and is Judaism—launched millennia ago, sustained against Greeks and Romans and in continuing defiance of Christians and Muslims, with no abandonment of our claim to the Land wherein Judaism is to flower. Indeed, we forget too frequently that even in the Middle Ages there were Kabbalists who tried to accomplish by miracles what in the twentieth century was accomplished by the World Zionist Organization with a program—also dotted with miracles. Thus, it is insulting to our forebears to brand Zionism a modern movement when its beginnings were already in Abraham's vision and Jews never despaired of that vision's fulfillment. According to Nachmanides, Judaism—the entire Torah heritage—was designed for life in the Land of Israel. And, if Jews adhered to Judaism in the lands of their dispersion, it was only so they might be in perpetual readiness for their eventual return to the land of their progenitors. In the thirteenth century, in the eighth decade of his life, Nachmanides accomplished aliyah and achieved maximum Judaism. Many more accomplished it in the twentieth century. But even those of us who are not yet there must never forget that as God's being and righteousness are one, so Judaism and Zionism are one—inseparable, and unintelligible, one without the other.

▪ Israel and the Diaspora ▪

Jewish settlements and communities outside *Eretz Yisrael* are called, collectively, the Diaspora. The word is applied only to the Jews in their dispersion, a word from the same Greek root. In Hebrew it's called *galut*, which also means exile. Thus the term conveys the idea that the natural condition for Jews is to live in their special land, the Holy Land. Anything else is abnormal and diminishes the meaning of being Jewish. Little wonder that the tug of *Eretz Yisrael* on the soul and psyche of every Diaspora Jew never abated, even after many centuries. Little wonder that to live in the Land of Israel, even to visit it, fulfills a *mitzvah.*

The following reading recounts the development of the bond between Jews and *Eretz Yisrael*, how that link was strengthened and transformed during significant epochs in Jewish life in the Diaspora, and how that attachment is still expressed today in Diaspora communities. This selection pays special attention to a developing new relationship, the interaction between two powerful Jewish communities: renascent Israel and the North American Diaspora. Explain why this relationship requires unusual consideration. What should that relationship be? Explain.

▪ Israel and the Diaspora   BY RAPHAEL PATAI ▪

Emotionally the centrality of *Eretz Yisrael*, the Land of Israel, in Jewish consciousness has been constant, as basic to Judaism as the belief in God. According to the biblical narrative, the attachment to the Land began the moment God first spoke to Abraham saying, go "unto the Land that I will show thee" (Gen. 12:1). The divine promise that Abraham's seed would inherit "the Land" was repeated several times to Abraham and then to Isaac and Jacob and formed the basis of the everlasting covenant between God and the Children of Israel. It was the desire to take possession of the Land of Promise, as much as the wish to be freed from slavery, that was concretized in the awesome scene of the Burning Bush, in which God's promise, by then centuries old, was repeated in the form of an imminent divine plan to lead the Children of Israel "unto a land flowing with milk and honey" (Exod. 3:8, 17).

An Unbreakable Bond

The six centuries from the conquest of Canaan under Joshua until the destruction of the kingdoms of Israel and Judea and the Babylonian Exile (586 B.C.E.) were the period of fulfillment as far as the emotional attachment of the People of the Land was concerned. In the course of those centuries the bond between the people and the Land became so strong as to prove unbreakable ever after.

The special, intensely emotional quality of the relationship between the Jews and *Eretz Yisrael* became first manifested with the Assyrian and Babylonian exiles. When Jews first experienced the trauma of being forcibly separated from their land, the yearning for return arose, and it has remained ever since a powerful motivating force in Jewish life and history. For centuries the inability to return was compensated for by a channeling of the desire into messianic dreams. From the time of the demise of the Second Jewish Commonwealth (70 C.E.), for almost two millennia the Jews of the ever-widening Diaspora lived in two worlds: in the actual world of their existence in exile and in the imaginary world of a future, messianic kingdom in the Land of Israel. And the harsher the reality of the exile, the sweeter was the promise of the dream of redemption and return. But whatever the actual conditions in exile, the emotional primacy of *Eretz Yisrael* over the Diaspora remained unchanged. It became weakened only in the nineteenth century among Jews who succumbed to assimilation.

Rise of Political Zionism

Without the age-old Jewish emotional fixation

on Zion and Jerusalem–as expressed in, and nurtured by Jewish religion and liturgy–political Zionism could not have won the support of the Jewish masses, and consequently the rebirth of the State of Israel would not have come to pass. Yet, even though the establishment of Israel was for most Jews (with the exception of such ultraorthodox groups as the Natorei Karta) the realization of the millennial Jewish yearning for Zion, its existence has not signified the end of that yearning. On the contrary, the emotional attachment of the majority of the Jewish people who have remained in the Diaspora to the land, the people, and the State of Israel is today as strong as ever.

In contrast to the constant emotional tie of the Diaspora to Israel, the intellectual relations between the two have historically manifested great variations.

To begin with, as laid down in biblical tradition, the greatest early intellectual achievements–the recognition of God and of God's covenantal relationship with the people of Israel–took place not in *Eretz Yisrael* but first in Mesopotamia (with Abraham) and then in Egypt (with Moses). However, from the conquest of Canaan until the end of the Second Temple period, and for more than a century thereafter–a period of fourteen centuries during which most of the people of Israel lived in their country–*Eretz Yisrael* was not only the center of the Jewish people but practically its sole locus. This was the time and the place of the creation of the everlasting foundations of Judaism: the Bible, with its evolving universal, ethical, and prophetic monotheism; and the Mishnah, the first codification of Jewish law and the basis of all later religious developments in Judaism. Thus the Land of Israel was established once and for all in Jewish consciousness as the place in which the Jewish people reached the summit of their intellectual achievement.

Babylonian Talmud

From about 200 C.E. the center of gravity began to shift from *Eretz Yisrael* to Babylonia. Although the sages of *Eretz Yisrael* retained cer-

tain religious prerogatives, the Babylonian Talmud outshone its smaller counterpart compiled in the Land of Israel, and it, rather than the "Jerusalem Talmud," became the standard source of Jewish law and the subject of study for all Jewry for all times. After the end of the talmudic period (500 C.E.) Babylonia-Iraq remained the religio-intellectual center of Judaism for another six centuries (the Gaonic period), during which the small Jewish community of *Eretz Yisrael* produced nothing that could compare with the output of the great Iraqi talmudic academies of Sura and Pumbeditha.

The Golden Age

From the ninth century on, another shift became noticeable, this time from Iraq to the far west, to Andalus, as the Arabs called Spain. The Jewish Golden Age of ninth-to-eleventh-century Spain is so well known that it only has to be mentioned to make one aware that no comparable intellectual flowering existed in contemporary *Eretz Yisrael*, or in any other Diaspora community, for that matter. In fact, at that time, and well into the twelfth and thirteenth centuries, there were other important Jewish intellectual centers in several Arab countries (Iraq, Egypt, North Africa), but *Eretz Yisrael* was not one of them.

From the eleventh century on another highly significant move in the center of Jewish intellectual activity began–the emergence of Ashkenazic leadership in Jewish scholarship, first in northeastern France, where the great Rashi lived in the twelfth century, and then in the Rhineland, and from the fourteenth century on in Eastern Europe.

Center of Kabbalah

Eretz Yisrael regained its position of religio-intellectual primacy for a short time in the sixteenth century, when the little town of Safed in the Galilee became the center of the Kabbalah, the great Jewish mystical movement whose most important work, the *Zohar*, had been produced in Spain in the late thirteenth century. It was the sixteenth-century Safed masters whose writings made the Kabbalah a popular mass movement among all three major divisions of the Jewish people, the Oriental Jews in Arab lands, the Sephardim in the Ottoman Empire and north-western Europe, and the Ashkenazim in Central and Eastern Europe. Sixteenth-century Safed was also the place where Joseph Karo (who, incidentally was also a leading Kabbalist) wrote his *Shulchan Aruch*, the last great code of Jewish law.

The Safed center disappeared as quickly as it arose, and from the seventeenth century *Eretz Yisrael* played no role in the intellectual life of world Jewry. By that time the religious-scholarly preeminence of the Oriental and Sephardic Jews had been a thing of the past, and from then on all the great Jewish religious and intellectual movements took place within the Ashkenazic orbit. The last flare-up of Sephardic élan was of an emotional rather than intellectual nature: it took the aberrant form of a messianic movement, created by Shabbatai Zevi (1626-1676), who lived in Egypt, *Eretz Yisrael*, and Turkey, and whose claim to messiahship inflamed Oriental, Sephardic, and Ashkenazic Jews alike, proving once more the unbreakable attachment of the entire Diaspora to a messianic *Eretz Yisrael*.

Eastern Europe was the environment in which the Ashkenazic religious movement of Chasidism arose (eighteenth century), partly in reaction to talmudistic elitism and partly in response to the popular desire to express one's joy in loving God in a simple, immediate fashion. Significant for the continued prestige of Safed Kabbalism in the eyes of the Eastern European Chasidim is their adoption for everyday use of the *siddur* (prayer book) of Isaac Luria, the greatest of the sixteenth-century Safed Kabbalists.

Since Chasidism was an Eastern European movement, it was to be expected that opposition to it should also arise in the same quarter. The fight of the Mitnagdim ("Opponents") of Chasidism was led by the greatest Talmudists of the age and was at times characterized by great bitterness. That this struggle did not lead to a break-up of Judaism into two separate denominations can be attributed to a considerable extent to the emergence of a new movement in which both the Chasidim and the Mitnagdim discerned a common enemy.

The Enlightenment

This new development was the *Haskalah*, the Jewish Enlightenment, spearheaded by Moses Mendelssohn in the late eighteenth century, which quickly spread from Germany to the neighboring countries. The *Maskilim* ("Enlighteners") objected to the traditional tenet upheld equally by Chasidim and Mitnagdim: that Jews must keep themselves separate from the Gentiles, not only in religion, but also in language, education, custom, and costume, and that their lives must be dedicated to, and circumscribed by, Jewish law and lore. The *Haskalah* preached that, while adhering to their religion, the Jews should acquire the language and culture of the country in which they lived.

Religious Reform

The *Maskilim* were also in the forefront of the struggle for Jewish emancipation, which was achieved, beginning with the nineteenth century, in one European country after the other. It was the Haskalah that made the emergence of Jewish religious reform possible, resulting in the establishment of Reform and liberal congregations in several Central and Western European countries, and soon also in America. In all these movements, which within two generations completely transformed the physiognomy of European Jewry, the concept of *Eretz Yisrael* played a very subordinated role. The traditional Jewish ties to Zion and Jerusalem were weakened, and from Reform prayer books even the references to the messianic hope of a return to Zion and the reestablishment there of David's throne were excised.

Political Zionism

The most recent movement made possible by

the *Haskalah*, political Zionism, was created by Theodor Herzl at the First Zionist Congress in Basle, Switzerland, in 1897. This movement was based on the millennial emotional attachment of the Jews to *Eretz Yisrael*, but it used political methods to achieve its aim, which was the establishment of a Jewish national home in Palestine. With it, suddenly, the age-old messianic dream of a return to the Land of Israel was transformed into a modern political movement, using diplomacy, technical and economic planning, and international organization–all features of modern Western culture inaccessible to Jews until the emancipation and enlightenment. Zionism not only resuscitated the old Jewish longing for *Eretz Yisrael*, it gave it a new form: It was henceforth political action not prayers (or not only prayers) that was to bring about the return. No wonder that the extreme Orthodox (whether Chasidim or Mitnagdim) rose up in alarm against Zionism. Their ranks were joined by some of the leaders of Reform Judaism.

After fifty years of Zionist work, of Jewish settlement in *Eretz Yisrael*, of laying the foundations there of a new Hebrew cultural center, the United Nations voted on November 29, 1947 for the partition of Palestine and the establishment of a Jewish state. During those fifty years the Jewish people experienced the greatest of cataclysms ever to befall it: the extermination of six million Jews by Nazi Germany and its Axis collaborators. There are those among modern historians who believe that it was the blood of the six million that moved the nations of the world to give their legal consent to the establishment of a state for the surviving Jews.

Since the establishment of Israel, the Jewish people comprise two great centers: that of Israel and that of America. There is still a large Jewish population in the Soviet Union; however, its position is so precarious that its very survival in the long range is in doubt, and it certainly is not able to be Jewishly creative. And there are the smaller Jewish communities of France, England, and several other European countries. There are remnants of the Jews in a few Muslim countries,

such as Morocco and Iran. And there are vital Jewish communities in Canada, Mexico, and Argentina. But the future of Jewry depends on the two largest and most vigorous Jewish communities of the United States and Israel, and on the interrelationship between them. At present they supply vital needs in each other's lives. American Jewry furnishes Israel with indispensable economic and political support and with a sprinkling of highly skilled specialized labor. Israel radiates toward American Jewry increasingly important cultural influences. Despite the six-thousand-mile distance, visiting between the two countries is intensive. Israel is an ever-present feature in the American Jewish consciousness. Because Israel exists and is what it is, American Jews are more proud to be Jews, while in the feelings of the Jews of Israel, American Jewry plays an important and vital role. In the midst of continuing Arab hostility Israel is more secure in the knowledge that American Jewry stands solidly behind it. Because of the powerful cultural role America plays in the world and the share of American Jewry in it, practically all Israeli Jews speak English as a second language, and Israel is one of the most avid consumers of American culture. And as for cultural production, Israeli and American Jewry mutually cross-fertilize each other in many areas, including Jewish scholarship.

In the field of religion, although Jewish Orthodoxy still dominates the Israeli scene (and this despite that only twelve percent of Israeli Jews are Orthodox), it is because of the influence of American Jewry that, gradually, Conservative and Reform Judaism have begun to gain footholds in Israeli religious life and increasingly attract adherents.

In the past the relationship between *Eretz Yisrael* and any Diaspora community was never one of equals. Either the one or the other had predominance. Today, for the first time, the Jewish community of Israel and the largest Jewish Diaspora community, that of America, occupy equal, balanced positions. It is on this balance that the survival of the Jewish people rests.

The Land and the People

▪ Theodor Herzl ▪

For some two thousand years Diaspora Jews nurtured one dream: to return to the Promised Land in fulfillment of ancient prophecy. An assimilated Viennese Jew brought that dream to the brink of reality at the twilight of the nineteenth century. Theodor Herzl was an unlikely candidate to galvanize ancient, slumbering Zionist aspirations to redeem the homeland. Yet he did so by the sheer power of his obstinacy and his single-minded effort. He created a process and an apparatus that, fifty years later, brought the Jewish Commonwealth into being. Estranged from his family, his health failing rapidly, Herzl, often standing alone, changed the course of Jewish history.

The following recounts Herzl's and Zionism's dramatic story, starting with the French court-martial of Captain Alfred Dreyfus and concluding with Herzl's untimely death. Herzl's efforts were fueled by the anti-Semitism he saw around him. He believed political Zionism was the key to the Jewish future. Why? Herzl the assimilated Jew returned to his people in response to anti-Semitism. What might bring today's assimilated Jews back to their roots? Explain why Herzl encountered opposition in most of Western Europe to his ideas and efforts.

▪ Theodor Herzl BY STEVEN SCHNUR ▪

Pressed against the iron gates, French mobs fought for a glimpse of the prisoner, shouting, "Death to the Jews!" In the courtyard of the Ecole Militaire, Alfred Dreyfus, a French army captain convicted of treason, cried "I swear and declare that you are degrading an innocent man" as his fellow officers stripped him of his insignia, broke his sword, and led him away in chains. Among the handful of journalists permitted to witness the humiliation that January day in 1895 stood Theodor Herzl, the Paris correspondent for the *Neue Freie Presse*, Vienna's most influential newspaper. Horrified by the screams of the surging crowd and by other outbursts of anti-Semitism throughout France, Herzl left the courtyard a changed man. Within two years this assimilated Jew, who once had been thrashed in grade school for failing to learn the biblical story of Exodus, would be celebrated throughout Europe as a prophet and vilified as a madman for his plan to save the Jews.

As anti-Semitism surfaced in Germany and Austria, and repressive policies in Eastern Europe made life for Jews intolerable, Herzl proposed a solution to this hatred and violence–a Jewish state. Though he did not live to see it established, he wrote, "The state is already founded in essence, in the will of the people to be a state. . . ." As he predicted in his diary, the State of Israel was created fifty years later.

Worshiped German Culture

Born in Budapest in 1860 to a middle-class family of assimilated Jews, Herzl, like his immediate forebears, all but ignored his religious heritage until rising anti-Semitism forced him to confront it. He declared while in high school that all religion was fraudulent. In its place he worshiped German culture, particularly its literature, music, and nationalist aspirations, and joined a Teutonic fraternity while studying law in Vienna. There, in 1882, he first learned of the sudden outbreak of murderous attacks upon Jewish villages in Russia.

In the minds of many assimilated Jews living in Western Europe the antiquated dress and customs of Orthodox Jews to the east were not only repugnant but, they believed, responsible for anti-Semitism. Enlightened Westernized Jews, they reasoned, had nothing to fear. Nevertheless, some middle-class Jews converted in the belief that by becoming Christians they could achieve full and equal status among Gentiles. Herzl himself wrote, "There was perhaps a time when I would have gladly slipped over into some corner of the Christian fold." In fact, he once thought he could "eliminate for all eternity the relentless prejudice against Jews by traveling to Rome and asking the pope: 'Help us against the anti-Semites and I will lead a great movement for the free and honorable conversion of Jews to Christianity.'"

Disdained the Synagogue Jew

Moody and theatrical, Herzl feverishly pursued dreams of literary fame, writing essays and plays that slowly gained him a reputation as a man of letters. Though the burgeoning number of anti-Semitic tracts being published disturbed him, he nevertheless agreed with certain of their prejudices, particularly those accusing Jews of illicit financial practices. Wishing to project an image of secular sophistication, Herzl disdained both the Jew of the marketplace and the Jew of the synagogue, stereotyping them in his plays.

Like many middle-class Viennese Jews, Herzl believed that "anti-Semitism will educate the Jews," by making them aware of their worst traits. But as the slurs turned violent and spread throughout Europe, his attitude changed dramatically. Though the Dreyfus Affair convinced him of the urgency of a concerted Jewish reaction, a decade of pogroms, prejudice, and persecution had slowly opened his eyes to the dangers facing all Jews.

Pogroms in Russia

Following the assassination of Czar Alexander II in 1881, pogroms swept through Russia, resulting in the deaths of thousands of Jews and the destruction of countless homes and businesses. As Russian Jews migrated west, so did the violence that had driven them from their homeland. Vienna's lord mayor, Karl Lueger, whose anti-Semitic policies were to inspire Hitler, declared: "The Jews, they are robbing us of everything we hold sacred! Fatherland! Nationality! And finally our property, too!" In the streets Jews were openly insulted. In Germany, Herzl himself was ridiculed in a beerhall. In France, Edouard Drumont's *La France Juive*, accusing Jews of responsibility for all of France's misfortunes, became a best-seller. During this period the infamous anti-Semitic forgery, *The Protocols of the Learned Elders of Zion*, was written by a Russian secret agent in Paris and later distributed around the world.

Though aware of the growing danger these events portended, Herzl was too preoccupied with dreams of literary fame to respond to them. He married in 1889 and two years later moved to France, where he wrote plays and served as Paris correspondent for the *Neue Freie Presse*. So removed was Herzl from Judaism during his early years that he did not have his son circumcised. His ignorance of Jewish history, customs, and rituals contributed to the secular nature of the Zionist movement he later founded.

Anti-Semitic Hysteria in France

In 1892 the French company building the Panama Canal suddenly declared bankruptcy, plunging France into financial panic, anti-Semitic hysteria, bombings, and riots. Though only two of those implicated in the massive swindle were Jewish, newspapers claimed that the collapse was engineered by an international conspiracy of Jews seeking to enrich themselves at the expense of France. Writing to a friend, Herzl remarked of the tense atmosphere in Paris, "There will be a revolution here this year. If I don't escape in good time to Brussels, I'll probably be shot as a German spy, as a bourgeois, as a Jew, or as a financier, whereas I am really just a worn-out, used-up trapeze artist." The metaphor was appropriate for a man on the run from an unhappy marriage, obsessively pursuing an elusive literary success. Though his essays gained him a wide readership, his plays achieved only limited critical recognition.

Following the Dreyfus Affair, Herzl became convinced that neither assimilation nor conversion would eliminate prejudice. He no longer believed that education would lead to an era of enlightenment in which Jews would be accepted as full and equal citizens. Such had been the attitude among emancipated Jews for almost a century, but at the very moment that Europe was supposed to be ushering in such an era, the French Assembly was deciding whether or not to ban all Jews from public service.

Writes Blueprint for Jewish State

As Herzl recognized "the emptiness and futility of trying to 'combat' anti-Semitism" intellectually, a new thought began to take shape in his mind. What the Jews needed was a country of their own, a modern state with all the variety and vice of Vienna, Berlin, or Paris, one in which they would not have to rely upon the whim of others for full freedom.

In a rush of creative energy Herzl closeted himself in his Paris apartment and began writing *The Jewish State*, a blueprint for Israel. In his diary he noted, "I have been pounding away for some time at a work of tremendous magnitude. . . . It bears the aspects of a mighty dream. For days and weeks it has saturated me to the limits of my consciousness; it goes with me everywhere, hovers behind my ordinary talk, peers at me over the shoulders of my funny little journalistic work, overwhelms and intoxicates me. . . . What disappointments if I fail, what grim struggles if I succeed." Overnight he reversed his opinion of conversion, calling those who rejected their Judaism "halfhearted, cowardly, and self-seeking Jews."

To those close to Herzl, the change that overcame him was both baffling and alarming. "The look in his face frightened me," his physician remarked upon seeing him during that period of intense creativity. "In the few days that I had not seen him, his face had changed into that of a sick man, suffering from a long disease." Several of his close friends feared for his sanity, believing that his notions of a Jewish state were the product of a diseased mind.

Well aware of the magnitude of his vision and the promise it held for world Jewry he wrote, "I think that for me life has ended and world history has begun. . . . I shall be counted among the greatest benefactors of humankind. Or is this belief already megalomania?" For nine feverish years amid failing health, he would pursue his dream in every European capital, seeking the support of monarchs, financiers, intellectuals, and the whole of the Jewish people.

Sets Up World Zionist Organization

Though he briefly considered other lands, Herzl's dream revolved around Palestine, long under the jurisdiction of the Ottoman Empire. Convinced that the territory was little prized by the ruling Turks and believing it to be sparsely populated, he planned to offer to buy Palestine from Sultan Abdul Hamid II with the help of the Rothschild fortune. When Rothschild and other wealthy Jews refused to support such a scheme, Herzl took his case to the Russian czar, to the German kaiser, and to the English Foreign Office. Until his premature death in 1904 he crisscrossed the Western world in search of sponsorship. Though he did not succeed in creating a state during his lifetime, he did establish the machinery to carry on his work in the form of the World Zionist Organization.

Ironically, Herzl received self-serving support from some of the very anti-Semites he sought to escape. In their eagerness to assist any plan that would rid Europe of Jews, they praised Herzl's Zionist efforts and wrote favorable reviews of *The Jewish State*. Most Western European Jews, however, were critical of Herzl for drawing attention to anti-Semitism and airing Jewish grievances in public. "No man in Vienna was so derided as Herzl was, except perhaps Sigmund Freud, his great brother in fate, who also tried, single-handedly, to create a grand world concept," wrote the author Stefan Zweig, who knew both men. To middle- and upper-class Jews who felt secure in cosmopolitan Europe, the suggestion that they belonged not in Vienna or Paris but in a land of swamps, desert, and widespread disease was ludicrous. They insisted that prejudice would disappear if Jews kept a low profile. Men like Herzl, they argued, did the Jews great harm. In the opinion of Edmond de Rothschild, all Diaspora Jews would be viewed as disloyal foreigners if a Jewish state were created.

Hailed as Messiah in East

But in Eastern Europe, where Jews had long begun to realize that the only solution to persecution was mass migration, Herzl's efforts gained wide support. From all over Russia veteran Zionists made their way to his doorstep. They flocked to train stations to catch a glimpse of him as he traveled through Europe, hailing him as the Messiah. For fifteen years, while enduring pogroms under the new czar, they had created their own vision of a return to Palestine and believed that Herzl had been sent to deliver them. As Herzl opened the First Zionist Congress in 1897, he was criticized by rabbis from Berlin to New York not only for attempting to bring about politically what they maintained only God would–the ingathering of the Jews to Zion–but for interfering with their belief that the moral mission of the Jews was to disseminate the ethical teachings of the Torah among the nations.

The critics were by no means confined to his enemies. At the First Zionist Congress convened in Basle, Switzerland, various factions attempted to wrest control from Herzl, who later commented, "I felt as if I were playing thirty-two games of chess simultaneously." Nevertheless, he succeeded in establishing and presiding over an organization that could represent world Jewry and negotiate with the great powers for the purpose of resettling the Jews.

Viewed Palestine as Uninhabited

In 1898 the Congress sent a delegation to Palestine to report on the feasibility of establishing a state. Noting that the most fertile lands were occupied by Arabs, the emissary reported to the Second Zionist Congress that "there have been innumerable clashes between Jews and incited Arabs." Large areas of desert and swamp land,

however, remained unsettled, prompting Herzl and his colleagues to view Palestine as largely underpopulated and available for settlement (even though as early as 1881 the Ottoman government specifically barred Jewish immigrants from Palestine).

Arabs and Jews Clash

Despite efforts by the Mufti of Jerusalem to forbid land sales to Jews, the Jewish population in Palestine doubled between 1882 and 1897. Tension arose between Jews and Arabs when the new settlers, unfamiliar with local customs, fenced in their lands and prohibited Arab peasants from grazing their animals on private property. In 1899 the Mufti proposed that all Jewish newcomers be terrorized and expelled, a symptom of the growing atmosphere of distrust that later resulted in riots and wars.

Ignorant of these conflicts or indifferent to them, Herzl sought to convince wealthy Jews to fund the Turkish national debt in exchange for a charter permitting a Jewish state in Palestine. In his bid for political support Herzl even attempted to convince the kaiser that such a state would increase German influence in the Middle East. After preliminary negotiations in Berlin, Herzl was invited to meet the German monarch in Palestine, and made the long, arduous journey, despite failing health. Disheartened by the poverty he found among both Jews and Arabs throughout Palestine, Herzl was strengthened in his belief that the Rothschild colonies had failed and that statehood was world Jewry's only hope. Addressing Kaiser Wilhelm outside the city of Jerusalem, Herzl assured him, "No [one's] rights or religious feelings are threatened by our idea. We understand and respect the piety of all faiths for the soil on which, after all, the faith of our fathers arose as well." But the kaiser dismissed Herzl without giving him the guarantees of support he had hinted at months before in Europe. Despondent over this failure, exhausted by the journey, Herzl wrote, "The tempo of the movement is slowing down. The catchwords are wearing out. . . . The well is running dry." Suffering from a diseased heart, estranged from his wife and children, he began having premonitions of an early death. Though only thirty-eight he looked and felt twenty years older.

The Uganda Plan

Despite his failures the number of delegates to the annual Zionist Congress doubled within three years and Zionist societies burgeoned from a handful in 1895 to more than 1,300 by the turn of the century. Frustrated in his efforts to acquire Palestine, Herzl turned to other territories in the hope of providing at least a temporary haven for the hundreds of thousands of Jewish refugees fleeing Russia. Encouraged by the British Foreign Office, he sent a delegation first to the Sinai and then to East Africa at the suggestion of Colonial Secretary Joseph Chamberlain. To many delegates, however, the idea of establishing a Jewish homeland anywhere but in Palestine was unthinkable, a "death blow for Zionism." Herzl, understanding such sentiment, told friends, "Palestine is the only land where our people can find rest. But hundreds of thousands need immediate help." He was thinking in particular of the Jews of Kishinev, who had been devastated by a pogrom in April 1903 in which forty-nine Jews were murdered, five hundred wounded, and more than a thousand homes and businesses destroyed. But, threatened with a revolt among the delegates, Herzl withdrew his support for the "Uganda Plan."

Rejected by Pope

In one of his last attempts to achieve his dream Herzl traveled to the Vatican and asked Pope Pius X for the Church's goodwill and understanding in exchange for international control of the holy places in Palestine. "We cannot prevent the Hebrews from going to Jerusalem," the pope told him, "but we could never sanction it. The Hebrews have not recognized our Lord, therefore we cannot recognize the Hebrew people."

Three months before his death Herzl convened a special session of world Zionist leaders to prevent a possible division of the movement. During what was to be his last meeting, he responded to critics who accused him of being autocratic, saying, "Here in this city of Vienna, I one day tore myself loose from the entire circle of my life, from all my acquaintances and all my friends and, as a lonely man, stood up for what I considered right. I do not feel the need for a majority. I need only to be in harmony with my own conviction. Then I am content, even if no dog accepts a piece of bread from me."

On July 3, 1904 Herzl died from pneumonia and heart disease. Tens of thousands of mourners converged on Vienna, making his funeral among the biggest in the city's history. At his grave his thirteen-year-old son, Hans, recited *Kaddish* as thousands pushed forward to catch a glimpse of his coffin.

In his will Herzl requested that he be buried beside his father "until the day when the Jewish people transfer my remains to Palestine." In 1949 his body was reinterred upon Mount Herzl in Jerusalem by the people of the State of Israel.

▪ Ahad Ha-Am vs. Herzl ▪

Herzl negated the Diaspora. He believed it to be an aberration that would lead ultimately to Jewish destruction. He posited therefore the return of all Jews to the Jewish homeland. Ahad Ha-Am, deeply involved in the early Zionist movement, had a different view. He believed the Diaspora was an eternal reality. At the same time he envisioned a small cultural and spiritual center (Israel) at the hub of a wheel whose spokes connect with the rim (Diaspora). The hub and rim need and support each other; each contributes to the strength and vitality of the whole wheel. Unlike Herzl,

Ahad Ha-Am believed a Jewish state could not protect against anti-Semitism, which is an inevitable concomitant to Diaspora.

The following reading compares these two giants of Zionism. Which, if either, has been proved right? Explain. Has the presence of the Jewish state eliminated anti-Semitism, as Herzl believed would happen? Why? Why not? Has the State of Israel produced a cultural and spiritual renaissance as Ha-Am believed it should? Explain. Why did Diaspora Jews not flock to Israel, as Herzl imagined they would? Does the existence of Israel strengthen or weaken Diaspora Jews and their communities? Explain.

■ Ahad Ha-Am vs. Herzl   BY RONALD S. MASS ■

Asher Ginsburg, better known by his pen name Ahad Ha-Am ("one of the people"), was one of the preeminent Jewish thinkers and Hebrew stylists of his generation. From the publication of his first article, "This Is Not the Way" (1889) until his death in Palestine in 1927, Ahad Ha-Am stood at the center of the Zionist movement, embroiled in its most crucial debates.

Ahad Ha-Am was born in 1856 in a small, predominantly Jewish village near Kiev. His parents, middle-class chasidic Jews, reared him in strict piety and sent him to a *cheder* for a traditional Jewish education. Possessing extraordinary scholarly gifts, he excelled in the study of Talmud. His father expected him to become a rabbi, but Asher, captivated by the intellectual fervor of the times, refused to be confined by tradition. Self-taught, he mastered a wide array of secular subjects, including Russian, German, French, English, and Latin, while attaining a solid understanding of the philosophy and literature of Western culture.

Uncompromising Moral Standards

By age thirty Ahad Ha-Am emerged as a man liberated from the parochial world of his childhood but secure in his identity as a Jew. His ability to blend traditional learning with modern thought, his refined Hebrew prose style, uncompromising moral standards, and unique understanding of the problems of the Jewish people provided him with the tools necessary to become a leading voice of his people.

In 1884 Ahad Ha-Am settled in Odessa, the heart and geographic center of the Hebrew Enlightenment. Thrust into the ferment of Jewish public affairs, he became a member of the Hibbat Zion ("Love of Zion"), a group dedicated to encouraging the establishment of agricultural settlements in Palestine, and quickly made a name for himself by writing a controversial article in which he criticized its settlement policies. His critique spawned a secret order called the "B'nai Moshe," which sought to reshape the program of Hibbat Zion according to Ahad Ha-Am's ideas.

In 1891, following Ahad Ha-Am's first visit to *Eretz Yisrael*, he wrote an article entitled "Truth from Palestine," which exposed the economic inefficiency and spiritual barrenness of the Jewish settlements. His critical survey aroused a storm of indignation but gained him a position of respect as an astute analyst and skilled essayist. After a second visit to Palestine in 1893 he became manager of the Ahiasaf publishing house and editor of the monthly *Hashiloah*, the most important publication of the Zionist movement and of Hebrew literature in Eastern Europe.

For seven years, from the First Zionist Congress until Herzl's death. Ahad Ha-Am was obsessed with the need to expose Herzl's program of political Zionism as ill-conceived and destined for disaster.

Herzl's prescription for the Jewish problem was founded upon his assumption that anti-Semitism could be put to constructive use. He insisted that the creation of a Jewish state would both stamp out anti-Semitism by ridding Europe of its Jews and solve the financial problems of the Jewish people. Because his solution was a political one, Herzl argued that the proper way to proceed was by diplomatic action, to convince the great powers of Europe and the Middle East of the necessity of establishing an independent Jewish homeland in Palestine.

A Mourner Among Bridegrooms

In a series of essays Ahad Ha-Am launched a stinging, well-reasoned assault against Herzl's political remedy. Nevertheless, he accepted Herzl's invitation to attend the First Zionist Congress, though not as a delegate. While the majority of those assembled greeted Herzl with rapturous applause, Ahad Ha-Am remained aloof from the proceedings, unmoved by the exaltation of the crowd. He would later remark that he felt at Basle "like a mourner among bridegrooms."

The contrasts between Herzl and Ahad Ha-Am were striking. Ahad Ha-Am was a man of the East, Herzl a man of the West. Ahad Ha-Am was the son of a chasidic family; Herzl was born into an assimilated Austro-Hungarian family. Ahad Ha-Am's mother tongue was Yiddish; Herzl spoke German. Ahad Ha-Am was by nature introverted and uncomfortable in the public eye; Herzl was a born leader, a man of action who projected an image of self-confidence, charm, and personal warmth. Ahad Ha-Am was a man of unflinching integrity who refused to compromise his views. Herzl was a skilled political maneuverer who viewed compromise as a necessary tool in achieving his aims. It is no wonder that two men so different in background and character would arrive at divergent conclusions.

Ahad Ha-Am believed that Herzl, as a Western Jew, was ill equipped to evaluate the needs of the majority of the world's Jews. In simplest terms Ahad Ha-Am argued that the mere creation of a Jewish state would not end the material suffering of the Jews. It was madness, he maintained, to expect that "as soon as the Jewish state is established millions of Jews will flock to it, and the land will afford them adequate sus-

tenance." Even if large numbers of Jews did come, he reasoned, the new immigrants would leave the state as soon as they realized that the land could not solve their economic problems. Thus, the new state would be impotent in its battle against anti-Semitism. The political ideal conceived by Herzl would not only miscarry, it would contribute to the spiritual barrenness of the Jewish people: "If the political idea is not attained," he wrote, "it will have disastrous consequences, because we shall have lost the old basis without finding a new one."

The Plight of Judaism

Whereas Herzl's main thrust was to alleviate the suffering of Jews, Ahad Ha-Am was most concerned about the plight of Judaism. Distressed by the social and moral malaise that had weakened the Jewish national sentiment and fragmented its people, Ahad Ha-Am feared that political Zionism, by ignoring the spiritual needs of the people, would seduce Jews from their heritage and break the thread that united them with the past.

Ahad Ha-Am did not negate the idea of national revival but went beyond what he felt was the narrowness of Herzl's vision. The first stage, he believed, had to be the establishment of a large Jewish settlement in Zion organized around the spiritual and cultural needs of the Jewish people. The flowering of the Jewish soul in Palestine would inevitably lead to the reestablishment of the Jewish state and to the global regeneration of Judaism: "Then from this center the spirit of Judaism will go forth to the great circumference, to all the communities of the Diaspora, and will breathe new life into them and preserve their unity; and when our national culture in Palestine has attained that level, we may be confident that it will produce those in the country who will be able, on a favorable opportunity, to establish a state that will be a Jewish state, and not merely a state of Jews."

Statehood Not Enough

For Ahad Ha-Am statehood was not enough, especially a state not firmly based on Jewish values. In his view a state built upon the principles of Western European nationalism that ignored the moral attributes of Judaism and naively promised a complete ingathering of the exiles was not only unrealistic but doomed to mediocrity and possibly extinction.

The Diaspora played a significant role in Ahad Ha-Am's system. Unlike others who denounced the Diaspora as a negative and dying entity, he believed that Jews would continue to live and thrive outside Palestine. Once a Jewish cultural renaissance occurred in Palestine, however, the Diaspora would be viewed in a new context. He likened the relationship between Palestine and the Diaspora to the heart and its circulatory system. The revitalized national heart would renew and replenish the outer network with fresh inrushes of living blood. In this way the Diaspora would be uplifted and transformed: "The influence of the center will strengthen the Jewish national consciousness in the Diaspora; it will restore our independence of mind and self-respect; it will give to our Judaism a national content that will be genuine and natural, unlike the substitutes with which we now try to fill the void."

Respected Herzl

Despite basic differences with Herzl, Ahad Ha-Am did not fail to recognize Herzl's importance as a leader. In fact, as much as Ahad Ha-Am disagreed with Herzl's brand of Zionism,

he privately respected Herzl's ability to put theory into practice and to attract the masses. Ahad Ha-Am realized that every movement needs a hero, and he acknowledged that for Zionism Herzl was ideally suited to the task. He even perceived that Herzl's death had the timeliness of heroic tragedy: "He died at the right time. His career and activities during the past seven years had the character of a romantic tale."

In 1903, after a wearying decade as editor, Ahad Ha-Am resigned from *Hashiloah* and took up a post with the Wissotzky tea company in the hope of devoting more time to his own writing. In 1907 he was transferred to the company's London office, where he played a role in obtaining the Balfour Declaration. In 1922 Ahad Ha-Am settled permanently in Israel, devoting his last five years to organizing his letters, essays, and the first chapters of his memoirs. He died quietly in Tel Aviv on January 2, 1927 after a long illness.

If Herzl was destined by the force of his vision and the magic of his personality to establish a Zionist organization and mobilize the nationalism of world Jewry, it was Ahad Ha-Am's calling to be the conscience of the movement. Ahad Ha-Am grappled with questions that remain as troubling today as they were in his time. If anything, contemporary Jewish experience has borne out many of his insights and implores us to examine even more closely the merit of his ideas.

▪ David Ben-Gurion ▪

A legend was interred when David Ben-Gurion was buried in the Negev, at Sde Boker, in 1973. That legend had been instrumental in creating the nation where he now rests. History has not yet taken Ben-Gurion's full measure. At best we can judge the work of his hands. *Medinat Yisrael*, the State of Israel, is at the core of that assessment. Would there be a Jewish state had Ben-Gurion not been its architect and godfather? Perhaps. But that the state owes its existence to Ben-Gurion is beyond dispute.

As the following reading shows, Ben-Gurion bestrode two centuries and connected their driving spirits in his own persona. At the same time, the decades carried his imprint. Knowing him is a way to get close to the late-nineteenth and early-twentieth-century forces that were reshaping Jewish destiny. Ben-Gurion was a man of strong conviction, and many of his beliefs engulfed him in controversy with both Israeli and Diaspora Jews. Examine those opinions. With which do you agree? Disagree? Explain your answer.

■ David Ben-Gurion   BY ALLEN S. KAPLAN ■

On a hill in the middle of the barren Negev Desert lies the grave of the first Prime Minister of the State of Israel, David Ben-Gurion, "father of his nation." Before he died in 1973 he had chosen to be laid to rest in this arid section of the state he helped to create because of its symbolic value. To Ben-Gurion the Negev represented the land he had first journeyed to in 1906, a desert waiting to bloom. Just as the earliest pioneers had drained the swamps of northern Israel, so, too, he predicted, would future pioneers create a garden in the sands of the Negev.

The history of David Ben-Gurion is the story of a vision so persistent that it exemplifies the challenge of Theodor Herzl–"If you will it, it is no fable." Possessed by the idea of a Jewish state in *Eretz Yisrael*, the Land of Israel, Ben-Gurion never once veered from his goal.

Who was this modern-day Moses and David, this prophet and warrior? He was born David Green in 1886 in Plonsk, a small village forty miles north of Warsaw, in what was then Russian-dominated Poland. His father, Avigdor Green, had joined the Hibbat Zion (Love of Zion) movement that had developed in Russia in the late 1870s and early 1880s.

Because of Avigdor's good relations with the occupying Russian administration, he was able to open his home to Zionist meetings, but his infatuation with building a Jewish state in Palestine earned him the enmity of the upper-class Jews of Plonsk, who were primarily Chasidim. A Jewish state in *Eretz Yisrael*, they argued, could only come into being when the Messiah came. God alone could build it, not humans.

Revolutionary Fervor

Influenced by his father's Zionist activities and the revolutionary fervor of the period, David joined Poale Zion, an outlawed Socialist-Zionist group. In constant danger of arrest (he was once imprisoned for ten days in Warsaw), he joined the general exodus of Jews from Russian Poland in the wake of the Kishinev pogroms of 1903 and the abortive socialist revolution of 1905–events that contributed to the so-called Second Aliyah, or wave of Jewish immigration to Palestine.

The land Ben-Gurion first encountered in 1906 was a barren, sleepy land of seven hundred thousand Arabs and fifty-five thousand Jews. Some of the Jewish residents of Palestine, as the region was called under the Ottoman Turks and later the British, were the descendants of Jewish families that had lived in *Eretz Yisrael* since biblical times. Others were scions of families that had arrived in the Middle Ages, fleeing Christian and Muslim persecution. And increasing numbers were recent arrivals, part of the first wave of migration that began in the 1880s as a result of the assassination of Czar Alexander II and the pogroms that followed.

First Day in Palestine

Ben-Gurion's first day in Palestine was overwhelming. Pulled off the boat by Arab stevedores in the dirty, sleepy town of Jaffa, he was met by fellow Zionists who hauled him and his companions to their meeting hall for a debate on socialist theories. "Is this what I came here for?" he later wrote. "This dirty town with these people debating theories when they should have been working in the fields." That same day he and his friends fled the town and walked across the sand dunes to Petach Tikvah to begin a new life. There the harsh realities of pioneering in Palestine soon dawned upon him.

The builders of Petach Tikvah had become financially secure but had lost their pioneering spirit. They no longer worked in the fields but hired others, primarily Arabs, to work for them. These first pioneers had become, Ben-Gurion angrily wrote, "speculators and shopkeepers trafficking in the hopes of their people and selling their own youthful aspiration for base silver. . . . In their eyes we were a living indictment. . . . They could not bear the sight of us."

The Ethic of Labor

Ben-Gurion believed that the physical work of building a Jewish state should be done by Jewish workers. To rely on Arab labor was to violate a principal tenet of pioneering Zionism–that Jewish hands would create a Jewish state. But repeatedly he was frustrated by the failure to make the ethic of labor dominant among the Jews. Determined to campaign for what he considered vital to the national structure of the state he would one day lead, he sought to merge the two Zionist labor parties, Poale Zion and Hapoel Hatzair. Only a united movement supported by the whole *Yishuv*, the Jewish community of Palestine, would be strong enough "to fight the landlords who had sold out their ideals for money and to build an independent socialist nation." Beginning his unity campaign within his own party, Poale Zion, he eventually succeeded in creating the foundation of the state.

But it took many years for Ben-Gurion to achieve his dream. Traveling from town to town, he worked where he could, often going hungry because he was too proud to ask for help. He contracted malaria and suffered greatly but said, "I was thrilled that I had the fever." To him it was a badge of honor, proof that he was willing to sacrifice all to build a Jewish state.

In 1910 Ben-Gurion left those swamps and moved to Jerusalem after joining the editorial board of *Achdut*, the new Hebrew language newspaper of Poale Zion, founded by his good friend Yitzhak Ben-Zvi. Living in the city forced him to forgo the practical Zionism of a farm laborer and to concentrate instead on uniting the labor movement and winning Zionist support among Jews abroad. During this period he left Palestine several times in search of worldwide Jewish support. In 1913 he began to study law in Turkey (which controlled Palestine) in preparation for political leadership, but when World War I broke out a year later, the university was closed. Then, in 1917, he and Ben-Zvi went to the United States to build the Socialist Zionist movement there.

During that first visit to America Ben-Gurion met Paula Munnweis. Their courtship was brief, culminating in a lunch-hour civil wedding ceremony in the Municipal Building in New York City. Immediately after the ceremony, he kissed his bride and ran off to a political meeting. His eldest daughter, Geula, was born in America. Two more children followed, Amos and Renana. Paula, considered by many as eccentric, was known for her dedication to her husband. She watched his food, his health, and protected him from those who attempted to monopolize his time, while he, as he had warned her when proposing marriage, continued to devote most of his time and energy to nation building.

British Rule

The great statesman of Zionism during this period was Chaim Weizmann, a British scientist who was instrumental in convincing Great Britain to issue the Balfour Declaration in 1917. Named after its principal author, England's Foreign Minister Lord Arthur Balfour, the declaration stated (with some reservations) that the British government looked with favor upon the establishment of a national Jewish home in Palestine. It also gave the British, after having conquered Turkey and occupied the territory in 1918, a reason for continuing colonial rule in Palestine until such time as an independent government could be established.

As soon as the English assumed control of Palestine, however, they began to whittle away the terms of the Balfour Declaration, even though the first civilian administration of the British Mandatory Government was headed by Herbert Samuel, a Jew and a Zionist. With the arrival of Samuel in Palestine the Arabs, instigated by Haj Amin el-Husseini, launched a series of attacks against both the Jews and the British and frequently closed their shops in general strikes. Succumbing to the pressure of strikes and terrorism, Samuel appointed el-Husseini to the post of Grand Mufti, highest authority on Muslim law, and issued an order temporarily limiting Jewish immigration. Ironically, the Arab strikes helped the Jewish economy in Palestine become self-sufficient.

Haganah Organized

In response to the violence Jewish leaders organized an underground self-defense force, the Haganah. When the first riots against Jews broke out, Ben-Gurion crisscrossed the country trying to increase membership in the Haganah and wrote letters to leaders in the Diaspora pleading for greater Jewish immigration to Palestine to help form a Jewish police force capable of protecting the settlers. Ben-Gurion insisted it be guided by the concept of *havlagah,* "restraint," avoiding bloodshed. He argued that "violence for the sake of violence is sheer insanity. We will show the world that we are not animals, we are human beings." But other forces within the Jewish community looked with derision upon his idea. The Irgun, a paramilitary organization inspired by Vladimir Jabotinsky and led by Menachem Begin, who would later become prime minister, refused to be guided by such restraint, attacking not only the British but also Arabs in reprisal for attacks against Jews. Ben-Gurion and Begin would remain political adversaries for life.

In Ben-Gurion's quest for unity he resolved to build a nonpolitical organization of laborers, gathering all workers into a labor federation called the Histadrut. Such an organization would not be able to govern the new nation, he realized, but "it could build factories and settlements in the wilderness, furnishing the money as well as the muscle." It would become a labor enterprise

involved in every area of the economy. "A state would evolve not from the fine talk of the diplomat but from the sweat and ingenuity of the worker," he later wrote.

Proclaiming Statehood

The day-to-day governing of the Jewish community in Palestine was conducted by the National Committee of the *Yishuv.* The broader work of immigration, economics, politics, and international affairs was in the hands of the Zionist Executive of the World Zionist Organization. In 1935 Ben-Gurion was appointed chairman of the Jewish Agency Executive, which effectively made him the "prime minister" of the Jewish shadow government in Palestine and the dominant figure in World Zionism. His brilliance and perseverance had alienated many along the way. His detractors had called his plans for the Jewish state a hopeless dream. But now the dreamer was the leader of a powerful and growing movement, and on May 14, 1948, the dream became reality as he proclaimed the establishment of the State of Israel.

When independence was declared, Chaim Weizmann was in the United States lobbying together with Rabbi Abba Hillel Silver and Moshe Sharett for support of Israel's statehood in the chambers of the United Nations and the corridors of Washington. In Israel, Ben-Gurion was rallying the people to the military challenge that was about to confront them. He had mustered an army of citizens, outfitted them with a handful of guns, and inspired them to defend their vulnerable cities and settlements against Arab attack. World leaders pleaded with Ben-Gurion not to declare the new state, fearing that the well-armed Arab armies would destroy it. But they underestimated the resolve of Palestinian Jews under Ben-Gurion's leadership.

The Altalena Affair

Ben-Gurion took great pride in *Tzahal,* the Israel Defense Force, which he helped fashion from the Haganah. He saw a united citizen army as indispensable to forming and securing a Jewish democratic state. Insisting that the various armed groups established before independence now be abolished, Ben-Gurion signed an agreement with Irgun leaders on May 31, 1948 incorporating its right-wing forces into Tzahal. But when the *Altalena* (an Irgun ship) arrived with 800 immigrants and large quantities of weapons on June 20, 1948 in the middle of the first truce with the Arabs, Irgun officers deserted their stations in many parts of the country and converged to unload the cargo, which they refused to hand over to the Tzahal representative ashore. In the general melee shots were fired and casualties resulted. Irgun leader Menachem Begin boarded the ship, which then steamed away carrying some of its military cargo. The next morning the *Altalena* was sighted off Tel Aviv. Still, the ship refused to surrender to government forces. In a new exchange of gunfire the ship was set ablaze. Ultimately the arms were lost and the revolt crushed. Members of the Irgun were eventually incorporated into Tzahal, and a few weeks later Ben-Gurion dissolved the left-wing Palmach, the commando units that had helped Israel survive militarily during the first weeks of the War of Independence. It was his firmness with the right as well as the left that preserved the unity of the state at its most vulnerable moment. Repeatedly during his political career Ben-Gurion demonstrated that he was not afraid of the Arabs, the British, or the various factions of his own people.

The Lavon Affair

Because he took such pride in Tzahal, Ben-Gurion risked his government and his political future to protect it. In 1954 an Israeli intelligence officer recruited a handful of Egyptian Jews to carry out acts of sabotage in Egypt against American and British targets in an attempt to embarrass the Egyptians and drive a wedge between them and the two Western powers. After several bombs went off, the plot was uncovered and two Jewish agents were arrested, tried, and hanged by the Egyptians.

Ben-Gurion had retired from office a year earlier to Kibbutz Sde Boker in the Negev, suc-

ceeded as Prime Minister by Moshe Sharett. Pinchas Lavon, a protégé of Ben-Gurion, had been appointed Minister of Defense and was in office when details of the sabotage in Egypt were made public. As the Israeli government and Tzahal came under national as well as international attack, members of Ben-Gurion's Labor Party urged him to return to power. He agreed, provided Lavon left the government. But Lavon insisted on his innocence and the "Lavon Affair," as it came to be known, almost brought the government to a standstill as Ben-Gurion tried to shield Tzahal from accusations of wrongdoing. His stand alienated many of his closest colleagues. Finally in 1960 Ben-Gurion resigned once more from government, this time permanently.

Ben-Gurion returned to Kibbutz Sde Boker because he wanted to awaken a sense of idealism among younger citizens of Israel, hoping they would follow his example and settle this last frontier. He also sought a respite from the relentless pressure of guiding his people. The younger generation was of great concern to Ben-Gurion. He saw in them the hope and future of the nation and cultivated such talented figures as Moshe Dayan, Shimon Peres, Teddy Kollek, and Yitzhak Navon, bringing them into government. He especially wanted those born in Israel to emulate the pioneering spirit of his generation.

The Eichmann Trial

Ben-Gurion also felt that it was important to teach the young, especially the Sabras, about the Holocaust. Thus when Israeli agents in Argentina located former Nazi SS officer Adolf Eichmann, responsible for carrying out a large part of the Final Solution in which six million European Jews died, he ordered Eichmann captured and secretly brought to Israel. The war criminal's trial, which received extensive media coverage, served to educate a new generation in Israel and abroad about the Holocaust and the need for a militarily secure Jewish state.

Unlike many other Zionists, Ben-Gurion did not believe the Arab population would be satisfied by better living conditions and higher wages. He recognized that the success of Jewish nationalism had given impetus to the development of Arab nationalism. Ben-Gurion believed that Zionism did not have the moral right to harm a single Arab. He always encouraged attempts to meet and negotiate with Arab leaders and sent Golda Meir on a perilous peace mission to Emir Abdullah of Transjordan (now Jordan) only a few days before the proclamation of the state. But Abdullah opposed an independent Jewish state and offered instead his protection in an Arab Palestine.

As early as 1925 at the Fourteenth Zionist Congress held in Vienna, no one was more emphatic than Ben-Gurion on the necessity to "find the way to the heart of the Arab people." He insisted that empty phrases about peace and camaraderie were not enough; what was needed was a genuine alliance between Jewish and Arab workers. After the 1967 war, living in retirement in Sde Boker, Ben-Gurion advocated the return of most of the "territories" on the West Bank and the Gaza strip conquered by Israel. His reasons were moral as well as demographic. Israel could not absorb one million Arabs and remain both a Jewish and democratic state, he insisted.

A Light unto the Nations

Ben-Gurion often stressed that the State of Israel would not long survive if it did not establish a model society based on high Jewish and moral values. Only such a society would inspire national pride and attract Western Jewish immigrants, becoming "a light unto the nations." Like the prophet Amos, Ben-Gurion believed that the Jewish people was chosen for righteousness, insisting, "The existence of Israel depends upon her moral force and her righteousness." He meant it and he lived by it.

Ben-Gurion walked across the pages of history, associating with the great personalities of our century. He admired Churchill for the courageous leadership he gave the English during the darkest days of the Second World War. De Gaulle was to him the symbol of true statesmanship, a man of stature with a sense of destiny. And he respected Konrad Adenauer, the leader of the new, free Germany, despite the emotional maelstrom that surrounded any relationship between the leader of Jewish Israel and the head of postwar Germany.

It was Ben-Gurion's total commitment to the Jewish state that prompted him to agree to negotiations with the German postwar government, resulting in reparations for the property of Jews murdered by the Nazis during the Holocaust who had no surviving heirs. Despite opposition from the Herut (formerly Revisionist) and Orthodox parties, Ben-Gurion accepted reparations for the sake of the economic future of Israel, reparations that helped to finance Israel's developing industries.

After the Second World War Ben-Gurion developed a friendship with General Dwight D. Eisenhower, who was sympathetic to the plight of survivors of the Holocaust. Ben-Gurion was impressed by his compassion. Later, however, when Eisenhower became president of the United States, he felt that Ben-Gurion betrayed him by allying Israel with France and England during the 1956 invasion of Egypt and the Suez Canal. Thereafter, neither Eisenhower nor his Secretary of State, John Foster Dulles, could be persuaded to give Israel the arms necessary to offset those the Arabs were also able to procure. Ben-Gurion had sought aid for his dream of a Jewish state from Turkish officials, English prime ministers, Soviet dictators, Burmese leaders, and African statesmen. Some responded, but most made Ben-Gurion painfully aware that Israel's survival could only be based upon self-sufficiency.

As the principal architect and builder of the State of Israel, Ben-Gurion had little tolerance for those whose commitment was not as total as his own. He looked with disdain upon those Jews who called themselves Zionists but refused to make *aliyah*. He had labored in the orange groves of Petach Tikvah, trod on grapes for the wine industry of Rishon le-Tzion, and, as the retired prime minister of Israel, fed the sheep on Kibbutz Sde Boker. He was tough on himself and tough in his judgment of others.

Loved the Bible

Ben-Gurion never considered himself an observant Jew. He made alliances with the religious parties in Israel because without their votes he could not govern. He meticulously observed the rules of *kashrut* in the homes of Orthodox families where he roomed during the War of Independence, and he was careful not to be seen driving on *Shabbat*, even if it meant giving up seeing his grandchildren. He loved the Bible and studied it lovingly and diligently, seeing within it the mandate for the State of Israel and its development.

Ben-Gurion respected scientists and scholars, never refused requests to meet and speak to student groups, and for years spent every *Shabbat* evening at the home of his youngest daughter, Renana, a microbiologist, where he met her friends and colleagues with whom he discussed how to further scientific developments in Israel. He felt his lack of formal education and tried to make up for it by prodigious reading. He had no ear for music but was proficient in nine languages. He delved into matters of the mind and spirit and maintained a prodigious correspondence with thinkers, religious leaders, and historians from all over the world. His only close friend, Berl Katznelson, rightly called him "the great gift of history to the Jewish people." In addition to tremendous successes he also knew bitter failures. He did not succeed in settling the Negev, did not complete shaping the "just society," and grieved for the many lives lost in the wars of Israel.

David Ben-Gurion was indeed a Moses and a David. He was a prophet and a warrior. His enemies were many, yet thousands loved him. He was a brilliant, dedicated leader with a unique historic vision. Although short in stature, he was a giant in Jewish history and will remain the dominant spirit of the State of Israel for generations to come.

▪ Jerusalem and the Jews ▪

Jerusalem, the Holy City in the Holy Land, compels every Jew to confront Jewish history and personal identity because *Yerushalayim* has been central to Jewish thought and existence for some three thousand years. Jews never entirely left Jerusalem despite exile, war, and internal pressure from Muslims. Hardships and disabilities imposed by the Ottoman Turks failed to keep Jews away. In fact, Jews have outnumbered Christians and Muslims in Jerusalem since the mid-nineteenth century. Jerusalem's central historical reality is exceeded only by its symbolic importance: Jerusalem, the City of Zion, is metaphor for all of *Eretz Yisrael* and is the banner of the hope of redemption: "Next year in Jerusalem!"

The following reviews the relationship between the Jewish people and Jerusalem down through the ages. Because Christianity and Islam derived from Judaism, the parent religion, Jerusalem has significance for those faiths as well. That sets the stage for the modern struggle in which Jerusalem united, the eternal capital of the Jewish nation, is prominent. No longer a divided city, Jerusalem is nevertheless considered by many non-Jews still to be two Jerusalems. Why? Although it is open to all residents and tourists, accessible in all aspects to all who come in peace, many clamor for Jerusalem to be an independent, "open" city. Why? Israelis who espouse the idea of trading land for peace say that all lands reclaimed in 1967 are negotiable as part of a peace process–all except Jerusalem. Why the exception?

The Land and the People

▪ Jerusalem and the Jews   BY CHAIM RAPHAEL ▪

Why should Jerusalem mean so much to the Jews? It seems enough at first to look at the immensely long historical association, something unparalleled in the world. Jerusalem was won as the capital city of the Jewish people three thousand years ago, in the days of King David. For a thousand years from this time, Jerusalem was the battleground of Jewish experience as recorded in the Bible, the forge of Jewish faith, the rallying point of Jewish identity. When the city was destroyed by the Romans in the year 70 C.E., the loss of the Temple was the symbol of a *galut*, "exile," that was to last for nearly two thousand years; but this, far from weakening the link, made it even more intense. Centuries of wandering by the Jews gave added poignancy to the memory of their eternal city. Their daily prayers recalled how the psalmists and prophets had sung of its beauty. In joy and sorrow, in legend, folklore, and poetry, Jerusalem was always with them. Life would have become meaningless without the hope that one day they would live again as free people in the city their ancestors had created as "God's dwelling place."

Meaning for Humankind

This extraordinary passion of the Jews for Jerusalem is more than nostalgia. It is a unique way of expressing their feeling that there is some meaning–not only for themselves but for the world at large–in their emergence as a separate people and their survival through the ages.

To understand this, one has to go back to the prophet Isaiah. It was Isaiah, speaking to his fellow Jews more than seven hundred years before the common era, who saw with extraordinary power how Jewish "distinctiveness," symbolized by the existence of their own Temple at Jerusalem, could give this people a lasting role in world history. To Isaiah, there was a moral principle in the universe that humanity on earth had to grasp. Against the primitive polytheism around them he argued that the God whom the Jews worshiped at Jerusalem was the creator of all humankind. To "walk in the paths of God" would lead, ultimately, to world kinship. Isaiah's words have rung throughout history:

Nation shall not lift up sword against nation,
Neither shall they learn war any more.

In saying this, he was speaking as a Jew: his vision is announced as "the word of Isaiah concerning Judah and Jerusalem." The two are inextricably linked: "From Zion the Torah will go forth, and the word of God from Jerusalem."

Heart of the People

The idealism of the prophets found its way in later centuries into other religions; but the power of this message would not have come through unless it had been given a national basis in the first place. Even the modern historian Arnold Toynbee, who was not always sympathetic to Jewish ideas, recognized this in his book *The Crucible of Christianity*. It was only when Jerusalem became the undisputed center of Jewish worship, he says, that Jewish identity was given the strength to survive. This will to live emerged triumphantly during the Babylonian Exile. Other nations in these circumstances disappeared. The Jews survived because they had been entrusted, Toynbee writes, with "a unique spiritual treasure." They could not have preserved this "without preserving also the identity of their own community."

Jerusalem was the "home" of this community. In exile the Jews remembered it as the living symbol of what was most precious to them. A famous psalm (Psalm 137) expresses it movingly:

By the rivers of Babylon . . . we wept
When we remembered Zion. . . .
We hanged up our harps. . . .
How shall we sing the Lord's song
In a foreign country?

If I forget thee, O Jerusalem,
Let my right hand forget her cunning.

It was a psalmist also who expressed in one sentence (in Psalm 125) the extraordinary power that the physical presence of Jerusalem has always had over Jews:

As the mountains are round about Jerusalem,
So God is round about God's people,
From this time forth and for ever.

Sacred Shrines

The Jews are not alone in having a deep feeling for the majesty of this city. Christians and Muslims have been moved over the centuries by a power that seems to spring, in some mysterious way, from the purity and beauty of its site. Jerusalem became sacred to them as the place where real or legendary events basic to their faiths found enduring expression. Jesus preached in Jerusalem and died there. Muhammad was believed by his followers to have been taken to heaven in a mystic flight from the rock that was once the site of the Temple and is now the site of the great domed Mosque of Omar. Pilgrims and visionaries of these faiths have left powerful evidence of their devotion. The beauty of the city is immeasurably richer because of the churches, mosques, and other historic places that are now part of its tapestry. They have a holiness of their own that the Israelis, ensuring completely free access and protection, deeply respect.

The Only Capital

There is, however, a special element in the Jewish attachment to Jerusalem. The point has been made with great force in a Roman Catholic magazine:

Jerusalem has always been the only capital for Judaism . . . Judaism does not look upon itself exclusively as a people with a religion but as a people who have a religious link with a specific land, the Land of Israel. While Jerusalem has primarily, even exclusively, a religious value for

Islam and Christianity, for Judaism it has also a national significance.*

The need to hold on physically to Jerusalem never left the Jews. Throughout the long exile there was, in fact, an almost unbroken Jewish presence in the city. Often it was very small, and sometimes nonexistent, as, for example, after the massacres by the Crusaders at the end of the eleventh century. But the urge to set foot on this sacred soil and to live on its hills was too strong to be denied, even though constant persecution made it precarious. From the eighteenth century on the number of Jewish inhabitants increased steadily. The Jewish quarter of the Old City included many beautiful synagogues. By the middle of the nineteenth century, as the city expanded, the Jews were becoming a majority. Before the outbreak of World War I in 1914 they had risen to 70 percent of the population.

Under British rule, from 1917 on, Jerusalem continued to have a large majority of Jews, though it was a city open to all faiths. How did it happen that when the State of Israel came into being in 1948, the Old City–the most sacred part of Jerusalem–fell into the hands of an unfriendly government, Jordan, which actually barred access to all Jews?

1948-1967: Divided City

It was a tragedy that lies at the heart of the present crisis over the city. After the 1948 Israeli War of Independence the Armistice Agreement left each fighting country in possession (broadly) of the areas it was then occupying, *but under carefully defined conditions.* The kingdom of Jordan, whose forces held the Old City, agreed that access would be granted to all holy places and that the Jews would, in addition, have access to their ancient cemetery on the Mount of Olives and to the great new Hebrew University and hospital buildings on Mount Scopus. Sadly it has to be recorded that these conditions were not fulfilled. The Jordanians set up barbed wire to keep the Jews out of the Old City. Inside its walls the Jewish quarter was pillaged and sixty-two syna-

*Service International de Documentation Judeo-Chretienne, Vol. IV, No. 2, 1971.

gogues were ruined or destroyed. Outside, the old cemetery was desecrated; the precious buildings on Mount Scopus fell into ruins.

For centuries the vision of a return had been expressed in an ancient prayer: "And build Jerusalem, the Holy City, speedily in our days." With an independent state now in being the area of Jerusalem in Jewish hands was indeed built up magnificently. By 1967 the population of the city as a whole had risen to almost 300,000, of whom 226,000 (or 76 percent) were Jews. Yet this was a city divided by barbed wire, with the Old City shut off.

In their daily occupations people are not always aware of the true forces within them. It sometimes takes a crisis to bring them out. There was so much constructive work to be done in Israel in those early years that the paradox of a divided Jerusalem was lived with. The full significance emerged, however, during the Six Day War.

For the soldiers who sprang into battle on the first of the six days–June 5, 1967–the issue could be defined in normal "patriotic" terms. They were fighting for the lives and homes of their people. But when, on the third day, the word came that the Old City was to be liberated, something quite extraordinary seemed to grip these people. Their passion to free the Old City transformed them. For nineteen years exclusion from the Old City had been the price of peace. But now that Jordan had launched an attack on Israel the wrong could be righted. The barriers would come down, and Jerusalem would be whole again. When these Jewish soldiers, after deeds of incomparable bravery, stood at last facing the Western Wall, the last surviving relic of the Temple, they knew they had not just won a battle, they had been united with their history. It was a moment of holiness. As the *shofar* sounded, many of these tough soldiers found themselves in tears.

It was the same outside Israel. Jews throughout the world had trembled for the outcome as the Arab nations surrounding this little country had mobilized for the attack. A great sigh of relief went up when the astonishing victories of the first day were announced. But something beyond all this happened when the Holy City was freed. Jews everywhere felt their hearts open as to a miracle. The prayers of all the Jewish people, past and present, had been answered. Jerusalem had been restored to Jewish care and was now once again a united city.

Open to All

The central purpose of Israeli policy since the Six Day War has been to reaffirm the determination that never again shall Jerusalem be divided, as it was so tragically between 1948 and 1967. Politically Jerusalem is the capital city of the State of Israel; but all who love and revere this city are completely free to celebrate this feeling. The holy places of Jerusalem are open to the world under guarantees that are visibly being kept. As for the *administration* of the city, it is a matter for the people who live there, whatever their religious faith. All are given full democratic rights, not because of "world interest" as expressed by the United Nations but because Israel is a democratic state. Social and economic benefits for all residents are extended equally to all. In effect, the State of Israel is expressing the intention of the U.N. resolutions of 1948-49 that Jerusalem should be a unified, peaceful, "open" city. This was frustrated in the intervening years without any action by the U.N. This time the unity of Jerusalem is to be maintained. To preserve the Holy City as a single entity is to preserve civilization.

Living City

But the preservation of Jerusalem, with all its sacred associations, does not mean that the Old City and its immediate surroundings have now to be "frozen" and made unresponsive to human needs. The marvel of Jerusalem is that it is a jewel of the past and, at the same time, a living city of human beings. Its citizens fulfill their role as heirs to a complex tradition, not as "fossils" but with flexibility and imagination. Changes have been taking place all through the centuries. Even in the Old City itself, it is the rich mixture of history and humanity that is so engrossing.

The winding streets have a clutter of mixed buildings of all periods. The squares, courtyards, and arches frame vistas of infinite variety. All this bears witness to the adaptability of the many people who have thronged to the city over the years. The settlements and villages outside have also become part of a continuously unfolding scene.

The magic of Jerusalem is that it can absorb and transfuse change. It can continue to grow as a city as long as two absolute priorities are observed.

The first is that nothing new must dominate the vision in a crude way. One must still be able to lift up one's eyes unto the hills. The skyline may change, but it must always be a skyline that communicates the peculiar beauty of this area.

The other priority is that Jerusalem must never again be divided. It is a city that must exist, and be governed, in unity. When the Israelis in 1967 removed the barbed wire, allowing people of all faiths to walk freely again from one part of the city to another, it was as if the ancient "Destruction" had at last been annealed. In countless numbers the visitors of all nations now turn again toward the city whose stone walls glow golden in the sun. All the visitors have their own memories and receive their own inspiration. For Jews history itself is restored. The psalmist has said it all:

I was glad when they said unto me:
"Let us go into the House of God."
Our feet shall stand within thy gates, O
    Jerusalem;
Jerusalem is builded as a city that is compact
    together. . . .
Pray for the peace of Jerusalem:
    they shall prosper that love thee.

(Psalm 122)

IV

OF JEWS AND LANGUAGES

JEWS CHERISH AND STUDY HEBREW, THE LANGUAGE OF THE JEWISH PEOPLE. A people's language conveys culture and traditions from generation to generation. A language mirrors the soul of its people and, in turn, the language is itself part of that culture. Words, idioms, and patterns absorb and resonate the shades and hues of the values informing the culture.

Words are also symbols to express, in a shorthand way, clusters of meaning that help define the culture. Words like "house," "mansion," "igloo," "tent" express the idea of a place in which to dwell. But each presents a different and specific picture of the structure, where it is, who uses it, and how it is used. Another example: while we know what the word "charity" means, Hebrew language has no such word. Hebrew relies instead on the word "*tzedakah*" from the root *tzedek*, which means justice or righteousness. Thus, for Jews, helping others is not noblesse oblige, acts done out of kindness; it is, for Jews, the path of justice, an obligation encased in a command from God. Charity is voluntary. *Tzedakah* is not. Such ideas basic to Jewish religion are incorporated into and expressed by the language Jews use. To know the language is to penetrate the value system to its most profound depth.

This chapter discusses three languages of the Jewish people. Each is an integral part of Jewish life, a bearer of Jewish values and ideas. Hebrew, the language of our earliest Jewish ancestors, is the language of the Bible, the *siddur*, and much of our religious literature. It is, as a revived language, the most direct link with our formative past. (Aramaic, however, the language of Talmud and of some biblical material, is not discussed in these articles. You may read about Aramaic and the Jews in a source like *Encyclopaedia Judaica*, Vol. 3, pp. 259-287.) Yiddish, the *mama loshen* (lingua franca!) of generations of European Jews, has often been pronounced dead only to rise, like the phoenix, literally often from ashes. It has a glorious literary past and, once again, a promising future. Ladino, the least known, is the language of Sephardic Jews. Ladino reminds us that the Jewish people boasts many faces and many languages. Wherever in the Diaspora Jews lived, they borrowed from and adapted local languages to serve the Jewish spirit and to express Jewish values. From such syncretism have emerged the languages of the Jewish people.

■ Hebrew: The Voice of the People ■

The modern renaissance of the Hebrew language is no less miraculous than the rebirth of the Jewish nation in its Land. Long considered to be "*halashon hakodesh*," the "holy tongue," reserved for prayer and study, Hebrew had ceased to be a living language for daily communication. Many believed that the ancient Hebrew language had served only an ancient people whose later vernacular tongues were, legitimately, of the Diaspora. Yet Jewish Bible study and prayer preserved Hebrew. It hovered in the wings waiting to be called again to serve the Jewish people.

The following suggests that the fortunes of Hebrew had waned even in ancient times and even within the Jewish state. Why? Even then, however, the decline was not universal, as the Bar Kochba letters attest. In modern times, Eliezer Ben-Yehuda's unbending determination to revive the Hebrew language marked a fanaticism that makes him one of the most passionate dissidents of our era. Why was the Hebrew renaissance opposed with such vehemence by some Jews? Explain how Hebrew helps to define the Jewish state. Would the state be Jewish if English, for example, were its official language? Explain.

▪ Hebrew: The Voice of the People

BY HILLEL HALKIN ▪

Historians and linguists are agreed that no other language besides Hebrew has ever "died" in ancient times and again been miraculously "resurrected" in our own, but there is a great deal less agreement on just when and how Hebrew's "death" and rebirth took place. (We are speaking here of Hebrew as a medium of everyday speech since as a purely written language it continued to be used intensively by Jews nearly everywhere during the long centuries of the Exile—for prayer, rabbinic commentary, works of theology and philosophy, even for romantic fiction and love poetry.) Let us briefly take a look at each of these questions.

A generation ago most scholars believed that sometime during the period of the Second Temple (538 B.C.E.-70 C.E.) Hebrew disappeared completely as a spoken language among the Jewish inhabitants of Palestine to be replaced by its Semitic cousin, Aramaic. Today, however, extensive research of both an archeological and literary nature has convinced the scholarly community that, while Hebrew may well have died out in most of Palestine–Jerusalem included–considerably before the destruction of the Second Temple in the year 70, it continued to be spoken in the outlying villages of Judea for centuries after.

Bar Kochba Documents

One of the most interesting demonstrations of this fact was the discovery a decade ago in caves of the Judean desert by the Israeli archeologist Yigael Yadin and his team of a number of documents by and relating to Bar Kochba, the leader of the bloodily unsuccessful Jewish revolt against the Roman occupation in 132-135 C.E. Some of the documents are in Hebrew, others in Aramaic. The Hebrew items (including letters written by Bar Kochba to his officers and deeds or leases of land) were startling to Dr. Yadin. Not only are the letters written in fluent Hebrew but their language comes complete with previously unknown colloquial expressions and even spelling mistakes based on popular pronunciation, leaving no room for doubt that Hebrew was the copyist's native tongue. Moreover, though the collapse of the revolt led to the widespread devastation of rural Judea, a careful study of literary sources reveals that, as late as the third and fourth centuries, Jewish farmers in the countryside stubbornly clung to Hebrew speech. In this respect the disappearance of spoken Hebrew followed the pattern by which most doomed languages "die." The Irish language (Gaelic) is an example in modern times. At the opening of this century Gaelic had for so long been displaced by

English in the cities of Ireland that it was considered to be doomed and dying, but in the rural areas it continued to linger on.

Fanatical Hebraist

As for the revival of spoken Hebrew in modern times, nearly everyone knows the story of the fanatically devoted Hebraist Eliezer Ben-Yehuda (1858-1922) who settled as a young man of twenty-three in Jerusalem. There, by stubbornly refusing to speak a word of anything but Hebrew to anyone, he became the first to reintroduce the language as a tool of everyday communications.

Ben-Yehuda's dedication to Hebrew was certainly nothing short of remarkable, yet the belief that he singlehandedly brought about its spoken revival is something of a myth. There is clear evidence that Hebrew was often used as a daily language among Palestinian Jews long before Ben-Yehuda arrived on the scene–especially among Ashkenazic Jews from Eastern Europe whose native tongue was Yiddish and among Sephardic Jews from North Africa, the Middle East, and the Balkans, who spoke Arabic and Ladino. Indeed, it would be difficult to overestimate this factor of *mizug galuyot*, the blending together of diverse exiles who had only one common language in which they could communicate, as the dominant force behind the successful revival of spoken Hebrew in the Land of Israel. To take the contrasting example of the Irish language again, it, too, was the object of a nationalist campaign of revival in the first decades of this century. [*While it was introduced into the country's school system in 1922, fewer than a third of the citizens of the Republic of Ireland spoke the national language after four decades of much national effort. Today there is a weekly newspaper in the Irish language; the dailies, which carry a column in Gaelic, are in English.–Ed.*] The revival of Gaelic fell far short of success above all because practically all Irish could already talk to one another in English. Hebrew alone, however, was capable of uniting the different strands of the Jewish people regathered in the ancestral home.

New Words

When we think of the enormous problems facing people like Ben-Yehuda in their struggle to make Hebrew once again into a spoken language fit for everyday use, we think first of all the many words needed to describe the concepts and ordinary objects of modern life–words that were lacking in the literary Hebrew of the exile and had to be supplied. Indeed, the revival of spoken Hebrew in Palestine led to an enormous outpouring of new words that soon enabled Hebrew to catch up with other modern languages.

Ben-Yehuda himself was responsible for many of these coinages. For example, his word for a "watch" was *shaon*, based on the Hebrew word *sha'ah*, which means "hour" or "time." For a "railroad train," he used *rakevet*, which he fashioned from the biblical word *rechev*, meaning "chariot" or "horse-drawn vehicle." In certain cases the new Hebrew words now invented replaced lengthy and sometimes even comic circumlocutions, such as *mishkefet* (from the verb *shakaf*, "view") for "binoculars," which had been occasionally referred to in nineteenth-century Hebrew literature as *hazechuchit hamegadelet et ezovei hakir liarzei halevanon*, "the glass that makes the mosses on the wall resemble the cedars of Lebanon." Literally thousands of such new words were introduced in the early years of the Hebrew revival, and many of these are still standard usage in Israel.

Putting Words Together

Strange as it may seem, though, the greatest problem with the new spoken Hebrew from a linguistic point of view has not been one of finding much-needed words but of the ways in which Hebrew speakers put these words together to form sentences and thoughts–that is, with what a linguist would call the grammatical and idiomatic structures of the language. When one considers it carefully, however, this does not appear so strange after all. All those who have ever learned a foreign language–think of French or Spanish or perhaps even Hebrew–know that, even after mastering a great deal of basic vocabulary, one still has a natural and often unconscious tendency when speaking to translate word by word from one's own native tongue. Thus, for instance, beginning students of French who want to ask "What is your name?" may find themselves saying *"Quel est votre nom?"* instead of *"Comment vous appelez-vous?"* ("How do you call yourself?") as the French do.

Imagine now the hundreds of thousands of Jewish settlers in Israel–from Russia, Poland, Germany, Rumania, Hungary, the Arab countries, from North and South America–each group learning to speak Hebrew by instinctively translating from the expressions of its own native tongue! One might expect the results to be a tremendous confusion in which various usages from a variety of foreign languages would compete with one another in a Hebrew guise–and, in fact, this is more or less what has actually happened.

What Kind of Hebrew?

Thus, if the battle for Hebrew has been definitely won in the sense that it is today the undisputed language of the Jewish people in Israel in all walks and corners of life, from the grocery store to the university, the battle has yet to be decided in another sense, namely: what *kind* of Hebrew is the Hebrew spoken in Israel going to be? Will it be a Hebrew that is a continuation in spirit, if not in all its linguistic details, of the Hebrew spoken and written by Jews in the past? Will it be the kind of Hebrew that echoes the spirit and texture of that of the *Tanach* and the other great books of Jewish history? Or will it be a Hebrew that is little more than a conglomerate reflection of the many non-Hebraic languages the incoming Jews brought with them?

No language exists apart from the culture it is a product of and that it helps shape. On the contrary, the way we speak and the ways we think, act, and believe are so interrelated that it is difficult to say where one ends and the other begins. And so the very same questions that can be asked about Hebrew today apply as well to the culture of the new State of Israel as a whole. Will the Israeli people develop a way of life that is uniquely its own and in some way a continuation of the Jewish heritage that gave birth to it? Or will it simply come to form another modern society where people live and think not very differently from the ways they do elsewhere in the West?

"Global Village"

It is certainly no accident that many of the foreign words that have entrenched themselves most firmly in Hebrew speech–despite attempts to find native equivalents for them, words like *radio, televizia, supermarket, autostrada,* and so forth–represent precisely those aspects of modern technology that are increasingly having a leveling effect on local traditions everywhere and tending to produce a single worldwide culture. The Canadian writer on mass communications Marshall McLuhan has labeled this culture "the global village." Many of the developments in Hebrew today could well be cited as evidence of the correctness of his phrase "global village."

In any case, however Hebrew grows and changes in the years ahead–as, like any living language, it must–one thing seems clear: just as the Jewish people could not possibly have regained its national and political independence in any other country than its historical homeland, the Land of Israel, so it could only regain its true independence of mind and thought in its historical language. Throughout their long and varied history, Jews have been the speakers of dozens of different languages, some of which–Aramaic, Yiddish, and Ladino, for example–they have made uniquely their own. Yet only Hebrew can claim to have been an uninterrupted repository of Jewish life all over the world from the time of the patriarchs and matriarchs on down. No less than the Jews have preserved and protected Hebrew over the centuries, the Hebrew language has preserved and protected them. As it has been in the past, so it will undoubtedly continue to be in the future.

▪ A Fresh Look at the Poet (Chaim Nachman Bialik) ▪

Chaim Nachman Bialik has been called the greatest and leading Hebrew poet of modern times. He was a complex, neoprophetic, nature-loving Zionist. His poetry expressed the anguish of a sensitive soul seeking to reconcile, for himself and for his people, the clash of two cultures. Almost singlehandedly he achieved the renaissance of spoken and literary Hebrew. A man of vision and dreams, he was also a practical man. For example, he inspired the creation of Jewish self-defense organizations. The demands on him from an adoring and expectant public clashed with those he made on himself for privacy and introspection. His was the eloquent voice of his people; the voice was virtually stilled almost thirty years before his early death.

This brief biography questions whether Bialik's poetry, judged against high literary standards, is really great. Conclusion: One side of Bialik, the quiet, lyric, romantic side, is greatness in its own right–and is sufficient measure of the man. For this, his place in literary history is firm.

At the same time, his writings cannot be assessed so simply. Even his seemingly straightforward lyric works must be read and understood on three levels: personal, national, and universal. Whether the personal, introspective romantic, or the national and universal public prophet to others, Bialik saw himself this way: "My soul stoops to the dust/Under the burden of your love;/Alas! I have become/A clinking penny in your empty barrel." What do you think should be the role of poets and other artists? By what standards should their greatness be measured?

▪ A Fresh Look at the Poet (Chaim Nachman Bialik)

BY HILLEL HALKIN ▪

I might as well begin with a confession: Chaim Nachman Bialik–the famous, the revered Bialik, Bialik the "Hebrew national poet"–has never been a favorite of mine. Perhaps this is because I was forced to memorize too many poems of his in too many classes of the Hebrew day school I attended as a boy: long, endless poems, so it seemed to me, which we read in the headlong Ashkenazic rhythms of the Eastern European Hebrew they were indeed written in but that today sound foreign to my ears. Maybe, too, in the years gone by since, I have seen too many stuffy articles and listened to too many speeches about "the great Bialik" that left me with little desire to return to his work.

Writing this article about Bialik gave me the opportunity to take a fresh look at his poetry. Was Bialik really the unparalleled master-poet of the Jewish people in our time that he has been made out to be? Or had he rather become, as I suspected, the object of an exaggerated cult that existed because it served to make readers of modern Hebrew feel that they, too, could claim as a national hero one of the great figures of world literature, just as the English could claim Shakespeare, the Italians Dante, the Germans Goethe, and so forth? (One must remember that in nineteenth-century Europe, where Hebrew nationalism, that is, Zionism, first arose, a "great" literature was considered to be a characteristic mark of true nationhood.) With this question in mind I took down my old edition of Bialik from the bookshelf, blew off the dust–there was plenty of that!–and sat down to read.

Rereading Bialik

Was I able to answer my question? In a way I think I was, but in a way, too, I was forced to come to the conclusion that it was not a very good question to begin with. On the one hand, I am now more convinced than ever that Bialik is not one of the world's great major poets when judged by the highest standards. In fact, those of Bialik's poems that are mostly written in a "major key," that are concerned in a grand way with great national themes, are those that on the whole I found I cared for least–and since these were the same poems I had been made to learn by heart as a boy, I must say that I felt a certain sense of vindication.

On the other hand, I made an even more satisfying discovery than this in the course of reexploring Bialik, and this was that there is another, a "minor key" Bialik, as it were, whom I decided I liked very much. This is a Bialik whose poems were never read in school presumably because our teachers either thought they were too "grown-up" for us (and some indeed were) or not really "Jewish" enough: the quietly meditative Bialik of such nature poems as *Morning Watch*; the tender, romantic Bialik of love songs like *Take Me under Your Wing* and *At Sunset Time*; the melancholy, somewhat cynical Bialik of *The Summer Is Dying* and *Those Eyes That Hunger*; the bitter Bialik of *Twilight Piece*; the self-pitying Bialik of *After My Death*. In short, I discovered a very private Bialik, a Bialik intensely concerned with his own purely personal emotions, a Bialik far removed in a sense from the celebrated figure of the "Hebrew national poet" whose anniversary we are currently marking.

The "Split" Poet

Bialik himself was sharply aware of this double aspect of his personality, of the split within him between the introspective and lonely lyricist and the extroverted public figure who was expected by his readers to reflect in his poetry the great and often terrible events of the age then taking place in the Jewish world and to become, as it were, the recognized voice of a nation. He often referred to this conflict in his own poetry, frequently with a note of regret. If one looks, for instance, at the last stanza of his short lyric *Twilight Piece*, it is clear that the "penny" he has looked for symbolizes his role as a "national poet" while the "crown" he has lost is his own inner world, which he feels he has sacrificed in order to write "public" poetry of the sort his audience demands.

Why has he done this? Because Mephistopheles (in the original Hebrew *Ashmodai*)–that is, the devil–has succeeded in his ancient stratagem of tempting people to betray their true selves for the most honorable of motives–in this case, speaking for one's fellow Jew. Now, the poem implies, nothing has meaning anymore: even the gray of twilight that follows a beautiful sunset can only make the poet think of "an imbecile evening scattering ashes on the earth and sea."

Mysterious Silence

Twilight Piece was written in 1908, when Bialik was thirty-five years old, shortly before he stopped writing poetry almost completely and lapsed into a mysterious silence that was broken only by a few scattered poems until his death. Many explanations have been offered for this silence, which began when he was seemingly at the height of his poetic powers, but perhaps the real answer is to be sought in this little lyric. Did Bialik already sense at the time of writing it that, having lost the "crown" of private inspiration while looking for the "penny" of public utterance, his poetic career was drawing to a close? It could be; indeed, in another poem written four years earlier and called *After My Death*, he had already hinted that buried deep within him in a hidden corner of his soul lay feelings so personal that he would never be able to express them anymore in his poetry.

At this point I had better avoid being misunderstood. I do not wish to say that Bialik wrote what I have called his "public" poetry–that is, his poetry based on collective, national, Jewish themes–simply out of a sense of duty or because he thought it was expected of him even though his heart wasn't in it. One need only read a few lines from *The City of Slaughter*–the only one of Bialik's long, "public" poems for which there is space enough here to print excerpts–to see with what real and furious passion it was written. The poem was composed in 1903 after Bialik, as a leading young Hebrew literary figure, had been sent by the Russian Jewish community to write a report on the brutal pogroms that had taken place in the spring of that year in the district of Kishinev in southwestern Russia. Horrified by what he saw, he put aside the document he had been asked to draw up and wrote this long, angry poem instead, which, while describing the pogrom in all its bestiality, points the principal accusing finger at the Jews of Kishinev themselves, who, Bialik felt, did nothing to defend themselves against their attackers and resigned themselves to their fate with a combination of religious fatalism and physical cowardice that was bound to invite more such outbreaks in the future.

Tremendous Impact

The City of Slaughter had a tremendous impact on the Hebrew reading public in Russia, particularly on the Jewish youth, which it helped inspire to create a series of Jewish self-defense organizations throughout the country. The poem is written in semibiblical style, and the reader will notice that in the very last lines the poet compares himself to a biblical prophet ("Son of Man" is the epithet given to himself in the Bible by the prophet Ezekiel) whose message goes unheard and might as well be shouted into a howling storm. In fact, however, Bialik's message *was* heard: *The City of Slaughter* was received with wide public acclaim and the image of the prophet, of the fearless poet dedicated to telling his people the painful truth about themselves, became affixed to Bialik for good.

But it is difficult to have to be a prophet, espe-

cially if one is still a young poet who wishes to write about love, and sunsets, and nature, and the joys and sorrows of the heart. Bialik was, I think, highly ambivalent about this role in which he was cast: On the one hand, it undoubtedly flattered him, as it well might have anyone, but at times it also seems to have become a terrible burden. We get a hint of this conflict in his poem *Prophet, Run Away*, whose theme was suggested by the verses in Amos 7: "And Amaziah said unto Amos, 'O prophet, go, run away into the land of Judah and prophesy there. . . . ' Then answered Amos, 'I was no prophet, neither was I a prophet's son; but I was a herdsman and a gatherer of sycamore fruit. And God took me as I followed the flock, and God said unto me, Go prophesy unto my people Israel.'"

In this poem, in which it is clear that Bialik was writing about himself as well, a number of emotions commingle in the prophet at once: pride in his prophetic mission, relief at the thought of returning once more to the "valley" and "sycamores" of his private life, and anger at the Jewish people for failing to understand him or appreciate what he has sacrificed for them. When Bialik writes, "My hammer found no anvil when it fell/My axe went splintering through rotten timber," he seems to be complaining that his own poetry has suffered from the need to adapt it to the level of a wide and not necessarily discriminating audience. This theme of the prophet who would gladly be rid of his public mission occurs in several other poems of Bialik's, too.

Personal Sadness

And yet this is not to say that Bialik's private life was always a happy one, either. In fact, if we were to judge solely by his poetry–and because Bialik was reticent about himself apart from his poetry, it is often all we have to go on–we would have to conclude that the contrary was more often the case. This is especially true of his poetry written after 1900, and it would almost seem that the more his outward life was crowned with honors and admirers, the more his inner one was filled with disappointment. Disappointment with what? His poems give only tantalizing hints: with love (Bialik was married young, at the age of twenty, but his love poems were quite clearly not written to his wife), with the conviction that his readers never really understood him, with the feeling that somewhere, he, Bialik, the celebrated "Hebrew national poet," had failed to live up to his own highest goals. . . . Bialik's mature love poems, for example, are all sad ones. Either, like *At Sunset Time* or *Take Me under Your Wing*, they are about the terrible loneliness of a man who cannot really love at all but can only relate to a woman as to a fellow sufferer or a mother figure–or else, like *Those Eyes That Hunger*, they are about the revulsion from sexual passion experienced by the satiated lover.

Bialik's nature poems tell a similar story of disillusionment. Whereas at the age of twenty-six, when he wrote *Morning Watch*, they are still full of hopeful images of dawn, dazzling sunlight, blossoming, and spring; six years later, when he wrote *The Summer Is Dying*, we find them dominated by the shades of sunset, autumn, and night. (Perhaps one might say that the summer of this poem is the summer of youth itself, which is followed by the autumn of middle age, in which adventurous dreams and high ambitions must give way to the petty realities–the "potatoes"–of daily life.) Soon after this, as we have said, Bialik practically stopped writing poetry altogether. Perhaps someday, when a serious biography of him is written, we will know more about what happened to him during this period of his life when he wrote his most beautiful–and unhappiest–poems.

Grimness of Life

The sadness of life is not a theme that we find in Bialik alone among the Hebrew poets and authors who were brought up in that cradle of modern Hebrew literature, late nineteenth-century Eastern Europe. On the contrary, no theme is as common in the works of Bialik's Hebrew-writing contemporaries–nor should this surprise us when we consider the grimness of Eastern European Jewish existence at this time, with its backwardness, its grinding poverty, the fanaticism of its religious life, its anti-Semitic

surroundings, and the seeming hopelessness even of the one practical solution–Zionism–that had been proposed for its plight. Bialik's greatest importance for Hebrew literature, it seems to me, was not that he, too, wrote about these problems in his "public" poetry, or at times played the part of the prophet his audience wanted to see him as, but that more than any other Hebrew poet of the age, he was willing to bare his private soul to the reader, too–and to do so in poetic language that was richer, stronger, and more natural than any Hebrew poetry had been since the time, some eight centuries earlier, of Judah Halevi.

Revolution in Poetry

To appreciate this stylistic side of Bialik, one need only compare those poems of his already discussed in these pages with the first poem he ever published, *To the Bird*, which appeared in print in 1892 when he was nineteen years old. [*Bialik himself later called it "childish and immature" and felt it owed its success to its atmosphere and spirit, which contrasted vividly with the reality of nineteenth-century Jewish life–Ed.*] It is not such a bad little poem in its way–yet how stilted and clichélike, really, is the language in which it was written. And yet this was the style–heavily dependent on the Bible and other traditional sources–in which practically all Hebrew poetry was still being written at the time Bialik began his career! In the space of seven or eight years (in a poem like *Morning Watch* we still see him in the middle of this process), Bialik managed to discard this old style completely in his private lyric verse and to forge a new, personal one of his own. The simplicity and freedom of Bialik's new style brought about a revolution in Hebrew poetry whose effects are still felt to this day. (His longer, "prophetic" poems like *The City of Slaughter*, on the other hand, continued to be written in a more conservative, ornate, biblical style, and this is perhaps one reason why I care for them less.) For this alone Bialik truly deserves to be called the father of modern Hebrew poetry.

The Many Bialiks

One must not imagine that when Bialik gave up writing poetry halfway through his life he retired from literary pursuits altogether. Rather, he now devoted himself with characteristic energy to other literary tasks. This is the period of his life in which we encounter, as it were, first in Russia and then in Palestine, a veritable multiplicity of Bialiks who have taken the place of the original Bialik the poet. There is Bialik the balladeer, who wrote marvelous facsimile folk songs, some of which, like *Two Steps from My Garden Rail*, have subsequently been set to music and become real folk songs; Bialik the prose writer, who penned several delightful short stories and memoirs of his childhood in a pastoral Russian village; Bialik the critic, who astutely commented on the literary trends of the day; Bialik the scholar, who collaborated with his friend Y. H. Ravnitsky to compile the monumental anthology *Sefer ha-Aggadah*, a definitive collection of the rabbinic folktales and legends found in the Talmud and Midrash; Bialik the brilliant conversationalist, who held audiences spellbound with his reminiscences and his opinions on literature, art, politics, Zionism, Jewish history; and Bialik the friend and literary patron, who generously lent an ear and gave advice and encouragement to many a younger writer. Each of these Bialiks made an invaluable contribution to Hebrew literature and life; each deserves an article, many articles, of his own.

In a sense these were happier Bialiks than Bialik the poet; certainly they seem to have been more at peace with themselves and less tragic. And yet it is not the Bialik of these latter years-described by his young friend and translator into English, Maurice Samuel, who knew him in Tel Aviv, as looking "rather like a successful businessman"*–whom I find that I cannot get out of my mind ever since beginning to work on this article. No, it is the tragic Bialik who is the unforgettable one for me, the poet whose conflict with his poetic role made him abandon it in the end like a man who gives up a woman whom he loves but knows he cannot go on living with, the lonely, romantic Bialik who at the pinnacle of his fame and powers sat down and wrote:

The pale stars cheated me.
I had a dream–it too has flown,
And left me behind by myself,
All alone.

What was that dream?

---

*"In company," Samuel wrote, "there was a perpetual good humor about Bialik that was utterly incomprehensible when one remembered certain of his poems that could only have issued from a deeply tormented soul." Many other acquaintances of Bialik also commented on his conviviality and enormous zest for life and observed how different he seemed in person from in his poetry.

▪ The City of Slaughter ▪

Spring of 1903 saw one of the most vicious of the many pogroms through which Eastern European Jews suffered for decades. Thirty-year-old Chaim Nachman Bialik, already a published poet, went to Kishinev at the behest of Russian Jewry to report on the massacre. What he saw outraged and inflamed him. Instead of an official report, he penned this poem, in Hebrew. The poem excoriates Kishinev's Jews for seeking refuge in passive resignation rather than in militant self-defense. Some have argued that the defenders of the Warsaw Ghetto might well have gone to their heroic deaths reciting Bialik's stirring words. Certainly, in his own time, the poet of the Jewish people spoke to the hearts and minds of young Jews and impelled them to action in Jewish causes. There is evidence among some contemporary writers as well that the national-prophetic aspect still inspires and elevates Jews and spurs them to action. Read some of these modern poets and decide for yourself.

▪ The City of Slaughter BY CHAIM NACHMAN BIALIK ▪

Arise and go now to the city of slaughter;
Into its courtyard wend thy way;
There with thine own hand touch, and with the eyes of thine head,
Behold on tree, on stone, on fence, on mural clay,
The spattered blood and dried brains of the dead.
Proceed thence to the ruins, the split walls reach,
Where wider grows the hollow, and greater grows the breach;
Pass over the shattered hearth, attain the broken wall
Whose burnt and barren brick, whose charred stones reveal
open mouths of such wounds, that no mending
Shall ever mend, nor healing ever heal.

There will thy feet in feathers sink, and stumble
On wreckage doubly wrecked, scroll heaped on manuscript,
Fragments again fragmented–

Pause not upon this havoc; go thy way.
The perfumes will be wafted from the acacia bud
And half its blossoms will be feathers,
Whose smell is the smell of blood!
Unto thy nostrils this strange incense they will bring.
Banish thy loathing–all the beauty of the spring,
The thousand golden arrows of the sun
Will bid thy melancholy to be gone;
The seven-fold rays of broken glass
Will bid thy sorrows pass;

For God called up the slaughter and the spring together,–
The slayer slew, the blossom burst, and it was sunny weather!
Then wilt thou flee to a yard, observe its mound.
Upon the mound lie two, and both are headless–
A Jew and his hound.
The self-same axe struck both, and both were flung
Unto the self-same heap where swine seek dung;
Tomorrow the rain will wash their mingled blood
Into the runnels, and it will be lost
In rubbish heap, in stagnant pool, in mud.
Its cry will not be heard.
It will descend into the deep, or water the cockle-burr.
And all things will be as they ever were. . . .

Lift then thine eyes to the roof; there's nothing there,
Save silences that hang from rafters
And brood upon the air:
Question the spider in his lair!
His eyes beheld these things; and with his web he can
A tale unfold horrific to the ear of man:–
A tale of cloven-belly, feather-filled;
Of nostrils nailed, of skull-bones bashed and spilled;
Of murdered men who from the beams were hung,
And of a babe beside its mother flung,
Its mother speared, the poor chick finding rest

Upon its mother's cold and milkless breast;
Of how a dagger halved that infant's word,
Its *ma* was heard, its *mama* never heard. . . .

Descend then, to the cellars of the town,
There where the virginal daughters of thy folk
were fouled,
When seven heathen flung a woman down,
The daughter in the presence of her mother,
The mother in the presence of her daughter,
Before slaughter, during slaughter, and after
slaughter!
Touch with thy hand the cushion stained; touch
The pillow incarnadined:
This is the place the wild ones of the wood, the
beasts of the field
With bloody axes in their paws compelled thy
daughters yield:

Beasted and swined!

Note also, do not fail to note—
In that dark corner, and behind that cask
Crouched husbands, bridegrooms, brothers,
peering from the cracks,
Watching the sacred bodies struggling
underneath
The bestial breath,
Stifled in filth, and swallowing their blood!
Watching—these heroes!–
The ignominious rabbis tasting flesh,
Morsels for Neros.
Crushed in their shame, they saw it all;
They did not stir nor move;
They did not pluck their eyes out; they
Beat not their brains against the wall!
Indeed, each wretch then had it in his heart to
pray;
A miracle, O Lord,–and spare my skin this day!
Those who survived this foulness, who from their
blood awoke,
Beheld their life polluted, the light of their world
gone out—
How did their menfolk bear it, how did they bear
this yoke?
They crawled forth from their holes, they fled to
the house of the Lord,
They offered their thanks to Him, the sweet

benedictory word.
The Cohanim sallied forth, to the Rabbi's house,
they flitted:
*Tell me, O Rabbi, tell, is my own wife
permitted?*
The matter ends; and nothing more.
And all is as it was before. . . .
And thou too, greet them not, nor touch their
wound;
Within their cup no further measure pour.
Wherever thou wilt touch, a bruise is found.
Their flesh is wholly sore.
For since they have met pain with resignation
And have made peace with shame,
What shall avail thy consolation?

They are too wretched to evoke thy scorn.
They are too lost, thy pity to evoke,
So let them go, then, men to sorrow born
Mournful and slinking, crushed beneath their
yoke
Go to their homes, and to their hearth depart—
Rot in the bones, corruption in the heart.
And when thou shalt arise upon the morrow
And go upon the highway,
Thou shalt then meet these men destroyed by
sorrow
Sighing and groaning, at the doors of the
wealthy
Proclaiming their sores, like so much peddler's
wares,
The one his battered head, t'other limbs
unhealthy.
One shows a wounded arm, and one a fracture
bares.
And all have eyes that are the eyes of slaves,
Slaves flogged before their masters;
And each one begs, and each one craves:
Reward me, Master, for that my skull is broken
Reward me, for my father who was martyred!
The rich ones, all compassion, for the pleas so
bartered
Extend them staff and bandage, say *good rid-
dance*, and
The tale is told:
The paupers are consoled.
Avaunt ye, beggars, to the charnel-house!

Of Jews and Languages

The bones of your fathers disinter!
Cram them within your knapsacks, bear
Them on your shoulders, and go forth
To do your business with these precious wares
At all the country fairs!
Stop on the highway, near some populous city,
Your customer, and spread on your filthy rags
Those martyred bones that issue from your bags,
And sing, with raucous voice, your pauper's ditty!
So will you conjure up the pity of the stranger
And so his sympathy implore.
For you are now as you have been of yore

And as you stretched your hand
So will you stretch it,
And as you have been wretched
So are you wretched!
What is thy business here, O Son of Man?
Rise, to the desert flee?
Thy tear upon the barren boulders shed!
Take thou thy soul, rend it in many a shred!
And feed thou thy heart to rage, as to a worm!
Thy tear upon the barren boulders shed!
And send thy bitter cry into the storm!

(This excerpt translated by
Abraham M. Klein, 1903.)

▪ A Living, Breathing Language ▪

At its zenith Yiddish embodied a profound literature, a rich and varied cultural context, a way of life to millions of Jews. Transplanted to America in the immense migratory waves of the late nineteenth and early twentieth centuries, Yiddish remained, for a while, the guardian of the special Jewish culture it spawned and expressed. But the immigrants sought to be "yenkees" and wanted their children to be bona fide Americans, not "greeners." As a result, Yiddish fell on hard times. It was destined to fall on even harder, cataclysmic times, as much a victim of the Holocaust as the Jews who spoke it. Despite the blows it has suffered in recent decades, Yiddish hangs on to life. Although the Yiddish press is minuscule by past standards, the language survives in small Yiddishist groups, in yeshivot, and in a tiny literary effort.

In the following, the author predicts a rebirth of Yiddish even while it is being pronounced dead by many observers. Identify the forces that have worked/are working in both directions.

▪ A Living, Breathing Language ▪ BY AMOS SCHAUSS ▪

Yiddish, like Tom Sawyer, has had the fun of being at its own funeral. In fact, Yiddish has had this pleasure many times. Long ago the world lost count of the number of these sad farewells. Over a century ago, in 1862, Alexander Zederbaum, the editor of the Hebrew weekly *Hamelits*, informed the czarist authorities that Yiddish was on its last legs. In 1898 Professor Leo Wiener of Harvard prophesied that Yiddish would soon be dead. Similarly, Ahad Ha-Am, the famous Hebrew essayist and philosopher, predicted the imminent disappearance of Yiddish, as did Abraham Cahan, the editor of the *Jewish Daily Forward* for over fifty years.

The list of prophets of doom includes many famous literary figures and community leaders, many of whom made their living by means of Yiddish and could express themselves best in that language. One might thus have expected from them a more optimistic attitude. The latest in this litany of lamenters is I. B. Singer, the world-famous Yiddish novelist and short-story writer, who feels that the tongue he writes in will soon be muted. He ends his article on "Yiddish Literature" in the new *Encyclopaedia Britannica* (fifteenth edition): "The soil for Yiddish in the United States is growing ever thinner, and the hope for the emergence of great writers in Yiddish ever more doubtful."

Dead Wrong

The amazing thing is that these sages and seers have all been wrong! Yiddish is still alive, and doing better than it has in a long time.

It is perhaps ironic that Yiddish has been kept alive by those very same factors that have made it *seem* Yiddish was at death's door. Those factors have included powerful historical forces such as: (1) the destruction of Eastern European Jewry by Hitler's Germany and thus the loss of millions of Yiddish-speakers; (2) the renaissance of the Hebrew language, the spread of the Zionist movement, and the establishment of the State of Israel, all of them advancing Hebrew over Yiddish; (3) the ongoing process of assimilation throughout the world, which leads to the use of vernacular languages and the shunting aside of Yiddish as well as Hebrew; and (4) the strangulation of all forms of Jewish culture and especially Yiddish in the Soviet Union.

All of these potent pressures have *seemed* to be smothering Yiddish to death, but they have actually helped to revive interest in Yiddish and have given it a new lease on life. Clearly, the tragedy of the Holocaust, the miracle of the State of Israel, the spread of enlightenment and general education among Jews, and, more recently, the suffering, courage, and struggle of our Soviet Jewish brothers and sisters have all had their effects. What are those effects? Jewish awareness generally among our people, young and old, has been aroused; and, in particular, these events have stimulated a renewal of interest in Yiddish language, literature, folklore, and culture.

Clearing Away Myths

There is a great deal to be said in the short space at our disposal about the Yiddish language. First off, we should know that the name of the language is *Yiddish* and never *Jewish*. There are *various* Jewish languages, of which Hebrew, Yiddish, and Ladino are examples.

Second, we should settle, early in the proceedings, that there *is* a word for "disappointed" in Yiddish, a perfectly simple and normal word, *antoysht*, and "disappointment" is thus *antoyshung*.

In this vein, we might continue with another misconception, prejudice, or myth we would do well to clear away, like ugly weeds from a garden. It is completely incorrect to think that Yiddish is only a "jargon" and not a language. Those who erroneously refer to Yiddish as a "jargon" (in my Oxford Dictionary, "jargon" is defined as ". . . a speech or dialect arising from a mixture of languages . . . ") would, by the same reasoning, have to call English a "jargon," too, because English has adopted a great many words from a long list of languages. But English is a language and not a jargon because its borrowed words have been thoroughly assimilated and are used in conformity with an inner consistency and distinctiveness. The very same applies to Yiddish. Just as English is a language, so is Yiddish, with its own grammar, syntax, and spelling. Others say that a language is a "jargon" (or a "dialect") with a literature, and in this sense Yiddish is a language of the first order.

Who Speaks It?

Before World War II there were about eleven million speakers of Yiddish in the world, of whom approximately half were killed in the Nazi Holocaust. Today it is estimated that there are perhaps five million Jews who use Yiddish. Most of these are concentrated in the U.S., the USSR, Latin America, and Israel, and there are Yiddish-speaking Jews also in Canada, Mexico, France, Australia, England, and the Republic of South

Of Jews and Languages

Africa. It is quite clear that to this very day, even with all the defeats and diminutions Yiddish has suffered over the years, when a Jew travels to a foreign country and is unable to speak the local language, communication with the Jews in that country is generally through Yiddish. The overwhelming majority of Jews in the world, allowing for a small percentage of exceptions, still are bound together by means of the Yiddish language. The Yiddish press is still the best means of information on Jewish life all over the world, and Jewish public leaders of different countries communicate most effectively in Yiddish.

One Thousand Years Old

Yiddish had its beginnings around the year 1000. Thus, like most of the European languages, it is roughly a thousand years old. The history of Yiddish is a reflection of the history of European Jews for the last thousand years. It was born in the upper and middle Rhine basin in Germany and in an area that used to be called Loter (today it is "Lorraine"), when Jews from northern Europe and northern Italy took over the German language of the tenth century. Some of the famous communities where all this started are Cologne, Mainz, Worms, Speyer, Trier, and Metz. There are still many Jews whose names indicate their connection with these towns–names like Shapiro (Speyer), Mintz (Mainz), and Dreyfuss (Trier or Treves).

The Crusades and the persecutions brought on by the Black Plague forced the Jews of the Rhine–and their newly developing language–to move toward central and southwest Germany, toward what today are Bavaria, Austria, and Czechoslovakia. By the thirteenth century Jews had reached Slavic territory. They settled in growing numbers in Poland, Lithuania, and the Ukraine, and in the course of time Eastern Europe became the major center of Yiddish. By the seventeenth and eighteenth centuries cities such as Cracow, Lublin, Brisk, and Vilna had become the trading hubs of Jewish life and Yiddish usage. Yiddish had become the language of practically all the Jews of Europe, except for the Sephardim, and this was the situation until Hit-

ler. During the nineteenth century the Jews of Western Europe gradually drifted away from Yiddish until, in the twentieth century, it was active again but only in Alsace. But, at the same time, Yiddish gained a very large increase in the number of Yiddish-speaking Jews in Eastern Europe, and when the great migration of the Eastern European Jews took place, from about 1880 to 1920, Yiddish spread to almost every country of the world. To this very day the most numerous single-language group among the Jews of the world is still the Yiddish-speaking group.

This history of Yiddish is usually divided by scholars into four periods: Initial Yiddish (1000-1250), Old Yiddish (1250-1500), Middle Yiddish (1500-1750), and Modern Yiddish (1750 and later). Since Jews have been a highly literate people from the very origin of the language on, literary monuments of each period have survived, although there are very few for the actual beginning.

Elements in Yiddish

Just as good English consists of a balance between the two historic elements, the Germanic and the Romance, good Yiddish constitutes a unique blend of its two main elements, Medieval German and Hebrew. There are other elements, too: Romance words of the initial period are still present in today's Yiddish; and, as the center of gravity of the Yiddish language community shifted into Slavic lands, many Slavic influences in the vocabulary and especially in word formation and syntax were stamped onto Yiddish. We can thus clearly see in the composition of the Yiddish language an accurate reflection of its history, as well as the history of a large part of the Jewish people for almost a millennium. Slowly a new language came into being with its own patterns and laws–a Jewish language comparable to Hebrew and Aramaic. Yiddish reflects directly all of Jewish life of the last thousand years, and through it the whole of Jewish tradition. But, at the same time, Yiddish has also served as a means of expression for many new trends and schools of thought in recent centuries: Chasidism, *Haskalah*, the Jewish Labor movement, and Zionism.

As everybody knows, Yiddish is written in Hebrew characters. The present-day spelling of Yiddish came into use around 1900, but many modifications have been and are being introduced. The rules of spelling Yiddish established by the Yivo Institute for Jewish Research are generally accepted as standard in the scholarly world and in many of the better journals and magazines, although the *Jewish Daily Forward* and many other periodicals still stay with the older spelling habits, claiming their readers are used to it. In the Soviet Union, where there has always been hostility to the Jewish people and to the language of the Bible, Hebrew, the traditional spelling of the Hebrew elements in Yiddish has been shunted aside.

Predictions and Prophecies

In spite of all the prophets of doom whom we mentioned at the beginning of this article, Yiddish survives very nicely today. It survives on various levels, both actively and passively. It survives as a living language great numbers of Jews can actively use to make themselves understood, and even greater numbers can understand passively even though they may not be able to speak it. But the most important and vital level on which Yiddish survives is in being a vehicle for the thoughts, hopes, ideals, and creativity Jews continue to express. On this level Yiddish can never die. For Yiddish literature and poetry, Yiddish writings on Zionism, Jewish socialism, the Jewish Labor movement, Chasidism, the Musar movement (study of moral and ethical literature), the Holocaust experience, the struggle of Soviet Jewry, and the world of Eastern European Jews—all of these will always claim the attention and interest of those wishing to know something about Judaism. So, in this sense, and on this level, Yiddish will live, just as almost nothing Jews have created through the centuries has ever died.

A famous Yiddish writer, Chaim Zhitlowsky, once said, perhaps exaggerating slightly: "One who does not know *loshn kodesh* [Hebrew] is an *am horetz*. One who does not know Yiddish is a *goy*." Surely another Chaim—Chaim Weizmann—was not exaggerating when he said that, just as Hebrew is our *loshn kodesh*, Yiddish is our *loshn hakdoshim*, the language of our martyrs. And, as long as there will be Jews and a Judaism, the Yiddish language will continue to live.

▪ The Rebellion of the Young Poets ▪

The turn-of-the-century young Yiddish poets labored on the streets and in the sweatshops of immigrant New York. Their writings, in Yiddish, brought a new dynamism to Yiddish literature. For them Yiddish poetry was for lyric, romantic, personal expression, not for serving social causes. Moreover, writing in the land of freedom, they opted to express themselves on Jewish themes. Thus, although America enabled them, if they chose, to ignore Jewish particularism in favor of universal concerns, they nevertheless drew deeply from their Jewish heritage, which, in turn, helped to define who they were.

The following introduces these young Yiddish poets—*di yunge*. You will explore why they rebelled against the then-popular use of Yiddish that had become a vehicle to express social and political concerns. Describe the common elements in their varied backgrounds. How did those elements influence their poetry? Despite its puristic tendencies, the poetry was widely read. Why? Compare the attitudes of these poets with Bialik's beliefs about Hebrew discussed in the second article of this chapter.

Of Jews and Languages

■ The Rebellion of the Young Poets

BY RUTH R. WISSE ■

Evening. A crowd of men and a few women, most of them in their late teens and twenties, gather to discuss new directions in literature. Bitter toward the newspapers and magazines that seek sensation and show no interest in good writing, they decide to pool resources and put out an independent publication, *Youth*, that will express the real feelings and aesthetic passions of these young poets and writers. (Despite a short-lived career of only two issues, the thin magazine earns its contributors and followers the literary nickname *di yunge*, "the young," which sticks with them even after they are in their sixties.)

The scenario, which could describe the beginnings of any number of modern literary movements, took place in New York City in 1907. The young men and women were very recent immigrants from Russia and Poland, often the first members of their families to arrive in America, and just as often refugees from the Russian czarist police. During the day they had worked at any job they had been able to find: bootmaking, hatmaking, paperhanging, sign painting, even waiting on tables. But they regarded themselves as poets and writers, and, familiar as they were with contemporary writing in Russian, German, and French, they were determined to find their own voices in their own vernacular, Yiddish.

Their native tongue was Yiddish, the language of the Jewish masses then streaming to America, and the language of more Jews than had ever spoken a Jewish language at any given period in history. It may seem odd that English-speaking America should have become the cradle of modern Yiddish poetry, but, to these young writers, aware as they were of American culture, Yiddish remained the natural language choice. The masters of modern Yiddish literature–Mendele Mocher Seforim, Sholem Aleichem, and I. L. Peretz–had already demonstrated the rich possibilities of Yiddish as a literary medium, and the

Americans were among hundreds of other talented writers in all parts of the world eager to take the literature in their own directions.

Variety Among Rebels

Though from the outside they may have looked like a group, the young people who clustered around the magazine *Di Yungt* ("Youth"), and especially those who gathered around the magazine's attractive successor, *Shriftn* ("Writings"), were a varied bunch of individuals. There was Mani Leib, a bootmaker from the Ukraine, who considered poetry one of the miracles of life and thanked fate for making him, not a shoemaker-poet, but a poet-shoemaker. Zisha Landau was a bit of a cynic, fanatic about high standards in poetry, and merciless to anyone who wrote a bad line. Reuben Eisland's best work was about everyday actions, like going off to work with lunch in a paper bag and then feasting on it in a private corner of a crowded workshop. Around this nucleus others gathered and then went their separate ways. Like all literary "groups," this one often quarreled or broke into open war. Moishe Leib Halpern was unhappy with the gentle sounds of *di yunge*'s verse; he called himself a "street drummer" and pounded out noisy rhythms on not-so-genteel subjects. Curses, garbage pails, and mocking laughter sounded through his poetry along with the stillness of setting suns and the ripple of the seashore. H. Leivick, an escapee from life imprisonment in Siberia, wrote highly serious, prophetic–what his detractors called pompous–verse. There were prose writers, too: the prolific Joseph Opatoshu, who took his subjects out of Jewish history and right off the New York streets; David Ignatoff, experimenting with combinations of symbolism and realism and always at the center of every literary battle. The women, like Anna Margolin and Celia Dropkin, wrote more erotically than the men, but their output was smaller. If this list of poets could be extended for pages, there would still be omissions. . . .

Mani Leib's Influence

The key figure in this experimental American Yiddish poetry was Mani Leib Brahinsky or, as he signed himself, Mani Leib. He didn't theorize much, but he produced a new melodious sound in Yiddish verse, much as Wyatt and Surrey had done for English poetry back in the sixteenth century. When he came to New York in 1905, he had already spent six months in prison for revolutionary, anti-czarist activities, and even in America he joined an organization to help the revolutionary struggle back home. But he did not consider poetry a vehicle for political ideas. And, although he worked at bootmaking ten to eleven hours a day, six days a week, for all of four dollars, he didn't want his poetry to protest this either. Poetry–in his view–should not be the weapon of social and national struggle but an end in itself, the poet's private expression. He carved out small poems: some of them so simple as to suggest "children's verse"; others based on Yiddish folk songs about the prophet Elijah, a family of many brothers, or a snowfall; still others, deeply personal lyrics of loneliness and guilt.

This may sound entirely innocent, even too innocent, as a poetic philosophy. But, in the Jewish immigrant environment of which Mani Leib and his fellow *yunge* formed a part, it was quite as revolutionary as the poet's former opposition to the czar. The current poetry featured in the pages of the daily Yiddish press or in the powerful weekly *Di Zukunft* ("The Future") consisted of rhythmic calls to labor solidarity or heartrending laments on the plight of the sweatshop workers. Yiddish literature was expected to be *public*, expressing the *national* sufferings of the Jewish people or the social abuse of the workers. It was expected to arouse the Jew in the worker or the worker in the Jew and to goad him into a stronger sense of group identity. Naturally the ears trained on this kind of verse would resent the deliberate softness, the gentle assonance, and the avowed privacy of Mani Leib's experi-

ments. A prominent reviewer called his first volume of collected poems "decadent."

In contrast with this cool official reception, however, was the acclaim of younger "educated" readers on both sides of the Atlantic. Shmuel Niger, who later became a major literary critic, wrote of his first enthusiastic reading of *Shriftn* (1912) when he was still a boy in Russia: "We felt that in America there had appeared writers who wanted to set themselves apart from their drab surroundings, writers who couldn't stop to pray–that is, "create"–right in the middle of the street but who wanted a separate literary synagogue for their *minyan*, an artistic holy place." Although we tend to consider "the old country" the source of American Jewish culture, the influence in his case went in the opposite direction, from America back to Europe where budding Yiddish writers admired the new styles and themes of Mani Leib and others and adapted them in their own work.

Admirers of Walt Whitman

The American Yiddish writers tried to keep English words and syntax out of their language. Unlike the Yiddish newspapers and most Yiddish speakers, who opened the language indiscriminately to every English word and sound, they kept Yiddish free of the surrounding influence. But they were alive to America and to its writers. Walt Whitman was the favorite poet. He seemed to embody the new freedom, the endless variety, abundance, and contradiction of the United States, and he was widely translated into Yiddish by his admirers. The country itself was a perpetual source of artistic inspiration. Isaac Raboy went out West to work as a cowboy and wrote vigorous short novels about life on the edge of the badlands. I. J. Schwartz wrote one of the finest Yiddish epics, "Kentucky," about the intriguing "bluegrass" country and a Jewish peddler who sinks his roots into that hospitable soil. Ironically it was the curse of urban life, tuberculosis, that introduced many Yiddish writers to the Rockies. A certain doctor, who was also a lover of Yiddish literature, invited the sick writers to take their cure at his TB sanitarium in Denver,

Colorado. As a result, the poetry of Yehoash, H. Leivick, and others is rich in praise of the red mountains.

The Golden Peacock

For the most part, however, America was New York City, the section of the Lower East Side that housed the Yiddish theaters, printing shops, and the "literary cafés," those inexpensive restaurants where you could sit all evening over coffee and a roll, arguing about the latest issue of this or that new magazine. On the one hand, the writers wanted to write about the real American scene, about the subways, the neon lights, the hard work and dirt, the blacks and Irish whom they had never known in Eastern Europe. On the other hand, they also longed to escape from the oppressing all-too-present reality by dreaming of the past, the life of nature, of the impossible "golden peacock" that flies through so many Yiddish songs. This clash between the "sober and the drunk" or the "realists and the fantasists" produced very different kinds of poetry, but it was often a battle that raged inside one and the same person.

Moishe Leib Halpern describes himself as torn by almost continuous inner conflict. Of his past he wrote a poem beginning: "Long for home and hate your homeland," admitting in the same breath his nostalgia and his refusal to lie about the hatred that drove him from home in the first place. He saw America as the "golden land" but recognized the greed that any gold rush inspires. A talented artist as well as a poet, he loved beautiful sounds and images, but he mocked himself for thinking of beauty when the world was so filled with injustice and pain. One of his most powerful poems, "Salute," re-creates the lynching of a fifteen-year-old Southern black boy who is innocent. The final anger of the poem is directed not against the spinster who makes the false accusation, not against the crazy mob that tars and feathers the victim, not against the racist preacher, but against himself, the poet, who stands around making beautiful poems about a lynching. Like all the *yunge*, Halpern turned his back on the poetry of the sweatshops and

insisted that art must serve only itself. But, whereas they declared the *nobility* of poetry and spoke of it in religious terms, Halpern considered it a wicked temptation, taking the artist's attention away from important social problems into the safe atmosphere of aesthetics. His poetry grew ever more complex and bitter, mostly against himself.

The Mixed Blessing

Halpern was not the only one to recognize the mixed blessing of America. It was a pressing issue in Yiddish literature long before its prominence in the works of Philip Roth, Bernard Malamud, and other American Jewish writers. One of the greatest Yiddish short story writers, Lamed Shapiro, launched his literary career in the new land with a horrifying story about a Russian pogrom in which America appears as the birthplace of a new, heroic Jew. After many years of disappointment and chronic unemployment in America, Shapiro created very different images of his chosen land. The main character of "Doc," for instance, is a dull but ambitious young man who sees a medical career as the road to wealth and fame, but he ends up as a lonely, second-rate doctor in a run-down neighborhood, taking morphine to kill the reality of his failure.

It was painful for the Yiddish writers who struggled over the purity of artistic utterance to see the Jews they wrote for speaking broken English and abandoning their native tongue as fast as they could. It was even worse to believe in an age-old Jewish cultural community when its members seemed to care only about getting their kids into college and themselves out of the slums of the Lower East Side and into the Bronx—at this time, it was roughly the equivalent of our suburbia. The writers realized that America did indeed offer freedom of expression, but it only *listened* to those who addressed it in English.

Nevertheless, despite the growing "defection" of Yiddish-speaking Jews so eager to exchange their cultural treasures for more material ones, Yiddish literature in the 1920s and 1930s developed a momentum and dynamism of its own. *Di yunge* began to seem like the "establishment" and younger writers challenged their sort of literature.

The victory of communism in the Soviet Union in 1917, and the overthrow of the czarism that had been so hateful to the Jews, was–in some circles–a cause for real rejoicing. Along with intellectuals in all parts of the world some Yiddish writers felt that a new age of equality had begun, and they expressed their solidarity with communist ideas and ideals. Their stories and poems attacked the poor living conditions of workers and the "vicious greed" of capitalists; they supported reform based on the model of what was supposedly happening in Russia. These so-called leftist writers turned back to public, realistic social literature and, until their own disappointment in the Soviet "paradise," opposed *di yunge* for hiding in their individualism and shirking their duty to help build a better life.

New Young Poets

From an opposite direction *di yunge* were found wanting by a younger group that felt the older poets were not individualistic *enough*. To emphasize their own wholly personal approach, they called themselves *Inzikhstn*, or Introspectivists, from the Yiddish words *in zikh*, "in the self." They insisted on free verse instead of the regular rhymes and stanzas of their elders because, according to their view of poetry, only free verse could express the unique rhythm of each individual subject. Their emphasis on precise, sometimes disconnected, images reminds us of the similar experiments of the American imagist movement of the same period. They wrote on every kind of subject–a Jewish gangster's funeral or the memory of a girl on a bus on a summer's day–but they objected even more strongly than *di yunge* to writing that was propaganda and socially relevant.

Oddly enough, all the writers seemed to agree on one point: Yiddish poetry and prose do not have to deal with specifically Jewish themes but are free to rise "above nationalistic concerns."

As the Introspectivists put it, the very fact of their writing in Yiddish was sufficient proof of national identification.

Drama of Jewish History

And yet, as so often happens, they said one thing in theory and did another in practice. The Yiddish writers were certainly free to choose any subject, but, being Jews, they got caught up in the drama of Jewish history and wrote some of their most powerful work on national events and themes. There was Moishe Leib Halpern's *A Nakht* ("A Night"), a terrifying, nightmarish poem on the slaughter of entire Jewish communities during World War I. There are erotic lyrics about the landscape of Palestine and countless works on the seemingly inexhaustible subject of the ancient-new homeland. A. Glanz-Leyeles, one of the leading "Introspectivists," wrote a great national poem on "Homer and Isaiah" that was like a duel between the Greek ideal of beauty and grace and the cutting Hebrew insistence on morality. Jacob Glatstein, another spokesman for "strictly individualistic literature," became the "liturgist of the Holocaust," creating the most remarkable range of prayerlike poems in which the survivors accuse, confront, deny, and ultimately comfort the Jewish God. As the Yiddish language was weakened by the dominance of English in America and Russian in the Soviet Union, and by the annihilation of Polish Jewry, the language itself became the subject of its literature, the incredible beloved, now so vulnerable in her beauty.

It was necessary, at the beginning, for the writers to insist on their literary independence, but the more genuinely they expressed their own feelings and thoughts the more they found themselves voicing a national identity and concern. Today, the brilliant literature produced by the American Yiddish writers is studied in schools and colleges and analyzed by new groups of scholars. For the time being, however, there does not seem to be another bunch of rebels in the wings.

Of Jews and Languages

■ Judeo-Spanish: A Language of the Sephardim ■

Jewish settlement in the New World began with the arrival of Sephardic Jews. They played important roles in American colonial life and were a significant group in early American economic, cultural, and religious developments. They brought with them high levels of culture and tradition dating, some believe, from Solomon's time. They brought as well a language expressing that rich and varied background. Like Yiddish, so also did Judeo-Spanish, Ladino, flourish after Jews were forced from the land in which the language had originated. In that sense Ladino, too, became guardian and conveyor of the Jewish culture it shaped and expressed.

The following discussion relates the developments of Ladino to the vicissitudes of Sephardic Jewish history. The language survived, indeed flourished, through trying and perilous times. Why, then, is it on the verge of extinction now?

■ Judeo-Spanish: A Language of the Sephardim

BY MARC D. ANGEL ■

One of the greatest eras in Jewish history was the thousand-year period in which Jews flourished in Spain. Spanish Jewry achieved cultural heights hardly if ever matched by any other group of Jews at any time. The amazing genius of the Sephardim (Hebrew for "Spanish Jews") manifested itself in poetry, philosophical, biblical, and talmudic scholarship, diplomacy, medicine, science, and, indeed, in nearly every area of creative endeavor. But in 1492 King Ferdinand and Queen Isabella decreed that all Jews be expelled from Spain, and five years later, after many Spanish Jews had fled there, Portugal followed the cruel Spanish example.

Thus an estimated 200,000 Jews were suddenly uprooted and forced to find refuge in a hostile world. The majority started life anew in the Turkish (Ottoman) Empire and North Africa, in such places as Constantinople, Turkey; Salonika, Greece; Safed, Palestine; and Tetuan, Spanish Morocco. The language these Jews spoke in their new homes was Spanish.

Ladino Explained

But whenever Jews have spoken a language, they have inevitably given it some recognizable Jewish elements. This was true of the Spanish of the Sephardim. Their language became known as Judeo-Spanish, or Ladino, a general term meaning "translation." It is for the most part Old Spanish, or the Castilian of the fifteenth century, but it also includes Hebrew words and phrases as well as terms drawn from the countries in which the Sephardim settled. Thus, there are Turkish, Greek, Slavic, and even English words in their vocabulary.

As an example of this expansion process, American Sephardim have taken the English verb "drive" and incorporated it into Judeo-Spanish as "*drivear.*" They would say, "*Está driveando el caro,*" meaning "He is driving the car." The verb "to march" becomes "*marchear.*"

"Rashi Script"

A vast Judeo-Spanish literature developed in

the centuries following the expulsion from Spain. The print used in Ladino publications has always been the so-called "Rashi script." The Hebrew letters *"alef," "vav,"* and *"yod"* serve as vowels. Because Judeo-Spanish has sounds not represented in the Hebrew alphabet, certain diacritical marks are used to indicate "ch," "j," and "zhe" and also to note whether a letter is pronounced *"peh"* or *"feh," "bet"* or *"vet," "shin"* or *"sin."* Hebrew letters written in the Judeo-Spanish cursive are far different from the widely used cursive of the Ashkenazim (the German and Eastern European Jews).

The first works to be published in Judeo-Spanish were translations of the Bible and of Jewish legal codes printed in Constantinople in the sixteenth century. These were followed by books of apologetics, homiletics, philosophy, and grammar. One of the most important works in the language is *Me'am Loez*, an encyclopedic, biblical commentary dealing with all aspects of Jewish life, with material drawn from the Talmud, the Jewish legends, and rabbinical literature. It was first published in Constantinople in 1730. Judeo-Spanish newspapers at one time enjoyed wide circulation throughout the Levant. In the U.S., too, Ladino papers were printed during the first half of this century. The most famous was the recently closed *La Vara*.

"Romanceros"

Perhaps the richest treasures of Judeo-Spanish literature are to be found in the folkloric material. The Sephardim have been important repositories of medieval Spanish folklore, and a growing number of Spanish and Jewish scholars are making studies of Sephardic folklore. The Sephardic genius produced sensitive poetry and stirring music. The folk songs they sing are known by such names as *coplas, cantares, romances*, and *romanceros*. I remember how as a young boy in Seattle I heard my grandparents (one set came from the island of Rhodes, the other from a town near Istanbul) and parents singing them. There are songs for every occasion: the birth of a child, the circumcision ceremony,

marriage, Jewish holy days, etc. There are also many beautiful love poems and songs that display a deep awareness of the wonders of nature.

One of my favorite songs is the following ballad, *"La Rosa Enflorece."*

La Rosa Enflorece
(The Rose Blooms)

La rosa enflorece
Hoy en el mes de mai.
Mi alma se escurese,
Firiéndose el lunar.

Más presto ven, palomba,
Más presto ven con mí;
Más presto ven, querida,
Corre y sálvame.

Los bilbilicos cantan
Con sospiros de amor;
Mi alma y mi ventura
Está en tu poder.

The rose blooms
Today in the month of May.
My soul darkens,
Like an eclipse of the moon.

Come more quickly, dove,
More quickly come with me;
More quickly come, beloved,
Run and save me.

The nightingales sing
With sighs of love;
My soul and my future
Are in your power.

Far-Flung Communities

Judeo-Spanish-speaking Sephardim live in communities throughout the world. Many are settled in the State of Israel. Other communities can be found in Canada, South Africa, Rhodesia, South America, Turkey, and Western Europe. In the U.S. the largest concentrations of those Sephardim are in New York, Los Angeles, and Seattle, in that order. Smaller groups have set-

Of Jews and Languages

tled in Atlanta, Cincinnati, Detroit, Highland Park, Indianapolis, Miami Beach, Montgomery, and Portland, Oregon.

Although Judeo-Spanish once occupied a central role in the lives of Sephardim, the language is suffering a considerable decline in modern times. Most second- or third-generation American Sephardim speak English as their main–and practically only–language. As a consequence, many young Sephardim are growing up without Judeo-Spanish.

Yet, the language represents an important aspect of Jewish culture and should not be allowed to be completely forgotten. Judeo-Spanish contains treasures for any seeker.

The Sephardic Studies Program of Yeshiva University in New York City issues this guide to Judeo-Spanish to students of the language.
Method how to learn to write and read in Spanish-Hebrew or in English
מיטודה פור אימביזאר אה איסקריב׳יר אי מילדאר אין גודיאו-איספאנייול אי איננליז

English	English Cap.	Spanish-Hebrew Hand written	Rabbinic or Rashi	Hebrew Characters
a	A		ﬡ	א
b	B		ﬖ	ב
w, v	W, V		ﬕ	ב׳
g	G		ﬔ	ג
ch	Ch		ﬓ	ג׳
d	D		﬒	ד
e	E		ﬡ	ה
a	A end of word		ﬠ	ה
o, u	O, U		ﬡ	ו
z	Z		ﬡ	ז
j	J		ﬡ׳	ז׳

V

JEWS SEEK GOD

JEWS VALUE AND PRACTICE PRAYER. The idea of *tefilah*, prayer, implies that just as someone offers prayer there is Someone to "receive" the prayer. Jews believe that God is that Someone and that God "wants" prayers, "hears" prayers, is affected by prayers in ways we cannot explain. Praying is natural to the Jew, as to all who acknowledge God's presence. How God receives or responds to prayer is unknown; that's part of the mystery of revealed religion. But that it is mystery does not stop Jews from seeking God through prayer as well as through deed. Jewish tradition emphasizes *mitzvah*, obedience to God's commands, and *ma'aseh*, acting properly. Nevertheless, Jews pray.

Judaism encourages public prayer, hence synagogue and *minyan*. Judaism also provides for private devotion "when you sit in your house, when you go on your way, when you lie down, and when you rise up." Whether in public or alone, the praying Jew expresses a God-relationship that affirms the *berit*, recognizes God's love for the people Israel, and acknowledges dependence on a greater Power. In prayer, as in Jewish thought, we presume God's reality and presence. How, why, and whether God exists are questions left to theology and philosophy. For the practicing Jew God is a constant presence, and prayer affirms that fact.

Over the centuries the prayers used by Jews evolved structure and phrasing in the *siddur* and *machzor* (prayer books for daily, Sabbath, and holiday use). The Passover Haggadah is a specialized prayer book that is also governed by a developing structure. Jews use specific prayers, some long, some brief, for every occasion: for the great moments like birth and death and (seemingly) lesser moments like washing hands and seeing something lovely. Because all of life is sacred, every moment is an occasion for prayer.

This chapter analyzes the characteristics of prayer and discusses how prayer is used. It explores values expressed through Jewish prayer. The chapter also considers several Jewish views of God, the One to whom we pray. Why does Judaism countenance multiple ideas about God's nature and relationship to the universe, God's creation? Finally, you will see how the *siddur* developed and how it continues to change today. What factors influence changes in the prayer book? Who can alter a prayer or the prayer book? How are changes or new prayers accepted or rejected by Jews?

▪ Some Reflections on Prayer ▪

A Jew prays daily, frequently, and unself-consciously because God and Judaism expect it. At the same time we are encouraged to think about why and to whom we pray. In fact, we are asked to pray with *kavanah*, serious intent and devotion: like life itself, prayer should never be taken for granted. We are in a two-way relationship with God in which we direct words and deeds toward the Divine who, in turn, requires our prayers for God's own fulfillment. Explain the idea that God "needs" human attention. The topic is taken up again in the next selection.

The following emphasizes that prayer helps to remind us of our place in God's universe: we are not self-sufficient. We acknowledge that reality in one type of prayer, *berachah*, blessing, which is attached to each of the many little actions constituting a day's activities. Why is so much of prayer devoted to blessing God? A prayer like the *Shema*, on the other hand, contains a commandment. What is it? Why is it imposed on Jews? Prayer is a victim of the limitations of language. This results in a prayer practice that today confuses many people: the use of masculine terms to describe God. Do you see this as a problem? Explain. Would nonsexist prayer language hinder or enhance the prayer experience? Explain.

■ Some Reflections on Prayer   BY JULES HARLOW ■

We take a lot for granted. Travel in jet airplanes, for example, or watching television, or taking miracle drugs. We are even casual about the fact that some human beings have walked on the surface of the moon and somersaulted in space, that we have seen photographs of the surface of the planet Mars. Much closer to our private life there are miraculous worlds known as human beings, as well as trees and sunsets, that we also take for granted. We even take ourselves for granted. A contemporary poet, Peter Davison, has stated the problem succinctly: "There's only one surprise–/to be alive–and that/may be forgotten daily/if daily not remembered."

A way of remembering daily is programed into Jewish tradition, a way of *not* taking the world or ourselves for granted. It is called a blessing, a *berachah*, a benediction, the simplest and most basic form of Jewish prayer. A *berachah*, like all Jewish prayer, is a declaration of dependence, praising God as the Source and Creator of all that we experience. Reciting a *berachah* thus reflects a special awareness of the world, a world we share with other creatures. It is a special kind of reaction to the world, a special way of being alive and realizing it.

Unfamiliar Blessings

Early in the morning service each day there are benedictions praising God for sustaining us, body and soul. Many people are familiar with only a limited number of special benedictions, such as those blessings recited before eating bread or drinking wine, before lighting Shabbat or holiday candles, or upon being called to the Torah. But a great number of blessings remain almost unknown, certainly far less familiar than the moon and Mars have become. These benedictions should be redeemed; we should be aware of them and use them. There are benedictions to be recited upon hearing thunder, smelling spices, upon seeing a sunset or a beautiful or a learned person, or upon seeing the first buds on a tree in spring, to cite a few examples. Here is a translation of that last-mentioned *berachah*: "Praised are You . . . our God, Ruler of the universe, who has created within it pleasing creatures and pleasing trees for mortals to enjoy."

The blessing itself, as well as the act of reciting it, is a blessing. I have a vivid memory of a special blessing on Shabbat in Jerusalem. I recall a man in his sixties, wearing a tattered coat, standing outside a small synagogue. Each Shabbat he stood there, holding a bunch of fragrant greenery, offering each person who came out after services an opportunity to enjoy the aroma and to recite another blessing (praising God who creates various spices), heightening our awareness of yet another aspect of creation. Dressed almost like a ragpicker though in his Shabbat best, he had the stature of nobility as he went about his Shabbat joy.

The Gift of Torah

Another aspect of life that Jewish prayer refuses to take for granted is the gift of Torah. There is an elaborate blessing in the daily morning service declaring gratitude for this gift and celebrating love as well. (A similar blessing with the same theme is included in the evening service.) The first words of this morning blessing mean "deep love" (*ahavah rabbah*). The main point of this blessing is reflected in the name given to it by those who composed it, the rabbis of ancient, talmudic times. They referred to it as "the blessing of Torah." Here is a translation of this blessing, close to the Hebrew text but not strictly literal:

Deep is Your love for us, Lord our God, boundless Your tender compassion. You taught our ancestors the laws of life. They trusted in You, our Father, our King. For their sake graciously teach us. Father, merciful Father, show us mercy; grant us discernment and understanding. Then will we study Your Torah, heed all its words, teach its precepts, and follow its instruction, lovingly fulfilling all its teachings. Open our eyes to Your Torah, help our hearts cleave to Your commandments. Unite all our thoughts to love and revere You; then shall we never be brought to shame. For we trust in Your awesome holiness. We will delight in Your deliverance. Bring us safely from the four corners of the earth, and lead us in dignity to our holy land, for You are the source of deliverance. You have chosen us from all peoples and tongues, drawing us near to You that we may offer You praise, proclaiming Your Oneness lovingly. Praised are You, Almighty who loves God's people Israel.

Although we will confine ourselves to a limited number of thoughts about this prayer, it could be the subject of an extended essay. It is important to realize that this prayer, like the rest of the prayer book, is a statement of Jewish theology, stating what the Jews do, or should, believe, as well as consisting of words directed to the Holy One.

God is referred to as both Father and King. He is near and far, approachable as a father and also removed as a king in a distant castle. While God is both, clearly beyond our grasp as the Creator while we are all creatures, it is significant that God's nature is described here with the words: love, compassion, and mercy. Furthermore, God loves us. How do we know? God gave our ancestors (and through them gave us) a most precious gift: Torah. We ask that God teach us as God taught them, if not because of our own merit then through the merit of our ancestors whose lives so clearly showed that they deserved God's blessing.

We also see from this prayer that knowledge and understanding of the Torah must not be an exercise in theory. The Torah must be reflected in our lives. We should study it; but that is not enough. We must teach it and live by it as well. We not only want to know Torah in the abstract; we want to fulfill its commandments in practice.

Still another Jewish value in this prayer focuses upon the Land of Israel as a place of ingathering for the Jewish people, emphasizing this ingathering as a sign of God's power of deliverance and calling upon the Eternal to use that power. The Land of Israel and Jerusalem are often included in specific Jewish prayers and are reinforced as basic values in the prayer book as a whole. They are inseparable from Jewish destiny.

Finally we come to a concept often misunderstood: the Jews as chosen. The interpretations of this concept as one perpetuated by a people with either a superiority or an inferiority complex are misleading, misrepresenting the meaning of chosenness in Jewish tradition. How did God choose us? By giving us the Torah as a sign of the divine love. This concept of having been chosen is one reflecting the historical fact that the Bible, the Torah, and God's Revelation all came into the world through the Jewish people who therefore praise the Creator, who has manifested the divine love in that way, and who pledge to embrace and perpetuate the teachings of the Torah.

The Shema

This blessing of Torah is followed by one of the most familiar parts of the prayer book, popularly known as *Shema* or *Keriat Shema* (the *Shema* reading), the first verse of which declares, "Hear, O Israel, the Lord our God, the Lord is One." This follows naturally from the blessing of Torah, which contains the hope that our hearts will be united as well as a commitment to God's unique Oneness. (Perhaps only after our hearts are truly one can we acclaim God as One.) Further, the blessing of Torah is an appropriate prelude to the recitation of words from the Torah of which the *Shema* consists. Then, too, the passage following the first verse of the *Shema* begins, "You shall love the Lord your God with all your heart . . ." which completes the theme of God's love for the people Israel with that of the people Israel's love for God. Ideally the love must be reciprocal.

The *Shema* itself is in danger of becoming a cliché, of being taken for granted, since it is so familiar and so often repeated. Very often it is described as "Israel's watchword" or as a statement of our monotheistic faith. It is, but it is also much more.

Words are commitments. Certainly the words of prayer are statements of our deepest commitments. If we would understand what we are committing ourselves to by reciting the words of the *Shema*, we must again look to the ancient rabbis who placed it in the prayer book (quoting the Book of Deuteronomy). They had a special name for the act of reciting the *Shema*: acknowledging the sovereignty of God, accepting the rule of God's authority. In reciting the *Shema*, we freely pledge our Maker our loyalty, declaring that our ultimate allegiance is to God alone.

To recapitulate, God's love for the people Israel is reflected in the Holy One's gift of Torah, God's Revelation. "Our love for the Holy One is reflected in our acceptance of this gift with joy and in our acceptance of God's sovereignty, which we declare by reciting some of the verses contained in that Revelation. In an imperfect world, where we are daily faced with choices, we must choose to show our love and acceptance through the quality of our lives as together we bear witness to our Parent, our Ruler, the Ruler of all humanity. Daily God renews Creation; daily must we renew our allegiance to God." (From *The Bond of Life*, edited by Rabbi Harlow. Published and copyright © 1975 by the Rabbinical Assembly.)

Study Is Worship

The first verse of the *Shema* is followed by other verses from Deuteronomy and by verses from Numbers. Thus, it is not a prayer as prayer is most commonly thought of. It is a reading of biblical verses. In Jewish tradition, study is a way of worship, and a person can also fulfill his or her obligations to study daily by reciting these verses.

The *Shema* and its accompanying verses are always preceded and followed by special benedictions in the service. These benedictions emphasize Creation, Revelation (partially discussed above), and Redemption. Thus, a Jew reciting prayers daily is brought to face these concepts daily, to express gratitude for them, and to attempt to relate them to life. Every Jew, young and old, unlearned and scholarly, has the daily opportunity of associating his or her life with specific enduring values of our tradition during the formal worship of God.

Prayers are not said in a vacuum; they are not isolated from problems. The sentiments expressed about God's love and mercy in the blessing of Torah are deeply moving and sustaining. Yet tragedy and pain jar us into questions about divine justice and compassion in a world that at times appears to be squeezed dry of such attributes. These questions are also a part of Jewish tradition. Ever since Abraham the questions have been legitimate. When Abraham learned that all

Jews Seek God

the people of Sodom would be destroyed, guilty and innocent alike, he challenged God with the question "Shall not the Judge of all the earth act justly?"

Adding Poetry

This challenging dimension of the tradition should be reflected in the prayer book as well. It should not appear as part of the standard, obligatory prayers, such as the *Shema* and its accompanying benedictions, but at other parts of the service where it could be included or deleted at will. There is a centuries-old tradition of adding liturgical poetry to a service. The medieval period was especially rich in such compositions. We believe compositions of this nature should be encouraged in contemporary times as well so our special and urgent concerns may be reflected within a service of prayer. To encourage this, and especially to give voice to a problem in faith, the Rabbinical Assembly edition of the *Mahzor for Rosh Hashanah and Yom Kippur* includes a poem written by Miriam Kubovy, a resident of Jerusalem who writes in French. In the *Mahzor*, her poem appears in a Hebrew translation, accompanied by my English translation, and is arranged for possible responsive reading in both languages. Here is an excerpt:

In Your image did You fashion us,
and You are obliged to be with us,

Thus we can worship You,
We can ask your forgiveness,

and we can hold You responsible,
we can struggle with You for all
that seems unjust and ugly.

We can contend with You, we
can refrain from resembling You,
we can reject what we do not understand

and we can turn to You more fervently, bound in gratitude

because You set the succession of seasons, change the day's divisions, arrange the stars in the sky, create day and night. . . .
(From *Mahzor for Rosh Hashanah and Yom Kip-*

pur, edited by Rabbi Jules Harlow. Published and copyright © 1972 by the Rabbinical Assembly.)

These lines pose the question of ambivalence in faith, which we often feel the need to express. It is significant that this harsh challenge is articulated in a framework of faith that makes it possible to be included in a service rather than only in a poetry reading or a lecture. The faith in God's essential dependability and concern is expressed in words (the last four lines of the above excerpt) taken from the first benediction before *Keriat Shema* in the evening service, the benediction whose theme is Creation. The entire poem is inserted at a point not long before that benediction. The poem ends as follows:

God of the faithless and God of the faithful,

God in all forms and formless,
who was and is and will be,
You are the Lord eternal.

Whether we pray with others in a congregation or alone away from all others, the language we use in Jewish prayer is expressed in the first person plural almost all of the time. Regardless of where we pray, using the Jewish prayer book, we are always part of the total community of the people Israel, we are always involved in the history and destiny of the Jews. But there is also a need for individual expression, for, while we find strength, consolation, and pride in identification with the community, each of us is unique.

First Person Singular

One example of prayer in the first person singular is found in the prayer following the recitation of the *Amidah* (Eighteen Benedictions, *Shemoneh Esreh*, or Silent Prayer). Part of this example reads as follows:

My God, keep my tongue from telling evil, my lips from speaking guile. Help me ignore those who slander me. Let me be humble before all.

Open my heart to Your Torah, so that I may pursue Your commandments. . . . Answer my prayer for the deliverance of Your people. May the words of my mouth and the meditations of my heart be acceptable to You, my Rock and my Redeemer. . . .

Although many people consider this prayer to be part of the *Amidah*, it is not, and its use is optional. It was composed by Mar bar Ravina, a sage of fourth-century Babylonia. We read in the Talmud that this was the personal prayer he recited after the *Amidah*. The Talmud also records the words of prayers written by other sages for their own use after the *Amidah*. The words of one person, used for personal expression as a sign of the flexibility of parts of the service, have become frozen into a fixed text everyone feels called upon to recite. I am not opposed to the recitation of these words of Mar bar Ravina. But I would like to encourage each of us to become accustomed to using our own words after the *Amidah*. Your own words at this point in the service are just as authentic as those of an ancient sage.

In the Rabbinical Assembly edition of the High Holy Day *machzor*, we have tried to encourage this personal practice by adding a note reading, "At the conclusion of the *Amidah*, personal prayers may be added, before or instead of the following." Following this note we sometimes print the commonly accepted text. At other times we print other personal prayers, including the following excerpt from a long prayer by Rabbi Elimelech of Lizhensk (of eighteenth-century Galicia) whose words are especially appropriate at the end of the *Amidah* for Yom Kippur:

Keep me far from petty self-regard and petty pride, from anger, impatience, despair, gossip, and all bad traits. Let me not be overwhelmed by jealousy of others; let others not be overwhelmed by jealousy of me. Grant me the gift of seeing other people's merits, not their faults. May the One who brings peace to the universe bring peace to us and to all the people Israel. And let us say: Amen.

Personal words add a precious dimension to prayer. It is difficult to express our own thoughts when we are not accustomed to it in the framework of a service of prayer. We must begin to develop this practice as a habit, inserting our own words at appropriate points in a service, if we are not to become a frozen people in this significant part of religious life. We must begin to articulate our own thoughts, just as we must begin heretofore-neglected benedictions, if we are to contribute to the vitality of the life of prayer and if we are to make it more of a reality in our own lives.

▪ A God Who Hears Prayer ▪

Praying is sometimes voluntary. Sometimes involuntary prayers escape our lips. Either way, to pray is to assume the prayer is "going" someplace, to Someone. Otherwise prayer would be just another way to talk to yourself, to share ideas with others, to create a sense of Jewish community. While those may be outcomes of prayer in which you can clarify your own thoughts and ideas, they are not the sole or even primary purposes of praying.

The following selection looks at a fundamental assumption about prayer–namely, there is a God who "hears" what we say aloud and silently. Especially, God hears and is present to us when we pray with conviction and out of habit. Why might this be so? Doesn't "habit" imply a mechanistic attitude that runs the risk of making prayer less meaningful? Explain. The article says God doesn't need our prayers. Do you agree or disagree? Explain. What does it mean to say God needs, or does not need, our prayers?

Jews Seek God

■ A God Who Hears Prayer
BY JAKOB J. PETUCHOWSKI ■

"What is God?" asked the commissar at an examination in a Communist university. "God," answered the student, "does not exist. God is a prejudice fostered by the upper classes to exploit the workers." "You have passed the examination," said the commissar. The student breathed a sigh of relief and said: "Thank God!"

Whether this story is true or not, it aptly illustrates a point once made by the psychologist William James: "The reason why we pray is simply that we cannot help praying." Prayer comes to us so naturally, and often we are not even aware that we actually are praying. Think of this next time *you* say "Thank God!" or, in a moment of anguish, cry out, "Oh, God!" Sometimes, indeed, you even start a conversation with the Almighty, though you may not know it. Have you ever said, "Why did this have to happen to *me*?" You were not really talking to anybody in the room. You were alone. You merely felt impelled to speak out loud. But the way you said it was already a kind of prayer. The Bible gives striking examples of this kind of prayer in the story of Jeremiah, and in many a psalm.

Many people, without necessarily believing in God, have recognized the value of prayer. Prayer, they say, gives us self-confidence. It helps us deal effectively with the crises in our lives. "The family that prays together stays together."

Jewish Prayer

But none of this is truly *Jewish* prayer. Certainly Judaism believes in the value of prayer. It even maintains that prayer is a *duty*. It sees in prayer an effective weapon used by Israel in the millennial fight for survival. Yet the important Jewish affirmation goes much further: it is that there is actually a "God who hears prayer." When you pray, you do not talk into a void. You do not even hold a monologue with yourself. You *are* speaking to God, and God listens.

"What?" you say. "Is God a person?" And Judaism answers: "Yes, God is!" God is not an old man with a long beard, the way many children imagine God to be. But, if even we can boast of having personality, then the One who made us must certainly have that particular quality. God may be much *more* than a "person," but God could not be *less*! If we speak of a God who loves, who cares, and who commands, then we are speaking of a God who can reach humans, and who, in turn, can be reached by humans.

Our attempt to reach God–that is the purpose of prayer. Mind you, the attempt is not always successful. Sometimes we make it without the necessary preparation. Sometimes again, God chooses not to be available. God may answer our request with a "No!" But at other times, particularly once you have cultivated the *habit* of prayer, you can actually feel the Divine Presence while you pray. Then your prayer will have been crowned with success.

Opening Our Hearts

Does not God know what we need without our telling? Of course, Judaism answers God does. But by telling God our needs we truly open our hearts to the Almighty. What is more, if we voice our desires before the Holy One, our desires themselves will be refined. Nobody prays: "O God, let me succeed in stealing my neighbor's apples." That would be a prayer in direct contradiction to what we know God wants us to do. If, then, we train ourselves to follow only such desires as we feel free to lay before God, the prayer of petition, as Judaism understands it, will already have achieved one of its main functions.

And just as God does not have to be told what we need, God can also do without the praises we offer. Yet it is precisely our praises and thanksgivings that bring God into our lives. A meal with a *berachah* is more than the performance of an animal function. It becomes an occasion when God is present. And that goes for all those other moments in our daily lives, accompanied by blessing and praise, when "the One that inhabiteth the praises of Israel" (Psalm 22:4) answers our prayer for the Divine Presence.

▪ The Power of God ▪

Some believe God is omnipotent. Others believe God is as powerful as it is possible for any being to be. There is a vast difference between these views. The second has an awesome consequence: God diminished God's power to share some of it with us. But we are not gods, to know, a priori, what to do with the might we have been given. Having power, we are burdened with the responsibility to use that power wisely in God's service. God challenges humanity to be God's partner to perfect the world.

The following examines other consequences of the shared-power view of God. If God's power is not absolute, if the Divine does not have all the power there is, does it make sense to petition God through prayer? Explain. A God of limited power needs us. Such a God has to depend on us for some things. That concept, in the present context, continues a discussion started earlier in this chapter. Does this reading change your previous thinking about this idea? Explain.

▪ The Power of God   BY CHAIM STERN ▪

What do you imagine God to be?
God is Creator. God is Redeemer. But, in between, God is a friend who is rooting for us but who needs us to accomplish Her/His final purpose. So God is in process.

How is God in process?
God is that Being who is supreme–not in power but rather in loving relatedness. God is the one Being who knows us so perfectly that we could not be better known. You couldn't possibly know yourself that well. In the wildest transports of love you don't know another human being, you only know the skin. God is the One who knows you and grows from knowing you. You are feeding God. Giving God your love, your strength, and your hope makes God more divine, more powerful.

Can we know God?
We begin to know God when we know love and know one another. God is the supreme principle of love but also of justice–which is embraced by love. There cannot be love without justice. Fairness, kindness, generosity, decency–all are attributes we value most highly. And we value them most highly precisely because we didn't invent them, but because they are revealed to us by Creation; they are divine. In one sense, it is a silly question: How do I know God? In another sense, I know God through relationships with other people. The principle of holiness is the bond that joins us. It is created through our linking, but, at the same time, we can't link without its being there to start with. Thus God makes it possible for us to be together. That's what God is all about.

Is God beyond our reach?
One has to understand that finally there are two ways of looking at God. God is remote, apart, transcendent, but God is also in need of us. God is "wholly" other, so far beyond us that the greatest word of the greatest poet is incapable of expressing more than the tiniest fragment of

meaning when speaking of the Divine. But, at the same time, the other side of God is the dependent side. When we ourselves change, we change God in turn. God is supremely relative, not absolute. I'm not absolute; you're not absolute. We are contingent upon air, food, and upon people. God is also in need of us. God has no choice about it anyway. God gave it up at Creation.

So God is not all-powerful?

It is not possible for me to understand how anyone can believe the conception of God as all-powerful and all-seeing. In the first place, what is the evidence for these compliments? Does common sense tell you God is all-powerful? If I say to God I'm going to kill six million Jews and one million of them are going to be babies below the age of four, will God do something to me? Demonstrably not. If I'm going to kill 200,000 Vietnamese this month, who is going to stop me? God does not stop anybody.

Doesn't this disturb you?

The Supreme Lover wants you to be free and loves you even when you use that freedom to hurt others. But I find it unbearable and unacceptable to say, beyond that, that the Supreme Lover would sit there and do nothing, if by one simple act, namely, by assassinating Adolf Hitler, the Holocaust could have been prevented. So I have to conclude that God would like us to be different from what we are but can't make us different–that freedom is our human dignity. If we really could be manipulated by God, God could cure us of cancer. But God created us so that the curing would be left to us. God has a share in all of this or I wouldn't be talking about it, but I think it is blasphemous or just mindless to speak of God's omnipotence and omniscience. It is unnecessary. There is little in the Bible that speaks of it. Biblical religion is my religion. It is very straightforward and clear. God says: "I hope things go well with you." When they don't, God gets very angry, but what can God do? Stop the Babylonians? Or does God say to Pharaoh: "If that's the way you feel about it, do your worst"? I wouldn't want to be Pharaoh. This is my notion of reward and punishment. To be Pharaoh is the punishment; to be Moses is the reward.

Then what ultimately is God's power?

The power of God is the worship God inspires. What power is greater than the power that simply says: "I love you and for that reason I want you to be the best you can be"?

▪ Your Word Is Fire ▪

Jewish mysticism, Kabbalah, originated in the Jewish longing to come closer to God, to bridge the chasm that separates us from our Source. In Kabbalah, therefore, and in later Chasidism, prayer is essential. It is the way to transport yourself to God, to become one with the Divine Presence. It is not easy to reach that ultimate state, to achieve *hitlahavut*, intense dedication, enthusiasm, inspiration. Once reached, however, the experience of all-consuming prayer can transform you forever.

The following describes stages or levels of prayer. The highest stage you can achieve unites you with God's very essence, from which the universe was and is being created. To reach this sublime level is the goal of chasidic prayer. It is a level of intimate experience where language is superfluous. How might you achieve the goal? Would you want to have such an experience? Explain.

■ Your Word Is Fire

BY ARTHUR GREEN AND BARRY W. HOLTZ ■

The masters of chasidic prayer, like most of their predecessors in the Jewish mystical tradition, were hesitant to write down any sort of systematic guide to the ways of contemplation. While they did have a clear sense that there were specific ordered steps to be taken that could lead one up the devotional ladder, the composition of such a guide would have been a particular affront to their ideals of spontaneity and wholeness. By what steps in a manual can you guide a person to *hitlahavut*, that state where ecstasy fills one's heart like a burning fire? Can any studied method really lead one to know that one's own soul is nothing but an outpouring of God's light?

Yet despite this lack of systematic introduction the works of the early chasidic masters are filled with hints as to the various rungs of inner prayer and how they are to be attained. From these references, scattered throughout early chasidic literature, a composite picture of their approach to contemplative prayer can be reconstructed.

Two Types of Prayer-State

There are two types of prayer-state generally described in chasidic sources. *Katnut*, the "lower" or ordinary state in which one generally begins one's prayers, as opposed to *gadlut*, the "greater" or expanded state of mystical consciousness. Prayer recited while in a state of *katnut* may contain within it great devotion; it is generally the simple prayer devotion of giving oneself to God and accepting the Almighty's will. It may contain both the love of God and human awe before the Divine Presence, the two essential qualities for authentic prayer in Chasidism. In *katnut*, however, a person is not transported beyond the self, does not "ascend" to a world where consciousness is transformed or where self-awareness is transcended.

The ascent from this state to that of *gadlut* is

one of the central themes of chasidic prayer literature. While the simple devotions of the *katnut* state are highly valued, the true goal of the worshiper is to enter that world where "one may come to transcend time," where "distinctions between 'life' and 'death,' 'land' and 'sea,' have lost their meaning." The worshiper seeks to "concentrate so fully on prayer that he (she) no longer is aware of self . . . to step outside the body's limits." Rapturous descriptions of the state of *gadlut* abound in chasidic writings.

The first step in the attainment of *gadlut* is the involvement of the entire self in the act of worship. There must be no reservation, no holding back of a part of the person. The body is to be involved along with the soul in the act of prayer: the rhythmic movement of the body, the sometimes loud outcry of the voice, the training of the eye to the page–all these externals are aids, in the first stages of prayer, to the involvement of the entire self.

Letters Become Liberated

As the ecstatic power of this involvement begins to overwhelm the worshiper, he or she may begin to dispense with the externals, one by one, as he (she) feels ready to do so. The body may become still, shouts may become a whisper, and he (she) may put the book aside and see the letters of his (her) prayer with the mind's eye alone.

At this point the winged ascent of the soul and word to the upper worlds begins in earnest. Prayer must ever be accompanied by the love and fear of God, the two emotions Jewish teachers had long seen as the "wings" that allow one's prayer to ascend to God. Each moment of true prayer contains within it the moment of standing before the Eternal at Sinai, when the consuming love of God and the total awe before God's tremendous power were most fully combined. As love and fear accompany the word upward the letters become liberated from their verbal patterns and lead the soul back from the "World of Speech" to their higher source in the "World of Thought." Verbal prayer gives way to abstract contemplation, to a liberation of the worshiper's mind from all content other than attachment to God. First, all of one's energies are concentrated on the word as spoken with fullness; now the word itself is released, and nothing remains with the worshiper but the fullness of heart that, paradoxically, also marks him (her) as an empty vessel, ready to receive the light from above. Even the self-conscious feeling of this fullness must be transcended, for "a person who still knows how intensely he (she) is praying has not yet overcome his (her) awareness of self."

This emptying of the mind of all content, which chasidic prayer shares with many other meditative techniques, finally leads one to that place within God known as the "Nothing" or the realm of Primordial Nothingness. According to kabbalistic theology, this Nothingness *within* God is the *ayin* or *nihil* out of which the world was created. All things are rooted in the divine "Nothing." As prayer ascends to God, the creative energy is returned to its predefined source in the One. Creation, however, is viewed in Chasidism as a constant ongoing process: the world is ever pouring forth anew from this state of Nothingness that lies at the innermost core of divinity. As the worshiper's mind is emptied, he (she) stands ready to be filled once again, having returned to that source from which creation takes place.

The Moment of Transformation

Here one has reached the moment of ultimate transformation. In all change and growth, say the masters, the mysterious *ayin* is present. There is an ungraspable instant in the midst of all transformation when what is about to be transformed is no longer what it had been until that moment, but has not yet emerged as its transformed self;

that moment belongs to the *ayin* within God. Since change and transformation are *constant*, however, in fact all moments are moments of contact with the *ayin*, a contact that humanity is usually too blind to acknowledge. The height of contemplative prayer is seen as such a transforming moment, but one that is marked by awareness. The worshipers are no longer themselves, for they are fully absorbed, in that moment, in the Nothingness of divinity. In that moment of absorption the worshipers are transformed: as they continue their verbal prayer, it is no longer they who speak, but rather the Presence who speaks through them. In that prayerful return to the source, human beings have reached their highest state, becoming nought but the passive instrument for the ever self-proclaiming praise of God. Through their lips the divine word is spoken.

The purpose of all prayer is to uplift the words,
to return them to their source above.
The world was created
by the downward flow of letters:
The task of humans is to form those letters into words
and take them back to God.
If you come to know this dual process,
your prayer may be joined
to the constant flow of creation—
word to word, voice to voice,
breath to breath, thought to thought.

The words fly upward and come before the Holy One.
As God turns to look at the ascending word,
life flows through all the worlds
and prayer receives its answer.
All this happens in an instant
and all this happens continually;
Time has no meaning in the sight of God.
The divine spring is ever-flowing;
one who is ready can make oneself into a channel
to receive the waters from above.

GLOSSARY
Prepared by Lawrence Kushner

HITLAHAVUT
Literally "setting yourself on fire." Being so joyous as to feel newly created. Like the times you dance with such energy that you stop being aware you're dancing.

CONTEMPLATION AND "CONTEMPLATIVE PRAYER"
You look into yourself and search for the secrets of the universe. You are seeking from yourself and God answers about the meaning of life.

KATNUT
Literally "smallness"–being low. You get so busy or bogged down in everyday affairs that you forget your holy purpose. There is not enough of you to get done what needs to be done.

GADLUT
Literally "greatness." Feeling full and tall and expansive, like there is more than enough of you to go around.

UPPER WORLDS
Higher levels of consciousness–(inside yourself, inside the universe, and inside God). Like when suddenly you get the sensation of looking down and seeing the person who you just were. Being wiser and able to see farther than before.

PRIMORDIAL NOTHINGNESS, AYIN, NO-THING
After a seed stops being a seed but before it becomes a plant, for that second it is nothing. From this nothing every new thing grows from plants to people to the universe itself. To allow yourself to be empty of all things, to return to this *ayin* (nothing) point is to come very close to God.

TRANSFORMING MOMENT
A split second after you are who you were but before you are who you are yet to become. In Genesis, Jacob wrestles with an angel and becomes Israel, a new person with a new name. Since every transforming moment is also a great struggle, he is limping. But he is now fit to be our father.

Jews Seek God

▪ The Roots of the Siddur ▪

The *siddur*, prayer book, is the fruit of a dynamic process. In fact, it was not until the ninth century that a *seder*, fixed order, of prayers appeared. Nevertheless, because it mirrors Jewish life, the *siddur* continued to change from then to the present time. Moreover, because the *siddur* embodies customs long established, Ashkenazic and Sephardic Jews have their own *siddurim*. For all Jews, however, the *siddur* is an essential and precious possession that guides individual and group prayer and provides religious instruction. The *siddur* links us to our ancestors and their search to come closer to God.

In the following the author demonstrates that the *siddur*, while not immutable, provides boundaries within which we are free to make changes. Unlike the Bible, the *siddur* was never canonized. Explain why. Despite internal changes and the appearance of new prayer books over the centuries, the *siddur*'s basic structure has not changed. Why?

▪ The Roots of the Siddur   BY LAWRENCE A. HOFFMAN ▪

Some people have strange ideas about the siddur, our prayer book. One of the strangest is the notion that all our basic Jewish prayers were composed eons ago in some imaginary period of Jewish greatness, a time of brilliance and creativity when Jewish teachings, laws, and customs were set once and for all—and that these prayers were then put into order and "frozen" for all time in what became known as the siddur, our "order" of prayer.

In fact, the earliest known comprehensive collection of Jewish prayers was not compiled until the ninth century. Thus, the first real written siddur is only about 1,100 years old. However, Jewish worship services existed long before that—at least another thousand years, even longer if one includes biblical prayers. If we want to find the roots of the siddur, we have to ask three separate questions: (1) What was Jewish worship like before that famous first siddur was issued? (2) How did Jewish prayer services change once that siddur appeared? (3) What happened to the siddur and the worship that accompanied it during the 1,100 years that have since passed? We shall see that the answers to these three questions are like three chapters in a story we might call "Freedom within Bounds."

Opposite Poles

The early rabbis (in the first two centuries of the Common Era) worried about reconciling two conflicting requirements of worship services. On the one hand, they knew true worship demanded the spontaneous outpouring of the human heart. Praying could not be mechanical, else worship would deteriorate into mere words, empty of emotion and sincerity. On the other hand, the rabbis realized that a gathering of individuals, each praying in a different way, is not a community. Therefore, some regulations were necessary to harness absolute freedom in praying.

Slowly but surely the rabbis constructed a framework of Jewish worship services—a kind of blueprint setting down certain themes essential for the services in the same way that a blueprint establishes the shape and character of a building. Just as the final appearance of the structure was determined by the choice of paint and building material, so the nature of the worship service would depend upon the way the themes would be expressed in words chosen by the individual Jew.

The blueprint of the rabbis supplied the "order" of the daily worship service. They designated certain Torah portions that had to be read, and they established various basic themes that had to be expressed in the prayers of the congregation. This daily service, in turn, was expanded or otherwise altered to form the structure of the prayer service for the Shabbat and the Festivals. The daily service was subdivided into three separate services: morning (*shacharit*), afternoon (*minchah*), and evening (*'arvit* or *ma'ariv*). Each of these services followed a certain thematic logic, progressing from (1) preparation for prayer to (2) affirmation of belief to (3) requests for divine assistance and, finally, to (4) concluding prayers of praise and thanksgiving.

Morning Service

The morning service, which contains all four of these elements in very clear form, began, for example, with some psalms. These were the preparation for formal worship, "mood setters," designed to move people's minds from the mundane to the holy. When the people were ready, the leader called them formally to congregational prayer by saying something like our *Barechu* (Praise the Eternal who is to be praised!); and the people answered, as we do, indicating that they now were really a congregation of worshipers, not just isolated Jews who happened to be gathered in one place. Next came the recital of the affirmation of Jewish belief, in the form of the *Shema* and some accompanying benedictions, two before and one after. The two blessings preceding the *Shema* asserted God's role as Creator of the universe and God's selection of Israel as the people to whom the Torah would be given. The *Shema* itself affirmed the unity of God and God's absolute rule over the universe. The third blessing declared God's presence in all of history and in the lives of God's human creations. This is symbolized by God's entrance into history to save the Jewish people from Egyptian slavery. After reciting the *Shema* and its blessings, the people were given the opportunity to petition God for both personal and communal favors. (We now call that section of the service the *Tefilah*, the *Amidah*, or the *Shemoneh Esreh*.) The worshipers concluded their service with final words of praise.

By the end of the second century the thematic structure of the worship service was very largely settled. The *Shema* passage was a biblical quotation and could not be altered. But most of the remaining prayers were not hallowed by being of biblical origin, and, as long as worshipers expressed the themes laid down by the rabbis—creation, God's covenant with Israel, God's presence in history, etc.–they were free to say the prayers in their own language. In this way Jewish prayer was both structured and free: "Freedom within Bounds."

The Second Question

We come now to our second question: Under what circumstances did the first siddur, or "ordered" prayer book, appear, and how did Jewish prayer services change once it appeared?

When we think about it, having the theoretical freedom to recite a given blessing differently every day of the year, depending on the whim of the individual prayer leader, is quite extraordinary. Throughout the centuries, great poets called *payyetanim* abounded. We even have records of some who composed enough different poetical embellishments of particular prayers as to make it possible not to repeat the prayer in exactly the same way for three to four years running!

But such great artistry in prayer was the exception, not the rule. Most congregations tended toward the opposite extreme. Daily creativity is hard, and most communities began reciting their prayers in much the same manner every day. In other words, local customs developed. People in a particular town expressed a required theme with one phrase rather than another, inserted this poem and not that one, bowed here rather than there, and so on. The theoretically endless range of possible expression had crystallized within the various Jewish communities into different local preferences depending on where you happened to live.

The Gaon of Sura

Now, perhaps the most outstanding authority in the Jewish world around 1,200 years ago was the intellectual leader of the leading Jewish academy at Sura, in the vicinity of Baghdad. He bore the title "Gaon" (plural: Geonim), a technical term roughly equivalent to "Your Excellency." Since about the year 760, the various men who held the lofty office of Gaon had noted the disparity in the prayer customs of the scattered Jewish communities. They were receiving an increasing number of letters inquiring about the origin or the permissibility of various prayer customs, and they made it a practice of responding to them. Since the Sura Academy was located in Babylonia, the Gaon had a record of the thinking of the Babylonian rabbis who had preceded him—the record of the Babylonian Talmud. Many of the questions a Gaon received dealt with matters of Jewish law; and, as any lawyer today would do when faced with a question regarding the permissibility or the legality of a particular practice, the Gaon relied on his record of legal precedent, the Babylonian Talmud. He also depended on what he himself knew to be customary in his own and surrounding academies. When the customs he learned about in letters ran contrary to these guides, he declared them illegal and urged his correspondents to adopt the Babylonian way of Jewish worship instead.

The eighth and ninth centuries provided the opportunity for thousands of such "responsa" (as the gaonic answers came to be called; "responsa" is the plural, "responsum" is the singular form), each of which then became yet another precedent for later Geonim to consider when answering Jewish legal questions put to them. By the year 857 the number of set responsa to the many Jewish communities around the world had become enormous. And, in that year, a man named Amram bar Sheshna became the Gaon at the Academy of Sura. It was he who wrote down the first comprehensive collection of Jewish prayers, along with instructions on how, when, and where to recite them. This is our first-known written siddur.

Seder Rav Amram Gaon or "The Order of Prayer composed by Rav Amram Gaon" is simply another answer (responsum) to another question about prayer. But it is a long answer, explaining to a relatively new Jewish community somewhere in Spain all the rules and regulations that had grown up through the centuries and now gov-

erned worship services in the Babylonian Jewish academies. It contains, not only the daily, Shabbat, and Festival services, but also a Pesach Haggadah and descriptions of lifecycle ceremonies and blessings for special occasions. In his collection are many biblical quotations, particularly psalms; benedictions of illustrious rabbis of preceding centuries; and poetry and hymns composed by past generations. The wording for all of this is given, along with introductory remarks regarding common errors people make and the proper way to say the prayer in question. That "proper" way was, in fact, simply the Babylonian way, supported by precedents from the Babylonian Talmud, "proper" according to actual prayer practice at the Babylonian academies of the time, and "proper" according to the growing body of legal decisions made by previous Geonim.

Rav Amram's book was handwritten, since the printing press had yet to be invented. The book could not be mass-produced for entire congregations: copies had to be made one at a time by scribes working slowly and methodically. At most, Rav Amram's siddur found its way into the hands of rabbis and *chazanim* (cantors), who used it as their guide in leading prayer services. But it became the most trusted work on the subject of Jewish prayer. In the centuries that followed its regulations would be cited in the writings of eminent rabbis throughout Europe.

Rav Amram's Influence

We now arrive at our third question: What happened to Jewish worship after Rav Amram wrote his book? Since scribes cannot compete with high-speed printing presses, we can imagine that nothing changed immediately, especially since old communities, such as those in Palestine, which had long-standing prayer customs of their own, were not always willing to change them simply because someone in distant Babylonia had not considered them "proper" according to Babylonian standards. But in the ninth and tenth centuries new Jewish centers began springing up all over Western Europe. They had no old, established customs to fall back on, and so they accepted Rav Amram's teachings. Eventually *Seder Rav Amram* became the basis for European and–much later–for American prayer books. The acceptance of his book in Europe guaranteed that nearly all Jews thereafter, including ourselves, would be the spiritual descendants of the Babylonian Geonim.

The consequences of this acceptance have been enormous. The freedom of Jews to express required themes in their own way was now gone. Language for prayers that had not been fixed before Rav Amram's siddur came later to be regarded as fixed and unchangeable. Customs that had been merely Babylonian preferences were now considered to be binding on every Jew. What had begun so many centuries before Rav Amram as an attempt by the rabbis to build merely a structure for Jewish worship, a progression of themes that individuals and congregations might flesh out in their own way, was now a rigid prayer book with fixed wording and detailed instructions.

Every group of Jews since Rav Amram's time has had to struggle with the tension between the structure–now rigid and unyielding–and the ideal of spontaneity in prayer. In various times and places Jews have been able to add to the fixed prayers in Amram's siddur by writing new prayer material. Those that stood the test of time were added to the siddur and were later considered to be just as authoritative as Amram's prayers had been. The *Kabbalat Shabbat*, or service introducing Friday evening, for example, is almost entirely the work of sixteenth-century mystics living in Palestine. Memorial prayers for the *Yizkor* service speak plaintively of Central Europe after the Crusades and the pogroms in Poland of

the seventeenth century. The poem "Yigdal" is the philosophy of Maimonides (twelfth century) set in prayer form in Italy in the fourteenth century.

New Versions of Siddur

Thus, over the ages, many new modifications of Amram's siddur were composed, nearly all of them based substantially on Amram's original but enlarged and invigorated with the spiritual expression of new generations. Particularly after the introduction of low-cost printed books, when everyone in the congregation could own a siddur, people tended to think of the prayer book they were raised on as timeless and eternal, going back perhaps to Sinai. But the truth is otherwise. The basic themes and structure of the prayer book do go back to antiquity (although certainly not to Sinai!), but the language of our most familiar prayers was composed in later centuries. Usually the words we say are merely the Babylonian versions popular during the Gaonic Age, versions Amram set down in his book. Other prayers and prayer practices used by some congregations may be old or new, reflecting the thinking and experience of Jews living in Spain, Poland, Germany, or America.

To know the siddur is to know ourselves through our own past. To use the siddur in any of its versions is still to struggle with the task of the earliest rabbis: to take the structure and the themes of Jewish prayer that have been handed down to us and to make them uniquely our own.

▪ Creating New Prayer Books ▪

Amram's ninth-century *siddur* established a framework for Jewish prayer. Other versions followed as compilers incorporated *piyyutim* (liturgical poems) and prayers reflecting concerns of Jews in Diaspora communities. In its early days the Reform movement's *siddur* departed from accepted structure and deleted prayers deemed incompatible with new understandings about Judaism. The *Union Prayer Book*, Newly Revised (1940), inherited the structure and content of those early Reform versions. It served English-speaking Reform/liberal Jews for over a quarter century.

The following selection brings the process of Reform *siddur* evolution to the present with the appearance of *Gates of Prayer* (1975), and of other non-Orthodox prayer books. In *Gates of Prayer*, Reform editors confronted contemporary concerns such as the use of Hebrew, Israel, and the Holocaust. They also confronted social concerns such as sexist language and the status of women. Moreover, they produced a *siddur* providing for wide choice in service style and content. Why is this, perhaps, the most significant achievement of the new *siddur*?

▪ Creating New Prayer Books   BY CHAIM STERN ▪

It has become noticeable, in recent years, that the Jewish community has been experiencing a liturgical renaissance, a renewal of prayer and worship. In a time when many have been wondering about the direction or lack of direction being taken by religion in general and Judaism in particular, this is perhaps a surprising turn and one worth exploring.

The latest process of renewal began at the end of 1967 in London with the publication of *Service of the Heart*, the first Liberal prayer book since the beginning of World War II. This became the official prayer book of the British Liberal (Reform) movement. It was very different from the prayer book that, until then, had been used by our British Liberal cousins. Its language was contemporary. It made reference to the State of Israel and the Holocaust. It contained more Hebrew.

This was the beginning. Since that time the American Conservative and British Liberal movements have published new prayer books for the High Holy Days, and the Reform movement has published one for weekdays, Sabbaths, and Festivals. The worldwide community of non-Orthodox synagogues, Reform and Conservative, has renewed its liturgy, testifying to a rebirth not merely of liturgical creativity but of religious vitality.

Awareness of Change

Progressive (Reform and Conservative) Judaism is Judaism that has always felt the need to reconsider itself from generation to generation and to express its truths and aspirations in a manner appropriate to the times in which we live. The Reform movement in Germany began as a movement of liturgical reform. This has remained a central part of the identity of that movement. The way we have looked at the world can be discovered by studying our different prayer books. The way we have understood ourselves is best seen in those prayer books. So it is that new prayer books continue to be published. And, so long as we remain committed to the idea that change is a significant fact of life and religion, we will continue to express ourselves through new prayer books or–at the very least–revisions of our old ones.

One charged with the responsibility of preparing a new prayer book finds a host of thorny problems in the way. What shall be the main sources of the new text? How should we relate to a tradition that began in the Bronze Age? Is there a simple way of balancing the demands of the past and the present? What about the divisions among contemporary Jews–shall these be ignored, covered up, accepted, or even encouraged? Do our current problems belong in a prayer book? Since our vernacular is English, how shall we balance its claims with those of the Hebrew language?

These are some–only some–of the questions I was compelled to face when I accepted the responsibility of preparing a new liturgy for the American Reform movement. Before my eyes were the traditional prayer book of our people (the siddur), the traditional prayer book of the Reform movement (the *Union Prayer Book*), and *Service of the Heart*, of which I had been coeditor. I had also the advice of the Liturgy Committee of the Central Conference of American Rabbis and of hundreds of other people, some of whom were rabbis, many of whom were not. I suppose I held a number of these questions before me simultaneously. For the purpose of this article I must deal with each separately.

The Siddur

The siddur is the great classic of our prayer tradition. It deserves our reverence and admiration. It has developed over the course of many centuries and reflects differences of thought and feeling among Jews to a surprising degree. You will find in its pages rationalism and mysticism, great pain and boundless joy. Some of its prayers are not "prayers" at all but passages of Torah included for didactic purposes. Here, psalmist, rabbi, and kabbalist rub shoulders. No prayer book can claim to be Jewish that does not base itself on the siddur. At the same time, however, the siddur contains passages few, if any, progressive Jews can pray with sincerity. The Reform movement especially has made changes in classic prayers in order to enable worshipers to say what they mean. We have, in some cases, emended the text; in others, we have made abridgments. Like my Reform predecessors, therefore, I was committed to a balancing act—basing the prayer book on the siddur without sacrifice of integrity.

The *Union Prayer Book* has served Reform Judaism in America for the first three-quarters of the twentieth century. The main questions facing someone preparing a new Union prayer book are: what to retain, what to delete, what to revise from among the many prayers in the old book that have spoken to and for generations of Reform Jews. And what of the English style of that book: Should it be retained, modified, or abandoned? Similar questions arise in the preparation of any prayer book in the English-speaking world.

English and Hebrew

The English-speaking world! Gradually the Reform movement has been reclaiming Hebrew as its language of prayer—without abandoning English. Make a chart of the Hebrew in successive editions of the *Union Prayer Book* and you will observe a line moving upward from one edition to the next. The line moves upward even more swiftly in *Gates of Prayer*. There was never much debate on this subject while the prayer book was being considered—all seemed in agreement that the more Hebrew the better. Our principle was that the Hebrew ought to be available in the hope that it would be used more and more as Hebrew became better known to Reform Jews.

This was not a particularly controversial issue. But controversy did arise when the question became one of precisely which Hebrew was to be restored. One example is all I have space for, but it will suffice. The well-known passage from Exodus 31:17, called "*Veshameru*" after its first Hebrew word, is, in the old prayer book, abridged. (See *UPB*, Vol. I, p. 19.) In *Gates of Prayer* (p. 133), it is given in its complete form. The two versions differ by reason of the inclusion of the following sentence in *Gates of Prayer*: ". . . For in six days the Eternal God made heaven and earth, and on the seventh day God rested from God's labors." One may suppose that this was deleted from the old prayer book because it speaks of the world's creation in six days. We believe this no more literally than did those who came before us, but we felt able to use the biblical Creation language more freely because we saw it as poetry. The language of myth, fantasy, or fable is, for us, a perfectly legitimate way of expressing the way we feel and hope about this world.

And this view also led us to use English differently. It seemed clear to us that the archaic English of earlier prayer books would not fulfill the needs of modern worshipers. We preferred "You" to "Thee" as a way of addressing God. In this we were fortified by the knowledge that Hebrew itself, from the Bible to the present, makes no distinction such as the one in old English. If we could address God simply as "You" in Hebrew, why should we suddenly feel different when using English? This was a matter of controversy, but I have no doubt we made the correct decision. All modern liturgies have chosen to use modern English. We have perhaps erected more than enough barriers between ourselves and God; we don't need this one as well.

Respect for Tradition

The great respect we have for our tradition dictated our decision to stick as closely as possible to the traditional structure of the service, retaining or restoring the Hebrew that has always preceded and followed the *Shema*, for example. The themes that surround the *Shema* were laid down many centuries ago: Creation, Revelation, and Redemption–that is to say, God as Creator of the natural order, God as Revealer of the moral order (Torah), and God as Redeemer of Israel (and the world). This attention to the traditional thematic order of our service is maintained throughout *Gates of Prayer* with little change from service to service. It is a major element, though far from the only one, of our "return" to tradition.

We intended to create a siddur for our time–and this involved the content of the prayer book, the more subtle matter of the way in which it would be used, and the very appearance and "feel" of the book.

For Our Time

A siddur for our time. If one side of that sentence is the word "siddur," the other side contains the words "for our time." No prayer book produced in the last half or quarter of this century can fail to attempt at least to reflect upon and to "live through" the events that loom so large upon our consciousness. Let us consider some of them.

Jews and others have suffered in many ages, yet the Holocaust was an event unique, unprecedented in the chronicles of suffering humanity. Earlier instances of Jewish suffering have led to the inclusion of prayers of lamentation and consolation in our traditional liturgy. It did not seem to us enough simply to reproduce those passages. Our own responses cried out for articulation. For this reason you will find in *Gates of Prayer* passages beginning: "How can we give thanks when we remember Treblinka?" and "The universe whispers . . ." and "All peoples have suffered cruelty. . . ." We have attempted to express our pain in order to find a way to pass through it. Our answers–if they can be called "answers"–move in realms of feeling, not of logic. The very act of expression, it has seemed to us, begins the healing of our spirits. In addition to individual passages on the Holocaust, we have included two complete sections: one "In Remembrance of Jewish Suffering," the other a service for Tishah Be'av and Yom Hashoah (Holocaust Remembrance Day).

Everyone knows Reform Judaism was at one time "anti-Zionist." It was a reflection of the view that Judaism is a universal religion that has transcended "nationalism." We remain convinced of this, but we do not quite draw the same conclusions today. The State of Israel is a reality for whose well-being almost every Jew prays. The Jewish community of Israel is part of the worldwide Jewish community. The sense of Jewish peoplehood is very strong in us. That peoplehood is religious at its center–"You shall be to Me a kingdom of priests, a holy nation." But we feel a special link to all Jews, whatever their religious attitudes may be at the moment, for they are part of this potentially holy people. Our concern for Zion, therefore, is not political but religious. Our concern, to quote the prayer book, is with the Divine Presence in Zion. We pray for a restoration of the sense of that presence. And not in Zion alone–in our hearts as well. For Judaism is a universal faith, and its God knows no boundaries and plays no favorites. Yet, however much we love humanity in general, we are entitled to hold our own family more closely. So there is no final contradiction between universalism and particularism. Both find expression in *Gates of Prayer.* And Israel, the reality and the dream together, is a fact in our time. *Gates of Prayer* celebrates Israel–or Zion–and prays for the welfare of our people in the Land of Israel. It celebrates its birth as an independent state with the hope that this independence will lead to a flowering of the Jewish spirit. And, in the service celebrating Israel Independence Day, we have done something unique, reviving the old Palestinian liturgy from the neglect of many centuries. So doing, we link our past and present hopes and realities.

Diversity of Views

There has always been diversity of thought in

Jewish life, more than we are inclined to suppose. And yet, surely, no time has seen such diversity as we take for granted, especially–though not exclusively–in the Reform movement. Indeed, it was said for years that a new liturgy for the Reform movement would have to await a time when our diverse views were reconciled. In other words, a new prayer book was out of the question in the foreseeable future. This made sense as long as we thought a prayer book ought to express a single point of view about God and the universe; but then we began to ask: Should it? Why should it? No doubt there are boundaries; should they, however, be quite so narrow as they have been? It dawned on us that a prayer book expressing a variety of moods was precisely what we needed.

Gates of Prayer makes room for the classical service with its classical God language. But it also contains a service whose language is "equivocal" and whose meaning therefore depends on the individual worshiper's viewpoint. It contains a service that is mystical in orientation and one religious humanists will find congenial. One of its Sabbath evening services comes from passages in the *Union Prayer Book* of 1940, and another echoes that prayer book's emphasis on social justice. Still another speaks the language of "covenant-theology," while yet another confronts our alienation from Shabbat and from God.

To further enrich our worship possibilities, we have provided many meditations from classical and contemporary literature, most of them Jewish in origin, all of them Jewish in spirit. What is Judaism at the end of the twentieth century? One answer–I believe a persuasive one–is found in the pages of this prayer book. The rich variety it provides speaks not only for the differences we find within our own minds and hearts. For there are times when we are mystics and there are times when we are rationalists. We believe, and we doubt. We care about the needs of our neighbors, and we look to our own souls. We feel like rejoicing, and we want to weep. *Gates of Prayer* speaks for all these moods. It recognizes and,

yes, it validates our own changing spirits openly and honestly. It unites us by making possible and legitimate the expression of different modes of "truth."

Equality of Women

A prayer book–any prayer book–is a mirror of change and continuity. As I was working on the English of *Gates of Prayer*, another change in our consciousness began to make its impact: the movement for equality of women.

Though a prayer book is not a political manifesto, it *is* a moral document. I came to see that language is not a neutral instrument. It reflects our social attitudes and influences our behavior. For this reason I found it necessary to look back upon the language of the prayer book I was working on and concluded that, by its very nature, current English usage carries into our time attitudes toward women that reflect the pat view of women as inferior creatures. I therefore decided that certain words and phrases must be altered. For example: "Our God and God of our fathers" may seem innocuous still to many people. Not so to me–and to many others. "Mankind" plainly excludes "womankind," and so on. References to humanity are no longer, in *Gates of Prayer*, exclusively masculine. I am confident that this is the usage that sooner or later all English-speaking Jews will insist upon.

What of tomorrow? How long will the new liturgies last? Will they serve our needs in the twenty-first century? I cannot say. I do know that we have paved a way. Some changes will be made by each successive generation–it takes no clairvoyance to say that much. I *think* we have built a new foundation on solid rock rather than on shifting sands. I hope we have. But our prayer book tradition, from the very beginning, is one of innovation, alteration, addition, subtraction. "Each generation has its interpreters" is a very old Jewish saying. I will be content to know that our new prayer books, and those yet to come, speak for us in what remains of this century. Something of what we have done today will be a part of tomorrow. That will do.

VI

JEWS MAKE THE WORLD BETTER

JEWS PURSUE RIGHTEOUSNESS, JUSTICE, AND LOVING DEEDS. Judaism says you may choose how to act: God will not interfere with what you want to do. In fact, some Jews believe God diminishes God's own power to share it with us so we can help God, through our acts, to complete and perfect the work of creation. That's a grave responsibility: power should be used wisely. Therefore God gave us guidelines about how to act so as to make God's world better. That's what "completing creation" means. However, we are free to follow the guidelines or ignore them.

Having such power is a mixed blessing: power makes you strong and puts you in control of situations and people. Most human beings like that. Power also makes demands on you and renders you responsible for what you do. Not everyone likes that. But, like it or not, power, and the responsibility that comes with it, are God's gifts to each of us. We are free to do what we want with them. That's where the guidelines come in. And the challenges. And the opportunities.

Tikun olam, repairing the world's imperfections, is the framework for the guidelines. Jews are obligated to further the creative process by using their God-given power to carry out God's plan: to make things better for others and to preserve the physical world. We are expected to pursue and sustain justice and to bring its benefits to all people. We are obliged to protect and extend freedom for everyone. We are compelled to work to achieve peace among individuals and nations. In doing these things we might be motivated by self-interest, but we are also responding to God's demands that we be God's creation partners. The Jewish response to God and our God-given power is to be good.

The readings in this chapter will offer Jewish replies to questions like "Who is a good person?" and "Why should I be good?" Think about your answers before you read the articles. How do your ideas differ from those of the authors? This chapter will also analyze the meaning of *mitzvah*. You know, and others can see, how your *mitzvah* performance affects other people; how does it affect you when you obey God's commands? We are enjoined in the Torah to pursue *tzedek*, righteousness. How can you practice daily *tzedakah*, aside from giving money to worthy causes? Leo Baeck is considered by many to have been one of the *tzadikim*, righteous ones, in our time. What can we learn about righteousness from his life? Finally, you will be asked to confront some prejudices about aiding individuals who seek your help. How do you determine whether or not to respond?

· Who Is the "Good" Person? ·

Most of us say we want to be "good" people. That generally means we'd like to do things that are good and refrain from doing things that are bad. The problem is not

Jews Make the World Better

everyone always agrees on what's good or bad. Some people believe good and bad are relative and depend on the specific circumstances. To complicate matters, we sometimes have to choose between two acts, each of which is good in and by itself. That means you have to choose what appears to be better at that moment. Being good turns out to be not so simple.

The following offers some suggestions you might consider in trying to be a good person, one who keeps the moral law. What's the difference between moral law and moral principle? How does each originate? Are we ever justified in going against a moral rule? Explain. Leo Baeck sought justice even for Nazis who had violated cardinal moral principles. Did that make him a good person? Explain. What guidelines can we use to determine whether a person deserves to be called good?

■ Who Is the "Good" Person?

BY NORMAN D. HIRSH ■

Who is the "good" person? Is it the human being who loves all kinds of people or the individual who keeps the Ten Commandments or someone we can trust, whose word is good? But wait. How can we even talk about the good person? Don't different societies have different ideas about who and what is "good"?

We believe a good husband should have sexual intercourse only with his wife. But in some societies a husband is expected to offer a male guest one of his wives for the night. How can we say who is the "good" husband? The fascist dictator of Italy during the Second World War, Benito Mussolini, argued that war is better than peace. He abhorred the peacemaker and honored the aggressor. We honor the peacemaker and abhor the aggressor. Who can say who is right?

Perhaps the clearest example of our difficulty occurred in real life not too long ago. A group of Colombian cowboys massacred sixteen nomadic Indians in the prairies east of the Andes Mountains. The leader of the cowboys argued: "For me, Indians are animals like deer or iguanas, except the deer don't damage our crops or kill our pigs. Since way back, Indian hunting has been common practice in these parts." In the culture of these Colombian cowboys it is acceptable to hunt Indians. We call it murder.

Finding Yardsticks

Are there some universal measures of right and wrong we can apply? Standards that would allow us to determine who is a good person? I believe such principles can be discovered.

In the branch of modern philosophy that deals with human conduct, a crucial distinction is made between moral principles and moral rules. Moral principles are broader than moral rules and they permit no exceptions. Moral rules allow for certain exceptions. What are some moral rules? Thou shalt not steal. Keep your promises. Honor your father and and mother. These are moral rules. We can all think of exceptions to them. A parent may be justified in stealing milk for a starving child. To save a life we should break a promise. Those few parents who are truly sadistic should not be honored. A moral rule almost always binds us. But not always. In some situations in our society or in another society, we may be justified in breaking a moral rule.

Moral principles are the source of moral rules. We sometimes speak of the principle underlying a rule. What are some moral principles? "What is hateful to you do not do unto another." This is the Golden Rule as formulated by Hillel. Killing for the sake of killing is wrong. This is the principle of reverence for human life. "Thou shalt have no other gods before Me." This is the Second Commandment. When faced with a decision, ask yourself what if everyone in similar circumstances should do as I propose to do? This is the Categorical Imperative. Now, how do we apply these principles to human conduct? Why shouldn't we steal? Let us use the Golden Rule. We certainly wouldn't want someone else to steal our prized possessions. Or apply the Second Commandment. Stealing is an act that makes greed the idol we worship over the One good God.

Moral principles go deep. They are the foundations of ethics. They also, and this is most important, permit no exceptions. A thousand years ago as well as today, in America, as well as in China, moral principles apply.

Applying Standards

Are we now in a position to say that the Colombian cowboys who massacred the sixteen Indians were wrong? We are. Their act violated at least three basic moral principles–the Golden Rule, the principle of reverence for human life, and the Categorical Imperative. For example, let us apply the Categorical Imperative. If we all hunted down human beings we despised, the world would be reduced almost totally to a jungle.

What standard can we apply to Mussolini, who preferred war to peace and acted on that belief? Anyone who glorifies and provokes war violates the principle of reverence for human life. We cannot consider him or her a good person. The case of the husband who offers one of his wives to a male guest for the night is more difficult. Even though his society may consider this proper conduct, if we look at it from a wider viewpoint, he is probably breaking the Golden Rule. For there is an element of inequality here. His wife may be forced to have intercourse against her will. We may assume the husband would not like to be forced to have intercourse against his will. The Second Commandment, which tells us to keep our priorities straight, is also violated in this situation. After all, this commandment insists that our primary loyalty be to God and to God's moral

laws. Offering a wife to a guest for the night makes too much of hospitality and too little of the special relationship that should exist between husband and wife. The host who offers his wife to a guest confuses his priorities. However, his sin does not compare, either in intent or in harm done, to that of the Colombian cowboys or of Mussolini.

I am convinced it is possible to talk about the good person. Certain basic and universal standards *do* exist. Beyond these basic standards, different styles of goodness are fully legitimate. The Jewish, Buddhist, Muslim, and Christian conceptions of the good person differ significantly. Yet a common core of agreement remains. Goodness can still be recognized across traditions. I recall meeting Dr. Martin Luther King, Jr., during a civil rights struggle and, even though I did not agree with his philosophy of non-violent resistence to evil, I still deeply felt that this was a good man!

Example of Leo Baeck

Who is the "good" person according to Judaism? Life itself offers us a model. Rabbi Leo Baeck was one of a few hundred survivors of 45,000 Jews at Theresienstadt concentration camp. When the Russians liberated the camp, they turned over some of the Nazi camp officials to the survivors for slaughter. But Leo Baeck stood up and pleaded for the lives of the officials. Despite what they had done, Rabbi Baeck could still remember that they were human beings and deserved a fair trial. Even they deserved justice! What enabled Rabbi Baeck to defend the rights of these Nazis? In that crisis I believe Leo Baeck managed to hear within himself the old biblical commandments: "Thou shalt not take vengeance," and "Thou shalt not murder." The moral law heard by a moral man explains Leo Baeck's noble decision.

In the Jewish view the person who hears and keeps the moral law is good. The moral law includes both moral principles and moral rules. It includes the Ten Commandments, the Golden Rule, and all the other ethical teachings of the

Torah such as "Thou shalt not follow a multitude to do evil" and "A stranger shalt thou not oppress."

The moral law commands us. Nevertheless, under the pressure of circumstances, it is sometimes one thing to hear and another to do. What enables us despite all the difficulties in life and our own destructive impulses to do the right? At bedrock it is our moral self-identity. There are certain unethical acts that as moral human beings we just cannot allow ourselves to do. There are ethical acts we feel we *must* do. We are, for example, not honest because honesty is the best policy. It isn't always. In the last analysis we are honest because we abhor dishonesty in ourselves. The ancient hero Job expressed it perfectly: "Till I die I will not put away my integrity from me." Thus, even in a losing cause, a good person may be able to do the right and preserve his or her moral self.

Words Vs. Deeds

Judaism believes that the person who hears and keeps the moral law is good. This is probably the best answer to our question, yet it is subject to dangerous abuse and oversimplification. Too often have I heard people glibly say: "I am a good person. I keep the Ten Commandments." They neither understand the commandments nor do they in fact actively carry them out in their lives.

Judaism therefore emphasizes good *deeds*. Specific *actions* are required, not words. In his stirring defense of his integrity Job (see Job 31) mentions loyalty to but one moral principle, yet he piles on example after example of his good deeds. He has been loyal to his wife, fair to his servants, generous to the poor, the widow, the orphan; he has not abused his power to influence the judge; he has not practiced idolatry; he has not stolen the land of the poor; indeed, he has delivered the innocent from the grasp of the unrighteous. Job's whole defense expresses a down-to-earth Jewish practicality. The person who accomplishes good deeds is good.

Yet an emphasis on good deeds alone may neglect motivations. Many Christian writers sum up our ethical duty in one word–love. Should we not say the loving person is good? Judaism, after all, does speak of the love of one's neighbor.

Pitfalls of "Love"

For two reasons Judaism refuses to define the good person in terms of love alone. First, the word "love" is subject to massive confusion and abuse. It is far too often reduced to a level of sentimental feeling having no solid results in ethical action. Second, love by itself is an inadequate guide to the ethical life. Love must be balanced by justice.

It is the nature of love to prefer. Love sees the uniqueness of the other. It says: "There is no one like you in the whole world." It is the nature of justice to resist preference. Justice sees the common humanity in all. It says: "All men are created equal."

Love is the special sacrifice one makes for one's children. Justice is the Jewish cook in the Nazi concentration camp–it was Dachau–who refused to look at the prisoners before him lest he favor his friends with an extra portion of soup.

Both are blind. But love is blind to fault while justice is blind to preference.

Love and justice are different in their source, too. Love wells up from the irrational. Justice rises from a more rational source–conscience. Both are necessary. Justice needs the warmth and renewal of love. But love needs the clear sight and limits of justice. Love led Jacob to favor Joseph over his other sons. Justice would have restrained Jacob and saved the family much grief.

Mercy and Justice

Judaism believes in both love and justice. But, when we describe them as a pair, we usually speak of "mercy" instead of love. Mercy is one of the expressions of love. It is love where there is frailty or misdeed. The word itself is more down-to-earth than the word "love." So in our tradition we speak of the balance of justice and mercy. In a famous verse the prophet Micah summed up our ethical duties as doing justice and loving mercy. (Micah 6:8) The medieval commentator Rashi told us that God first tried to create the world by justice alone, but society could not endure. Then God created the world by mercy joining justice to it, and society endured. Both are necessary. We may say the just and merciful person is good.

Who is the good person from the Jewish perspective? Several answers have merit. Perhaps the best answer is the person who hears and keeps the moral law. But we also have sufficient grounds to argue for the person who either performs good deeds or who is just and merciful.

The "Amen" Person

One more answer should be given. It goes back to the old biblical Hebrew word "*Amen*." In the Hebrew, "*Amen*" means: "I will stand firm. I will be loyal." When we say "Amen" we mean we will hang on, hold on, persist in the relationship no matter how difficult sticking it out becomes. So our people have persisted in our relationship with God. So we have persisted in our loyalty to our fellow human beings. Undismayed by every revelation of human hatred and division, we still try to make relationship work. A Leo Baeck does not deny the human bonds. Nor do we reject the long-held dream of our people. There still lives within us the hope to repair and build up the human connections so humankind will be one. *Amen.* "I will stand firm. I will be loyal." The person capable of persisting in relationship is good. Here then is another Jewish definition of the good person: Not the person who *says Amen*, but the person who *lives Amen*. The Amen-living person is good.

▪ The Bridge to "The Good Life" ▪

Many think to be good consists merely of refraining from being bad. Judaism guards against that simplistic notion when it requires positive, deliberate actions to do good things. Performing such acts defines "good" as much as refraining from bad things does. For most of us, after all, it's easy not to murder, not to steal, etc. That's why that's not enough. Judaism demands, in addition, that we give form and substance to our pious intentions through appropriate actions. Such actions are part of the *mitzvah* system, actions commanded by God.

The following selection considers *mitzvot* that are *ma'asim tovim*, doing good things. However, while exceedingly important, they are not the only *mitzvot*. Describe the difference between ritual *mitzvot* and *ma'asim tovim*. Does Judaism value either above the other? Explain. How does the article understand the term "spark of holiness"? What does that have to do with being good? The *mitzvah* system contains 613 commandments, both positive and negative. How does each type help you to be good? Are there limits to being good? Explain.

▪ The Bridge to "The Good Life"   BY HERMAN J. BLUMBERG ▪

Most of us want to be good and to do good. Some make the effort daily. Others try in fits and starts. And then there are those who have to be reminded of when and how to do good. The Jewish concept of *ma'asim tovim*–the term means "good works" or "good deeds"–helps to clear up

Jews Make the World Better

any misunderstandings about the meaning of "good" as Judaism defines it. It also spells out a number of ways of doing good that perhaps have never occurred to some Jews. The more we learn about *ma'asim tovim*, the better we grasp the basic idea of "right conduct" and the Jewish view of "the good life."

Built on Mitzvot

We must begin with *mitzvot* (plural of the familiar *mitzvah*), commandments in the Torah that reflect our understanding of God's will for humanity. Jews perform *mitzvot* in response to God, in an attempt to reach toward the goodness God represents to us. Jews perform *mitzvot* to fire the spark of holiness within themselves and to live lives of goodness.

There are many kinds of *mitzvot*, and they are divided into various categories. One category, *mitzvot bein adam lamakom*, speaks of the obligations between humans and God. Another category, *mitzvot bein adam lechavero*, speaks of the obligations between humans to each other. *Ma'asim tovim*, "good works," fall into the second group of duties, between humans–in today's jargon these duties might be pompously termed "human relationships."

Moses reminded the people of Israel (in Deut. 12:28): "Be careful to heed all the commandments that I enjoin upon you . . . you will be doing what is good and right in the sight of the Eternal, your God." And the rabbis explain: "The good" refers to what is good in the sight of God; "the right" is a reference to what is right in the sight of humans. (*Sifre*) In other words, both kinds of *mitzvot* matter greatly.

Failure to perform *ma'asim tovim*, despite other manifestations of piety and exemplary religious behavior, prevents a Jew from being regarded as "a good person." The Talmud rejects the offering of wheat that has been stolen. (*Sanhedrin* 6) One who studies Scripture and Mishnah and serves the learned but who is dishonest in business and discourteous in his relations with people is considered corrupt, ugly. (*Yoma* 86a) Acts of injustice or brutality, or dishonesty, deception, of slander, of unkindness to a fellow are all *religious* transgressions against God. (Cf. *Bava Kamma* 30)

Conversely the active performance of *ma'asim tovim* carries enormous weight. Here is an anecdote in which a single good deed is balanced against a life of sin:

Rabbi Abbahu questioned a man called Pentekaka, known for his five sins. Abbahu asked him, "What is your occupation?" The man replied, "I work as a laborer for the harlots. I deck the theaters. I take the harlots' garments to the baths. I clap and dance before them. And I beat the tympanum for their orgies."

Abbahu said to him, "Have you ever done one good deed?"

"Once," the man replied, "I was decking out the theater when a woman came and wept behind one of the pillars. When I asked her why she was crying, she told me her husband was in prison and she was going to become a prostitute to raise the money for his ransom. So I sold my bed and coverlet and gave her the price and said, 'Go, redeem thy husband.'"

Abbahu then said to him, "Worthy art thou to pray and to be answered!"

Jerusalem Talmud, *Ta'anit* I, 4, 64b

There is a debate in the Mishnah about whether one good deed can avert punishment for many transgressions. There is also a question about whether the balance is drawn in this world or in the world-to-come. Fine arguments aside, the point is made: *ma'asim tovim* are very important. With them the good life is possible; when they are absent, one cannot call oneself "good."

It is easy to compile a long list of good deeds. We are all of us full of noble impulses, and, when (or if) we have the chance, we act decently. But usually there is a gap between our ideals and our ability to realize them. We mean well, but opportunity doesn't always knock, or perhaps sometimes we don't quite manage to hear it. *Mitzvot*, for the Jew, provide a clear code of action with a built-in self-propelling impulse. The impulse rouses you, and the code then guides you to move from good intentions to specific good deeds.

Bikur Cholim

Take, for example, the *mitzvah* to visit the sick: *bikur cholim*. It is a religious duty. God himself provides the model: God visited Abraham soon after his circumcision. If God performs such a deed, the rabbis teach, surely humans should do likewise. It is an important act, praiseworthy and effective: "Whoever visits a sick person helps that person to recover. One rabbi declared boldly, "One who visits an invalid takes away one sixtieth of that person's pain." (*Nedarim* 40a, 39b) *Ma'asim tovim* are more than deeds casually performed when we feel up to it, when we have a spare moment, or when others are looking. For believing Jews, such acts, derived from Torah, are what life is all about, the very purpose of human existence. Jews look for them, aggressively seek them out in their quest to become good people.

Moreover, the *mitzvah* code provides practical, how-to-do-it rules for implementing the idea. Consider these eleventh-century guidelines:

Visit the sick and lighten their suffering.
Pray for them and leave. Do not stay long, for you may inflict upon them additional discomfort. And when you visit . . . enter the room cheerfully.

Orchot Chayim

In many instances the Jewish community created institutions or agencies to help Jews fulfill their religious obligations. *Bikur cholim* societies served shut-ins and the ill, caring for their medical and human needs. Today "meals on wheels" and neighbor-help-neighbor programs are carried out in the synagogue and Jewish community, based on the *mitzvah* of *bikur cholim*.

Does this process work? Perhaps this is not a question for Jews to answer. Certainly it is difficult to gauge the effectiveness of a religious way. Outside observers of Jewish life, more objective than insiders, have spoken of Jewish contributors to society, of the humaneness of Jewish life, the values in the Jewish family and home, the breadth and the liberality of Jewish social con-

cern. Perhaps observant Jews can say "We must be doing something right!" But then observant Jews would not care to consider the question at all. For them performing *mitzvot* is as natural as breathing. They are divine commandments, and the process of carrying them out is part of their very being.

A Rabbinic Tale

The rabbis tell a story:

A man going along the road sees his enemy's ass fallen down under its burden. He goes forward, lends a hand, and helps his enemy to unload and reload the animal. Then both men go into an inn and the latter says, "So-and-so is my friend after all, and I thought he was my enemy." They fall into talking with each other, and peace results.

What was it that caused the two men to make peace and become friends? It was that the first man kept what was written in the Torah: "If thou seest the ass of him that hateth thee fallen down under its burden, thou shalt forbear to pass by him, thou shalt surely release it with him."

(Exodus 23:5)
Midrash on Psalms 99:3

The story illustrates several *ma'asim tovim*: kindness to others even when you dislike them; compassion for the dumb beast straining under its load; and making peace. *Ma'asim tovim* include simple, human, everyday acts, undramatic, seemingly insignificant in the grand scheme of the world.

We also gain a crucial insight into the relationship between conduct and the study of Torah. The sacred teaching suggests the good deed and impels us toward it.

Some people say, "It is more important to be a good person than a good Jew." And they will quote chapter and verse like "Not learning, but doing is the chief thing" (*Avot* 1:17) or "One whose deeds exceed one's wisdom, one's wisdom shall endure; but one whose wisdom exceeds one's deeds, one's wisdom shall not endure." (*Avot* 3:12). Such people distort the narrow distinction between religion and ethics, between Torah and acts of goodness. In fact, they eliminate the former and talk about the latter. Our story suggests another way: Yes, the deed is supreme, but see how knowledge of Torah informs one's act, serving as a model, a guide–perhaps as an imperative–for right conduct. It is curious, by the way, how some Jews deceive themselves into thinking that being "good" can be separated from being a Jew. Their standards for being a "good person" come directly from the greatest Jewish source possible–the Bible!

The Story of Rabbi Adda

Once Rabbi Adda bar Achwah was approached by his colleagues. "What good deeds have you done?" they asked. Rabbi Adda cataloged a number of such deeds, like spending much time in the synagogue and thinking constantly about Torah. (Yes, *ma'asim tovim* include more than ethical rules.) Then he continued:

I have never strutted among my fellow scholars, or given one of them a nickname, or rejoiced when they stumbled. No curse of any one of them ever occupied my bed (that is, before nightfall he would forgive anyone who did him wrong). I never walked by the side of my debtor (to avoid embarrassing him).

Jerusalem Talmud, *Ta'anit* III, 13, 67a

For Rabbi Adda good deeds were not only the familiar ones, like doing justly, feeding the poor, pursuing peace. He lingered instead on the quiet, the personal, the "ordinary" acts of ordinary life–restraining the inclination to boast, to speak derisively, to gloat, to carry a grudge, to embarrass, or to give discomfort.

The Vast Mural

Our tradition enunciates vast, majestic enduring values: peace, justice, freedom, love, compassion. It's as though each one of those ideals were eternal symbols painted on some enormous but unfinished mural circling the globe. The very size and grandeur of the ideals make ordinary people timid about their ability to help work on that mural. But the process of performing

mitzvot enables all Jews to step up to the canvas and fill in their own brushstrokes every day. Thus, it is not only the diplomats and the generals who are concerned with peace, *shalom*. The youngest child in a Jewish home can help fulfill the *mitzvah* of *shelom bayit*, the peace attained by everyday acts of kindness, thoughtfulness, self-restraint, and self-giving within the family circle. The *mitzvah* of *gemilut chasadim*, the practice of goodness, kindness, or benevolence, can be carried out by such acts as visiting the sick, feeding animals before you sit down to eat your own meal, extending hospitality, returning lost objects to their owners, keeping a cheerful smile on your face, sympathizing with a friend, showing tact and understanding. The performance of the *mitzvah* of *tzedakah* can be carried out not only through acts of personal generosity but also through acts such as being fair to employees and employers, not cheating in business, not spreading gossip, not closing your eyes to the misdeeds of others, or not following the crowd bent on doing wrong.

In every catalog of right conduct prescribed by Judaism, restraint or acts of self-control are also considered "good deeds." We are already familiar with the notion of "Thou shalt not" in the Ten Commandments. The rabbis enumerated 365 negative commandments, one for each day of the year (together with 248 positive obligations, we have a total of 613 called *taryag mitzvot*). The conclusion is clear: to be a good person requires extending the hand with deeds of love and–with equal love–holding back the hand, word, and gesture that so often wound and destroy.

Can One Be Too "Good"?

Given some of the realities we have all seen in recent decades, the question "Can a person be too 'good'?" is not so strange. We know that too much permissiveness–parents with children, teachers before a class–can bring about chaos. When individuals demean themselves and violate their own principles in serving others, they are diminishing their own worth and dignity. When a group subordinates its highest self-interest for the good of others, it may suffer.

The clearest Jewish insight into this potential dilemma is stated in Leviticus 19:17: "Love your neighbors as yourself." In order to love others, you must first have a healthy regard for your own needs, desires, opinions, feelings, and attitudes. Only when we see ourselves as total human beings can we understand the subtlety of others' humanity.

Judaism does not demand sainthood, that one should say "What is mine is yours and what is yours is yours." (*Avot* 5:13) While acts of loving kindness have no limit, practical matters must be considered:

It was decided at Usha that a man should give a fifth of his possessions for good works. . . . But if this means a fifth of his whole possessions, then in five years he would have nothing left. . . . They finally agreed that after the first year it meant a fifth of his increase.

And similarly:

Rabbi Jeshabab gave all his possessions to the poor. Rabban Gamaliel sent to him to say, "Do you not know that the rabbis have ordered that a man should not give more than a fifth?"

Jerusalem Talmud, *Peah* I, 1, 15b

The Bridge

The *mitzvah* system, in the last analysis, has attempted to help people negotiate the contradictions of real life: a concern for self was balanced with a deep concern for others. The need for maintaining a just society, without favoring one group over another, was tempered by *chesed*, grace or charity. By committing themselves to a *mitzvah* system that embraced a wide range of right conduct, Jews built a bridge for living. This bridge, paved with positive "good deeds" and negative "good deeds"–all of them thoughtful considered acts in the service of God or *ma'asim tovim*–has helped the Jew to pass through the difficult mountains and abysses of daily living. As one proceeds step by step, one is continuously being a "good person" and living what Judaism calls "the good life."

▪ Why Choose to Be Good? ▪

The drive to "get ahead" in school or business or social situations often works against being good. After all, who can blame you for wanting to do what seems best for you, even if someone else gets hurt? In the end, however, you'll blame yourself because most of us want to do what's right and want to avoid doing what's wrong. Jews have another reason: God and Judaism expect us to be good, expect us to keep faith with the teachers and sages of our ancestry. You are free to do otherwise; but the consequences of choosing not to be good are great.

The following essay explores a variety of reasons for "being good," reasons based on the teachings of our tradition. "Being good" does not come naturally; neither does "being bad." We must learn to be good. Only through study can we comprehend why God wants us to be good. In obeying God we can be holy, gracious, and merciful. Why should we want to be like God? In what ways is being good an "act of faith"? How might you protect yourself against not being good? Why should you seek such protections?

■ Why Choose to Be Good?

BY SEYMOUR ROSSEL ■

Everywhere we turn it seems that the prevailing philosophy is "Me first." People say, "It's a dog-eat-dog world." Those who cheat at a poker game–and who are so clever and skillful at cheating that they don't get caught–have all the advantages. They know where the cards are; they know, too, what cards are up their sleeves and how to wait for the big winnings. They are totally in command. Those who trust them are being robbed–cheated of their money and of their faith. Why shouldn't the other players cheat, too? Why should we choose to play honestly–to do right–when there is a chance that someone else may be cheating? Why should anyone choose to do good?

You, or someone you know, may feel that way about life itself. Perhaps you think the winners in the game of life are the ones who are the biggest and best cheats. They are the ones who will drive the biggest cars; they are the ones who will wear the diamond necklaces.

Glorifying Cheating

In many ways cheating has become a way of life. We expect nations and their governments to cheat one another and sometimes even their own citizens. We are no longer innocent enough to believe that an American president would not cover up burglary, bribery, and election-fixing. We even glorify cheating when it seems in our own interest to do so. When newspaper reporters use the very same methods they claim to detest–wiretapping, information-peddling, bribery, and theft–to secure information for what they consider "the public's right to know," we applaud them. When passing an examination in school may mean the difference between getting into a top-notch college or having to attend a state school, many are willing to pay for the answers to the exam if only some brave soul–tried and and true–will pilfer them from the teacher's locker. When the cashier at a local restaurant makes a mistake and gives too much

change, many hold their breath while the incorrect amount is rung up. It has come to the point where some define "good" as "what we can get away with without being caught."

However, there is another side to the coin. For the great majority of us cheating is uncomfortable at best. Some of us do it so badly that we prefer not to do it at all. Some of us choose not to cheat or lie or steal. Which is to say that some of us–probably most of us–choose to do what is good. We are sometimes misled–talked or cajoled into doing something that is wrong–but mainly we stick to the straight and narrow. Most people prefer to think of themselves as "good." The question is: "What is 'good'?"

Refining Ideas of "Good"

This matter of the "good" and what it means is one of humanity's most complex problems. With the passing of years definitions have changed in some ways and remained unchanged in other ways. For example, the command "Thou shalt love thy neighbor as thyself" (Leviticus 19:18) was "good" in biblical times and remains "good" in our modern world. But the biblical law, "eye for eye, tooth for tooth, hand for hand, foot for foot" (Exodus 21:24) may now be viewed as cruel and primitive. As a matter of fact, the rabbis of the Talmud amended the law to mean that, if a person put out the eye of another, a monetary sum had to be paid in compensation. (To the best of our knowledge, this law–the law of *talion*, or exact repayment–was never carried out in ancient Israel except for the crime of murder, which was punishable by death–"life for life," Exodus 21:23.) The point of these examples is: human beings have to *learn* what is "good." Infants do not come into the world with the knowledge, experience, or wisdom to choose "good." People have to learn it over a lifetime. Further, over many generations, there has been a large accumulation of wisdom. So learning what is "good" requires not only constant study but also reconsideration and refinement of ideas that have come down to us.

The rabbis of the Talmud had a simple view of good and evil. If a person suffered, they said (*Ber.* 7a), it was because that person was in some way imperfect. If a person prospered, it was because that person was in some way deserving. They admitted that, as humans, we cannot always know in what ways a person is deserving or faulty, but they believed sincerely that God is always just. The simplicity of their belief is best expressed by Hillel, as it is told of him:

Moreover, he saw a skull floating on the surface of the water. He said to it: "Because you drowned others, they have drowned you; and, at the last, they that drowned you shall themselves be drowned."
–Pirke Avot 2:7

This simple faith in the righteousness of nature and the world and the justice of God in all cases was unfortunately difficult to maintain. Time and again, as the people were subject to one misfortune after another, doubt crept in.

The Middle Way

Much more acceptable was the explanation of good offered by the physician and philosopher Moses Maimonides (1134-1204). Maimonides combined the best thinking of the Greeks with his vast fund of Jewish knowledge and spoke of finding good in "the middle way." He argued that we can identify what is "good" by seeing the extremes and finding the middle; the middle is the good path. He explained this in the seven chapters of *Hilchot Deot*, a part of his gigantic masterwork *Mishneh Torah*, known as the Code:

1. Every human being is characterized by numerous moral dispositions that differ from one another. . . . One person is haughty to excess; another humble in the extreme. One is a sensualist whose lusts are never sufficiently gratified; another is so pure in soul [so as] not to even long for the few things our physical nature needs. . . . In the same way people differ in other traits. There are, for example, the hilarious and the melancholy, the stingy and the generous, the cruel and the merciful, the timid and the stouthearted, and so forth.

2. Between any moral disposition and its extreme opposite, there are intermediate dispositions, more or less removed from one another. . . .

3. To cultivate either extreme in any class of dispositions is not the right course. . . . If one finds one's nature tends or is disposed to one of these extremes, or if one has acquired or become habituated to it, one should turn back and improve so as to walk in the way of good people, which is the right way.

4. The right way is the mean in each group of dispositions common to humanity; namely, that disposition equally distant from the two extremes in its class, not being nearer to the one than to the other. . . .

So now we have one Jewish definition of what is "good." In truth this definition, which since the time of Maimonides has been one of Judaism's basic guideposts, is derived from the work both of the rabbis and the ancient Greek philosophers who developed the idea of the "golden mean." It is highly doubtful that the ancient rabbis understood the Torah and its laws this way.

Through this example from the work of Moses Maimonides, we see that Judaism is not basically a religion fearing influences from the outside or the wisdom of non-Jews; it is a religion willing to listen to reason. There are times when we are stubborn and, as the Torah pictures us, "stiff-necked," but basically the problem of the Jew is not how to be a good Jew but how a Jew can be a good human being.

Why Be Jewish?

Now you might say, if the problem is being a good human being, why should we bother being Jewish? Many have asked that question with the hidden meaning "Wouldn't there be peace in the world if we could all simply be human beings?" What might surprise you is that this unity of all humanity is one of our cherished hopes as Jews—that, if we work to bring about a time of peace, the world will be united under dominion of God alone, and each of us will be free to live without fear of war, crime, poverty, disease, or hunger. We often find this idea in the Bible. Here is one example:

Jews Make the World Better

That Your way may be known upon earth,
Your salvation among all nations. . . .
O let the nations be glad and sing for joy;
For You will judge the peoples with equity,
And lead the nations upon earth.

–Psalms 67:3, 5

Until this ideal has been fulfilled, however, being Jewish still serves many purposes. For example, the traditions and values of Judaism provide a kind of test for us. They provide goals and are designed especially to meet our needs in our particular time and place. These traditions, folk customs, and laws protect us from associating with the kind of people who cheat, lie, steal, or murder–like those who cry "Peace! Peace!" as they brandish swords and machine guns and murder the innocent in the marketplace. When being "plain human" might mean that we'd be in the same class as the terrorist and murderer, one begins to think twice about what "simply being human" really means.

All of this helps to shed some light on just what "good" is, but it does not answer the more difficult questions: "Why should I choose the good?" and "Why do those who are wicked so often succeed?" There are several ways to think about this second question. (It's a very old and troubling question; the prophet Jeremiah asked it some 2,500 years ago.) One way is to inquire: "Do the wicked succeed?" Sometimes they do seem to. But sometimes we also tend to exaggerate the number of successes. After all, what we see in newspapers and on TV in news programs is based primarily on what is evil. A good deed rarely gets news coverage, whereas a startling murder is front-page news.

Outlook on Life
Basically there are two ways of looking at the world. In *Pirke Avot* Rabbi Eliezer points out that the good way to hold to is "a good eye," and the evil way is "an evil eye." We can easily understand what is meant by "an evil eye. It's a way of looking at the world and seeing an ugly, unhappy, miserable place in which to live. The evil eye stands for envy, jealousy, constant complaining, and unhappiness.

A man once appeared before his rabbi and said: "I am finished with this business of being good. All my life people have said if I was good I would succeed. But look, here I have a list of twenty names of people who were evil and successful. Now I am going to cheat my customers and I will be rich, too." The rabbi smiled, "I see your list of those who were evil and succeeded," he said. "But where is your list of those who were good and succeeded?"

When people look at the world through an evil eye, they naturally see only evil and are disturbed by everything. It is just the opposite for those with "a good eye." The world seen through a good eye is a place of joy and cheer, of satisfaction and enjoyment. The good eye is our ability to see what good can be brought into the world through us. "Those who have a good eye will be blessed, for they give of their bread to the poor." (Proverbs 22:9) In other words, even if those with "a good eye" are themselves poor, they will find someone poorer to whom they can give charity because their good eye allows them to see themselves as rich!

In God's Image
There remains the first question, which we have saved for the last: "Why should I choose to be good?" There can be only one answer (although there are many ways of saying it): Being good is an act of faith. It is an act of faith in oneself, in one's neighbors, and an act of faith in God. It is the act we choose when we realize that we are not alone in this world, that others are a part of us, and that God watches over us. We choose to be good when we realize that doing evil to others hurts us as well.

This idea that we are all tied together is one Judaism shares with other religions and systems of thought–for instance, Hinduism and Buddhism; even with the German philosopher Arthur Schopenhauer (1788-1860). In a brilliant essay Schopenhauer posed a simple question: If our first primal instinct is to save ourselves and to preserve our own lives, why do human beings who see someone in trouble (drowning or being hurt) rush to help without stopping to think of the danger to themselves? He answered it:

When a person reaches saintliness, one no longer makes the egotistical distinctions between one's person and that of others but takes as much interest in the sufferings of other individuals as in one's own and, therefore, is not only benevolent in the highest degree but even ready to sacrifice one's own individuality whenever such a sacrifice will save a number of other people. . . .

–*The World as Will and Idea,* Bk. 4, para. 68

We all know the feeling in a small way. For each of us there is someone for whom we care especially–a parent, a friend, a sibling, a child, a spouse. We value their lives sometimes even more highly than we value our own. If we had to make a choice, our lives or theirs, it would be a very difficult one.

Why Choose to Be Good

Judaism takes the same thread of an idea that Schopenhauer is weaving and passes it back through the needle. We are all reflections of the One God. The Midrash tells us that when a human mints coins by striking the metal with an image, the image never varies from the original mold. But when God mints humankind in God's image, each human being is unique. Yet they are all of one image, the image of God.

In other words, if you are seeking God, you do not have to look up at the sky or down into the sea; you do not even have to meditate with your eyes unfocused so all you can see is what is within you. God's image is all about us, reflected in every face we see whenever we see these faces as a part of us and not as objects "out there" somewhere. And, if you are seeking good, you will find it at the hands of others who are good to you and who will expect good from you. We Jews have a special faith in one another. As we say: "All Israel is responsible one for another."

Being good is an act of faith. The highest expression of this idea is:

Ye shall be holy; for I the Lord your God am holy.

Ye shall fear every one, one's mother, and one's father, and ye shall keep My sabbaths: I am the Lord your God. Turn ye not unto the idols, nor make to yourselves molten gods: I am the Lord your God. . . .

The passage appears in chapter 19 of the Book of Leviticus, which is called the "Holiness Code" because in it we Jews are commanded to be holy. The chapter specifies what is meant by holiness: "You must not hold back a laborer's wage, even until the next morning. You shall not curse the deaf nor put a stumbling block in the blind person's way, but you shall fear your God: I am the Lord."

The constant repetition throughout the Holiness Code of the words "I am the Lord" drives home the realization that God is the Source, the Authority, of all goodness. God is concerned not only with our behavior toward heaven but perhaps more deeply with our behavior toward other human beings. Good makes us feel better inside; but Judaism's special understanding is that being good is an act of faith. Returning to Maimonides (continuing the four points of the Code previously discussed), we read:

5. . . . We are bidden to walk in the middle paths, which are right and proper ways, as it is said, "and you shall walk in God's ways." (Deut. 28:9)

6. In explanation of the text just quoted, the sages taught: "Even as God is called gracious, so be you gracious; even as God is called merciful, so be you merciful; even as God is called holy, so be you holy. . . . "

7. . . . And as the Creator is called by these attributes, which constitute the middle path in which we are to walk, this path is called the Way of God. . . . Whoever walks in this way secures for themselves happiness and blessing. . . .

Doing what is right and choosing to do what is good is always an act of faith: on the deepest level, of faith in oneself; on another level, of faith in humanity and its basic goodness; and on the highest level, of faith in the righteousness and goodness of God. Or, as the Holiness Code puts it: "Ye shall be holy; for I the Lord your God am holy."

Jews Make the World Better

▪ Leo Baeck: Giant of Tzedakah ▪

History provides many models of the good person. Albert Schweitzer, Mahatma Gandhi, Martin Luther King, Jr., Mother Teresa, and a host of others have demonstrated how a life can be devoted to *tzedakah* and *ma'asim tovim*, to being good. Jewish role models begin with Abraham, who taught us to care for strangers, and continue through the righteous ones and martyrs of Jewish history who often gave their lives to ease others' burdens. Alex Goode, Andrew Goodman, Jonas Salk, Samuel Gompers, and countless other Jews down the centuries have shown us how to be good. Not least among them is Leo Baeck.

This moving biography introduces you to Leo Baeck, whom many consider to have been a saint, or the closest Judaism comes to saintliness. (You met Baeck briefly in the first selection in this chapter.) His life illustrates that being good requires a commitment and a decision to act according to ethical teachings, which, in Judaism, derive from God's demands on us. Which of Baeck's actions might serve as examples for your commitment to righteousness? Explain. Baeck's actions flowed from his "duty to the community." What does that mean? How might you arrive at such a sense of duty? Might you want to do so? Explain.

▪ Leo Baeck: Giant of Tzedakah

BY STEVEN SCHNUR ▪

Starving and riddled with disease, they stood shoulder to shoulder in the freezing attic, listening to a white-haired rabbi lecture from memory on philosophy and history. By the hundreds these Jewish prisoners of Theresienstadt concentration camp crammed together in darkness, "absorbed, in breathless silence," according to one survivor, "forgetting hunger and cold, going away with new strength–to suffer the torments of the camp." For just a moment Rabbi Leo Baeck enabled them to forget the inhuman present, recalling for them the life of the mind they had known before the Nazis destroyed a thousand years of German Jewish history. "In this day of sorrow and pain, surrounded by infamy and shame we will turn our eyes to the days of old. From generation to generation, God redeemed our ancestors, and God will redeem us and our children in days to come."

Vowed to Remain Behind

When the Nazis arrested Leo Baeck in 1943, he was nearly seventy. For more than thirty years he had been considered Germany's chief rabbi, had even been called by some the "pope of German Jews," and, since Hitler's rise to power, had held the title of president of the *Reichsvertretung*, the National Council for German Jews. In that capacity he had not only helped thousands of Jews to emigrate but had established a network of Jewish schools and welfare agencies to care for those remaining behind.

Although he declared as early as 1933 that the long and distinguished history of German Jewry had come to an end, he vowed to remain "as long as a *minyan* exists." Briefly arrested in 1935, Baeck refused to be intimidated by the Nazis and continued to preach at Berlin's

Fasanenstrasse Synagogue, imploring his congregation not to forget their proud history or succumb to fear, declaring, "Judaism must not stand aside" when confronted by persecution but must "rouse the conscience of humanity."

Arrested by Gestapo

As all but a handful of Berlin's Jews fled, Baeck received dozens of invitations to teach in England and America. But he remained in Germany, committed to teaching and caring for the remnant that clung to him, telling those abroad who begged him to save his own life and flee, "I will go when I am the last Jew alive in Germany."

By the end of 1942 most of his students and all of his colleagues on the Jewish Council had been deported. When the Gestapo finally came for him on January 27, 1943, he defied their command to leave immediately and instead sat down and wrote to his daughter in England that he was being taken to Theresienstadt. With characteristic meticulousness he paid his gas and electric bills and only then agreed to be taken to the concentration camp.

When he entered the bleak medieval ghetto of Theresienstadt, its narrow, filthy streets and crumbling buildings contained more than 60,000 Jews, six times the number the town was built to house. "Theresienstadt meant much to me even before I saw it," he later wrote. "Three sisters of mine had died there and a fourth died shortly after my arrival." At the age of seventy, suffering from dysentery, Leo Baeck pulled a garbage wagon through the typhus-infested streets.

But within weeks he was again teaching and organizing programs to care for the ghetto's elderly and sick. Daily he scanned the list of new arrivals, looking for a familiar name, someone whose shock of deportation he could ease with a visit and a few words of reassurance. He ministered to the sick and conducted Bar Mitzvah ceremonies and funerals.

Power of Caring

He prevailed upon those who received packages of food from outside to share them with their fellow prisoners as he did with the parcels sent by his daughter, Ruth. He smuggled newspapers into the camp at risk to his life, knowing that news of Allied advances kept hope alive. Survival, he said, depended on patience and imagination, on the ability to withstand present oppression and the willingness to envision a better future. It also depended on maintaining a sense of community in which people shared common ideals and cared for one another's welfare.

He achieved this through his lecture series, drawing together as many as seven hundred inmates, who came not only to learn but to participate in a community of like-minded Jews. "Is there another people on earth that has such a deep and true connection to the spirit as ours—that, although it is facing such humiliation and danger, it asks for the word of the philosopher?" Baeck asked in awe of his fellow prisoners.

Knew Fate of Transports

He alone knew with certainty that the weekly transports filled with Theresienstadt prisoners ended not in work camps as the Nazis insisted but in the ovens of Auschwitz. Yet he continued to hold out hope, refusing to share his knowledge for fear that what little strength remained among his fellow prisoners would collapse in the face of a reality as hideous as the extermination camps. He watched in silence as his nephew and niece boarded one of those death trains, knowing that the Nazis would have allowed him, as a community leader, to substitute two other Jewish prisoners for his family, a privilege he refused. And he knew that in all likelihood he, too, would soon board that train; yet he continued to lecture on the glories of Western civilization.

But fate spared him, even after a chance meeting with Adolf Eichmann, the mastermind of the Final Solution. Baeck had been attending to some business in the ghetto offices, he later recalled, when "the door opened and an SS officer entered. It was Eichmann. He was visibly taken aback at seeing me. 'Herr Baeck, are you still alive?' He looked me over carefully, as if he did not trust his eyes, and added coldly, 'I

Jews Make the World Better

thought you were dead.'" Baeck returned to his barracks, certain Eichmann would order his immediate deportation. "I gave my wife's and my wedding rings to a friend and asked him to hand them on to my daughter in England," he added. "Then I wrote farewell letters and was ready for what might come." But what came was freedom.

In May 1945 the Germans suddenly abandoned Theresienstadt, fleeing before the advancing Russian army. Baeck, together with the International Red Cross, took charge of the effort to quarantine and cure the thousands of prisoners suffering from typhus. Fearing a disastrous epidemic if the infected left the camp, he pleaded with them to stay in that city of death, promising he would remain with them until every last one received proper medical attention and was assured transportation out of the camp. For two months, the hardest days of his life, he later admitted, he cared for the sick despite the letters from friends and family and the pleadings of an American colonel waiting to escort him to England. When he finally passed through the medieval gates of the city in July, he was among the last to leave.

Not a Martyr

During the months following his liberation Baeck wrote hundreds of letters answering the anxious inquiries of those seeking lost relatives. He sent packages of food and clothing not only to Jews in desperate need but to his non-Jewish friends still living in war-ravaged Germany. Until he died in 1956, Leo Baeck traveled between London, where he served as the chairman of the World Union for Progressive Judaism, and Cincinnati, where, at the Hebrew Union College, he devoted the last years of his life to teaching. He believed, above all, in his duty to the community and had been willing to sacrifice his safety in the effort to hold the dwindling German Jewish community together. He was not a martyr; he simply refused to run from what life had set before him. As he wrote, "A life fulfills itself when it understands and accepts what is sent to it."

▪ Tzedakah: Q & A ▪

The first line of this chapter declares that Jews pursue righteousness. That means Judaism emphasizes your obligation to look for ways to be good. To wait passively for *tzedakah* opportunities to come your way is not enough. Many questions spring from the idea that the pursuit of *tzedakah* is required of you: To whom should you give? How much? In what priorities?

The questions that follow inquire into the meaning and practice of *tzedakah*. Try to develop your own answers to the questions before reading the replies offered. Compare your answers with those in the article. Other questions are suggested by the replies. Why is there no special biblical term for charity? Should you shun material goods because a person's worth is measured in *mitzvot*? Explain. Do you agree it is better to give to a potential deceiver than risk denying a deserving person? Explain. What other questions do you have about *tzedakah*?

▪ Tzedakah: Q & A ▪ BY ARON HIRT-MANHEIMER ▪

Q. What does the term *tzedakah* mean?

A. It is derived from the Hebrew *tzedek*, meaning "justice" or what is right. In the Torah it is also used to mean righteousness–in the sense of piety. One cannot be considered pious–a *tzadik*–unless one lives a righteousness and just life, and that requires devotion to helping the needy. Although the idea of charity appears throughout the Bible, there is no special term for it. Only later, in the Talmud and thereafter, did *tzedakah* generally come to mean charity.

Q. How are the poor regarded in Jewish tradition?

A. The underprivileged are not to be blamed for their condition. The Hebrew prophets held that social injustice is the cause of poverty. Ezekiel attributed the destruction of Sodom to its lack of charity. By Jewish law the poor have the right to receive *tzedakah*. And, according to the Talmud, those who give *tzedakah* get more out of it than those who receive it because the donors are given the opportunity to perform a *mitzvah*. This attitude is based on the belief that all earthly possessions belong to God and that one's worth is measured in *mitzvot*, not in material goods.

Q. Who is required to give *tzedakah*?

A. It is required of everyone, including poor people who themselves receive charity. The poor shall not be denied the feelings of joy and self-esteem that derive from performing the *mitzvah* of *tzedakah*. As the Talmud teaches: "When a person gives even a *perutah* (the smallest coin) he or she is privileged to sense God's presence."

Q. What categories of people get top priority in receiving *tzedakah*?

A. The Bible emphasizes the *mitzvah* of caring for the widow, the orphan, and the stranger. In the process of refining the laws pertaining to charity the rabbis of the Talmud determined that preference was to be given to women over men and one's poor relatives over strangers. The poor of *Eretz Yisrael* took precedence over everybody.

Q. Should charity also be given to the non-Jewish poor?

A. Yes, it should be given to all peoples, because in doing so we foster peace in the world.

Q. Should *tzedakah* be given to someone we suspect of deception?

A. It is better to give to a deceiver than to risk depriving the deserving of relief.

Q. Is it preferable to give *tzedakah* openly or anonymously?

A. Every effort must be made to avoid causing shame or humiliation to the recipient of *tzedakah*. As is written in the Talmud, when R. Yannai observed somebody giving money to a poor man in public, he said: "Better not to have given him anything than to have given and caused humiliation." The most famous formulation of laws concerning the relationship of donor to recipient is Maimonides' *Eight Degrees of Charity*. From the lowest to highest level they are to give (1) but sadly, (2) less than is fitting, but in good humor, (3) only after having been asked, (4) before being asked, (5) so that the donor doesn't know who the recipient is, (6) so that the recipient doesn't know who the donor is, (7) so that neither knows the identity of the other, and (8) in a manner so that the recipient becomes self-sufficient, thus avoiding the loss of self-respect that may result from receiving the lower degrees of charity.

Q. How much should one contribute to charity?

A. One is expected to give up to one-fifth of one's possessions to fulfill the *mitzvah* of *tzedakah* to its fullest degree. Less than one-tenth is considered miserly. The law cautions against giving beyond one's means, for it is no benefit to society if a person becomes impoverished by giving excessively.

■ Brother, Can You Spare a Dime? ■

Most of us practice *tzedakah* rather impersonally. We send checks to favorite Jewish and other charities, drop coins in boxes, contribute to various Keren Ami Funds, give a few dollars to door-to-door solicitors. That's a high rung on Maimonides' ladder: we don't know the recipients and they don't know the donors. It's also an easy way to feel good about fulfilling a *mitzvah*. *Tzedakah* gets less easy when we are face-to-face with someone who seems to need help, as when meeting a beggar on the street. Unfortunately that's getting to be a common occurrence in our cities. How do you feel when that happens? How do you respond? How do you know what's best to do?

The following elaborates on a topic considered in the previous selection and asks questions that might be occasioned by meeting a beggar on the street. The reply to each of the fifteen questions contains a Jewish teaching. What value does each answer embody? How might each help you to be a good person? Explain.

■ Brother, Can You Spare a Dime?

BY ARTHUR KURZWEIL ■

In my neighborhood in Manhattan there is hardly a day when I am not approached by an individual who asks me for spare change. These individuals come in various forms:

1. Some are bag ladies, dragging the sum total of their worldly possessions with them in numerous shopping bags.
2. Some are "street people" who most probably live on the street, in the subway, or other public places.
3. Some are idle welfare recipients who appear capable of holding some kind of job.
4. Some are alcoholics, with bottle in hand.
5. Some are obvious drug addicts.
6. Some show no immediately apparent reason to be asking for anything, as they are well-dressed, groomed, etc.
7. They are of all ages (literally from eight to eighty).
8. They are both men and women.
9. They are usually black or Hispanic in my neighborhood, but in Greenwich Village, where I often walk, they are mostly white and sometimes Jewish.

10. Ninety-nine times out of a hundred they are nonthreatening (though I am a male and I imagine if I were a female, I might have a significantly different perspective on this).

Though the organized Jewish community has gotten the *mitzvah* of giving *tzedakah* down to a science, and though I have also been a member of a *tzedakah* collective for four years, I was confused as to what I should do about the beggars I meet.

My habit regarding beggars was inconsistent:

1. Sometimes I gave nothing.
2. Sometimes I'd get into a giving mood and give to every beggar in sight.
3. Sometimes I got angry over the issue and thought, "They ought to get a job."
4. Sometimes I'd give consistently though selectively to people I decided were worthy recipients.
5. Sometimes I'd give enthusiastically to a familiar beggar, only to ignore that person the next day or week.

There were other inconsistencies as well, but those five listed above are enough to indicate that my thinking on the subject was confused. But more than confused, I was troubled by it. Two questions loomed in my mind: What should my attitude toward beggars be? And does Jewish tradition have anything to teach me on the subject?

The following are the results of my own exploration of those two questions. My approach to the question of "What should my attitude toward beggars be?" was to first sit down and list all of the questions I could possibly think of relating to my own personal dilemmas in regard to the subject. I came up with fifteen questions:

1. Do Jews give to beggars?
2. What if they are fakes of frauds?
3. What if they are nasty or otherwise offensive in looks, smell?
4. What if I feel I simply can't afford to give to beggars?
5. Aren't there better causes to give to than these people?
6. Shouldn't these beggars be supported by official or organized agencies?
7. Shouldn't I just ignore these people?
8. What if I am in a rush?
9. What if they aren't Jewish?
10. What if I have no money with me or no spare change?
11. If I do give, how should I treat these people? How should I approach them? What should I say?
12. What if I see the same people every day? Won't they get to know me as a sucker?
13. What if I already gave to a few beggars in one day?
14. If they ask for money, perhaps I should go buy them a cup of coffee instead. After all, they will probably spend it on booze anyway!
15. If I do give to beggars, how much should I give?

The fifteen questions seemed to cover just about every possible issue I could come up with regarding beggars.

I spent a frantic and exciting few days searching my shelves, grabbing books I thought might help. In the process I read a great deal and learned more than I had ever hoped. The following are but a few of the insights I gleaned from Jewish sources:

1. Do Jews give to beggars?
R. Isaac said, "One who gives a coin to a poor person is rewarded with six blessings. But one who encourages the person with friendly words is rewarded with eleven." *Bava Batra* 9a.

2. What if they are fakes or frauds?
Rabbi Chayim of Sanz had this to say about fraudulent charity collectors: "The merit of charity is so great that I am happy to give to a hundred beggars even if only one might actually be needy. Some people, however, act as if they are exempt from giving charity to a hundred beggars in the event that one might be a fraud." *Darkai Chayim* (1962), p. 137.

3. What if they are nasty or otherwise offensive in looks or smell?
Rabbi Shmelke of Nicholsburg said, "When poor people ask you for aid, do not use their faults as an excuse for not helping them. For then God will look for your offenses, and God is sure to find many of them. Keep in mind that the poor people's transgressions have been atoned for by their poverty, while yours still remain with you." *Fun Unzer Alter Otzer*, II, p. 99.

4. What if I feel I simply can't afford to give to beggars?
Even a poor person, a subject of charity, should give charity. *Gittin* 7b.

5. Aren't there any better causes to give to than these people?
While it is commendable to aid students of the Torah more than commoners, the Jewish law knows no such distinction. The latter must also be aided. Nachman of Bratzlav.

6. Shouldn't these beggars be supported by official or organized agencies?
In answer to an inquiry from a community

overburdened with beggars, Solomon b. Adret ruled that, although "the poor are everywhere supported from the communal chest, if they wish in addition to beg from door to door, they may do so, and each should give according to his or her understanding and desire."
Responsa, pt. 3, # 380.

7. Shouldn't I just ignore these people?

If one noticed poor people asking for something and ignored them and failed to give *tzedakah*, one has broken a prohibitive command, as it is written: Do not harden your heart and shut your hand against your needy sibling. (Deut. 17:7) Rambam, *Mishneh Torah*.

8. What if I am in a rush?

It is related to Nahum of Gamzu that he was blind in both his eyes, his two hands and legs were amputated, and his whole body was covered with boils.... On one occasion his disciples said to him, "Master, since you are wholly righteous, why has all this befallen you?" He replied, "I have brought it all upon myself. Once I was journeying on the road and was making for the house of my father-in-law. I had with me three asses, one laden with food, one with drink, and one with all kinds of dainties. A poor man stopped me on the road and said, 'Master, give me something to eat.' I replied to him, 'Wait until I have unloaded something from the ass'; I had hardly managed to unload something from the ass when the man died (from hunger). I then went and laid myself on him and exclaimed 'May my eyes that had no pity upon your eyes become blind; may my hand that had no pity upon your hands be cut off; may my legs that had no pity upon your legs be amputated,' and my mind was not at rest until I added, 'May my whole body be covered with boils.'" Thereupon his pupils exclaimed, "Alas that we see you in such a sore plight." To this he replied, "Woe would it be to me if you did not see me in such a sore plight." *Ta'anit* 21a.

9. What if they aren't Jewish?

Poor Gentiles should be supported along with poor Jews; the gentile sick should be visited along with the Jewish sick; and their dead should be buried along with the Jewish dead in order to further peaceful relations. *Gittin* 61a.

10. What if I have no money with me or no spare change?

If a poor person requests money from you and you have nothing to give the person, speak to him or her consolingly. Rambam, *Mishneh Torah*, "Gifts to the Poor," 10:5.

11. If I do give, how should I treat these people? How should I approach them? What should I say?

Those who give *tzedakah* in a surly manner and with a gloomy face completely nullify the merit of their own deed, even if they give a thousand gold pieces. They should rather give cheerfully and gladly, while sympathizing with those who are in trouble, as it is written: Did I not weep for the one whose day was hard? Was not my soul grieved for the poor? (Job 30:25) Rambam, *Mishneh Torah*, "Gifts to the Poor," 10:4.

12. What if I see the same people every day? Won't they get to know me as a sucker?

Though you may have given already, give yet again, even a hundred times, for it says, "Give, yea, give thou shalt...." (Deut. 15:10-11) *Sifre* Deut., *Re'eh*, 116.

13. What if I already gave to a few beggars in one day?

If you have given a *perutah* to a person in the morning, and there comes to you in the evening another poor person asking for alms, give to that person also.... *Avot d'R. Natan* 19b.

14. If they ask for money, perhaps I should go buy them a cup of coffee instead. After all, they will probably spend it on booze anyway!

Nehemiah of Sihin met a man in Jerusalem who said to him, "Give me that chicken you are carrying." Nehemiah said, "Here is its value in money." The man went and bought some meat and ate it and died. Then Nehemiah said, "Come and bemoan the man whom Nehemiah has killed." Jerusalem Talmud, *Peah*, VIII:9, 21b.

(In this example, the case is reversed: the person wanted an item of food rather than money. But the point is the same: don't decide what is best for the beggar.)

15. If I do give to beggars, how much should I give?

A poor person who goes begging should not be given a large donation but a small one. One must never turn a poor person away empty-handed, even if you give him or her a dry fig. Rambam, *Mishneh Torah*, "Gifts to the Poor," 7:7.

Each person's relationship to these texts is different. For me the texts represent an ideal, and one I confess I do not live up to regularly. Yet this research was not an academic exercise. The exploration of the text moved me–literally–to avoid passing up the opportunity of observing the *mitzvah* of *tzedakah* each day in the neighborhood. I often fail at seizing each opportunity offered to me, but I struggle to come closer to the ideal, and that is, in my opinion, the purpose of the teachings. As R. Assi observed: *Tzedakah* is as important as all the other commandments put together. *Bava Batra* 9a.

VII

A JEW CELEBRATES

JEWS OBSERVE SHABBAT, FESTIVALS, AND JEWISH LIFECYCLE CEREMONIES. Jews do not hallow places or sanctify structures. Even the presence of the Temple in Jerusalem did not preclude worshiping God in other places. The important thing is that Jews should worship God. Where that happens is of secondary interest. Places and buildings don't last. Time does. So time is an important component of Judaism. God can be approached anytime, but there are commonly defined times when Jews make special efforts to do that. Thus, Jews hallow time and look to its passage for defined occasions to praise God and express reliance on the Holy One.

Common parlance suggests that, for most people, time itself is neutral. We manipulate it, use it wisely, ignore or cherish it, thereby investing time with significance or insignificance. We kill time or use it well, waste time or savor precious moments. Seconds drag on or hours fly by; we lose track of time or count the minutes. God, however, used time to create the universe, thus informing each valuable moment with the creative act. God divided time into fractions. Measured by the heavenly bodies, those time segments became periods measured and marked by ceremonies and rites expressing human awareness of time. The circuits of heaven are thus reflected in earthly circuits that are observed by the community. The observances of time segments are major activities in Jewish communal life.

The Jewish people learned to sanctify time from the Creation drama itself: there was a beginning and there was a time to rest. Thus, *Shabbat* became the prime example for hallowing time, for making it *kadosh*, holy. The Jewish historical experience also teaches us to hallow time. For example, while God is present in all moments, sometimes we feel or want to feel particularly close to our Creator. Those special times mark significant moments in the saga of our people, times like the Exodus, the desert wanderings, the encounter at Sinai. We celebrate those moments each year. We also celebrate the time cycles of individual lives from birth through burial and, as in *Yahrzeit*, even beyond. These moments, too, we make *kadosh* with appropriate ceremony. So, also, do we celebrate the reading time cycle of Torah, source of Jewish life.

Although this chapter is about Jewish observances, it is not a study of Jewish holidays and lifecycle events. It is, however, about what Jewish celebration meant for our ancestors and what it means, or can mean, for us. The readings will also consider how it may be possible to ascribe new significance to rituals like *Shabbat* and other Jewish observances. Many Jewish holidays are related to agricultural events. Why did such celebrations persist among nonagricultural Diaspora Jews? The meaning of some rituals is shrouded in mystery. Why do they continue to appeal to us?

This chapter explores the idea of celebration and the magic moments when God and the Jew meet in the echo of history.

A Jew Celebrates

▪ The Festivals Are for Us ▪

Jews today celebrate the festivals in much the same ways our ancestors did. Though times have changed, centuries have not dimmed attachments to things that bind us with Jews of long ago. Those links contribute to Jewish identity and identification. For some Jews, however, it is not enough to rehearse past ways. Many Jews look for new forms in which to preserve the substance of ancient celebrations. That effort has resulted in beautiful new traditions for the Jewish people, thus enhancing the idea of *tam*, the good taste that should accompany *mitzvah*.

The following reading suggests some ways in which ancient ceremonies might be informed with new meanings to enrich holiday observance. Can you add to the list for the holidays discussed as well as for others in the Jewish calendar? Are there limits to the kinds of changes one can make? Explain. How might you decide what can be revised, added, or dropped? Can individuals institute changes, or do they require community or other approval? Explain.

▪ The Festivals Are for Us   BY HARVEY J. FIELDS ▪

Not long ago I was discussing with a religious school class how Jews have celebrated *Pesach* during the last several thousand years. I thought I was holding everyone's attention, until one student raised his hand and said, "Rabbi, I don't mean to be disrespectful, but very honestly–you want us to be honest, don't you?"

I nodded. "Of course I do."

"Well, we do a lot of talking about the Jewish holidays, but, truthfully, I find most of them boring."

"Boring?" I asked.

"Yeh," he continued. "I mean, I guess they're fine for adults. And I can understand why they are important to the Jewish community. But what are people our age supposed to do to make them interesting and fun?"

Some of his friends cheered. They agreed with him and believed he had asked an important question. So did I. I have written this article as a partial answer; partial because I am convinced that, once we start thinking creatively about how to make our Jewish festivals "interesting and fun," we will come up with all sorts of new possibilities.

"Nothing But Joy"

According to the Torah, the mood of *Sukot* is supposed to be "nothing but joy" (Deuteronomy 16:14). We should take that instruction as our theme for celebrating. Giving thanks for the harvests that keep us alive and focusing attention upon our human responsibilities to nature can make this festival a wonderful and memorable experience.

Building and decorating a *sukah* at home and at the synagogue is great fun. Look for a good set of plans. Sit down with your family or a group of friends and decide what themes and materials you are going to use for your decorations. Remember, the *sukah* is meant to be a temporary dwelling, so it can, and probably ought to be, different each year. One year you may want to emphasize the theme of "friendship," another year "great biblical quotes," and another year "our concern for the planet Earth."

Have a Sukah Party

Meeting in the *sukah* for meals and discussions is a *mitzvah*, as is inviting guests to share those meals. So plan a *sukah* party, develop a menu, ask your parents–politely–to get out of the kitchen, prepare your favorite foods, set and decorate the table to your own taste, and choose the games or topics for discussion that interest you.

In ancient times when Jews traveled to Jerusalem and lived in their *sukot* for seven days celebrating the harvest festival at the Temple, many of their prayers expressed the hope that the coming year would yield a bountiful harvest. In other words, their concerns were about nature. They hoped the rains would come in time, the crops would grow, and they would harvest enough food to sustain human life.

Today our concerns are also about preserving human life on our planet. *Sukot* is a perfect time to heighten our awareness and the sensitivities of adults in our community to what we can do about pollution, the use of our natural resources, and the dangers of a nuclear catastrophe. So take the initiative and organize a debate or forum.

Peace and Unity

In his book *Knesset Israel*, which was written in the early part of this century, Rabbi Yaakov Israel (1874-1934) made the following observation about the meanings of the *Sukot* symbols (*etrog, lulav, aravah,* and *hadas*). "The four species symbolize peace and unity. For, just as they differ in taste, odor, and form but are united together, so, too, the different parties of our people must form one alliance, and with one shoulder work for the good of their people."

We don't always do well. There are serious frictions between different Jewish groups. What about developing a *sukah* dialogue program with other Jews on the questions and issues of Jewish plurality and unity? We say "We are one!" What does that mean, and how do we accomplish it?

Four Tough Questions

We all know children are supposed to ask the Four Questions at the *seder.* So let's take that seriously. Think up the toughest questions facing us Jews and ask them at your *seder.*

Or go into the *seder* beautifying business, cre-ating *matzah* covers, *afikoman* holders, *seder* placecards, Elijah cups, and *seder* plates. All profits should go to a *tzedakah* project of your choosing.

Using a tape recorder, interview the three oldest members of your family about their favorite *seder* recollections. Limit them to four minutes, then play the results, perhaps with slides at your family *seder.*

Counting the Omer

Seven weeks separate *Pesach* from *Shavuot.* In Jewish tradition the period is called *Sefirat Ha'omer,* "the counting of the Omer," the fifty days until the first harvest of summer. But more is involved here than simply counting out days. Through the centuries *Sefirat Ha'omer* emerged as the way in which the Jewish people marked the journey from Egyptian liberation to the receiving of the Torah at Mount Sinai.

We can continue that process today. Create a *Sefirat Ha'omer* calendar. Illustrate it, choose quotations for each day, and sell it to every family in your congregation. It will be your contribution to bringing Jewish education into the home.

Shavuot is also known in the Torah as *Chag Hakatzir,* "the harvest festival" (Exodus 23:16), and as *Yom Habikurim,* "the day of first fruits" (Numbers 28:26). The emphasis of the holiday is on harvesting and on the importance of Torah to the Jewish people.

A Floral Parade

How can we bring both of these themes together? Perhaps through a colorful parade of flowering plants brought into the sanctuary and placed on the pulpit by young people in the congregation. After the reading of the Ten Commandments the entire congregation could plant the flowers in the temple garden, beautifying the building and the community.

We read the Ten Commandments on *Shavuot,* believing they are among the most significant statements of Jewish tradition, perhaps of Western civilization. Yet, how do they apply to our lives? You may wish to develop a debate around some of the commandments or on the topic "How does Jewish law work?" Or what about creating "Ten Commandments for Parents of Teenagers" and "Ten Commandments for Teenagers of Parents," and then inviting parents for an evening discussion.

On *Shavuot* we read from the Book of Ruth about a woman who became a convert to Judaism. In our congregations there are many people who are Jews-by-choice. They have much to teach us about what it means to make important religious decisions and about how to be proud Jews. Invite two or three Jews-by-choice to form a panel and share with you some of their experiences.

A Final Word

I have been back to that class I visited in our religious school and have shared with them some of the ideas suggested above. They have divided up the festivals and are busying making their plans for this year. Have you made yours?

▪ Praying for Rain ▪

Jewish agricultural festivals share a common concern: rainfall in *Eretz Yisrael*. For our ancestors belief in one God was inextricably linked to agricultural vicissitudes relying on the type of rain the crops required and when the rains appeared. Opposing forces in the rainy period had to be in balance so as not to destroy one or another of the delicate crops on which Israelite civilization depended. While the Canaanites looked to specific deities, each of which controlled a natural element, Israelites placed their faith in *Adonai*, who mediated balance and harmony in all of nature.

The following article describes the delicate water needs of the crops on which the Israelites so sorely depended. How is each of the crops that are so fundamental to Israelite survival commemorated in festival and other Jewish celebrations today? The festivals do more than celebrate natural phenomena. Each holiday has historical import as well. Why? Describe the connections between natural and historical meanings. Why did Jews continue to pray for rain in the Promised Land throughout nearly two thousand years of exile?

▪ Praying for Rain   BY MANUEL GOLD ▪

Rosh Hashanah and *Yom Kippur* were not always the High Holy Days. For hundreds of years, during and after the biblical period, the most important holiday was *Sukot*.

Why was *Sukot* special? And how did *Rosh Hashanah* and *Yom Kippur* become so important in our day? To answer those questions, we must journey backward in time, almost three thousand years, to the Temple in Jerusalem. *Sukot* and the other two important harvest festivals, *Pesach* and *Shavuot*, had their origins as agri-

cultural celebrations among the pre-Israelite inhabitants of Canaan. When the Jewish people settled among the Canaanites after the death of Moses, they began to celebrate these festivals, gradually adapting them to their own monotheistic belief in YHWH, the Jewish God. The holidays became their way of formally asking God for new growth and productivity from the soil of their new and difficult land. Crops in Canaan were not watered by great rivers as they were in Egypt along the Nile and in Mesopotamia along the

Tigris and Euphrates. In Canaan rain was the major source of water, and rain was scarce. Without sufficient rainfall there could be no wheat or barley, no flour, and, hence, no bread! Without rain there was famine.

The First Crop

Barley was the first major crop of the agricultural year. Though not as fine or desirable as wheat, it was heartier and easier to grow in that difficult climate. Since the winters in Canaan were usually rainy but mild, the grains planted in the fall could grow slowly during the winter months. In the spring, at the beginning of Passover, the barley would begin to ripen. Farmers would continue to harvest the crop for many weeks after Passover, and those Jews who lived close to Jerusalem would make a pilgrimage to the Temple, bringing the first cuttings of the barley crops as offerings of gratitude to God.

Three Types of Jews

Then, as now, there were at least three types of Jews. The first group came to the Temple diligently with their barley, giving thanks and praying for further blessings. For the priests these offerings were not only a matter of religious observance but their primary source of food.

The second group of farmers decided against making a pilgrimage to the Temple with their barley offerings, thinking to themselves: Why should we share this grain with anyone? We've harvested a good crop; we don't need to pray for what is already assured. So they stayed home.

The third group of farmers reasoned: We know we should bring the "first fruits" of our barley to Jerusalem to express our thanks to God, but it's a long trip. We don't feel so well and our wives and children need us. We'll go to the Temple for the next festival. We feel thankful, but we'd better stay home and tend to the chores.

It appears, according to ancient texts, that on Passover little more than one-third of the farmers journeyed to the Temple with their barley offerings.

"First Fruits"

Seven weeks after Passover, as every farmer knew from experience, the long-awaited wheat crop would begin to ripen in the region around Jerusalem. Again, one third of the farmers came to the Temple in Jerusalem with their first cuttings of the wheat crop (the "first fruits"–*bikurim*), this time on the holiday of *Shavuot*. One third or so, the "agnostics" of their day, stayed home. The remaining third found some excuse for not fulfilling what they truly felt was their obligation.

Then came summer. The rains had ended around Passover, followed by dry, hot, cloudless months during which the grapes and olives ripened, thriving in the arid climate. Figs, dates, and pomegranates–other staples of the Israeli diet–also flourished during this season.

Now the ground became hard as brick, baked dry by the summer sun. Soon it was fall, and all the crops, grains, and fruits had been harvested. If it had been a good year, all the farmers would feel the gratitude that comes with knowing there would be enough food to tide their families over until next year's crops ripened.

Sukot Was Different

Next came *Sukot*, and again the priests of the Temple in Jerusalem waited for the people to come with their offerings of thanksgiving. But, in contrast to *Pesach* and *Shavuot*, almost everyone came to the Temple. *Sukot* was different. On *Pesach* and *Shavuot* thanks were given for crops already harvested. But *Sukot* was not only for giving thanks for the past agricultural year and its seven basic products (barley, wheat, olives, grapes, figs, dates, and pomegranates) but for praying such bounty would continue. *Sukot* was the time to focus on the next agricultural year, particularly the beginning of the rainy season (fall and winter), which was absolutely crucial for the growth of future crops. Everyone worried about the unknown, whether there would be enough rain or too much. So on *Sukot* the special prayers for rain became the most important part of the holiday.

Torchlight Processions

The farmers came to the Temple believing they had to pray for rain. Even the "agnostics" probably reasoned, It may not do any good to pray for rain, but it certainly can't hurt, and, besides, you never know for sure. . . . So, they all came to the Temple in Jerusalem for the *Sukot* holiday, *the* Holiday. *Sukot* was a time of joy, torchlight processions, water libations on the altar, songs, and prayers for the future. In this society dependent on agriculture the people recognized many different kinds of rain, and for each they had a different name in Hebrew, just as the Arabs have many names for camels and Eskimos have many names for snow.

Three Types of Rain

Three types of rain were vital to the planting and growth of crops in ancient Israel:

1. **Early Rain** (*Yoreh*)–a light rain that came in the fall. It was essential in helping to soften the dry, sun-baked earth the summer heat had hardened, making it possible for the ancient one-pointed plow to churn up the earth and ready it for seeds. If the rain came down too hard, it washed away the seeds. If the light rain failed to fall, the hard earth could not be pierced by the plow and planted.
2. **Winter Rain** (*Geshem*)–the heavy midwinter rains that enabled the seeds to grow to their fullest. Too little rain could result in a poor crop and famine. Unlike many areas, where the winters are too cold for most crops and planting takes place in the spring, the area around Jerusalem experiences mild winters. Seeds planted in the fall grow during the winter and are harvested in the spring.
3. **Latter Rain** (*Malkosh*)–the light springtime showers that helped the barley and wheat grow to full maturity. If the heavy rains continued through the spring to Passover, the barley and wheat would be washed away, mildewed, or otherwise destroyed. If the rains stopped too early, before the spring, the crops would not grow to their fullest poten-

tial, resulting in shortages of the basic foods for everyone.

These descriptions clearly illustrate the three basic types of rainfall needed by the farmer in the area around Jerusalem. They did not just pray for rain. They had to pray for three different types of rain–early, heavy, and latter–to come at the right time of the cycle. Any variation from this rainfall curve could spell disaster. *Sukot*, which was celebrated at the start of the rainy season, became the Holiday (*Hechag*), the most important of all the Jewish holidays, because the prayers for rain, if answered, would enable the Jewish people to survive.

Rise of Rosh Hashanah

How did *Rosh Hashanah* and *Yom Kippur* become the High Holy Days? In ancient times the priests of almost every people observed a special day before their major harvest festival. On that day priests cleansed and purged their temples of all impurities, believing that such a ceremony of purification was necessary to make the harvest holiday prayers acceptable to their deities.

Priestly Holidays

Our ancestors accepted this priestly purification custom and created *Yom Kippur* in preparation of *Sukot*. Most of the Jews living in and around Jerusalem were not involved directly in the rituals of *Yom Kippur*. Ten days before *Yom Kippur*, on the first day of a day we now call *Rosh Hashanah*, the priests began their cleansing ceremonies. In other words, *Rosh Hashanah* was the day of preparation for *Yom Kippur*, which was the day of preparation for *Sukot*. The priests believed that something as important as *Sukot* had to be prepared for, and prepare they did.

Many years later the Jewish community began to change. Jews were no longer only farmers living in an agricultural society; many became merchants and traders. For the holidays to maintain their meaning for this new community, historical experiences, especially Exodus, were blended into each holiday observance. *Pesach* came to symbolize not only the barley harvest but also the Exodus from Egypt. *Sukot* began to symbolize not only the total harvest but also the Israelites' need to live in *sukot* (booths) during their wanderings in the wilderness. *Rosh Hashanah* became the symbol of the creation of the world. *Shavuot*, however, was not given a historical connection until late in the rabbinic period, when it was connected to the Revelation on Mount Sinai.

Historical Connections

That all these historical connections are later additions is clear from the specific symbols chosen. The *sukah* made of wood and branches could not have been used by the Israelites in their wilderness wanderings. They used tents of cloth or animal skins because wood was scarce. The *sukah* is actually similar to the booths that farmers built on their fields during the harvest season in which they stationed guards to protect their ripened crops from animals and thieves. Also, after the harvest, when pilgrims came to the Temple for the *Sukot* celebration, there were many more people in and around Jerusalem for the eight-day festivities than there were places to stay. So they built booths, temporary dwellings, in and around Jerusalem to meet their needs.

Origins of Matzah

The Passover *matzah* also had its origin in the agricultural life of pre-Israelite Canaan. Like the *sukah*, the *matzah* was given additional historical significance by its being linked with major historical events, in this case the hasty departure from Egypt. *Matzah*, however, was connected originally to the barley harvest, which took place in the spring at the same time as Passover. After the barley harvest the old barley flour that had been stored for a year was discarded along with the yeastlike leavening that enabled the dough to rise. In ancient times, before the discovery of yeast, the leavening was preserved in a clay jar and buried just below the surface of the ground inside the home. After a year of use it would begin to deteriorate. So, at Passover, when the new barley was tuned into flour for new bread, all the old leavening starter was discarded. The new bread would be made without leavening and look flat and dry, much like our *matzah* today, until the new leavening, made from the fresh flour, was ready a week later.

How did *Rosh Hashanah* and *Yom Kippur* become so important? After the Second Temple was destroyed in 70 C.E. a transformation took place. *Rosh Hashanah* and *Yom Kippur*, originally for priests, became holidays for all the people. Instead of being dedicated to the cleansing of the Temple (which no longer existed) and the priests (who no longer functioned), these days became a special time during which all Jews cleansed their souls and hearts from the impurities of sins and faults.

Revival of Sukot

Since no person is ever free of fault or error, and since we all need to feel we can improve and make a new start, *Rosh Hashanah* and *Yom Kippur* served to satisfy a basic human and Jewish need. Thus they became the High Holy Days, the most important days of the Jewish year. *Pesach* became the holiday during which scattered families reunited at the *seder*, expressing their togetherness, their ties to their Jewish past, and their hope for the future. *Shavuot* came to symbolize the Torah, the teachings of Judaism, and our recommitment to those moral and ethical principles that suffuse our tradition. But *Sukot*, which was once the most important of holidays, was all but forgotten, though its symbols apply to our age in a meaningful way. *Sukot* and its prayers for rain symbolize our dependence on nature. It awakens in us the fear of what could happen if we interfere with that life-sustaining system, allowing the pollution and destruction of our planet.

A renewal and revival of *Sukot* in our time could serve as a symbolic reminder of our need to preserve and protect our environment, so the rains, without acid, may fall and the earth continue to give forth its life-giving crops.

▪ Understanding Shabbat ▪

On *Shabbat* God, resting from the work of Creation, set aside a special occasion to hallow time. As we have seen, that act became the paradigm for sanctification of time daily and throughout the calendar. We are commanded not only to remember but also to observe *Shabbat*. A prime example of the dual nature of Jewish festivals, *Shabbat* celebrates Creation, an event in the natural order, and *Shabbat* commemorates the Exodus from Egypt, an event in history. *Shabbat* is doubly *kadosh*, holy; it is holier than any other day save *Yom Kippur.* Even the supreme holiness of *Yom Kippur* is expressed in *Shabbat* language: It is called the Sabbath of Sabbaths. The Safed mystics invested *Shabbat* with additional special meaning by naming it both Queen and Bride, the exalted holy companion of the Jewish people.

In the following the authors consider several aspects of *Shabbat*. How is *Shabbat* related to *berit*, covenant? What does *Shabbat* have to do with slavery? Describe ethical concomitants to *Shabbat*. *Shabbat* is supremely important. Why, then, has *Shabbat* been so prone to desecration by so many Jews? You are commanded to violate *Shabbat* to save life. Explain why. *Shabbat* observance is not fulfilled by being passive, by doing nothing on the day of rest. Explain.

▪ Understanding Shabbat

BY STEVEN SCHNUR, BERNARD M. ZLOTOWITZ, AND ARON HIRT-MANHEIMER ▪

Shabbat embodies the essence of Judaism, symbolizing the relationship of the Jewish people to God and to humankind. So important is the Sabbath that it alone of all Jewish festivals is mentioned in the Creation story and in the Ten Commandments; not even Yom Kippur shares that privilege.

The Ten Commandments appears twice in the Torah, once in Exodus and again in Deuteronomy. In the first instance the Fourth Commandment begins with the words: "Remember the Sabbath day, to keep it holy." The Sabbath refers to the day God ceased from the labor of creation on the seventh day. In imitation of God we are forbidden to work on the Sabbath. This prohibition extends to slaves, cattle, and strangers in our midst. (Exod. 20:8-11)

The Fourth Commandment in Deuteronomy differs in two significant ways from its formulation in Exodus. First, it begins with "Observe (and not "Remember") the Sabbath day, to keep it holy." (Deut. 5:12-15) Second, instead of referring to God's resting on the seventh day as a model for human conduct, it cites the Israelites' Exodus from Egypt as the basis for observing the Sabbath. The Jews are reminded: "You were a slave in the land of Egypt and the Lord your God brought you out from there with a mighty hand and an outstretched arm; therefore, the Lord your God commanded you to observe the Sabbath day."

Shabbat as Covenant

By referring to the Exodus from Egypt, the Fourth Commandment reminds Jews of their covenant with God, the lessons of their history, and the evils of slavery. The Torah, recognizing the ease with which humans enslave themselves to ideas, routines, and to one another, provided the Sabbath as a weekly counterforce. One who never experiences freedom may neither yearn nor strive for it, but the slave who tastes freedom even one day a week will eventually rebel against enslavement.

How the Sabbath was to be observed by the Israelites was first set forth in the Bible in the context of the forty years of wandering in Sinai. The first practical lesson in Sabbath observance involved the gathering of manna in the desert. Sent by God to feed the wandering Israelites, the dewlike sweet bread fell from the heavens every morning except the morning of the Sabbath. On Friday a double portion was provided to last the entire *Shabbat.* God, through the Sabbath, taught these former slaves how to plan ahead for their future, how to think like free people.

Following their conquest of Canaan, it became customary for the Israelites to offer animal and grain sacrifices on the Sabbath, in keeping with the laws of the Bible. (Numbers 28:9-10) It was also common practice on the seventh day to visit a "man of God" or prophet. (2 Kings 4:22-23)

Difficult to Observe

Although the Sabbath was deemed in the Bible to be among the most important of Jewish holy days, second only to Yom Kippur, the Fourth Commandment proved difficult to observe. Repeatedly the Bible echoes God's angry admonition: "You have despised My holy things and profaned My Sabbaths." (Ezek. 22:8) The prophets linked Israel's fate to Sabbath observance. The destruction of the First Temple and the subsequent Babylonian Exile, according to Jeremiah, were the result of Israel's failure to keep the Sabbath. (Jer. 17:21-27) Even after the Jews returned to Jerusalem to rebuild the walls of their holy city about a century and a half after its devastation, they continued to desecrate the Sabbath. Said Nehemiah: "Did not your ancestors thus and did not our God bring all this evil . . . upon us and upon this city? Yet you bring more wrath upon Israel by profaning the Sabbath." (Neh. 13:18) Shifting the emphasis from admonition to reward, Isaiah called the Sabbath a "delight," promising: "If you refrain from trampling the Sabbath. . . . / And call the Sabbath a delight. . . . I will make you ride upon the heights of the earth, / And I will feed you with the heritage of your father Jacob. . . . " (Isa. 58:13-14)

Saving a Life

In the early years of the Maccabean revolt at least one group of Jews refused to defend itself on the seventh day, preferring death to Sabbath desecration. (*1 Macc.* 2:32-38) Following this tragedy, Mattathias and his sons set a precedent that would be expanded in the Talmud: to save a life or to defend one's life it is permissible to violate the Sabbath. (*1 Macc. 2:41*)

Many of the Sabbath rituals originated during the period of the Talmud. Elaborating on the Bible's general and often vague Sabbath prohibitions, the Talmud sought to formalize and thereby protect its observance, listing in detail all acts prohibited on *Shabbat.* To the thirty-nine types of forbidden labor–modeled on the tasks performed by the priests in constructing the tabernacle (Exodus 31)–the rabbis added "fences" designed to minimize the likelihood of violating the Sabbath. Thus, since the rabbis interpreted the Bible to prohibit writing on *Shabbat,* they also outlawed the carrying of a writing implement on the seventh day.

In the process of clarifying biblical law, the rabbis sought to lessen its severity. For example, the Bible states: "You shall kindle no fire in all your habitations on the day of *Shabbat.*" (Exod. 35:3) A strict interpretation would have prohibited the use of fire or heat in any form for the duration of the Sabbath. The rabbis, however, permitted the use of fire for light or heat, so long as it had been kindled before the onset of *Shabbat.*

These laws, collected in the Talmud, formed the blueprint for *Shabbat* observance. Elaborating both on what should not be done in violation of the Sabbath and what should be done to enhance it, the Talmud provides laws concerning travel, work, lighting candles, eating, praying, caring for the sick, sexual relations, childbirth, circumcision, and virtually every aspect of human endeavor that might occur on the Sabbath.

A Jew Celebrates

Honoring the Sabbath

Central to the liturgical practices instituted by the rabbis were the recitation of *Kiddush* at the beginning and *Havdalah* at the end of *Shabbat.* These sanctify the Sabbath by setting it apart from the other six days. Honoring the Sabbath, the rabbis taught, consists of preparing for it as if for a royal visit, bathing oneself, cleaning house, and dressing in one's finest clothes. Delight, they said, consists of eating special foods, taking pleasure in one's spouse, resting, and studying Torah. "One who delights in the Sabbath," the Talmud says, "is given one's heart's desires." (*Shab.* 118b)

Intermingled with these laws are the sayings and legends that have enlivened Jewish culture, folklore, and literature for two thousand years. Never losing sight of the prophet Isaiah's description of the Sabbath as a day of delight, the ancient rabbis spoke repeatedly of it as a special inheritance from God, a gift, a blessing, a Bride, a Queen, a foretaste of the world to come.

The sixteenth-century Kabbalists of Safed in northern Israel and the Chasidim of eighteenth-century Eastern Europe enhanced the job of Sabbath observance by expanding on ideas contained in the talmudic literature. Favorite among these was the concept of the Sabbath as a Bride, which was later incorporated in the Sabbath poem "*Lecha Dodi*" written by the Safed mystic Solomon Alkabetz:

Come my beloved to meet the Bride
Let us welcome the presence of the Sabbath
Come in peace . . . and come in joy . . .
Come, O Bride! Come, O Bride!

The rabbis viewed the Sabbath as the royal road to redemption, saying, "If Israel were to keep two Sabbaths according to their prescribed law, they would immediately be redeemed." (*Shab.* 118b) That theme prevails to the present day, whether it be redemption from sin through Sabbath prayer or the redemption of one's humanity through rest and reflection.

This belief in the saving power of *Shabbat* found modern expression in the writings of Ahad

THE ROOTS OF SHABBAT

According to traditional Jewish belief, the Sabbath has its origin in God's divine command to observe the seventh day as a day of rest and sanctification. Scholars, on the other hand, are divided in their opinion concerning the origin of the Sabbath, though they all agree it was borrowed from another culture. Some scholars contend its origin is Babylonian. The Babylonians believed the seventh, fourteenth, twenty-first, and twenty-eighth days of the month (following the phases of the moon) were evil days and therefore the physician, the oracular priest, and the king ceased all labor on these days. The cessation of work on the day they called *Sabattu* was based upon fear and had no relation to the biblical concept of the Sabbath as a day of rest, joy, and refreshment of soul.

Other scholars contend the Hebrews borrowed the concept from the Canaanites, whose primitive agricultural calendar was based on a seven-day week. Here, too, the number seven was regarded as evil and unlucky, a potential source of ill fortune to be avoided at all costs. They viewed this final day of the week as a day when evil spirits abounded, and therefore as a day in which human labor would not prosper.

The ancient Hebrews, however, transformed this negative character of the seventh day into one of joy, refraining from labor because it was a day of gladness of spirit. None of the scholarly theories explain how and why the Jews, who were supposed to have borrowed the Sabbath from the Canaanites or Babylonians, accomplished this transformation.

Traditionally Judaism teaches that the Sabbath was unique to ancient Hebrew culture and not influenced by others. It contends that the Sabbath as a day of rest and joy is our special contribution to the world, a gift from the Jewish people to all humankind.

Bernard M. Zlotowitz

Ha-Am, who in 1898 observed: "More than Israel has kept the Sabbath, the Sabbath has kept Israel. Had it not been for the Sabbath, which weekly restored to the people "soul" and weekly renewed their spirit, the weekday afflictions would have pulled them further and further downward until they sank to the lowest depths of materialism as well as ethical and intellectual poverty."

Idols of Technical Civilization

"On the seventh day," wrote the modern sage Abraham Heschel, "[one] has no right to tamper with God's world, to change the state of physical things." On that day we should set aside our technological mastery of nature. Believing *Shabbat* to hold out our best hope for progress, Heschel described the seventh day as "one day a week for freedom, a day on which we would not use the instruments that have been so easily turned into weapons of destruction . . . a day in which we stop worshiping the idols of technical civilization. . . ."

In a recent booklet Rabbi Irving Greenberg called *Shabbat* "the temporary anti-reality of perfection." On the Sabbath, he wrote, "all things are seen through the eyes of love, as if all nature were perfect, in harmony with itself, and with us." In Greenberg's view this foretaste of the redemption is not a substitute for redemptive action. "Thanks to *Shabbat*," he continued, "there is enough fulfillment in the here and now to keep people in motion toward the final consummation. . . . The world was meant to be perfect. Says the *Shabbat*: "Experience that perfection. Now, go and make it happen!"

▪ Invitation to a Mystery ▪

Believe it or not, the Passover Haggadah has appeared in nearly four thousand different editions over the centuries. It is, arguably, the best-known of all Jewish prayer books. Yet, it is perhaps the least understood. It is a profound work of history, poetry, theology, moral teaching. It is a saga of redemption and of gratitude. It operates on many levels, including the disarmingly simple recital of the Exodus from Egypt and the birth of the Jewish nation. The term "Haggadah" comes from the Hebrew verb *lehagid*, "to tell." The Haggadah is the vehicle through which to fulfill the commandment to tell the story (Exodus 13:8). But, as you will see, there's a lot more to it than merely "serving up the facts."

The reading that follows encourages you to examine the Haggadah's secrets, to enter the pages on a detective search. Why are the Haggadah and the seder, together, "religion at the highest"? *Midrashim* are stories told by the rabbis to expand upon or illustrate a point in the tradition. What accounts for the many insertions of *midrashim* in the Haggadah right up to this day? Or for the many extant versions of the Haggadah? Your attitude toward the Haggadah and your knowledge about it are equally important to understanding its mysteries. Why?

▪ Invitation to a Mystery

BY LAWRENCE A. HOFFMAN ▪

What is the magnetic and never-ending appeal of the Passover Haggadah? Every year new editions roll off the presses–new translations, new versions, new formats, at times with brilliant art and illustrations. There are Passover Haggadahs in countless forms and languages. Some are very modern and streamlined, omitting some familiar portions and ceremonies. Others are very traditional, with all the old customs and symbols. There are even versions issued by kibbutzim that proclaim their atheism! What is the secret of the Haggadah's hold on the imagination of Jews?

There are so many answers that it is hard to single out *the* answer, the real reason for the deepest attraction of the *Haggadah shel Pesach*. The Haggadah is literally the "telling" of the Passover story, and, in the course of telling it, we conduct a *seder*, an "order of service," according to the instructions in the Haggadah. The Haggadah and the service go together, so it is impossible to separate one from the other. Everyone has a favorite part of the Haggadah and the seder. Children like the Four Questions, the hunt for the *afikoman*, or opening the door for Elijah. Everyone likes the joyful songs. People of all ages are delighted by the symbols, by the idea of a festive family banquet served with wine, or by the mood of the Haggadah–the fresh optimism of spring. All of these elements play some role in explaining the emotional appeal of the ceremony spelled out in the Haggadah. But they are not *the* reason for the eternal appeal of the Haggadah.

Sense of Mystery

The entire Passover seder that is spelled out in the Haggadah is a ritual. That is its secret. A ritual is like a large magnet in a sieve. The magnet attracts individual particles of human experience that are related to one another. It pulls them together and holds them together by a compelling and powerful force. As centuries of Jewish life pass through the sieve, a cluster of folk memories, customs, and legends collect, all of them representing eons of Jewish participation in that force at the core of the magnet.

The magnetic force at the very core of the Haggadah is the universal human yearning for freedom. For the Jew, this yearning is best expressed in the great Exodus from Egypt. But this particular event has been overlaid through time by countless other related incidents supplied by every generation up to and including our own. Each generation has left us symbolic representations of its own thoughts and feelings, and they are there clinging to the "magnet," the ritual of the Haggadah. So the Haggadah and the seder together are "religion" at its highest and best: a dramatic and self-contained ritual providing us with two precious things at the same time–a link with our ancestors and a rare depth of insight into ourselves. It is one of the few genuine rituals left to us in the modern world, and Jews who lose touch with it lose touch with themselves.

But ritual, as a rare form of communication, is not easily appreciated. It can best be compared to a slide show of surrealistic paintings flashing before our eyes. Each separate item, as each separate paragraph in the Haggadah, is a story in itself. Each section is more than it appears to be. Everything stands for something else. When the slide show is over, we realize we have just experienced something tremendously deep and have been touched to our core in a way that defies description.

That, at least, is what is *supposed* to happen at the seder, and sometimes it does; or, at least, it still can, providing we *want* it to happen. But everything depends upon having a bit of knowledge and the courage to enter the realm of religious mystery. If we are unwilling to come to the seder with a sense of mystery, we lose everything.

Reliving History

So our Passover Haggadah begins with the *Kiddush* and, on Saturday nights, with the *Havdalah*. Both are acts of separation by which we leave the world of the profane and enter the domain of the sacred. We even wash our hands, ritually, as a symbol of the transformation. Like Alice in Wonderland, we are about to enter a world where imagination is unfettered, where we have transformed ourselves into our own ancestors and relive their history, going–as the rabbis phrased it–"from degradation to glory." This past is not merely to be *read*, but it is actually to be *relived* and *felt*. Lifting up a broken piece of matzah, we imagine ourselves back in Egypt. "This is the bread of affliction . . . [and] now we are slaves."

The Four Questions that follow are meant to express the wonder of this mysterious night. They deal with relatively simple and obvious examples of the night's uniqueness, so they do not need any immediate and direct replies. The real question that underlies the Four Questions is unspoken. It is: "What are we doing in this night's strange performance? What is the play all about?" The answer is supplied by the remainder of the Haggadah.

This answer was originally in the form of a rabbinic embroidery on the story of how the Israelites descended to Egypt, were enslaved, and then redeemed, going from "degradation to glory." But, in the third century of the Common Era, the rabbis prefaced this embroidery with two insertions that help us to probe more deeply into the meaning of this extraordinary experience. What, after all, is "degradation"? What was the ultimate misery of the Jewish people?

The first section talks about physical slavery: "We were slaves to Pharaoh in Egypt." We were miserable and degraded because we were held in physical bondage; we were wretched, lowly slaves. But a few pages later the second section added by the rabbis gives us yet another interpretation. Physical slavery is bad, yes, but, when it is forcibly imposed from the outside, slavery is not in itself necessarily shameful. Powerful armies can subdue weak nations; but might is no guarantee of right. The worst kind of slavery, the lowest kind of ignominy, is self-imposed slavery of the mind. In other words, it is stubborn, willful, deliberate ignorance. To worship idols when the truth of the One God shines everywhere, to cling to idolatry when God's truth is evident, is like putting on a pair of blinders. To practice idolatry is to impose slavery on oneself. So, in the second section added by the rabbis in the third century, we read: "In the beginning our ancestors were idolators. . . . " That was our *true* degradation. We were enslaved by our own ignorance.

If we wish, we may pause here to ponder these

two sections. The Haggadah nowhere tells us we *have* to pause, but the Haggadah, remember, is no simple textbook. It is a *ritual*, and the instructions for that ritual are barely hinted at in a kind of very sketchy shorthand. For example, in the first section there are two anecdotes that invite us to speculate freely. One is the fascinating story of the five rabbis whose seder lasted until dawn–a story suggesting to us that, when we allow ourselves to celebrate ritual, we cannot place any arbitrary time limitations on our imaginations. We have to open ourselves up to the fullness of the night's promise. The second anecdote is the famous story of the Four Children. Each of them comes to the seder with a different attitude. The story invites each of us to ask ourselves, "What is my attitude?"

Levels of Meaning

The traditional Haggadah contains much midrashic lore, commentaries by the rabbis with many levels of meaning. How much simpler it would have been to tell only the plain, straightforward biblical story! But the rabbis did not read the Bible according to the plain meaning, and tonight's encounter with the past is no plain or simple recitation. The purpose of the Haggadah is not to serve up facts–which we probably already knew–but to celebrate ritual. As the Haggadah itself says at one point: "Even if we were all wise . . . it would still be a mitzvah to relate the Exodus, and to expand on the story is praiseworthy." For religious ritual is the discovery of the new in the repetition of the old. Last year's wisdom is no longer relevant. Tonight we relive history anew, engage in fresh speculation, and take part in our people's glorious deliverance.

One midrash in the traditional Haggadah raises a whole series of fascinating speculations. Who, you might ask, is the villain of the Haggadah? It is Pharaoh himself. But if we look at the traditional Haggadah, we discover there is another villain even more evil than Pharaoh. He is none other than Jacob's father-in-law, Laban the Aramean. Why? The rabbis remembered that Pharaoh ordered the death of male Hebrew infants but spared the female babies. (See Exodus 1:22.) But they also remembered that Laban the Aramean pursued Jacob when he finally fled from his father-in-law's service. (Genesis 31:23) He would actually have slain Jacob "root and branch" if God had not intervened for Jacob. Why is this story about Laban the Aramean in the Haggadah? Did first-century Jews perceive in the Hebrew word *Arami* (=Aramean) a veiled reference to the Hebrew word *Romi* (=Rome), the cruel oppressor who had just sacked and destroyed Jerusalem? Was this their way of expressing anger at murderous Rome?

The rabbis are careful to emphasize in the Haggadah the verse in Deuteronomy 26:8, "And the Eternal brought us forth out of Egypt with a mighty hand, and with an outstretched arm. . . . " It is God, and God alone, they insisted, who brings deliverance. Certainly that quotation belongs in the Haggadah because it is basic to the story of the Exodus. But did that quotation come to mean something *in addition* around the first and second centuries when Christianity was seeking converts? Should this passage be read as a rejection of, and a warning against, false messiahs? Against Christianity itself, perhaps? Was the need to warn against would-be human saviors so strong back in the first century that the rabbis went to the extreme of excluding even an *authentic* Jewish hero? The name of Moses himself, the great human leader of the Exodus, is omitted from the Passover Haggadah.

Masters of Ritual

First-century Jews were masters at celebrating ritual. They appreciated symbolic language and had no trouble seeing the Egyptian experience as a model for their own painful times. They, no less than their ancestors, saw the world for what it is: an imperfect residence for finite human beings who yearn for certainty and hope for better times. "Why is this night different from all other nights?" Because tonight, through story and legend and ritual, we recapture the essential Jewish experience of hope. No matter how difficult the world, we must always continue to hope.

Later ages in our history added to our Haggadah further sections that elaborate on the Passover theme: the recitation of the Ten Plagues, plus *midrashim* commenting on them: and the familiar song "*Dayyenu,*" which recounts each separate stage of deliverance, saying after each, "It [alone] would have been enough" to meet our gratitude.

Before we eat the Passover meal the Haggadah explains the three major symbols of the seder: the paschal lamb (*pesach*), matzah, and bitter herbs (*maror*). Before the year 70 such an explanation was not demanded. It is also likely that the actual meal, which now *follows* the recitation of the Haggadah, the "telling," was at that time eaten much earlier in the proceedings, probably before the asking of the Four Questions. But the rise of Christianity led to a restructuring of the seder. Since early Christians believed Jesus' last supper was a seder, many of them celebrated a seder but gave it novel Christian interpretations. They ate the meal at the beginning of the evening and, when they came to the special symbolic foods, they spoke of their significance to Christians. So the rabbis moved the meal to what was then the *end* of the Haggadah; and they prefaced the meal with a Jewish explanation of the symbolic foods that would be eaten.

By the second century the Haggadah and seder went from questions to midrashic answers, to a discussion of symbols, and then to the seder meal. Just before eating, a part of the age-old *Hallel* (Psalms 113-118) was recited, along with a benediction thanking God for redeeming us. After dinner and the grace after meals, the *Hallel* was completed. The night's festivities were ended with fitting words of praise from the Psalms.

Eating plays an important role in the celebration of ritual. Sharing a common meal has major implications for a people recollecting its very ancient origins. So ordinary foods were transposed into symbolic substances (for example, bitter herbs = the bitterness of slavery). At various times in history different foods became popular, but each one in its turn bore the same essential message of a people once enslaved, now dedicated to freedom. Eggs, for example, whose very roundness suggests time without end and rebirth, found their way into the Passover seder, into Jewish mourning customs, and also the Christian Easter. The *afikoman* came to be a replacement for the last bite of the paschal lamb with which Jews had once ended the evening.

But, as a living and growing ritual, this basic seder expanded steadily throughout the Middle Ages. Folk songs like *"Adir Hu"* and *"Chad Gadya"* were added. It was in the Middle Ages that the symbolic climax of the Haggadah and the seder was moved to after the completion of the meal. At that time Jews recalled an old custom of drinking a fifth cup of wine and saying along with it Psalm 136. (Our traditional Haggadah has retained the psalm but omits the fifth cup; the new Reform Haggadah has brought back the fifth cup.) According to one old interpretation, four cups of wine were sipped, each one of them marking a separate example of deliverance in Jewish history. Some Jews in the Middle Ages began to drink a fifth cup to signify the final act of redemption yet to come, the advent of the Messiah. Other medieval Jews chose not to drink the fifth cup, but they poured wine into the cup and left it ready on the table in case Elijah should appear suddenly to announce the arrival of the Messiah.

In the Middle Ages another old custom—opening the door for guests coming to the seder–was reinterpreted to mean a welcome for the prophet Elijah. This act of opening the door came to be accompanied by the recitation of certain biblical passages (beginning with Psalm 79:6, "Pour out Thy wrath upon the nations that know Thee not . . . "). In the time of the Crusades these powerful words were probably intended as a bitter comment on the massacres of German Jewish communities by marauding knights and other brutal persecutors. How many Jews waited anxiously in those harsh times for the prophet Elijah really to materialize on this seder eve! How many of them prayed to hear the news that ultimate redemption was finally at hand, that Israel's enemies at last would be punished, and that "next year"–as the concluding line puts it–we would celebrate "in Jerusalem"!

The essence of the Haggadah has always been the symbolic language of its religious ritual. The seder participants who are sensitive and alert to that language will discover the mystery of true liturgical experience. A rapid succession of associations evoked by the symbols has permitted us to plumb the very depths of our being. We rise from the table having *personally* been freed from slavery in Egypt, having *personally* fought Rome, and *personally* confronted the Crusaders. We are part of Israel, a people that has known degradation but still dares to hope and to pray for a glorious future.

▪ Plum Jam and Other Purims ▪

Despite its folk frivolity and pious pandemonium, *Purim* has a very serious side: it celebrates salvation and redemption. That's a sober theme for a playful occasion. Yet, what better way to remember survival than with merrymaking, song, and wine? God is not mentioned in *Megillat Esther.* Yet, God is assuredly at the core of the story. God saves God's people from the Hamans of history. That's reason enough to fire the imagination of a grateful folk.

The following reminds us that many Jews and Jewish communities, threatened with extinction, have been saved miraculously. Shushan and Persia thus became metaphors for happy outcomes in precarious circumstances. Jews attribute their redemption to God. Therefore, Jews continue to celebrate ancient and recent deliverances just as Mordecai ordered the first *Purim* to be observed forever (Esther 9:28). What can we learn about Jewish values from the custom of celebrating special *Purims*?

■ Plum Jam and Other Purims

BY DAVID ALTSHULER ■

Eighteen generations ago a miracle was done for the Jews, indeed for my own family. My relative Hanokh ben Moses Altschul escaped death at the hands of a wicked government, and from that day to this his fortune has not been forgotten. Hanokh, you see, created his own Purim–but first the story.

In the winter of 1622-1623 valuable damask curtains were stolen from the Prague palace of Count Charles of Lichtenstein, who was away on travels. The Jews of Prague were told that, if the curtains should turn up, they should immediately be handed over to the synagogue *shamash*, who happened to be my relative Hanokh. A certain Jew, Joseph ben Jekuthiel Thien, did exactly that, saying he had bought the curtains, without knowing they had been stolen, from two soldiers. Hanokh returned the curtains to the palace, but the mayor insisted on knowing who had turned them in.

"Curtain Purim"

Now Hanokh was in trouble, for the rules of the Prague congregation specifically forbade informing government authorities of the identity of anyone who voluntarily surrendered stolen merchandise. Hanokh refused to give in, and he was imprisoned and sentenced to hang the next day. In order to save the life of the innocent *shamash* the president of the congregation gave special permission for him to break the rules. Then the Jews of Prague, with the help of a righteous, prominent Christian, persuaded the mayor not to hang the Jew Joseph either.

The Jews did not escape persecution entirely, however. They were sentenced to pay a huge community fine of 10,000 florins. To add to their humiliation, this fine had to be delivered by ten Jewish leaders, each carrying a linen bag of silver coins to city hall, escorted through the streets by soldiers.

The story does not end there. Hanokh was so grateful his and other lives had been saved that

he declared the day of his release–the twenty-second of the Hebrew month Tevet–as "Altschul Purim," sometimes also called "Curtain Purim." He even wrote a special *megillah* for that holy day, and he urged his family–my ancestors–always to observe their special Purim every year on the anniversary of the miracle.

Plum Jam and Other Purims

Hanokh was one of many Jews in our history to create their own Purim, a second Purim, because of a miracle that befell their community or their family. Indeed, the *Encyclopaedia Judaica* lists some 110 special Purim celebrations created in the last thousand years. Here are a few interesting examples:

–"Snow Purim," created in 1891 by the Jews of Tunisia, when a Jewish neighborhood escaped harm from a blizzard that destroyed much property and took the lives of many non-Jews.

–"Window Purim," established in 1741 by the Jews of Hebron, who had been sentenced by a governor to be sold into slavery or burned to death unless they could deliver an enormous ransom in three days. The sum was more than anyone believed possible to acquire, so the Jews fasted and prayed for divine help. On the final day someone discovered on the windowsill of the local synagogue a purse containing enough money to pay the ransom, and this miracle saved the community.

–"Plum Jam Purim," began in 1731 by the Brandeis family of Bohemia, when they were cleared of a false accusation of having tried to poison a Christian family by sending them a jar of contaminated jam.

Even in our own times new Purim celebrations have been instituted as new miracles have occurred. Here are two such innovative holy days:

–"Hitler Purim," established in 1943 by the Jews of Casablanca, when they escaped violence and oppression by the Nazis. To commemorate this joyous occasion, they wrote a *megillah* that curses Hitler and all of his leading officers by name.

–"Frimer Family Purim," first celebrated in the spring of 1978 by Rabbi Norman Frimer and his family to recall the events of March 1977, when Rabbi Frimer and over a hundred other innocent people were held hostage at the Washington headquarters of B'nai B'rith (along with others at the District Building and the Islamic Center in Washington) by a group of fanatical Hanafi Muslims. The hostages were held for thirty-nine hours, threatened with death if their captors' outrageous and illegal demands were not met. The Frimer family resolved never to forget that their prayers were finally answered when police and three ambassadors from Middle Eastern countries convinced the kidnapers to give up their scheme. For the year following the miracle Rabbi and Mrs. Frimer, together with their children and grandchildren, labored to create a family observance suitable for the first anniversary celebration.

Remembering Miracles

Purim can be a very personal holiday when it recalls events significant in the lives of individual Jews, families, or particular communities. Yet the Purim all Jews celebrate on the fourteenth of Adar also began in one place–Shushan–and thanks to one Jew, Esther, and her uncle Mordecai. The custom of creating a second Purim is very old, and it is consistent with Judaism's tradition of recognizing and responding to the divine impact on history wherever and whenever it may occur.

The rabbis of the Mishnah state that one should bless God, who did miracles for our ancestors, whenever seeing a place where a miracle was done for Israel. The Talmud (*Ber.* 54a) goes on to explain that Jethro, on seeing his son-in-law Moses, blessed God for redeeming Israel from Egyptian slavery. (Exod. 18:10) The rabbis add examples from their own days of pious Jews who blessed God for saving them from wild beasts, drought, and the like.

Personal Holy Days

Thus, creating a second Purim naturally comes from the desire to praise and thank God for mercy and salvation. Individuals, families, and whole communities may create their own holy days, on which they recite special psalms and read a special *megillah* describing their miraculous fortune. The day prior to a special Purim there will often be a fast like the Fast of Esther on the thirteenth of Adar. And, on the holy day itself, a festive meal and distribution of food to friends and gifts to the poor are common.

What can we learn from this beautiful custom of the special Purim? First, we have occasions for learning about important events in the history of the Jewish people. Second, we may see how our own families and communities were themselves touched by divine destiny. Finally, we may appreciate the miraculous that enters life, and we give thanks for our lot and share our blessings with others. All this is important, "that the days of Purim should always be observed among the Jews, and that the memory of them should never cease among their descendants." (Esther 9:28)

• The Festival Megillot •

The Hebrew word *megillot* means scrolls; singular, *megillah*. When we say "the" *Megillah*, that usually means the Scroll of Esther, which is read on *Purim*. The Five Scrolls are the shortest books of the Bible section called *Ketuvim*, Writings. But length does not imply importance or the opposite: the Five Scrolls contain many of Judaism's most significant ideas and chronicle some of our most important experiences. Like the Torah itself, the books are often retained in scroll form to this day for easy access and to preserve their specialness. The Book of Esther, however, is always written on a parchment scroll.

The article that follows describes why and how Song of Songs, the Book of Ruth, and Ecclesiastes came to be associated with the pilgrim festivals of *Pesach, Shavuot,* and *Sukot* respectively. *Purim* has been considered in an earlier article of this chapter. Lamentations, not discussed here, is assigned for *Tishah Be'av* reading. Why?

■ The Festival Megillot   BY ALLEN S. KAPLAN ■

Among the Hebrew Scriptures is a group of books called the *Megillot*, the Five Scrolls. The most familiar of those is *Megillat Esther*, which is read in the synagogue on *Purim*. The other scrolls include Song of Songs (*Pesach*), Ruth (*Shavuot*), Lamentations (*Tishah Be'av*), and Ecclesiastes (*Sukot*). Each of these *megillot* is an important part of the liturgical celebration of the festivals.

In the synagogue, as part of the Torah service on each of the Pilgrim Festivals, one of the *megillot* is read. On *Shabbat Chol Hamoed Pesach*, the Sabbath of the Intermediary Days of Passover, the Song of Songs is read. On *Shavuot*, the Book of Ruth is read. Ecclesiastes, also known by the Hebrew word *Kohelet*, is read on *Shabbat Chol Hamoed Sukot*, the Sabbath of the Intermediary Days of *Sukot*.

Season of Rebirth

Passover commemorates the Exodus from Egypt. It is also a festival of thanksgiving for the barley harvest of ancient times and therefore a celebration of spring. During the seder, we dip *karpas* (parsley) and eat a roasted egg, both symbols of rebirth. For ancient people the arrival of spring meant that the earth literally was reborn after having died in autumn. The fields returned to life and new crops were planted. It was a season of promise and hope, and a time for love. The love between a man and a woman was thought to bring fertility to the fields and an abundant harvest to the farmer.

The Song of Songs, which we read during *Pesach*, is erotic love poetry. When the Bible was canonized, some rabbis were distressed by the lusty earthiness of this book. Others said it was not about a man and a woman but an allegory symbolizing God's love for Israel. However it is read, all agree it contains a joyous outburst of love. If spring is the time for lovers, and Passover a celebration of spring, then the Song of Songs is perfectly suited to the holiday.

My beloved is coming–hear his voice.
He leaps upon the mountains, he skips on the hills.
My beloved is like a stag or a young deer.
Now he is standing beyond our wall;
He is looking through the window;
He is peering through the lattice;
He speaks and says to me:
"Get up, my beloved,
My beautiful one, and come away,
For the winter is over;
The rainy season is over and gone.
The flowers appear in the land,
The time of bird songs is here,
And the voice of the turtledove is heard in the land.
The fig tree puts forth its green figs
And the grapevines in blossom
Send forth their fragrance.
Get up, my beloved, my fair one,
My beautiful one, and come away.
O my dove, in the clefts of the rock,
In the hidden place of the cliff

Let me see your form and let me hear your
  voice,
For your voice is pleasant and your form is
  beautiful."

(Song of Songs 2:8-15, translation by Dr. Samuel Sandmel,
The Hebrew Scriptures)

Portrait of Biblical Life

The Book of Ruth, which we read on *Shavuot*,
is so beautifully written, so pastoral in style, it
is a favorite among avid readers of Scripture. Set
during the period when the judges ruled Israel
(around 1200 B.C.E.), it paints a lovely picture of
biblical life. In it Ruth, a Moabite widow, has
returned with her mother-in-law, Naomi, to
Naomi's homeland, Judah. Ruth is determined to
cast her lot with her new people and their faith.
She supports herself and Naomi by gleaning the
fields of grain left behind. The Bible enjoins
farmers during the harvest season to be aware
of the plight of the poor by leaving for them any
grain that has fallen to the ground during the
harvest. In addition the Bible instructs farmers
to leave the corners of their fields for the
poor.

The picture of the harvest presented in the
Book of Ruth is perfectly suited to a festival that
offers thanks to our Creator for the abundance
that sustains rich and poor alike.

The last of the three Pilgrim Festivals, *Sukot*,
is the ultimate thanksgiving festival. The final
crops of the year are harvested as the season of
life comes to a close. *Pesach* is exuberant,
Shavuot is pastoral, and *Sukot* is introspective.
During this festival we are instructed to live in
frail booths symbolic of the huts our ancestors
lived in during the harvest time of biblical days
and during their trek through the Sinai
wilderness.

"A Time to Be Born, a Time to Die"

Why do we read Ecclesiastes on this holiday?
Full of pessimism, it speaks of everything being
"vanity," "a striving after wind," and of there
being "nothing new under the sun." Its skepti-
cism and cynicism are not prevalent in Hebrew
thought.

Perhaps if we were to equate maturity with
pessimism, we could say that Ecclesiastes is a
compendium of mature advice by a mature person for mature people. And, if we were to say
the hope of spring gives way to the despair of
autumn, then Ecclesiastes is well matched for
Sukot. But maturity is not properly equated with
pessimism, nor is autumn a time for despair.
When we pause in the midst of our bounty to
reflect upon life, we begin to count our blessings
and often we realize how fortunate we are. We
are able to place our lives in proper
perspective.

There is a time to be born and a time to die.
There is a time to plant and a time to pluck up
what is planted.
There is a time to kill and a time to heal.

(Ecclesiastes 3:1-3)

The *Megillot* read during the Pilgrim Festivals
enhance our celebration of the festivals and provide us with an opportunity to reflect on our individual lives and on God's creation.

VIII

A JEW LISTENS

JEWS CARE ABOUT THEMSELVES AND OTHERS, THEIR OWN FAMILIES AND FAMILIES OF OTHERS, THE JEWISH COMMUNITY AND THE LARGER COMMUNITY. The family, whether in one of its contemporary configurations or in more traditional patterns, is at the core of Western and other civilizations. Although an alarming number of children are born into dysfunctional family settings, most enter and are reared in a home environment that includes near and distant relations. That setting enables the growing, exploring child to acquire attitudes, values, and behaviors in a nurturing cocoon. More than fulfilling an idyllic aspiration, the family is the primary influence on and teacher of the next generation. The family preserves and transmits the essence of the ethnic and religious group of which it is part. The family is the filter through which cultural and socializing forces are allowed to affect the child, the succeeding generation.

The traditional family configuration has been joined by new variations. Many children are raised in single-parent families. Many are in families that include stepparent and stepsiblings. Many are children of intermarried couples. Large-scale mobility has made it difficult for children to interact with grandparents and other relatives except sporadically and briefly. Economic necessity and the advancing status of women have created large numbers of families where both parents work and children are reared by parent substitutes at home or in proliferating day-care centers. Some of these children are "latchkey" children, left pretty much on their own during the day. These new realities have severely affected the family's ability to nurture, support, and encourage its members or to console them in crisis. In Jewish families it has become increasingly difficult to convey what children need to know and do to ensure the continuity of Jewish life.

The same forces that strain the fabric of the family, as well as that very strain, affect individuals in the family. The children especially are vulnerable to false promises of security offered by drugs, promiscuous sex, street gangs, and cults. Many children seek surcease by running away from home. Many seek the ultimate release through suicide. Such problem-solving efforts add to the burdens of the emotionally overtaxed family, which is further disabled when children, succumbing to peer pressure, pull away from parents and look outside the family for love and values. One sad result of modern pressures and tugs on families and family members is alienation of people from one another. Worse, people are alienated from themselves and seem not to care when they harm themselves through substance abuse, inappropriate uses of sex, other destructive behavior, or suicide.

This chapter considers some Jewish views about self, family, and community. The readings will clarify Jewish understandings of how a family should function, elements in the parent-child relationship, inappropriate and destructive behaviors. The article on homosexuality suggests relationships and types of family that are little understood by most people.

▪ Love and Marriage: Some Questions for Jews ▪

What are Judaism's ideas about marriage? The Hebrew word for betrothal tells it all: *kiddushin*, from the same root as *kadosh*, "holy." The Jewish marriage contract is more than a legal document. The *ketubah* publicly affirms the intent of two people to create another Jewish home among the Jewish people. The Jewish family in that home is expected to help assure Jewish survival. Marriage is one of the goals voiced in the prayer recited at the *Berit Milah*, circumcision. The boy is asked to study Torah, marry under the canopy (which symbolizes a Jewish home), and perform *ma'asim tovim*, righteous acts.

The following considers historical and current Jewish views of marriage. You will evaluate your ideas on sex outside of marriage, zero population growth, interfaith marriage, the meaning of love. Why does Judaism value marriage above being single, having children above remaining childless? Intermarriage can weaken the links in the Jewish survival chain; it can also bring new Jews into our midst through conversion. Suggest other arguments for and against intermarriage.

▪ Love and Marriage: Some Questions for Jews

BY CHARLES A. KROLOFF ▪

Much has happened since 1960 when I started counseling couples before marriage and officiating at their weddings. During the first ten years not one engaged couple ever said they did not plan to have children. Today I frequently hear, "There are enough children in the world. We do not want to make more problems."

In my high school discussion groups students now ask, "What difference does a piece of paper make? If we love each other, a marriage certificate can't bring us closer. And, if we fall out of love, no legal document should hold us together."

Some feel religion should make no difference in marriage. Others list "Jewish" as the top priority in their choice of mate. When Jewish couples are insistent that "religion should make no difference," I as a rabbi and a marriage counselor conclude they probably know little about the Jewish view of marriage. What are some of the things that make the Jewish marriage a unique relationship?

In the Beginning

Basic to the Jewish concept of marriage is Judaism's view that life is a precious gift from God and that the "vessel"–that is, the whole human being–that God created to store this gift is inherently good. Genesis 1:27-31 describes the creation of humans: "And God saw all that God had made and found it very good." What are the implications of this idea?

Unlike early Christianity, which taught that the body is sinful, Judaism has always held that the body and bodily functions were given to human beings for their potential good. There is nothing "sinful" or "shameful" about the body, its organs, or its functions; on the contrary, the human being has the responsibility of caring for and preserving this precious vessel.

If the human body and the entire human being are potentially good, why, then, do we occasionally commit sins? The rabbis explained that we are born with the *yetzer tov* and the *yetzer ra*, the good impulse and the evil impulse, but we can master those impulses and direct our lives on the right path. Interestingly enough, the rabbis recognized that even the evil impulse is not literally always evil. They sometimes referred to the sexual urge as the evil impulse, but they also knew the urge can be used creatively or destructively. The Midrash says: "Were it not for the evil impulse, no man would build a house or marry a woman or engage in an occupation." Thus, the Jewish point of view celebrates life and the human being who was created "in God's image." Humanity was endowed with exceptional gifts: body, mind, spirit, abilities, functions, appetites, emotions, energies, senses—all of which can be directed toward the good. We also have the gift of free will—the capacity to choose. How, then, can we best choose to use these gifts for good, constructive, and satisfying lives?

The Necessity of Marriage

Judaism believes we can live the most creative life and make the best of all our potentials through marriage. " . . . God said, 'It is not good for man to be alone; I will make a fitting helper for him.'" (Genesis 2:18)

The rabbis considered marriage so important that they called betrothal *kiddushin*, holiness or sanctification. "An unmarried man," they taught, "impairs the divine image." Without a wife a man is "a homeless wanderer." He is "incomplete," he is "blemished." In his excellent book, *My Beloved Is Mine*, Rabbi Roland B. Gittelsohn tells the rabbinic tale in which God thought Creation was completed after Adam. But soon God was dismayed by the sound of a disturbance that marred the harmony of the universe. An angel was sent to investigate and returned to report the source of the disturbance—it was Adam sighing of loneliness. God out of love then created Eve as Adam's wife, and harmony was restored.

Love, in the Jewish tradition, is built into the very structure of the universe. God loved Adam and created a partner for him. In all relationships, and particularly in the intensely close love partnership of marriage, we cannot treat others as objects to be used, but we should treat them as subjects we respect.

But why build this relationship primarily with one person within marriage? Why not in a group, or with several concurrently, or with one for a few years, and then with another? These are questions I've been hearing in recent years. Getting to know another person well, establishing rapport, and developing understanding are very difficult tasks that take not months but years–or probably a lifetime. To relate fully to another person requires all of our emotional energy and complete trust. Only marriage offers the conditions for such relationships. If we have no long-term ties, we have less reason to work at reconciling differences. If we have another partner off in the wings, why bother even to make the effort?

Importance of Children

Judaism believes in the necessity of the family unit and the importance of having children. God's first command after creating the first couple was: "Be fertile and increase, fill the earth and master it." Why was this the first *mitzvah* God uttered to humankind? Why was procreation–in the form of the sexual urge–built into our biological nature?

Child-rearing has a profound spiritual dimension. When a man and a woman rear children together in a happy marriage, several things happen–the parents convey their values and ideals to the next generation and, in a real sense, achieve a kind of immortality. At the same time this joint effort intensifies their love for each other because children are their joint creation.

So important are children in the Jewish idea of marriage that traditional Jewish law permitted a man to divorce his wife if she did not bear him a child within the first ten years of marriage. While such a law would seem excessively harsh today, its underlying principle remains valid–marriage enables us to perform the *mitzvah* of having children. But, notice, this is not without limit! Rabbinic law states that once you have two children you have met your obligation. Except for the most traditional Jews, most Jewish families today do limit their family size.

Many Jews today not only practice sound family planning but are committed to Zero Population Growth (ZPG). They realize that the growing world birth rate is outdistancing efforts to solve humanity's problems. But we Jews have a special problem. In the past quarter century we have experienced not a net gain but a net *loss* of Jews. In 1939 there were 17 million Jews in the world; today we number about 13 million. Most of that loss resulted from the Nazi Holocaust, but intermarriage and assimilation have also taken their toll. Even without ZPG our Jewish birthrate is far below that of most other peoples. At the risk of appearing illogical or chauvinistic I believe ZPG is beneficial for most of the peoples of the world but potentially suicidal for Jews.

The Jewish Family

Without the family it is very difficult to live a full Jewish life. We began in the ancient Middle East as a closely knit tribal unit. We wove our religious traditions into the daily life of the family. In contrast to Christianity, where all the sacraments except one (the last rites) are performed in the church, Judaism is a home-centered religion. We emphasize a loving and a cohesive family unit for many reasons, among them that for a Jew living alone it is impossible to live a full Jewish life. Try conducting a *Pesach seder* alone, or building a *sukah*, or conducting *Havdalah* all by yourself!

A rabbinic tradition teaches that the most important of the Ten Commandments is "Honor your father and your mother." Why? Because it is they who transmit to us faith in God and the Jewish way of life. We begin life by loving and honoring our parents and our immediate *mishpachah* (family). From them, we come to love our extended *mishpachah*, the Jewish people. God, the Redeemer of Israel, is conceived of as the loving Creator of us all. From this we derive the idea that all humanity is interrelated.

Attitude toward Sex

Note well that the model for all these values is the *family*. This differs from the traditional Christian point of view. In 1952 (and the principle was reaffirmed recently), Pope Pius XII censured all Roman Catholics who would "give marriage a preference in principle over virginity." In other words, celibacy, abstaining from all sexual relations, is still a revered value among some Christians.

This clearly is the direct opposite of the Jewish view, which regards the sexual impulse as positive and creative when it is expressed in marriage. In the ancient days of the Temple, on Yom Kippur, the most solemn day in the Jewish calendar, the High Priest *had* to be married in order to officiate. For Jews the sexual relationship between husband and wife serves other purposes besides procreation. Sex is one of the most important ways a husband and wife express and deepen their love.

What about premarital sex? Some say "living together" is a good testing ground for marriage. I think not. If either partner can walk out at any time, then anxieties can build up. The trust or the motivation necessary to achieve sexual compatibility will very often be lacking, and the test may turn out to be harmful. It often takes a husband and a wife several years to achieve full sexual satisfaction. Most "living together" arrangements do not have the cement of patience. "Affairs" probably do more to confuse our emotions than to clarify our desires. In the animal world sex is primarily a biological drive, like eating and sleeping. For the human being it is more complicated because the mature person requires emotional satisfaction, affection, understanding, and respect as parts of the sexual experience. Without these other factors sexual release alone leaves the human being unsatisfied. Rabbi Stanley Rabinowitz has put it well: "It is love that makes intercourse a human rather than an animal experience."

The Nature of Love

What is love? When you become seriously interested in another person, how can you distinguish between infatuation and love? Between sexual attraction and an emotion that leads to an enduring partnership? What should you look for in order to have the best chance for a successful marriage? Here are the definitions of Alexander Magoun, a leading marriage counselor and sociologist:

Love is a feeling of tenderness and devotion toward someone, so profound that to share that individual's joys, anticipations, sorrows, and pain is the very essence of living.

Love is the passionate and abiding desire on the part of two people . . . to produce together the conditions under which each can be himself [or herself] and spontaneously express his [or her] real self; to produce together an intellectual soil and an emotional climate in which each can flourish, far superior to what either could achieve alone.

Do you agree with this definition? Can you improve upon it? Notice that Magoun emphasizes these factors in love: (1) we share sorrows as well as joy; (2) we can be our "real" self and do not have to act or fake it; (3) we have enough freedom to pursue our own goals; and (4) we enjoy a shared "climate" that brings out the best in us.

An old adage has it that "opposites attract." True, people who are shy and introverted may be attracted to outgoing people in order to compensate for what they feel they lack. But, for a lasting love relationship, you will do better if your areas of compatibility far outnumber your differences. That would include similar attitudes about money, socializing, sex, rearing children, career, each other's parents, and religion.

The more mature you are, the more likely your relationship will be based on enduring love rather than upon romantic infatuation. What characterizes mature people? Here are some criteria: (1) They are spontaneous and have a sense of humor. (2) They do not need to dominate others. (3) They like themselves. (4) They are not in rebellion against their parents. (5) They do not repeat their mistakes. (6) They accept what they cannot change. (7) They do not keep their emotions bottled up.

"Love at first sight" is nonsense. It takes time to determine how mature and how compatible you and your partner are. The younger you are when you marry, the more likely you are to marry for the wrong reasons. Some people marry to escape turmoil in their homes–marriage is their escape. But once independent of parents, they find their main reason for marriage–escape– is gone. Other people have a low opinion of themselves and are attracted to anyone who builds up their ego. But, if such persons grow and mature, they will have less need for the one they chose to prop them up.

Some people marry because of physical attraction. This by itself will carry them for about six months–not much more. One young woman I know married a young man because he was such a great party date. But, since the wedding, he hasn't stopped running from party to party, sometimes with her, sometimes without!

Generally the older you are, the better chance you will have of avoiding such pitfalls. You may stop growing physically in your late teens, but emotionally and intellectually many of you will continue to mature for years to come–possibly for as long as you live. That prospect presents both an opportunity and a risk for marriage. When Isaac and Rebekah were married, the Torah said: "And she became his wife, and he loved her." Does this mean that before the ceremony there was no love? No! This reversal of order teaches us that so much occurs *after* the marriage that our love either deepens–or vanishes completely. Marriages never stay the same as when they started out.

Problems of Religion

One of the great threats to successful marriages is religious conflict, when the husband and wife have different religions; or even though as adults they may not observe their religions, still they absorbed differing religious ideas as they were growing up. There are studies of marriage and divorce in California and Indiana in the 1960s revealing that the divorce rate is much higher for Jewish-gentile marriages than for Jewish marriages–sometimes 300 to 400 percent higher. (A 1985 study showed the rate to be 100 percent higher.)

What are the advantages of a Jewish man and a Jewish woman sharing a Jewish marriage together? Do Jewish students think seriously about the matter? If you haven't, here are some points to consider:

1. You will have similar attitudes toward the family, sex, education, in-laws, prayer, death, and much else.

2. The many traditions surrounding our holidays and lifecycle experiences will enrich your life. You and your partner will share the warmth of Jewish customs, ways of life, folk expressions, songs, foods, literature–without the need for explaining or interpreting.

3. The aspirations of the Jewish people become the shared goals of your marriage–rebuilding the State of Israel, working for the freedom and dignity of our people, and all people, and taking part in the history and religious and cultural life of our people.

4. When you have children, they will not be torn between two religious directions, or be denied any religious training, because of their parents' conflicting beliefs. Children are entitled to a positive and a happy identity as Jews from their earliest childhood.

5. You will be helping to assure the continuity of the Jewish people rather than assisting in its decline. From my own experience–which does not agree in many ways with the findings of the recent study on intermarriage–most of the mixed marriages I have seen lead to assimilation. Most of the children of these unions are not raised as Jews.

Many engaged Jewish-gentile couples try to underestimate their religious differences and insist these differences should not enter into marriage considerations. But religious differences often lie dormant until children are born or until other disputes arise. A few weeks ago a father phoned me to arrange a "quickie Bar Mitzvah" for his son of twelve and a half. "Why did you wait until now to call me?" I asked. He replied: "My wife is not Jewish and we have been discussing [read: arguing] this since the kid was born. I finally convinced her last night."

When that couple was married, both partners probably gave the stock answer to the question about the religion of their children: "We'll wait until they are ready for school," or "We'll let them decide." Both answers show an abysmal ignorance of healthy child-rearing.

Mixed Dating and Parents

Does mixed dating lead to Jewish-gentile marriage? The intermarriage rate among those who *never* interdated is zero. The more you interdate, the more likely you are to marry a non-Jew. Dating is the process of sorting out our feelings about members of the opposite sex. But it also establishes patterns for socializing, delineates our group of friends, and presents the opportunity to be "swept off our feet."

Should Jewish parents be fearful of objecting to interdating, lest their opposition boomerang? Will the children, out of rebellion, date Gentiles? According to the new study on intermarriage, they need not be afraid to speak up. Where parents were not at all opposed, or were only mildly opposed, to having their children interdate, the rate of mixed marriage skyrocketed. Where they were strongly opposed and voiced their views, the rate dropped radically.

Marriage Counseling

I see many couples in trouble who tell me they sensed problems before mariage or in the first few years but did nothing about them. Had they talked frankly with their rabbi or sought counsel from another trained professional, they feel they might have avoided tragic consequences. Years ago a twenty-year-old member of my synagogue and her fiancé came to see me to discuss their marriage only six weeks away. As I asked a few probing questions I noticed the young woman's eyes filled up with tears. Sensing her doubt, I arranged several sessions where I could talk with each partner alone. The young woman told me invitations to the wedding were already in the mail and gifts were arriving daily. But, despite all the embarrassment, she decided by the end of a week of discussions to call off her wedding. Two years later I officiated at her marriage to another man, and today they are happily married.

Many rabbis are very helpful at this time. If your rabbi cannot counsel you him- or herself, he or she will put you in touch with someone who can, and the earlier you see that person, the better. Six months to a year before the wedding is ideal because, if problems surface, you will be able to work at them without the pressure of a wedding date pushing you.

Some of the questions I raise in the premarital sessions are:

1. How long have you known each other? (If six months or less, warning! You haven't had enough experiences together to make such a decision, even if you have been together every day.)

2. How do you feel about the other's parents? (If he is hostile toward her parents, and she cannot deal with this hostility.)

3. What do you feel your shortcomings are? (If he cannot think of any, he has little self-understanding. Ask *her* to list *his* shortcomings and compare them to the response.)

4. How do you feel about your Judaism? (Wide divergence in attitudes suggests conflicts about values and lifestyle.)

5. How much economic security and how many material possessions are you accustomed to? How important are they to you?

6. Describe your home life. Was her father home most evenings? (Would she expect the same of her husband?) Does he have a dominant mother? (If so, is he looking for another strong woman? Or does he want a submissive wife? Or

has he worked through this problem so he can have a fifty-fifty relationship?)

Women's Liberation

Among the most recent pressures on marriage is the women's liberation movement. More and more, women intend to pursue careers throughout their marriage. I do not see this as inconsistent with a good Jewish marriage or with having children if the husband and wife plan for the children and both of them share in rearing them. Increasingly husbands and wives are sharing more of the domestic duties. I know a clergyman who could not accept a call to another pulpit because he and his wife had an agreement: whoever found a job first would determine where they would live. Yes, she was the first.

Jewish Marriage

Rabbi Akiba said: "When a husband and wife are worthy, the Divine Presence dwells in their midst. If not, a fire will consume them." I interpret this to mean that when both partners give their best to the marriage, without draining themselves in relationships that compete, they will be blessed.

Modern Jewish marriage gives both partners the setting and the opportunity to be blessed. Jewish values, traditions, and insights help to create warm, loving homes and warm, loving, stable families. Judaism's open, honest, and realistic attitudes toward the human being encourage each of us to grow individually and together. When a husband and a wife can prove themselves worthy of all these potentials, then the Divine Presence indeed lives in their midst!

▪ My Parents, Right or Wrong ▪

Many people believe that respect must be earned, that no one should be respected just for the asking. Judaism suggests an important exception to that belief: parents are always to be honored by their children. In fact, the Fifth Commandment is preceded only by commandments that govern the relationship between God and God's children. Honoring parents is among the chief *mitzvot* and is unconditional.

The following provides Jewish teachings about parent-child relationships. How might the texts be rephrased using contemporary examples? Are any of the teachings outdated? Explain. Jewish teaching cares about every family member, not only parents: parental responsibilities to children are also enunciated. What if the parent shirks those responsibilities, as in cases of abuse, neglect, desertion? Does the Fifth Commandment still apply? Explain.

■ My Parents, Right or Wrong

BY BERNARD M. ZLOTOWITZ AND STEVEN SCHNUR ■

Both the Torah and the Talmud explicitly detail the responsibilities of all family members: a husband's duties to a wife; a wife's duties to a husband; parents' to children; and children's to parents. They speak of honoring, revering, and fearing parents; of caring for and teaching children; and of loving one's spouse. Especially today, when only half of all Jewish families are traditional nuclear ones, the other half consisting of divorced and single-parent households, the teachings of Torah and Talmud provide invaluable guidance for conducting our often-difficult family relationships.

The vaguest of the Bible's Ten Commandments is the fifth: Honor thy father and thy mother. What does it mean to honor? How do we do so? The rabbis of the Talmud asked the same questions. "In what does reverence for a father consist? In not sitting in his presence, in not speaking in his presence, and in not contradicting him." They continued: "Of what does honor for parents consist? In providing for food and drink, in clothing them, in giving them shoes for their feet, in helping them to enter or leave the house." (*Kiddushin* 31b) "If [people] honor their father and mother, God says, 'I reckon it to them as if I dwelt among them and as if they honored me.'" (*Kiddushin* 30b) Several stories in the Talmud and Midrash illustrate this: "Wise men came to Dama ben Netina to buy a precious stone in the place of one that had fallen out and been lost from the breastplate of the High Priest. They agreed to give him a thousand gold pieces for the stone. He went in and found his father asleep with his leg stretched out upon the box containing the

jewel. Since he would not disturb his father, he went back to the wise men without it. Thinking he wanted more money, they offered him ten thousand gold pieces. When his father woke up, he went in and brought out the jewel. The wise men offered him the ten thousand pieces, but he replied: Far be it from me to make a profit from honoring my father; I will take only the thousand we had agreed on." For honoring his father, the story continues, God rewarded this dutiful son. If a father makes a mistake, should a son correct him? The rabbis taught: "Let not the son say, 'Father, you have made a mistake,' for this will pain him. Rather say, 'In the law we find...' thus correcting without humiliating his father."

So important is this concept of honor that the rabbis base the security and well-being of the family upon it. "Be careful about the honor of your wife, for blessing enters the house only because of the wife." (*Bava Metzia* 59a) "Of him who loves his wife as himself," the rabbis taught, "and honors her more than himself, and brings up his sons and daughters rightly, and marries them early, the Scripture says, 'Thou knowest that thy tent is in peace.'" (Job 5:24).

Parents are charged by Bible and Talmud with the responsibility of teaching their children. "He who denies a child religious knowledge robs him of his inheritance." (*Sanhedrin* 91b) Children, in turn, are commanded to be receptive to those teachings: "Hear, my son, your father's instruction and reject not your mother's teaching," the Book of Proverbs says. "A wise son hears his father's instruction." (Proverbs 13:1) "He who does violence to his father and chases away his mother is a son who causes shame and brings reproach." (Proverbs 19:26) "If one curses his father or his mother, his lamp will be put in utter darkness." (Proverbs 20:20) "When a son respects his parents, God accounts it as if the son respected God as well; but, when he vexes his parents, God says, 'I cannot abide you.'" (*Kiddushin* 30)

According to the rabbis, the responsibilities of the father to his son are explicit: "He is bound in respect of his son to circumcise him, redeem him (the first-born male), teach him Torah, take a wife for him, and teach him a craft." (*Kiddushin* 29a) Elsewhere in the Talmud fathers are directed to teach their sons to swim.

How a parent is to teach a child is also set forth. "We should not say to a child: I will give you something, and later change our mind, for this teaches the child to lie." (*Sukkah* 46) "Do not threaten a child, either punish or forgive him [or her]." (*Semachot* 2:6) "If you must strike a child, strike [him or her] with the string of a sleeve." (*Bava Batra* 21) "Discipline your son while there is hope; do not set your heart on his destruction." (Proverbs 19:18) And finally the Bible instructs: "He who spares the rod hates his son, but he who loves him is diligent to discipline him." (Proverbs 13:24)

So attuned were the ancient rabbis to the everyday struggles of family living and the natural instincts of both parents and children that they wrote that a father should provide his infant child with things to break, inexpensive things that would not anger the parent if broken. Later, when children begin to talk back to parents, the rabbis instruct fathers and mothers to listen. "[Humans were] endowed with two ears and one tongue that [they] may listen more than speak." (Chasdai, *Ben Hamelech* 26) Above all a parent must be caring. "A parent without sensibility is less than an ant." (*Leviticus Rabbah* 1:15)

Though marriage in Judaism is not considered indissoluble, the rabbis taught that it was a blessing, a "divine covenant" requiring nurturing and care. "If a man divorces his first wife, even the very altar sheds tears because of him." (*Gittin* 90b) "Man cannot exist without woman nor woman without man, nor both of them without God." (*Even Ha'ezer* 25) "Man must not cause his wife to weep, for God counts her tears." (*Bava Metzia* 59a) Above all is the gift of children, humans' greatest possession, which the psalmist says are "a heritage of God."

▪ A Jewish View of Sexuality ▪

Judaism holds that the human body and its functions, created by God, are neither good nor bad in themselves. They attain positive or negative value depending on how and for what purposes they are used. Sexual functions, therefore, are good if they are used to advance God's purposes. These include the sanctity of marriage and the joy that comes to husband and wife united in love. That union is a holy one; the community has sanctioned it by being present at the wedding ceremony. On these assumptions rest the Jewish value system about love, sex, and marriage.

In the following selection, the author suggests that marriage, in addition to its inherent holiness, helps people to feel and act with caring and responsibility. Children, the fruit of marriage, provide an awareness of the future. Sexuality is more and other than mere biological urge and function; otherwise, the body is nothing more than a machine. Do you agree? Explain. Define the relationship between sexuality and love.

▪ A Jewish View of Sexuality

BY HAROLD M. SCHULWEIS ▪

We do not normally speak about sexuality in the synagogue because we somehow deem it inappropriate. Matters of sex are aired outside the sanctuary, given over to psychologists and sociologists, not to those who deal with spiritual matters. But sexual silence in the synagogue is both un-Jewish and unwise.

We are not the children of Paul or Augustine or Luther. We are not the inheritors of a classical Christian or Gnostic tradition that regards sexuality as degrading lust. We are not Puritans, and we ought not behave like Puritans. Indeed, on the most awesome of all days, we read out loud about sodomy, transvestism, and adultery. On Yom Kippur afternoon we read the eighteenth chapter of Leviticus. The rabbis were remarkably astute in picking that section for a holy day when Jews behave like the angels, neither eating nor drinking. Is it perhaps to remind us that we have bodies or, more important, that we are bodies.

We are fortunately rooted in a biblical and a rabbinic tradition that deals explicitly and frankly with the most intimate sexual relations, for in Judaism there is no shame in the body. It is unwise to avoid speaking about the Jewish view of sexuality because that creates a vacuum filled with notions more appropriate to the Christian ethic. However ecumenical my spirit, I sense here the limits of speaking in terms of the "Judeo-Christian tradition." Some problems of Christianity are not Jewish problems.

If there is anything that clearly differentiates the perceptions of Christianity and Judaism, it is their respective attitude toward sexuality and the status of the body.

The central passage in the Christian Scripture's treatment of the body and of marriage is found in the sixth and seventh chapters of the first book of Corinthians. There we find Paul's idea of celibacy and virginity: "It is good for a man not to touch a woman . . . I say, therefore, to the unmarried and widows, it is good for

them if they abide even as I. But if they cannot contain, let them marry, for it is better to marry than to burn."

In classic Christian teaching the world is divided. There is a split between the body and the soul, the senses and the spirit, the inner and the outer, the human and the divine. The world is to be overcome and transcended. The Christian ideal of celibacy reflects man's decision to withdraw from Eve and reproductivity so as better to serve God. One must come to God unburdened by the concerns and responsibilities of the human family.

Marriage Ideal

A Jew, however, must be connected to the world and involved in its history. If the classic Christian ideal is celibacy, the classic Jewish ideal is marriage. Marriage is the way we enter the world of care and responsibility. God and humankind are not adversaries. Humanity is the co-creator with God in the repair of the world. To marry, to have a child, is a religious act reflecting one's commitment to transform the world. To have a child is to have a flesh and blood connection with the future. We have an investment in the future through our husbands and wives, through our children and children's children. Marriage, then, is not understood biologically but theologically and morally.

Motivations for Marriage

What in Judaism is the major motivation for marriage? It is a primary *mitzvah* to see to it that the world is continued. The classic text used by rabbinic commentators to sustain this moral stance comes from Isaiah 45:18, "[God] created it not a waste. [God] formed it to be inhabited." Interestingly the Hebrew term for bachelor is *ravak*, which means literally "emptiness," for the willful bachelor empties the world. Folk tradition further dramatized the point by denying the bachelor the prayer shawl, thereby making him something of a marked man.

But procreation is not the sole end of marriage. A remarkable statement from the tractate *Yevamot* (61b) reads, "Though [one] may have many children (and has thus fulfilled the *mitzvah* of procreation), [one] is not to remain unmarried because it is not good . . . to be alone." To be alone is the dreaded curse among our people.

Sanctity of Sexuality

In a thirteenth century treatise, "*Menora Ha-Maor*," written by Israel Ibn Nakawa and popularly attributed to Nachmanides, we find a chapter dealing with the sanctity of sexuality in the relations between husband and wife. In the "Epistle of Holiness" addressed to the husband, the author writes: "Engage her first in conversation that puts her mind at ease and gladdens her. Thus, your mind and intent will be in harmony with hers. Speak words that arouse her to passion, union, love, and desire. Never may you force her, for in such a union the Divine Presence cannot abide. Quarrel not with her . . . win her over with words of graciousness and seductiveness."

To those who lean toward the influence of Aristotle, such as Maimonides, and who disapproved of the sense of touch, our author admonished, "Let [one] not consider sexual union as something ugly or repulsive, for thus we blaspheme God. Hands that write a sacred Torah are exalted and praiseworthy; hands that steal are ugly." And so it is with the sexual organs of the body. All the energies are morally neutral. There is nothing that is intrinsically contaminating, nothing that is intrinsically holy except the use to which that energy is put.

The non-Jewish contemporaries of Ibn Nakawa and Nachmanides, Peter Lombard and Pope Innocent III, insisted that the holy spirit leaves a room even where a married couple has sexual relations, for such action, even if for procreation, shames God. There thus grew up a Church tradition that on Friday one is to abstain from sex in memory of the death of the Savior, on Saturday in honor of the Virgin Mary, and on Sunday in memory of the Resurrection. In this tradition holiness and sexuality are contradictory. Contrast this view with that of the tractate *Sotah* (17a), which asserts, "When a husband and wife unite in holiness, there the Divine Presence abides." The *Shabbat* is the celebration of the creation of the world. What more appropriate time to rejoice with one's spouse.

New Challenge to Jewish Sexual Morality

It is clear that today people are not struggling with the inhibitions of the Victorian era. The pendulum has swung the other way. The older morality proposed the ideal of loving without sex. The new sexual morality encourages sexuality without love. Both positions are dualistic and in conflict with Judaism.

In its bluntest form the new morality is articulated by the publisher of *Playboy*, Hugh Hefner. Hugh Hefner puts it on the line. "Sex is a function of the body, a drive [humans] share with the animals, like eating, drinking and sleeping; it is a physical demand that must be satisfied. If you do not satisfy it, you will have all kinds of neuroses and repression psychoses. Sex is here to stay. Let us forget the prudery that makes us hide from it, throw away those inhibitions, find a [female] who is like-minded and let yourself go." One of the typical cartoons in *Playboy* depicts a boy and girl locked in amorous embrace during which he cries out, "Why talk of love at a time like this."

Arguments against Formal Marriage

Four basic arguments are usually presented by those advocating the right and propriety of having sexual relations without marriage. The first argument maintains that being in love is its own justification. The important thing is "to feel." Feeling is more important than a marriage license.

The second argument insists that sexual relations openly arrived at by mutual consent are fine as long as "nobody gets hurt." No one advocates seduction or coercion.

The third argument asserts that sexuality is important as a means of determining marital compatibility. How will you know whether you are compatible without knowing if you are sexually compatible?

The fourth argument claims that sexuality is morally neutral. It is a biological phenomenon and not really different today from yesterday's holding hands.

Body Not a Machine

I, for one, cannot accept these four arguments because I cannot isolate the body from the total self, nor can I isolate the private self from the community. If sexuality is essentially a bodily function, the purpose of which is to relieve tension, then the body is merely a machine. Clearly, before you invest in a machine, you try it out. You see whether or not it works. If it doesn't work, you may discard it or trade it in or try to fix it up. Such a mechanical view of sex depersonalizes man and woman.

The body conceived of as a machine leads to serious consequences. Psychiatrists report a rising concern with impotence and frigidity. Patients no longer come to the psychiatrists with the old complaints of sexual inhibitions. They now come with a complaint of incapacity to feel, an inability to be moved, an inability to laugh or cry or love. The complaint of these emancipated men and women is of a numbness, a frozenness, an anesthetized self. When the other person is seen as an appendage of your body, as an instrument of physical gratification, as an object, you are alone with yourself. You do not experience love.

What Is Love?

To love is to see the world through the eyes of the other. It is to be patient with the temperament of the other. To love is to be willing to defer the gratification of the moment. When others argue it is all right to relate sexually with another as long as "nobody gets hurt," they mean something other than what I mean by love. To love is to suffer the hurt of another and open one's self to the possibilities of being hurt by the other. Who can hurt me more than someone I love? The stranger cannot hurt me. Many turn to sexuality without love, not out of lust, but out of fear. Behind much of the trivialization of sex, behind *Playboy* coolness, is a fear of authentic relationships, a fear to suffer, a fear of responsibility and of community.

The issue before us is not sexuality; the issue is character. How we express our sexuality reveals much about our moral character. A person who requires instant joy, instant contact, here and now, is devoid of frustration tolerance, gets angry with any demand to postpone immediate gratification, and becomes impatient with the need to understand the needs of the other. Such a person is little more than a spoiled child grown up. Erotic detachment, "without any strings attached," is not a rehearsal for marriage. It is a rehearsal for divorce. It is a rehearsal for the growth of moral coarseness and insensitivity.

Marriage and Community

What is most important is not the wedding, the *chupah*, the breaking of glass, the presence of the rabbi. The religious rite of passage takes on its proper significance when it expresses the virtues with which a community has endowed marital love. For Judaism marriage is not a private arrangement; marriage celebrates the formation of a moral community within a moral community. The vow declaring "be thou consecrated unto me" is not complete. It is completed by the statement " . . . in accordance with the law of Moses and Israel." When two people are covenanted for the purpose of marriage, there is a third presence. That presence is the Jewish community and its ideals of divinity.

The ultimate task of life is to overcome separation, to live with another because without the other one cannot become a whole human being. That love embraces body and soul.

▪ Jewish and Gay ▪

A scant decade ago homosexuality was a whispered word. Homosexuals hid their identities in sheltering myths. Identified gays and lesbians were ignored at best, persecuted at worst. With the sexual revolution of the seventies many homosexuals "came out of the closet" and compelled us to examine or reexamine deeply held personal and social attitudes. A spate of research was directed at understanding homosexuality. Acrid debates swirled around such issues as whether homosexual behavior was "sexual preference" or one's nature. Gay and lesbian rights movements sought to protect the civil and human rights of homosexuals.

Like society in general, Judaism, too, had to face homosexuality and respond to homosexual men and women in its midst. Gay and lesbian synagogues emerged. *Halachic* opinions on homosexuality were sought and issued. The debate within Judaism continues, as the following suggests. The article speaks also of the fear, shame, and loneliness young people experience when they discover they may not be like most of their peers. How would (did) you react after discovering a classmate was gay or lesbian? What if it's a sibling? What if it's you?

▪ Jewish and Gay   BY JANET MARDER ▪

In June 1985, on the night of his high school graduation, Robert Rosenkrantz shot schoolmate Steve Redman ten times with an Uzi semiautomatic rifle. What turns a white middle-class teenager into a murderer? In Robert's case, it was a blend of fear, rage, and desperate loneliness. Steve Redman and Robert's brother, Joey, had spied on Robert in an attempt to prove he was gay. When they caught him in a homosexual encounter, they told his parents what they had discovered. Robert testified at his trial that he had hidden his homosexuality for years for fear that he would be rejected by his family and friends. "I was not able to say 'I'm gay' until I was in custody," he admitted.

At Calabasas High School in Woodland Hills, California, where Redman and the Rosenkrantz brothers were students, hostility toward homosexuals is pervasive. "This is strictly a straight school," said sophomore Wendy Bell, 16. "If there are gay people at this school, nobody knows about it. If people found out, they would verbally torture you." Assistant Principal Robert

Donahue agrees. "I think a kid who is gay is probably in the worse position of any minority." Donahue is worried that Robert Rosenkrantz's violent behavior may reinforce students' hostility toward homosexuals. "To have a young gay man go out and do what he did just confirms their attitudes that homosexuals are crazy as hell," he said.

I have been trying to imagine what it must have been like for Robert Rosenkrantz to grow up gay. I know that when I was in high school the most painful way to insult a boy was to call him a "queer" or a "fag"—this despite the fact that few of us actually knew any lesbians or gay men. Fifteen years ago homosexuals were far less visible than they are today. Throughout my years in high school, college, and rabbinic school, I knew only generalizations and stereotypes. Most of my information came from newspapers, popular magazines, and the conversations of those around me. Thus I learned that gay people were perverted, sinful, and pathetic misfits. They dressed oddly. They molested children. They were promiscuous and hedonistic, caring only for their own pleasure; they had rejected marriage, children, and family life. They lived wretched, lonely lives, most of which they spent hanging out in bars and bathhouses, engaging in unspeakably sordid acts. Gay men were "swishy," effeminate wimps; lesbians were angry, unattractive, man-hating "dykes."

"Go for It"

That was my education about homosexuals. Why then did I find myself in late April of 1983 applying to be the first ordained rabbi of Beth Chayim Chadashim (BCC), a Los Angeles synagogue for gay and lesbian Jews? First, I believed that any Jewish congregation was entitled to responsible rabbinic leadership. Moreover, BCC had the support and recognition of the Reform movement. In 1973, the UAHC made history by becoming the first (and only) national religious body to accept a gay/lesbian congregation. (The Conservative movement voted in 1990 to welcome congregations with special outreach to homosexuals.) But most important was the advice of my husband, Shelly, also a rabbi. He had had professional contact with a group of BCC members who conduct monthly Shabbat services at a local nursing home. Shelly told me that the BCC volunteers led a service that was warmer and more spirited than any he had ever seen in a nursing home. There was clearly something special about these men and women who took such pleasure in giving. Being the rabbi of such a group, Shelly thought, would be exceptionally rewarding. "Go for it," he urged.

And so, eight months pregnant, I went to meet with the rabbinic search committee of BCC–but not without considerable anxiety. How, I wondered, could I teach Judaism honestly to a group I believed was Jewishly illicit? Leviticus 18:22 states that a man who lies with another man as with a woman has committed an abomination. Leviticus 20:13 adds that men performing such acts "shall be put to death–their blood-guilt is upon them." How could I ask gay men to love a Torah that condemns them to death? Moreover, Judaism emphasizes marriage and family as the

primary means of transmitting our heritage. Could I still affirm those values while ministering to a congregation whose very existence seemed to subvert them? Finally, I was filled with doubts about my ability to counsel men and women who lived, I thought, so differently from me and everyone I knew. How would I ever understand their problems and help them? In fact, I was rather embarrassed by the concept of public "displays" of homosexuality; the thought of two men embracing or dancing together made me quite uneasy. Worse yet, I fully expected to hear details about my congregants' lives that would make me feel morally queasy. In other words, I wanted them to be honest with me, but I was afraid of what they might say.

Today, after three years of many trials and many more errors, I hardly recognize myself. My beliefs have changed slowly, but in profound ways that affect my entire outlook on life. My thinking has shifted most significantly in three areas: the nature of homosexuality, the role of *halachah* in liberal Judaism, and the place of lesbian and gay Jews in our community.

Scientific Studies Inconclusive

As soon as I was hired by BCC, I set out to learn whatever I could about homosexuality by reading the works of psychologists, psychiatrists, sociologists, and physicians. I also read the accounts of "insiders," such as Howard Brown's *Familiar Faces, Hidden Lives: The Story of Homosexual Men in America Today* and Evelyn Torton Beck's *Nice Jewish Girls: A Lesbian Anthology.* Even these limited forays into the subject of homosexuality showed me that scientific studies were far from conclusive. Some regarded homosexuality as physiologically based, others traced it to environmental factors; some viewed it as "curable," others as predetermined and immutable.

I began to see that the main division in studies of homosexuality is between those who classify it as undesirable "deviant" behavior, regardless of origin, and those who accept it as natural, legitimate behavior in no way inferior to heterosexuality. I continued to read and learn, but I gradually found myself less interested in what the experts said, paying more attention to my own observations of the several hundred lesbians and gay men I came to know over the next few years.

The more I came to know my congregants, the less I regarded their way of life as unethical, unhealthy, and undesirable. I realized that my initial discomfort with public "displays" of homosexuality arose, not from anything inherently bizarre or "unnatural" in their behavior, but simply from my unfamiliarity with it. One who is different provokes suspicion and, sometimes, hostility–be it a teenager with a pink, punk-style haircut or a traditional Jew clad in *shtreiml*, beard, and *peyot*. Once I started examining my own prejudices more carefully, I began to see nothing "unnatural" about my congregants' behavior; rather, I saw differences to which I quickly became accustomed. Soon I was no longer struck by the oddity of two men holding hands or dancing together; I saw instead their very "natural" need for affection and companionship.

Similarly, as I came to know my congregants as individuals, I could no longer tolerate generalizations about homosexuality as pathology or sin. Certainly I met some gay people whose lives were wretchedly unhappy. But most of the misery in their lives seemed to be the result of family rejection, social bigotry, or internalized self-hatred–not of any misery endemic to homosexuality itself. Other gay people I met acted in ways that struck me as sick or immoral. But this is no less true of the straight people I meet, and few would condemn heterosexuality as immoral–despite the high incidence of rape, incest, child abuse, adultery, family violence, promiscuity, and venereal disease among heterosexuals. The sad, the sick, and the sinful are a minority in the gay community, as they are in the straight. My congregants are men and women as healthy, loving, and morally responsible as any I have known in my life.

My attitude towards homosexuality has moved from tolerance to full acceptance. I see it now as a sexual orientation offering the same oppor-

tunities for love, fulfillment, spiritual growth, and ethical action as heterosexuality. I still do not know what "causes" homosexuality, but I must confess that at this point I do not much care anymore than I care what "causes" some people to have a special aptitude for music, others for baseball. I simply accept with pleasure the diversity of our species.

Role of Halachah

My changing perceptions of homosexuality forced me to confront the role that *halachah* (Jewish law) plays in my life as a rabbi and liberal Jew. I began an intensive study of what our tradition has to say about homosexuality. Aside from the prohibitions in Leviticus, biblical references to homosexuality are few, and their exact meaning is not always clear, I learned.

The story of the destruction of Sodom in Genesis 19 is thought by many to reflect an abhorrence of homosexuality; in my view, it is not a comment on homosexuality *per se* but a denunciation of inhospitable behavior to the stranger, as manifested in an act of attempted gang rape. (So also for the similar narrative in Judges 19.) Interestingly, Ezekiel 16:49 calls the sin of Sodom arrogance and callousness toward the poor; there is no reference to homosexual acts. The Bible (Deut. 23:18) refers to a *kadesh*, or male cult prostitute, but it is not clear whether the *kadesh* engaged in homosexual or heterosexual prostitution. Another possible biblical reference to homosexuality is David's lament over the dead Jonathan: "I grieve for you, my brother Jonathan; you were most dear to me. Your love was wonderful to me, surpassing the love of women" (2 Sam. 1:26). Some theologians believe this verse indicates that a sexual relationship existed between the two friends. If this is so, it would be the Bible's only favorable presentation of homosexual relations.

Nowhere in the Bible is lesbianism prohibited or even mentioned. This may be because women are not bound by the commandment to procreate (and thus their offense is less serious), because no act of sexual penetration or "waste of semen" occurs, or because the male authors of the Bible were simply unaware of lesbianism.

Postbiblical references to homosexuality are relatively few and uniformly negative. In the Midrash, for example, homosexuality is called the cause of solar eclipses (*Sukkah* 29a) and the destruction of the Temple (*Tosefta Sotah* 6:9, quoted in L. Ginzberg, *Legends of the Jews*). Another midrashic passage states that Ham's sin, for which his descendants were condemned to slavery (Gen. 9:20-27), was a homosexual relationship with his father, Noah (*Sanhedrin* 70a). In the Midrash we find lesbianism prohibited. The prohibition is derived indirectly from Leviticus 18:3. "You shall not copy the practices of the land of Egypt where you dwelt, or of the land of Canaan to which I am taking you. . . . " This, according to a *midrash*, refers specifically to sexual practices: "The Egyptians used to marry a man to a man and a woman to a woman" (*Lev. Rabbah* 23:9).

A Rare Aberration

The *halachic*, or legal, portions of the Talmud treat homosexuality as a rare aberration. In the Mishnah, for instance, Rabbi Judah rules that two unmarried men may not sleep together under the same cover (*Kiddushin* 4:14); but the Sages overrule him and permit it, since "Jews are not suspected of homosexuality" (*Kiddushin* 82a).

The attitude is also reflected in medieval legal materials. The greatest medieval philosopher, Moses Maimonides (1135-1204), wrote: "A Jew is not suspected of homosexuality. Therefore, a Jewish man is allowed to be alone with another Jewish man. But if one takes care not to be alone with a male . . . it is praiseworthy. An adult who commits sodomy, either passively or actively, is to be stoned" (*Hilchot Issurei Biah* 22:2; 1:14). Rabbi Joseph Karo (1488-1575), author of the definitive legal code for traditional Jewry, was even more stringent: "In our century, when there are many lewd men around, one should refrain from being alone with another male" (*Shulchan Aruch, Even Ha'ezer* 24). A century later, how-

ever, Rabbi Joel Sirkes suspended that prohibition because "in our lands [i.e., Poland] such lewdness is unheard of" (*Bayit Chadash* to *Tur, Even Ha'ezer* 24). Homosexuality itself is not explicitly prohibited in the *Shulchan Aruch*, probably because its author believed that such behavior was virtually nonexistent among Jews.

"Spilling the Seed"

Why is homosexuality rejected by our tradition? First, it is an act of "spilling the seed" in which procreation is impossible; procreation is not merely a desirable Jewish goal but a *mitzvah*, a binding commandment (Gen. 1:28). As a *midrash* says: "One who does not fulfill the commandment of procreation is like one who sheds blood and diminishes the divine image." Second, homosexual behavior seems to violate the natural order of being as presented in Genesis, in which woman is created to fulfill and complete man: "God said, 'It is not good for man to be alone; I will make a fitting helper for him.' . . . Hence a man leaves his father and mother and clings to his wife, so that they become one flesh" (Gen. 2:18, 24). Third, in biblical and rabbinic sources homosexuality is associated with idolatrous pagan practices, which Jews are expected to shun. In the ancient world, as we have seen in the Sodom story of Gen. 19, homosexual rape was also a way of humiliating and degrading a vulnerable male.

Liberal Jews may analyze these reasons to determine how valid they are for us today. For traditional Jews, however, the reasons for the ban on homosexuality are not ultimately important. What matters is that the Bible forbids it and calls it "an abhorrent thing"; hence no traditional Jew can regard homosexual acts, even between consenting adults, as acceptable Jewish behavior. Writes Great Britain's Chief Rabbi Immanuel Jakobovits: " . . . Jewish law holds that no hedonistic ethic, even if called 'love,' can justify the morality of homosexuality, any more than it can legitimize adultery or incest, however genuinely such acts may be performed out of love and by mutual consent." Rabbi Norman Lamm, a contemporary Orthodox authority, states:

"Compassion should be stressed for the man or woman trapped in this dreadful disease . . . the homosexual who genuinely desires to emerge from his situation ought to be helped by all the means at our disposal, whether of medicine or psychotherapy or counseling. But the compassion and help extended by society should in no way diminish the judgment that *mishkav zachar* (male homosexuality) is repugnant. . . . "

Liberal rabbinic opinions on homosexuality vary considerably. Solomon Freehof, a prominent Reform rabbi and legal authority, calls homosexuality "a grave sin." He argues that liberal Jews are not permitted to discard the biblical prohibition of homosexuality, since it is not merely a legal enactment but reveals "a deep-rooted ethical attitude."

Hershel J. Matt, a Conservative rabbi, disagrees. He points out that the biblical prohibition of homosexuality is apparently based on the assumption that homosexuality is a free and conscious choice. The homosexual is thus one who willfully rebels against God and the Jewish people. However, since recent scientific evidence indicates that "homosexuality is deep seated and not something that one chooses to be or not to be," Matt suggests that it would be more appropriate to regard the homosexual as one who acts from "*ones*" (pronounced oh-ness), out of constraint and lack of freedom. Since a frequently invoked principle in Jewish law states that "in cases of *ones* the Merciful One exempts" (*Nedarim* 27a), Matt believes homosexuals should not be judged as sinners and must be treated with compassion, kindness, and friendship. He cautions, however, against regarding homosexuality simply as a valid "alternative lifestyle," for heterosexuality is clearly "the God intended norm" and homosexuality "a sexual deviance, malfunctioning, or abnormality–usually unavoidable and often irremediable."

Tradition Vs. Conscience

My study of Jewish views of homosexuality led me to a disturbing conclusion. While some rabbis urged tolerance and compassion for *homosexuals*, none regarded *homosexuality* as a fully acceptable Jewish way of life. And so I had to decide: how much did it matter to me that the voice of my tradition ran counter to the evidence of my experience and the deepest promptings of my conscience?

For me the choice was clear. I could not be guided by laws that seemed profoundly unjust and immoral. I believe, and I teach my congregants that Jewish law condemns their way of life. But I teach also that I cannot accept that law as authoritative. It belongs to me, it is part of my history, but it has no binding claim on me. In my view, the Jewish condemnation of homosexuality is the work of human beings–limited, imperfect, fearful of what is different, and, above all, concerned with ensuring tribal survival. In short, I think our ancestors were wrong about a number of things, and homosexuality is one of them.

I am also a fallible human being, and it may be that my judgments will one day be proven wrong. But, for now, I have no choice but to decide for myself which parts of our tradition I hold sacred. In fact, the Jewish values and principles that I regard as eternal, transcendent, and divinely ordained do *not* condemn homosexuality. The Judaism I cherish and affirm teaches love of humanity, respect for the spark of divinity in every person, and the human right to live with dignity. The God I worship endorses loving, responsible, and committed human relationships, regardless of the sex of the persons involved. There is no Jewish *legal* basis for this belief; my personal faith simply tells me that the duty to love my neighbors as myself is a compelling *mitzvah*, while the duty to kill homosexuals for committing "abominations" most certainly is not.

Life and Death Issue

These are not academic matters; they are life and death issues faced by real human beings. Synagogues across the country are filled with Jews in hiding–gay men and lesbians who live in perpetual fear of the sidelong glance, the whispers, giggles, and sneers that mean someone has discovered their secret. These Jews in hiding are in the pews at *Shabbat* services, on the *bimah* preaching sermons and chanting the liturgy, in the classrooms of religious schools, and behind the principal's desk. They sing in the choir, serve on the temple board, car pool their kids to youth group meetings. In other words, wherever Reform Jews gather to pray, study, and socialize, you'll find gay men and lesbians among them.

My three years with BCC have left me at times bewildered and frustrated. I have tried to understand why liberal Jews who say they are devoted to justice and equality balk at granting justice and equality to gay and lesbian Jews. I have tried to understand why they cling so tenaciously to denigrating stereotypes about "the homosexual lifestyle" and its alleged threats to the purity of Jewish life. I don't understand why homophobia is the last socially acceptable form of bigotry in our country—even among Jews, who should know better. I don't know why Robert Rosenkrantz and a thousand other kids like him should have to grow up feeling desperately alone and scared to death to be themselves.

But above and beyond my moments of frustration, I feel deeply blessed to have spent the last three years of my life working with my congregation. Apart from the intrinsic joys of working with an active, questing, and spirited group, I feel grateful for the education I've been given—a chance to see with my own eyes, to make up my own mind, rather than simply swallow the judgments and slogans of others. I'm grateful also that my daughters are spending the crucial years of their early childhood in the presence of hundreds of loving gay "uncles" and lesbian "aunts."

They, thank God, will grow up without the ugly myths and stereotypes that afflicted me. Perhaps that is the greatest gift I have received from my congregants.

[Rabbi Marder served Congregation Beth Chayim Chadashim for five years, until 1988. She is now associate director of the UAHC's Pacific Southwest Council. Since this article was published in 1986, the Reform movement has taken several important steps to acknowledge and affirm the presence of gay and lesbian Jews in our community. In 1987 the UAHC General Assembly passed a resolution urging all member congregations to "develop educational programs . . . that promote understanding and respect for lesbians and gays" and to "employ people without regard to sexual orientation." A resolution passed in 1989 encouraged congregations to "welcome gay and lesbian Jews to membership as singles, couples, and families." In 1990 Rabbi Alfred Gottschalk, the president of HUC-JIR (the Reform rabbinical seminary), stated that sexual orientation, in and of itself, would not disqualify a candidate from admission to the seminary. Finally, in June 1990, the Central Conference of American Rabbis approved a report urging that "all rabbis, regardless of sexual orientation, be accorded the opportunity to fulfill the sacred vocation they have chosen."]

▪ When Families Fail ▪

High school and college age suicide rates have escalated drastically. Some believe suicides result from inability to cope with the stresses of frenetic modern life. Some believe alienation from self and absence of strong value systems are to blame. Suicide may end the pain of the victim; the pain of friends and family, however, continues for their lifetimes. Suicide attempts are frequently cries for help. How should we respond? What can break through, or prevent, the cycle of depression-escape which, coupled with a faulty comprehension of what death is all about, so often leads to suicide?

The following discussion directs your thinking to the reality of suicide. What might you do if you hear someone talk of suicide? What might you do if you have thoughts of suicide? How is talking helpful? How can young people or adults be helped to feel better about themselves? How does that help prevent suicide?

■ When Families Fail   BY ALLEN S. KAPLAN ■

"I couldn't handle it anymore," he told me. "Mom and Dad were separating and using me as their messenger to carry threats and ultimatums between them. Neither had time to listen to my problems, to find out what was happening to me in school. I thought they didn't give a damn about me.

"Then Mr. Fisher told me I was flunking Geometry and would have to repeat the course. I knew what that would unleash: 'What do you mean you flunked Geometry? Nobody in our family has ever failed anything. We always got As in everything!' I expected them to tell me I was stupid, that I had disgraced the family name.

"The family name. Some name! My father was running around with other women and everybody in the neighborhood knew. He wanted me to be a doctor because he had always wanted to be one, but his family had been too poor to send him to medical school. Did he ever bother to ask me what I wanted to be? He didn't pay the slightest attention to my wishes. Neither did Mom. It seemed they really didn't love me. Maybe if I were dead, we'd all be better off."

The preceding is from an interview with a young man of sixteen, following his suicide attempt. Each year more than 6,000 young people end their own lives. Ten times that number attempt suicide but are not successful.

Suicide, the third leading cause of death among young people ages fifteen to twenty-four, has almost tripled in the last decade. Among the general population, regardless of age, suicide is only the ninth leading cause of death. The shocking truth is that too many of our youth are succumbing to the lure of suicide as a means of solving their problems.

Unhappiness

If there is any one characteristic that can be said to define the young person who is a prime candidate for suicide, it is *unhappiness.* Young people who contemplate suicide often hold themselves in low self-esteem, which, coupled with anger, makes them susceptible to depression. Depressed people often seek ways to punish the objects of their anger, perceiving suicide as one of the best means of inflicting that punishment. A young man breaks up with his girlfriend after a fight and thinks, "If I kill myself, she will forever be sorry that she broke up with me." Or after a stormy battle between mother and daughter, the young girl thinks, "If I were to die, she'd never stop blaming herself." Psychologists, social workers, the clergy, and the family physician can help get such troubled young people on the path to better mental health.

Friends also can help stem the tide of suicide by learning to spot the telltale clues. Recognize when a friend is feeling desperately low and give him or her needed moral support. You can do much by simply being a good friend. But, once you spot what you detect to be cries for help, seek professional intervention. Remember we are "our brother's keeper."

While Judaism has much to say about taking one's life, it has a more pertinent message about saving life. Our Jewish tradition tells us that, if we save even one life, it is equivalent to saving the entire world.

Cry for Help

For many people, attempting suicide is a cry for help. Those contemplating suicide usually give signs of their intentions that are easy to spot. If a close friend confides in you: "My friends don't appreciate me; they're always on my case; sometimes I want to die," this may not be idle chatter but a call for help. The problem can be dealt with successfully through psychotherapy. Where the suicide is successful, it means no one has heard these cries for help. One study reported that suicidal youth feel that their families do not understand or appreciate them. They feel unwanted and unloved. The perception of the child may be faulty, but the feelings cannot be denied.

The rising rate of divorce accounts in great

measure for the increase in the rate of suicide among youth. Separating parents often use their children as pawns, the means for one parent to inflict harm upon the other. Children are made to feel guilty for the break up. As a result some believe if they were to disappear, their parents would be able to reconcile their problems and save their marriage. Similarly children of an alcoholic, believing themselves in some way responsible for their parent's condition, have been known to commit suicide in order to resolve their parent's drinking problem.

■ To Spend the Time ■

The national and personal tragedy of substance abuse is also the tragedy of self-abuse. The effects of drugs on mind and body are sure, destructive, and addictive. No drug is "safe." Some people used to argue about the facts. The facts are no longer in dispute. The question is: Why do people of all ages, from all stations and walks of life, persist in such self-destructive behavior? How can they be helped? What does Judaism say about harming yourself?

The story that follows illustrates how easy it can be to fall into a pattern of drug abuse. Self-delusion fuels the downward spiral. Most people, however, will not be as lucky as Sharon; most need help to get out of the cycle. Remaining clean is a lifelong effort. What kind of help is available in your community? How could you help a friend, or yourself, stay away from drug abuse in the first place? Why should you?

■ To Spend the Time   BY JOY WEINBERG ■

"I'm stoned," Pat said, laughing.

"I think you're stoned, Pat," David said, passing him the bong.

"Hey, Pat, pass that when you're done," Sammy called, flinging open the door for a pretty brown-haired girl and walking in after her. They sat down.

"Who's this?" David asked.

"I'm Sharon."

"Hi, Sharon." Sammy claimed the bong. "Good stuff." He glanced at Sharon. She shook her head.

"No, not right now," she said.

"OK," Sammy shrugged. He noticed she was biting her lower lip. "Relax," he whispered. "No one's gonna make you do anything you don't want to do. It's here if you want it." He passed the bong to David.

She smiled at Sammy. He was living up to his word. When he had invited her to the party, he'd told her drugs would make her forget her problems, she'd have a good time–but he wasn't going to pressure her to take drugs. That was her decision.

What should she do? No one was forcing her to smoke. Everyone was having such a good time, smiling, laughing, enjoying the drugs. She stood apart, analyzing everything, as she always did. Why did she feel uncomfortable? Why couldn't she just have fun like everyone else? Why shouldn't she?

Why shouldn't she? She looked at Sammy again. "I'm ready," she said.

Sharon held the bong carefully, unsure of what to do. Sammy flicked the lighter, and she took a small puff. Nothing happened.

"You have to inhale more than that," David said. "Have you ever smoked before?"

"Sure, in high school everyone smoked joints." She tried to sound cool but felt foolish. She was telling the truth, but she knew he didn't believe her.

She tried again; this time she felt something. David and Sammy nodded their heads approvingly. She passed the bong to David.

"Here, watch this," he said. He inhaled for almost a minute. "How the hell can he do that!" she thought, impressed. "That would kill my throat." He passed it to her, and she drew a longer breath, passed it to Sammy. She was catching on.

"How do you two know each other?" David asked.

"We're old friends," Sammy replied, squeezing Sharon's shoulder.

"Yeah—that kind of friends."

"No, no!" Sharon burst in. "I have a boyfriend at home."

"Some boyfriend," Sammy said bitterly. He glanced at David, then back at her. "I'm sorry."

"No, it's OK." She looked at David. He was gazing at her attentively. "We've just been having some problems lately."

"I know you don't know me—but, if you want to talk about it . . ."

"No, thanks." She grimaced. She could feel Sammy's and David's eyes upon her, waiting for her to speak. "Hey," she said gaily, "we're not here to get upset. I want to be high!"

"I like this girl," David said, handing her the bong. "Take it away." She drew in sharply, waited, inhaled again. She passed it to David, who gave it to Sammy; then it was hers again. Around and around they passed it. She could feel the drug taking effect.

The rest of the night was little more than a blur to her—David and Sammy looking at her, watching her every move; she more aware of herself, her body, of them, than ever before. She felt good, at peace with herself, harmonious with the world around her. She thought of Richie, her boyfriend back home, who had just told her he loved another girl. For the first time since last Saturday, when he had broken the news, thinking about him didn't make her wince with pain. She could remember feeling destroyed, angry, humiliated, but her body felt too relaxed and wonderful

for her to experience anything but a delightful drowsiness.

At some inconceivable hour in the morning she kissed David good night on the cheek, kissed Sammy, too, after he took her home. Exhausted, but marveling at her ability to be flirtatious—and to enjoy it—she climbed into bed.

After a long, arduous day at the library, which, she had to admit, was spent more on thinking about Richie and running into friends than studying, Sharon returned home. David had left her a message: "Party at my place, seven-thirty tonight. Please come." Should she? At the library she had run into Marcy, who had asked her to see a movie, but she had seen it twice. Besides, the movie was about a "happy love" relationship—it would make her reflect on her own unhappy one. No, what she needed to do was to get her mind off Richie. For the first time in a long while last night she had forgotten all about him. At least when she was stoned, the pain of not having him subsided; she felt good about herself again. Besides, it was fun, having all that attention lavished upon her. Sammy and David fighting over her. She had to smile. If only Richie could have seen her last night! If only Richie would act that way. "No," she said out loud. She wasn't going to think about him. She changed out of jeans and a sweatshirt to a tight black blouse and white pants and headed toward David's room.

When she arrived, Sammy, Pat, and a few others were there. Strawberry incense permeated the room, Sharon's favorite. "You look good; make yourself comfortable," David said, placing a pillow under her. Lighting his pipe, he winked at her.

For a split second she wanted to get away. She felt uncomfortable, self-conscious around David's friends, who were so different from her own. She wasn't even sure of her feelings toward David. He was exciting, powerful, maybe too powerful. In her rush to attract him was she sacrificing a part of herself? Was taking drugs what she really wanted?

She shook herself. What was wrong with her? She'd had a better time last night than she'd had

A Jew Listens

in a long while. She had to stop thinking and start enjoying. Taking the pipe from David and inhaling deeply, she said to herself, "Tonight I'm going to get higher than high."

The smell of smoke filled the air, and David put on Pink Floyd's "The Wall." Everyone lay down and silently stared at the ceiling. Sharon continued smoking with David after the others had stopped. And she lay down to watch the light of the ceiling mingle with the strawberry essence. The room was alive and vibrant; the lights, the smells, were clear to her, closer than they had ever been. She felt at ease with the room, at ease with the others, at ease with David. She drifted off to sleep.

When she awoke, everyone had left. David was sitting up and looking at her, smiling. Noticing she had awakened, he plopped down beside her. "No," she said sleepily. "Hold me, then," he said, drawing her close to him, and she consented.

In the morning an awkward tension filled the room. Sharon wanted to speak to David, to talk about how she was changing, to understand him, but she didn't know what to say. David reached for the pipe, but Sharon pushed his hand away. "Let's talk."

David nodded, and she continued. "I feel like I know so little about you. I don't know where to start. God, this sounds stupid but–what's your major?"

"Biology." He laughed. "Couldn't you tell?"

"I'm majoring in Comparative Lit. Not that I can do much with it, except maybe drive a taxi-cab in New York City. . . . "

They heard a knock on the door. "Come in; it's open," David called. Pat and his girlfriend, Jeanne, walked in. "We're going to Johnny's Bar," Pat said, hugging Jeanne tightly. "Wanna come?"

"Sure," David smiled. He looked at Sharon. "Ready to go?"

"This early in the morning?"

"Why not?"

She paused. "I thought we were going to talk."

David smiled reassuringly. "We'll have plenty of time to talk after we get back–I promise. OK?"

"Sure," she said, caught off guard. She grabbed her purse, and they were off.

As time passed Sharon became happier and happier, or so she thought. Most of her time was spent with David. Life was a whirlwind of spontaneity and constant excitement. There was no time to sort through problems, to become depressed. All that mattered was what David called "pure hedonism," feeling good. Sometimes she thought twice about how her life had changed since she had begun taking drugs. Every once in a while it scared her. For the first time in her life she was losing control over her school-work, getting Bs and even an occasional C on exams. She felt alienated from her old friends. Sammy had started going out with Marcy, who had pressured him to stop taking drugs. She hardly saw them anymore.

Yet she was happiest when stoned. Whenever thoughts of Richie's rejection haunted her, being high made the pain go away. Whenever she was lonely, there were friends to get high with; there was David. It was a miracle cure.

A month after their first meeting Sharon and David threw a party to celebrate. Pat and Jeanne came, as usual, and Sammy brought Marcy along.

Sharon lit up right away. She had had a hard day.

Sammy sat down next to her. "Hi, Sharon," he said, smiling. "It's been a long time. How have you been doing?"

"Really well. David and I are highly happy. Light?"

"No thanks."

"I never thought I'd hear that word coming from your mouth," she joked.

"I don't need it anymore. Marcy gives me all the high I want."

"Not even one little puff?" She pouted.

"What are you trying to do–pressure me?"

"No." She laughed. "You look tense. I just want you to loosen up, that's all."

"What's with you lately? You seem to think you can't be happy without drugs."

She glared at him. "What are you going to do now, give me a speech about getting dependent on drugs?" She took a deep breath. "Look, Sammy, I've had a hard day. I don't want to discuss it."

"What's wrong?"

"Forget it."

"Can't we even talk? Sharon, you're like a stranger to me now. We used to spend so much time together, doing clarinet and piano duets, seeing plays. Now you're in your own little world, you and David. Tell me, when was the last time you went to the theater?"

"Not for a while."

"Well, Marcy and I have two extra tickets for *Waiting for Godot* at the College Playhouse tomorrow night at eight. Do you want to go?"

"I guess so. I'm not sure. David won't want to."

"But what do *you* want to do?"

Just then Sammy felt his hair being tousled and kissed. He looked back at smiling Marcy and nodded. "Sharon, I have to go. I didn't mean to upset you, but, please . . . think over what I said."

"OK–bye. . . . Wait!" she called, as he followed Marcy out of the room. He stopped. "Let me have those tickets," she said. "I'll see what I can do."

Sharon slept late. When she awoke, she took a long walk around the campus, thinking. She remembered a slogan she'd read: *Smoking pot is hazardous to your mental health.* She thought of David's simpler one: *Drugs are fun.* Were things easier now? Drugs gave her a temporary high, shielded her from pain. But Sammy was right, too. She was pulling away from him. And last night wasn't the first time she had gotten stoned to escape from reality. She wasn't even trying to work things out for herself anymore. She wasn't doing much besides drugs, and there was more to life.

What was the answer? Maybe she should stop–at least for a while, to pick up the friends and activities she'd left behind. Or maybe she did have to stop permanently. Even though she knew there was no such thing as physical addiction to pot, once she got started she couldn't stop. It was easy for her to become dependent, too easy.

Unsure of herself, but determined to discuss her feelings, she headed toward David's room.

As Sharon approached she could smell the sweet, pungent odor. It was David and Pat and Jeanne. "Hi, love, where've you been?" David said, passing her the pipe. She pushed his hand away. "I have something to tell you.""

"So do I," David chimed. "Gary and Pete are throwing a 'Drink All You Can' party tonight–starts at eight."

"That's what time the play is. I have free tickets to *Waiting for Godot.*"

"Waiting for who?" David, Pat, and Jeanne all doubled over with laughter.

She waited until the laughter had died down. "David, can I speak to you alone?"

Pat and Jeanne nodded at each other and left. As the door clicked Sharon took a deep breath.

"Sammy and Marcy gave me two free tickets to *Waiting for Godot* tonight. Do you want to go?"

"I've never heard of it."

"It's about these two characters who wait for someone named Godot who will change their lives."

"What happens when he comes?"

"He never does."

"Sounds pretty stupid to me. A play about people sitting around waiting for nothing is worth nothing."

She paused and suddenly blurted angrily, "But that's what we do, damn it! We sit around, not talking, not doing anything but getting high."

"Come on, Sharon, we do more than that. . . . " He chuckled softly.

"That's not what I mean. First, I'm not getting my schoolwork done: I can't concentrate anymore. Every time I try to study, people drop by to get stoned. And your friends! We can talk for hours when we're high, but otherwise we have nothing to say. That's not friendship."

"Do you feel that way about me, too?"

"No! Damn it, David, I'm not talking about you. I'm talking about *the drugs!*"

"I don't understand."

"Look at yourself. You told me you don't need them, you can stop whenever you want to, but

A Jew Listens

you're always smoking."

"It doesn't matter, Sharon. I can handle it. I'm in control. I'm not one of those people who don't know their limits."

"Maybe that's what I'm so angry about," she said. "About the pushers, the con artists, the fake friends. They're wrong. No one's to blame but me. I like getting high. It makes it easier to communicate, to forget–damn it, it just feels good! But you can't get high all the time."

"Since when have *you* changed?"

She heard the bitterness in his voice. "I'm sorry, David. I have no right to tell you what to do. All of a sudden I realized how angry I am with myself. It started last night when I spoke with Sammy . . . no, maybe it started a long time ago. But it wasn't until yesterday that I finally looked at myself. Was this what I wanted out of life–feeling good, forgetting pain, ignoring the outside world? No. I don't want to live that way."

"So you want to cut down on our drug use?"

"No, David, I have to stop for good. It's funny–I remember a guidance counselor in high school using the expression 'use is abuse,' and I never truly understood what he meant before now. I can't get stoned every once in a while–it's too easy for me to become hooked."

He sighed heavily. "How do you think this is going to affect our relationship?"

"I honestly don't know. The only thing I'm certain of right now is I need to find other things that make me happy–like seeing that play tonight."

"OK, Sharon, I think I understand."

"So are you going to come with me?"

"I can't. I promised Gary and Pete I'd be at the party. But, if you want to go, have a good time."

She looked at her watch–it was 7:45. "I have to get going."

"OK."

"Bye."

Slightly bewildered, she left in the direction of the theater.

Sharon entered the College Playhouse and took her seat. Sammy and Marcy weren't there yet. She waved at a few friends, but they nodded and walked past her. Sharon felt anger swell inside her. But what else could she expect? She hadn't made much effort to be friendly lately.

The lights dimmed. She felt alone. She was tempted to leave, to go to Pete's and Gary's party, to have David beside her.

But as the curtains opened Sharon's eyes were fixed on the stage. She no longer felt forced to stay. She wanted to.

IX

JEWS PROTECT
ONE ANOTHER

JEWS EXPRESS THEIR KINSHIP WITH OTHER JEWS. When a family member does well, we're happy. When a close relative is in trouble, we act out of concern. We help. The Jewish family shares a religious history that's almost 4,000 years old. We represent a common national history that goes back about 3,200 years to the days of Moses. All Jews worship God, celebrate the same holidays and lifecycle events. Despite a 2,000-year-old worldwide dispersion, Jews seek and enjoy close contact with one another. We accept and express the implications of *Klal Yisrael*, the unity of the Jewish people. We are family. We are responsible for one another.

Responsibility has many forms. We help other Jews by sending things to them or paying for things they need. We provide support and encouragement through letters and phone calls. Sometimes political action and advocacy are required. A visit to relatives in different lands shows family we care and helps ease their pains. Throughout history, Jews have relied on other Jews to alleviate harsh conditions Jews have experienced the world over. *Pidyon shevuyim*, ransoming captives, was an important Jewish communal responsibility in the Middle Ages. *Pikuach nefesh*, preserving an endangered life, is fundamental to Jewish religion. Historically, Jews were seldom powerful enough to intercede physically to save other Jews; however, the 1976 Entebbe Rescue by Israeli forces demonstrated that Jews could do that, too. Jewish community organizations constantly seek and preserve the welfare of Jews locally, nationally, and throughout the world. Synagogue action programs help other Jews wherever they are.

The American experience is but the most recent manifestation of Jewish concern for other Jews. In 1654 Dutch Jews made sure Peter Stuyvesant would allow refugee Jews from Recife to remain in New Amsterdam. The 1840 Damascus blood libel prompted American Jews to solicit and receive intervention by President Van Buren. Jewish reaction led President Lincoln to revoke General Grant's 1862 anti-Semitic edict. And not only in America. British Jews organized mass protest meetings against the czarist pogroms of 1881-82. Jews worldwide supported, morally and financially, the *Yishuv*, which struggled to maintain a Jewish population in Palestine at the turn of the century. Israel's heroic rescue of Yemen's Jews during the first years of statehood was accomplished under most difficult circumstances. Similar Jewish rescue efforts are under way in Russia and Ethiopia in more recent decades. American and Canadian Jews express their concern for Israel's security by lobbying with their respective governments.

Examples of Jewish actions to preserve and sustain Jews are abundant. *Kol Yisrael arevim zeh bazeh*, "all Jews are responsible for one another," is a serious obligation. It is accompanied by a parallel obligation to be informed about Jews wherever they live and especially about Jews who are powerless to control their destinies and who require our help.

This chapter will introduce you to some of the Jewish communities that rely on us for survival in their native lands or for emigration to hospitable shores. While the essays talk about the Jews of Ethiopia, Arab lands, Russia, and Israel, Jews in other communities also require our help. The remnant European Jewish communities are peopled mostly by the aged; they rely on us. Jews in South and Central America command our concern. Elderly and poor Jews in North America are frequently invisible. They, too, need us. *Kol Yisrael arevim zeh bazeh.*

▪ Beta-Israel–Lost and Found ▪

As recently as a decade ago we looked on Ethiopia's Jews as quaint or exotic, if we thought about them at all. That changed dramatically when political instability and civil war in Ethiopia threatened extinction of Ethiopian Jews, who often were trapped between warring factions. The Beta-Israel, as they prefer to be known, were further endangered by religious disputes in Israel that effectively sabotaged early rescue plans. In 1985, however, Operation Moses, financed by worldwide Jewry, brought large numbers of Ethiopian Jews to Israel in a gripping rescue effort. Today the Beta-Israel lead productive lives in Israel, preserving their unique culture while participating fully as citizens of the Jewish nation.

The following reading describes the Beta-Israel in their land, their plight over the centuries, their steadfast adherence to cherished Jewish traditions despite government persecution and persistent missionary activity. What kept the Beta-Israel, isolated from all other Jews, faithful to the Jewish tradition?

▪ Beta-Israel– Lost and Found

BY STEVEN SCHNUR ▪

Until recently, in a remote mountain region in Northeast Africa accessible only by foot or on horseback, lay 490 isolated villages inhabited by a dark-skinned people who observed the Sabbath as prescribed in the Torah, prayed in straw-roofed synagogues, ate only kosher food, and hoped one day to return to Jerusalem. To outsiders they were known as "Falashas," or exiles, but among themselves they were and are still called "Beta-Israel," the House of Israel. No one is certain where these black Jews came from, but some rabbinical authorities have traced their roots to the lost tribe of Dan.

When the Northern Kingdom of Israel was destroyed by the Assyrians in 722 B.C.E., ten of the twelve tribes of Moses were carried into exile and lost for all time, among them the tribe of Dan. Since then rumor and legend concerning the whereabouts of these missing Children of Israel have played an important role in Jewish folklore and history. Travelers and storytellers in ancient times claimed the tribes could be found in lands as remote as Arabia, India, Japan, and the Americas. One theorist wrote in 1786 that the American Indians were descendants of the ten lost tribes. But none of these groups had proved through its literature, traditions, or religious practices that it is a true descendant–none except possibly the Beta-Israel of Ethiopia.

Both the Jews and Christians of the country trace their ancestry to Menelik, the legendary son of King Solomon and the Queen of Sheba, and to his followers who, according to legend, helped him steal the Holy Ark from Jerusalem and transport it to Ethiopia. When, the folklore relates, they reached the banks of the mythic Sambatyon River, the Sabbath had arrived. Those who violated Mosaic law and crossed the river with Menelik became Ethiopian Christians. Those who remained behind in the mountains eventually became a mighty nation of Jewish warriors.

During the Middle Ages this nation of black Jews succeeded in conquering much of Ethiopia. Later, however, it was defeated by Christian tribes and persecuted by a succession of anti-Jewish Christian rulers. Queen Esthers and Judiths abound in Beta-Israel history as do King Gideons, all of whom were remembered for rescuing their people from enslavement. Because of an endless series of wars, virtually all records kept by the early Beta-Israel were destroyed. Only the Ethiopian Chronicle kept by the Christian kings remains as testimony to centuries of persecution and slaughter.

Earliest Accounts of the Beta-Israel

Apart from the Chronicle the earliest surviving account of the Ethiopian Jews appears in the writings of one Eldad ha-Dani, a ninth-century traveler who claimed to be a member of the lost tribe of Dan. According to him, the Danites had settled in Ethiopia together with the other lost tribes of Naphtali, Gad, and Asher in 681 B.C.E., but only the Danites had survived. Benjamin of Tudela wrote three centuries later about Jewish towns and fortresses in the land south of Egypt, and in 1438 Elijah of Ferrara recounted a meeting with an Ethiopian Jew in Jerusalem who spoke of their successful wars in Africa and of their unique language, Ge'ez. Fifty years later Obadiah of Bertinoro told of meeting Ethiopian Jews in Egypt who claimed the legendary Sambatyon River still flowed in Ethiopia and continued to separate the Children of Moses from Christians. With the exception of Jesuit mission-

aries who visited the Beta-Israel in 1541, however, no effort was made until the nineteenth century to authenticate the existence of these suspected descendants of the lost tribe of Dan.

In the intervening years the once-powerful nation of Jews was conquered and stripped of its rights by a succession of Christian rulers who attempted to annihilate them or forcibly convert them to Coptic Christianity. Like the Marranos in Spain, the fifteenth-century Beta-Israel were forced to practice their Judaism in secret. Then, in 1559, they suffered their own Masada at the mountain fortress of Mashaka. Rather than be captured and sold into slavery by the Ethiopian King Sarsa Dengel, the defending Jews slit their own throats or leapt from the fortress's great precipice. The king celebrated his victory by saying Mass atop the stronghold and burning whatever Beta-Israel texts he found there.

Exterminator of the Jews

In 1616, following the example of an earlier ruler who had called himself "The Exterminator of the Jews," the negus (king) Susneyos crucified the leader of the Jewish community and ordered the killing of all adult Beta-Israel and the enslavement of all their children. Declaring it illegal for Ethiopian Jews to own land, he forced them to become artisans and tenant farmers.

Since Susneyos's decrees, the Beta-Israel have lived an impoverished life as second-class citizens. Estimated to number nearly a million in the days of their independent kingdom, they dwindled to no more than a hundred thousand in 1900 and today number roughly twenty-eight thousand. Poverty, warfare, and disease are responsible for much of this decline, but so, too, are the efforts of Christian missionaries.

Christian Missionaries

In 1770 the Scottish explorer of the Blue Nile, James Bruce, reported meeting several Jews in their Ethiopian capital of Gondar. From them and their High Priests he assembled and published an account of Beta-Israel history from the thirteenth century. The result of his disclosures, however, was not an effort to save this vanishing people from extinction but a minor crusade by Anglican missionaries to convert the "heathens" to Christianity. Led by several Jewish converts to the Church of England, the London Society for the Promotion of Christianity amongst the Jews further diminished the number of Ethiopian Jews by baptizing them into the Ethiopian Orthodox Church, a practice that pleased the emperor.

Customs of the Beta-Israel

The most famous of these apostate missionaries, Henry A. Stern, carefully detailed his exploits in the jungles of Africa. The Beta-Israel he attempted to convert ate only the meat they themselves slaughtered, prayed twice a day in their *mesgid*, or synagogue, and washed so frequently, in accordance with religious laws, that their neighbors said they could always identify them by their smell of fresh water. Their dress and physical characteristics were similar to their Christian neighbors, but their *kohanim* (priests) wore a white headdress distinguishing them from the rest of the community. They celebrated the Jewish festivals of Rosh Hashanah, Yom Kippur, Sukot, and Passover, slaughtering a paschal lamb during the celebration of deliverance from Egypt and smearing the animal's blood over the entrance to the synagogue as prescribed in the Torah. The only religious writings known to the Beta-Israel, however, were the Five Books of Moses and several apocryphal books–which the talmudic rabbis, unknown to them, had excluded from the canon. Because they left the Land of Israel before the rabbinic period, the Beta-Israel, until modern times, had no knowledge of the Talmud and therefore practiced a purely Mosaic Judaism. Curiously the Christian practices of confession and monastic seclusion had been adopted by them.

Jewish Rescue Efforts

In 1869, determined to counter the effects of the missionaries, Professor Joseph Halevy of the Sorbonne journeyed to Ethiopia to strengthen their Jewish identity through education and contact with the world Jewish community. Returning to Europe with two promising Ethiopian Jewish students, he began a campaign to direct Jewish resources toward the dwindling African community. His efforts bore fruit in the person of Jacques Faitlovitch, one of his students, who absorbed his enthusiasm. In 1904 Faitlovitch made the arduous journey to the mountains of Ethiopia, where he set up mobile schools and medical clinics. But a controversy arose when a rabbi sent to verify their Jewishness returned to France convinced they were not authentic Jews. As a result most sources of financial aid were cut off. Faitlovitch overcame the difficulty by raising funds privately, particularly in America and Italy, through "Pro-Beta-Israel" committees. With the help of his sister, Leah, who said later of him, "His whole life was consecrated to assisting them," Faitlovitch improved health care, trained teachers, established a boarding school in the Ethiopian capital of Addis Ababa, and arranged European and Palestinian educations for a few who later became not only the leaders of their community but members of the government of Emperor Haile Selassie.

Beta-Israel Still Outcasts

Until 1975 the Beta-Israel were not fully accepted by the Israeli government, despite the fact that several prominent rabbis had recognized them as Jews. In 1921 the Ashkenazic chief rabbi of Palestine, Abraham Isaac Kook, called for the rescue of "fifty thousand holy souls of the House of Israel from oblivion." His successor, Rabbi Yitzhak Herzog, the first Ashkenazic chief rabbi of the State of Israel, also recognized their Jewishness. They live in the midst of war-torn Ethiopia, preyed upon by terrorists, and all but ignored by the rest of the world.

Then in 1982 thousands of the Beta-Israel began making their way on foot over the mountains and across the desert to refugee camps in Sudan. Slowly, and after great hardship, ten thousand eventually reached Israel, but many thousands more remained behind in squalid, overcrowded camps, prey to hostilities and disease. In 1984 the Israeli government organized Operation Moses, a secret airlift that transported seven thousand of these refugee Jews to freedom. A year later another eight hundred were rescued by Operation Joshua, a United States-sponsored airlift. But fifteen to twenty thousand Beta-Israel still remain in Ethiopia.

Of the 490 remote villages that once dotted the mountainous Gondar region only a handful survive, the result of forced resettlement and exile. Three thousand Beta-Israel now live in the Ethiopian capital of Addis Ababa, many as

"Marranos," fearing for their lives, hoping one day to escape to safety. Under a family reunification agreement reached in 1989 between the governments of Israel and Ethiopia, 550 Jews a month are now permitted to resettle in Israel, but for the thousands left behind, hope seems to be fading. Their life in Ethiopia amounts to little more than slavery, they say, and like the slaves of Egypt they hope they, too, might one day know deliverance from bondage.

▪ Eliyahu's Visit ▪

A Jew is never a stranger in a Jewish community, even in one like the Beta-Israel, which has been hidden from the Jewish world for generations. As a Jewish traveler soon discovered, innumerable points of reference in a shared history and destiny connect Jew to Jew. Jews feel at home with other Jews.

This reading is a compelling vignette of life in a Beta-Israel village in Ethiopia. The author's experiences lead to his immediate identification with his gracious and grateful hosts. Which experiences were most effective in identifying the bonds between Spira and the Beta-Israel? Explain.

▪ Eliyahu's Visit   BY ELI SPIRA ▪

I knew there was a small village of Beta-Israel a short distance out of Gondar. I did not know if they celebrated *seder* as we Jews of the West do. I did not know if their calendar was equal to ours and if indeed tonight was *seder* night for them. I did not know if they would welcome outsiders to their religious celebrations, and I did not know if I was an outsider to them.

I arrived at the small village by means of a rented horse-and-buggy escort. I looked around. Mud-and-stick huts stood in a disorderly fashion on a hillside. Some looked poor and pitiful; some looked worse. I heard voices coming from a mud building that looked a little better than the others. As I was nearing the building a man appeared in the door. He looked at me and said: "*Shalom*." The "*shalom*" sounded sweet, beautiful, comfortable, and welcoming. I answered "*Shalom*," and he asked: "*Ata medaber ivrit?* (Do

you speak Hebrew?)" I said yes and was glad we had a common language.

"I am the teacher Yair," he said in a fine, almost accent-free Hebrew. "I am a visitor from America and my name is Eliyahu," I answered. "Would you come in, please, into the classroom?" I followed the teacher into the schoolhouse. It was clean but terribly poor. Dirt floor, few wooden benches, two small tables, and over thirty kids, most in rags, most of them sitting on the floor. They were having a lesson in Hebrew.

Invitation to a Seder
Yair turned to me and said he must leave because he was especially busy today. "It's a holiday tonight–*seder*," he said. "Can I stay for the *seder*?" I asked. "Of course, Eliyahu; I'll be back soon," he said. He called to a small boy; "Daniel, come here. Show Eliyahu around." My guide,

nine-year-old Daniel, spoke beautiful Hebrew. Yair taught him, he said. "Let's walk around," I said, wanting to see the village. "There is nothing to see," said Daniel. "What's over there, across the street?" I asked. "The *goyim*," replied Daniel. "They don't like the Jews."

He looked up as if he wanted to say something but remained standing with his dark black eyes intensely looking at me and his mouth partially open. We kept walking quietly until he suddenly asked, "Are you Jewish?" "Yes," I replied, "I am." "How can you be Jewish?" said Daniel, and, touching my hand, added, "You are not black." "Daniel," I told him, "I am Jewish, and there are many Jews who are not black. The color of the skin is not what makes a person a Jew. It's the heart, and all the Jews have the same color in their hearts."

We visited Daniel's home, a one-room mud-and-stick building where five or six people lived in a four-hundred square-foot space. Daniel's father was a carpenter, and I admired his tools and craftsmanship. His mother offered me tea-the food was hidden because of the approaching holiday. While I was sipping the hot, sweet drink, Daniel's sister, who sat behind me, pulled my jacket. In a quiet voice, almost whispering, she asked, "Is it true, Eliyahu, that we are all going to go to Israel?" "Why is it so?" I demanded. "Yair said so," she replied. "If Yair said so, it must be true," I said.

Healing the Sick

While I was talking to Daniel's father about his occupation (he spoke only Amharic, and Daniel was the interpreter), the question of my trade came up. "A veterinarian," I said, and tried to explain, "doctor for animals." I don't think they got the "animals," but they got the "doctor," because I was right away asked to look at Daniel's aunt, who was in the next hut, sick. She was lying on the floor in pain. She obviously had abdominal cramps, the reason for which I could not diagnose. I took from the first-aid kit I carried with me two Probanthine tablets and gave them to the woman. The word that there was a doctor in the village spread like fire. I was next

called to see a mother with a few-months-old baby in her arms. The baby was more dead than alive, and the mother tried to press his lifeless lips to her dry nipple. She clutched her baby, looking like a cornered, frightened animal. We boiled milk, added sugar, and prescribed it for the baby because there was nothing else to prescribe. When I left the mother, I was choking from quiet cries and dry tears.

The woman whom I had seen first believed a miracle had happened. She had been in pain and could hardly get up for two days and now she was walking around feeling much better. She was praising God and kissed my hands. I was ashamed because I knew I had cured nothing. The drug dissolved the cramps and alleviated the pain, but whatever caused the illness was probably still there.

The men went down to the river to wash, and soon after they returned we went to the synagogue. The synagogue was a round building, twenty-five feet in diameter with no windows, only one door. To the north, facing Jerusalem, stood an ark with books in it, which the elders removed and read from.

After reading and praying we went down to the schoolhouse. It was packed. The wooden benches were against the walls, and the older men sat on them. In the middle of the room stood two small tables. Yair sat behind one table and asked me to sit behind the other. I protested that I had come to watch and learn, not to perform. "I don't know how you celebrate Passover," I said to Yair. "Just like the Jews anywhere," he answered me, pointing to the modern Haggadah in front of me.

Leading the Seder

I opened the book and started leading the *seder* as I do at home, as it is done in my father's home. It never had dawned on me that the Passover story starts with "Next year in the Land of Israel" and ends with "Next year in Jerusalem," but today it was different. It was not a Haggadah, it was not a Passover story, it was not a phrase, it was a cry, a petition, a question, a hope.

Jews Protect One Another

The kids knew all the melodies, and everyone joined in the singing. Men and women looked in through the windows. It was a *seder* for the whole village, but the room could hold only a quarter or a third of the people. It was a beautiful *seder*, but without a meal. After we finished reading the Haggadah, every family went to its house to eat. I went with Yair to his house, a simple mud hut, enforced with branches and with a metal roof. The meal consisted of *matzah* and a green salad. That was all. For me they boiled three chicken eggs, which I felt like devouring, because I had eaten nothing the whole day. When I saw that no one else had eggs, I ate only one and passed the other two along. They asked me to tell them about Israel, America, about Jews everywhere.

It was getting late and two young men offered to accompany me to Gondar. "It is not safe for you to walk alone at night on the road," they said. "If we leave now, you can be in your hotel in Gondar in less than two hours." "Can't I sleep here?" I asked. I saw Yair's face light up with joy. "You want to stay with us?" he asked, obviously surprised and happy. "Yes," I said. As the men placed some straw mats and rags on the dirt floor, Yair brought out a sheep's skin. "For you," he said. I realized I was the only one honored to sleep on a soft, woolen bedding. As the kerosene lantern was blown out, I said good night to the people in the room. Someone answered, "Next year in Jerusalem."

Eliyahu's Cup

I awoke early the next morning and knew I'd better start walking, for I had to be in Gondar no later than nine in the morning. I was very thirsty: the *seder's* spicy salad, I thought to myself. I looked around, and through the open door of the schoolhouse I saw on one of the tables the cup of Eliyahu. I knew it had been full of wine last night, and, even though I knew that all Yair had were two bottles, I could not resist my thirst. I walked into the schoolhouse and almost emptied the cup. As I left the room an old man was standing outside waiting for me. I knew he saw me drink the wine and I apologized, explaining I was very thirsty. He answered in a calming voice, "It's all right, Eliyahu, may God bless you. Is not the wine in the cup for Eliyahu? God sent you to us. I am an old man, but not until today did I see Eliyahu drink the wine from his cup. We have many visitors that come to look at us, but never did one share our food, sleep in our houses, teach our children, cure our sick, and lead us on *seder* night. I knew you would leave before daybreak, and I came to bid you farewell."

As I left, he said very quietly, barely audibly, "*Shalom*, Eliyahu." I could say nothing. I picked up my bag and walked slowly down the hillside to the road leading to Gondar. In the distance I saw the village. In front of the schoolhouse stood the old man clad in white on the same spot where I had left him. I knew all the time that he was looking at me. I knew he wouldn't let his eyes off me until I vanished around the mountain, and now I tried to catch his eyes with mine. We stood far apart and yet so close. I heard the old man praying to God. He was praying like he had a thousand times before, yet now there seemed to be more hope in his voice. He said. "Our Father who is in heaven, You made so many miracles. Please make one more. Help us."

▪ Foundations for Oppression ▪

For about 2,500 years Arab lands have been home to Jews who remained there despite persecution, conquest, pogrom. Denied equality, these proud Jews nevertheless participated in and contributed to the cultures of their host lands. In moments of official enlightenment, Jews rose high in their native lands under Arab rule. At best, however, Jews were a grudgingly tolerated minority. Why did they stay? Why have they now all but disappeared from lands that were their homes for over two millennia?

This selection reviews the inconstancy of Jewish life in Arab lands. Special emphasis is placed on the Muslim-Jewish relationship starting with the Muslim conquests of the seventh century. Is the Golden Age a good measure of Jewish achievement under Arab rule? Explain. What perpetuates the myth that Jews lived idyllic lives under Muslim rule? Why is the myth especially dangerous today?

■ Foundations for Oppression

BY MARTIN A. COHEN ■

In recent years Arab propagandists have painted an idyllic picture of the relationships of Jews and Arabs in the past. Their claim is that Jews and Arabs have always lived peacefully and congenially. With such propaganda the Arabs are trying to persuade people that the State of Israel today has nothing to lose by opening its doors wide to every Arab who would enter.

Like most propaganda, the Arabs' claims are not without some foundation. Jews have achieved position and wealth in the Arab world, as well as close professional, social, and cultural contacts with their Arab counterparts. Some of the greatest Jewish intellectual achievements took place in the midst of Arab society.

Jews and various Arabic peoples have lived together since biblical days. There were many Jews in the city of Medina when Muhammad , in the year 622, created a new faith called Islam (meaning "submission to God's will") and began to build an amazing empire. By the year 650 it stretched from Persia to Libya; by 750 from India and across North Africa to encompass Spain. Jews were present in most of these lands and, despite changes in governments and political boundaries, have remained in them until the present day.

Jews often welcomed the conquering Muslims, as the adherents to Islam were called, especially in Christian lands where they agonized under burdensome economic restrictions. Under the Arabs humbler Jews could usually freely engage in handicrafts, petty trade, and even agriculture, while the more sophisticated could devote themselves to international commerce, banking, medicine, and diplomacy.

Eras of Achievement

Some of the Jews' greatest achievements are concentrated in three periods under Arab rule—from the years 850 to 950 in the region around Baghdad, from 950 to 1140 in Spain, which the Muslims called Al-Andalus, and from 1500 to 1650 in the Ottoman Empire, especially in cities like Constantinople and Salonika. In Baghdad wealthy merchants like the Aaron and Netira families developed international trade and modern forms of banking, while the great rabbinic academies made the Talmud the constitution of Jewish life and sent learned letters of religious guidance (responsa) throughout the Muslim world. In Al-Andalus Jews furnished the Muslims with outstanding diplomats, like Hasdai ibn Shaprut (circa 915-970) and the amazing Samuel ibn Nagrela (993-1056), who served as special adviser to the king of Granada and commander of his army. They produced as well a golden age of Hebrew poetry and Jewish philosophers like Solomon ibn Gabirol (1021-1069), Yehudah Halevi (1086-1148 [?]), and Moses Maimonides (1135-1204). In the Ottoman Empire, Jews from Spain and Portugal developed commerce, administration, and the imperial army, which they introduced to the use of gunpowder. They also began to resettle the Holy Land, where the city of Safed became an important center. In their midst lived Joseph Karo (1488-1575), compiler of the *Shulchan Aruch* (The "Prepared Table"), the

·207·

Jews Protect One Another

great code of Jewish law; Solomon Luria (1534-1572), founder of a mystical movement in Safed that eventually influenced Chasidism; and countless other great scholars and teachers.

The Other Side of the Coin

Undeniably impressive as such achievements are, it would be erroneous to regard them as typical of Jewish experience in the Muslim world and, even more so, as typical of the experience of the average Jew.

Considering the total Jewish populations under Muslim control for all lands and centuries, we realize that the achievers of wealth, status, and culture were deceptively few. Glamorous and colorful, the exceptional few who enjoyed life under Arab rule are remembered, while the nameless majority who suffered from dire conditions, from which even the few were not always exempt, are often repressed and forgotten. Yet it is by turning to these conditions that we can appreciate what Jewish life under Arab rule was really like.

For this there is no better starting point than the Koran, Islam's holy book, the basis of its faith and behavior.

Jews in the Koran

Although it borrowed heavily from the Hebrew Scriptures and rabbinic tradition, and in places urges kind treatment of the Jews, the Koran brands Jews as insolent, depraved, hypocritical, and idolatrous. It charges that they "devour the property of people falsely." It accuses them of plotting against Muhammad and spying against the faithful of Islam. It insists that the Jews falsified the Bible to conceal proof of Islam's truth and references to the coming of Muhammad. It admonishes its faithful not to take Jews or Christians for friends and advocates the destruction of those who do not believe in Islam.

Such attitudes, embellished by Muslim tradition and polemics, explain the enshrinement of contempt for the Jew in Islamic law and practice from Muhammad's time to the twentieth century.

Restrictions on Jews

Jews were not permitted to dress like Muslims and frequently had to wear special patches on their clothing. A Turkish sultan once ordered the execution of all his Jews because their clothes were too beautiful. A healthy payment saved the Jewish community, but the sultan still imposed oppressive sumptuary regulations.

Jews could not build tall houses or ride horseback or testify against a Muslim, except under great restrictions. They were required to pay tax surcharges and special taxes, including a poll tax (a "*head*" tax for *protection*) and clothes tax. One Muslim jurist, Ash-Shafi, declared that a tax of up to two-thirds the value of Jewish property could be levied. In addition, Jews had to provision troops and traveling diplomats and stock harems with young women and food. One medieval Arab conquerer of Morocco even ordered the Jews to provide his slaves with wine.

Jews were compelled to behave submissively before Muslims. Hardly atypical in this regard is the degradation suffered by Algerian Jews from the Middle Ages to modern times, poignantly described by Henri Garrot in his book *Les Juifs Algériens* (1898):

If a Jew met a Muslim while traveling in the mountains on a donkey or a mule, he had to dismount, take the beast by the bridle, get over to the side of the road at a respectful distance from the Muslim, and could not remount his beast until the Muslim had entirely disappeared from sight.

The first Muslim on a scene had the right of requisition over the Jews. He could impose work on them he would not even have demanded of slaves or beasts of burden. He would make them bear heavy loads, without even being obligated to pay them in return.

Jewish women were powerless to refuse the erotic advances of Muslims.

A Muslim could take the first Jew he came across on the road and make him serve as a mount. At his pleasure he could even put a bit in his mouth and guide him like a packhorse. Any Jew who refused was brought to the judge and, after a beating, was thrown in jail and often sold as a slave, unless he became a Muslim.

Jews were not permitted to enter a mosque. In some places they had to doff their hats and shoes if they passed by a mosque and were subject to a drubbing if they forgot. They were forbidden to build new synagogues, though gifts into ever-open hands would often close the eyes of officials. They were occasionally permitted to repair existing synagogues that had been damaged by the elements or wanton attacks by Arab mobs who broke, tore, and desecrated everything in sight.

Victims of Mobs

Wherever they lived, Jews were at the mercy of mobs. Whenever it served a political end, the mob could be turned against them. Among the cases of such occurrence none is more tragic than the massacre of the Jews in Granada in 1066 following the execution of the Jewish foreign minister, Joseph, the son of Samuel ibn Nagrela.

They were also at the mercy of soldiers. The Janizaries (elite troops) of the Ottoman Empire, for example, outraged Jews and plundered their homes in city and country alike so regularly and mercilessly that until this century Jewish mothers bent on disciplining wayward youngsters could expect immediate success with the mere threat of calling the "janizaros." The Janizary corps, incidentally, had been disbanded in 1826.

And Jews were at all times subject to the whims of their Muslim overlords. "The deys and beys (i.e., the governors) inflict grave outrages upon them every day," writes a scholar of North African Jewry, "and often for acts that would bring a slave only a drubbing."

Among these outrages was expulsion from home, city, or country. The great liberal Muslim caliph of the ninth century, Al-Mamum, once capriciously expelled large numbers of Jews from Baghdad. Jews were ejected from the great Tunisian city of Kairowan in the eleventh century,

from countless cities of Spain in the twelfth, and from towns and villages in various times and places.

Even worse were the massacres inflicted upon them, particularly by warring armies in times of revolt and conquest. In one decade alone, the 1140s, countless Jewish settlements in North Africa were wiped out by the fanatical Almohades, who also demanded conversion or expulsion for the Jews of Al-Andalus. Among the refugees was Moses Maimonides. He later wrote a heartening letter to the Yemenite Jews who were burdened by guilt for their forced conversion to Islam. Up to the twentieth century Muslim authorities in Yemen kidnapped Jewish orphans and raised them as converts to Islam. No less frightening was the massacre by North African Arabs of countless Jewish refugees from Spain and Portugal in the 1490s and the starving of many of the survivors.

Pact of Omar

All these disabilities and afflictions were rooted in a revered document called the "Pact of Omar," after the great Muslim caliph of the seventh century (ruled 634 to 644), who forbade Jews from entering Jerusalem. The Pact of Omar prescribed the treatment of non-Muslims, who were called *dhimmis*, or "protected ones," a second-class status of toleration from which even the best and highest placed among them could never escape. A distinguished Muslim jurist of the seventeenth century, citing older authorities, expressed this status when he said of Jews and Christians alike: "The absence of every mark of consideration toward them is obligatory for us." Muslim lay people frequently said: "The Jew is no more than a dog."

To be sure, the regulations and implications of the Pact of Omar were not always rigidly enforced. Jews were not beaten or robbed or sadistically humiliated at every moment. But the foundations for oppression were ever present in tradition, law, and the precedent of practice. Even in trifling matters there was reluctance to jog these foundations. The Yemenites, for example, refused a request to forbid Muslim schoolboys from stoning Jews because such sport, they said, was an age-old custom and could therefore not be forbidden! Of such practices the distinguished Jewish scholar S.D. Goitein wrote (1955): "On the basis of my personal acquaintance with many Yemen Jews, I can vouch that they have had a very adverse effect upon the psychology of the people concerned." The same has always applied to the nameless majority of Jews in the Muslim world.

Even in the best of times the lot of the Jews was therefore insecure, their hopes limited, and their spirits fettered wherever they lived in the vast and complex Arab world. Even though this world produced times of peace, prosperity, and relative quiet for the Jewish people, even though it brought them to many peaks of cultural and intellectual achievement, it was not a utopia, not by any stretch of the imagination.

▪ Jews in Muslim Lands ▪

A decade ago many Jews, despite increasing hardship, still lived in Arab lands. Today only pitiful remnants can be found, and in only some of the countries. Most of the Jews have been killed or rescued. The lucky ones now live mostly in Israel and the United States. The once proud, vigorous, creative, and deeply Jewish communities in Arab lands are footnotes in history.

The following describes what Jewish living was like under a succession of oppressive Arab regimes. Personal safety was problematic. Communal survival was vulnerable. Are there lessons for today? Some Arabs, for example, suggest solving the Middle East situation by creating a "secular, democratic state" under Arab hegemony in Israel. Polemics aside, what can we learn from history about such an idea?

▪ Jews in Muslim Lands   BY GEORGE E. GRUEN ▪

Anxiety and concern for the future cast a constant shadow over the daily lives of the small Jewish communities that continue to exist in the Muslim countries of the Middle East and North Africa. This is true even in countries such as Morocco and Tunisia, where the Jews enjoy freedom and are under the protection of benevolent rulers, for no one can predict when the regime may be overthrown by assassination, coup, or popular uprising.

A recent example was the bloodless coup in which Habib Bourguiba, Tunisia's "president for life," was deposed in November 1987 by Zine el-Abidine Ben Ali, his prime minister. The ailing eighty-four-year-old "father of the nation" had ruled Tunisia since leading the country to independence from France in 1956. He had actively protected the Jewish community in the face of

anti-Israeli demonstrations in 1967. However, growing Islamic fundamentalism in recent years and virulent anti-Semitism, fanned by inflammatory broadcasts from neighboring Libya, resulted in several incidents against Jewish institutions. The most serious was the killing of three Jews and the wounding of eight others during services on Simchat Torah in October 1985. (This occurred a few days after Israeli forces had bombed the PLO headquarters outside Tunis.) The attack on the Jews was committed by a crazed guard who had been assigned by the authorities to protect the ancient synagogue on the island of Djerba. The perpetrator was captured as he was fleeing to Libya.

Within days of his assuming power, Ben Ali met with the leaders of the Jewish community to assure them he would continue to protect them.

While Ben Ali has maintained the country's generally pro-Western orientation, he has also recently restored relations with Libya, which had been broken off by Tunisia in protest against Colonel Qaddafi's campaign of subversion. Ben Ali has permitted opposition parties to function and has also eased up on the harsh crackdown on local fundamentalists, which he himself had earlier instituted as Bourguiba's minister of interior. Despite the governmental reassurances and the normal functioning of Jewish institutions, the population continues to dwindle through gradual emigration. Today fewer than 2,200 Jews remain, as against a pre-1948 total of 105,000.

The same pattern can be found in Morocco, where only some ten thousand Jews remain. This contrasts with the more than three hundred thousand who lived there forty years ago. Like Bourguiba, King Hassan has provided full rights to the Jewish community. The dynamic young king is pro-Western and has adopted a relatively moderate stand in the Arab-Israel conflict, even though he is chairman of the al-Quds (Jerusalem) Committee of the Arab League. The king played an important behind-the-scenes role in facilitating Egypian-Israeli contacts in 1977, has secretly hosted Israeli leaders over the years, and openly received Prime Minister Shimon Peres in July 1986. Moroccan Jews are free to travel, and those who have emigrated, including the 150,000 who have gone to Israel, are welcome to return on visits.

The majority of the Jewish population lives in Casablanca (6,500), with the others mainly in Marrakech, Tangier, Rabat, Meknes, Fez, and Kenitra. The local community boards are federated into a Council of Jewish Communities. As a result of mass emigration and the continual departure for study abroad of most youngsters upon completion of high school, the community has a disproportionate number of very young and aged. Educational, health, and other social services are assisted by the American Jewish Joint Distribution Committee (JDC), a well as such groups as the French OSE, Lubavitch, and Otzar Hatorah. The uncertainties of life in an increasingly Arab nationalist country where there have

been several attempts on King Hassan's life, together with better professional and social opportunities abroad, have prompted most of the young adults to settle in France, Israel, Canada, and the United States.

In Algeria fewer than 300 Jews remain as against 130,000 in 1948. The majority are over sixty years old and reside in Algiers. In May 1988 the last functioning synagogue was desecrated by vandals who tore Torah scrolls, ripped prayer books, and broke furniture. Interior Minister El Hadi Khedri met with the president of the local Jewish community, Roger Said, to promise that the police would seek out the vandals. The police arrested eight teenagers and charged them with robbery after stolen Jewish objects were found in local stores.

Only six Jews remain in Libya. Widespread anti-Jewish riots in the days preceding and following the outbreak of the June 1967 Arab-Israel war led to the evacuation of most of the 4,000 Jews who had not emigrated earlier. In Egypt, during the 1967 war, some 500 Jewish men, or most of the adult males of the community, were incarcerated and kept in prison for many months. Since the 1979 peace treaty with Israel, the tiny and aged Jewish communities in Cairo (83) and Alexandria (95) have been permitted to resume contact with their relatives in the Jewish state. In 1983 the JDC was permitted to establish a social welfare program in Egypt. (The JDC also assists the Jewish communities in Algeria; Melilla, a Spanish enclave near Morocco with 1,300 Jews; Tunisia; and Syria.)

Some 300 elderly Jews remain in Iraq, a pitiful remnant of a community that once numbered 125,000. Permitted to worship and no longer harassed, they live with bitter memories of pogroms and persecution, including the hanging of eleven Jews in 1969 on trumped-up charges of espionage.

The formerly affluent and flourishing Jewish community in Lebanon, which had been protected by successive Christian-dominated governments, now numbers only a few dozen. The civil war that broke out in 1975 accelerated the rate of Jewish emigration. Most of the remaining Jews left when the Israeli forces withdrew following the 1982 war. The old-age home in Muslim West Beirut was evacuated after four Lebanese Jews, including leaders of the community, were kidnaped in March 1985. A new radical Shi'ite group, "the Organization of the Oppressed on Earth," claimed responsibility and threatened to kidnap and kill other Jews unless Israel withdrew from "all occupied territories" and released Lebanese and Palestinian detainees. Eight Jews have reportedly been killed by this terrorist group, ideologically linked to the pro-Iranian Hezbullah (Party of God). Since the terrorists have released the bodies of only three of their captives, the fate of others remains uncertain. A glimmer of hope remains that two kidnap victims may still be alive. They are Isaac Sasson, president of the Lebanese community, who was abducted in March 1985, and Salim Jammous, secretary general, kidnaped in August 1984.

The overall trend among the Jewish communities in the Middle East and North Africa is the winding down and in many cases the disappearance of historic communities. Discrimination, persecution, mob violence, and more subtle political, economic, and psychological pressures, as well as positive factors–notably a desire to live in a reborn Jewish state in the Holy Land or to enjoy the opportunities in Western democracies–have combined to produce a sharp decline in the Jewish population in the Arab world from nearly 900,000 in 1948 to fewer than 20,000 today. Jews have voted with their feet.

But in Syria and Yemen, Jews are forbidden to emigrate. "Every time there is a knock on the door, mothers and fathers shake with fear for their children. Will the agents of the Mukhabarat (secret police) take us to jail or to some even more horrific fate? We are constantly spied upon by the authorities and our whole life is one big question mark." This was part of the testimony of "Esther," a young Jewish mother from Damascus, whose husband "Yaacov" and their daughter managed to escape from Syria within the past year.

Despite the possible risk to their families remaining in Syria, they came to Paris at the end of March 1988 to appeal to participants in the second International Conference for the Freedom of Syrian Jewry to "do as much as you can as quickly as possible." Turning to the members of the press in the audience, Esther urged them to write about the conditions of the Jews in Syria. "Your work is extremely important," she said, "because it has a big impact on the Syrian government."

In her testimony to the conference Esther stated that there are many young Jewish girls who would like to leave but cannot do so. Their mothers are worried and frightened for the fate of their daughters. (Another participant recalled that four young Jewish women were murdered when they tried to flee Syria in 1974. Their mutilated bodies were returned to their families in sacks by the Syrian authorities.) It is not only fear of the consequences that deters many young women from attempting to escape. Most Syrian Jews don't know what life in freedom is, Esther said. "They were born in shackles; they are like birds in a cage." Having lived all their lives in a police state, it is hard for them to imagine life in a free society.

Since more young Jewish men than women have successfully fled the country, and because a number of men are not marrying–hoping to start families in freedom rather than trying to escape with a wife and young children, many Jewish women are destined for spinsterhood if they are not permitted to leave to seek husbands abroad. As time goes on an increasing number may be tempted to marry Muslim or Christian men.

The Syrian authorities still employ draconian measures to enforce the ban on Jewish emigration. Even those permitted to go on brief trips abroad must generally leave behind a substantial monetary deposit and immediate members of their family as security for their return. The estimated 4,000 Syrian Jews, 3,000 of whom are concentrated in Damascus, with 800 in Aleppo and 200 in Qamishly, are in effect a hostage community.

Desperate attempts to leave the country continue. Those who are caught or suspected of planning to travel "illegally" are held in prison by the agents of the Mukhabarat. Nine Jewish men from Damascus were picked up in the second half of 1987. According to Amnesty International, they have reportedly been subjected to beatings and other forms of torture and denied access to legal counsel. In several cases even their families were denied permission to visit them. While four of the nine have been released, as of October 1988, five were still incarcerated. They are Albert (Ibrahim) Laham, 43; his son Yeheya (Victor), 18; Zaki Mamrout, 31; Eli Soued, 31; his older brother Selim Soued, 45. In July 1988 Jack Lalo, 50, was arrested on suspicion of planning to leave.

Although restrictions on the daily life of the Jewish community have been eased in recent years, and synagogues and Jewish schools function under the watchful eyes of the authorities, Jews are still barred from employment in government offices or public bodies, such as banks, and suffer from discriminatory economic and legal practices restricting their rights to dispose of property through sale or inheritance.

Given these restrictions and the ban on emigration, it may seem ironic that Syrian Jews fervently pray for President Hafez al-Assad's health. He suffers from a variety of serious ailments and has been the target of assassination attempts by the Muslim Brotherhood, a Sunni fundamentalist sect opposing the secularized regime of Assad, who belongs to the minority Alawite community. Assad's forces brutally crushed a Muslim Brotherhood revolt in Hama in February 1982, Jews fear that their position would be far worse should the fanatical Brotherhood succeed in overthrowing Assad.

The Yemen Arab Republic is another country that totally bars Jewish emigration. No one knows how many Jews were left behind following Operation Magic Carpet, which brought nearly all Yemen's Jews to Israel in the first years of the state. Current estimates are that between 1,200 and 2,000 Jews remain, scattered in more than forty villages in the mountainous northern part of the country. (Others believe there may be more than 5,000, including those nominally converted to Islam.) Yemenite Jews are not actively harassed and are "protected" by the local tribal leaders in return for payment of the traditional Islamic poll tax. They conduct day-to-day economic activities, but they lack spiritual leaders and are denied virtually all contact with their brothers and sisters overseas. Repeated requests from leaders of the Yemeni Jewish community in the United States to visit the country or to arrange for young Yemeni Jews to be trained in yeshivot in New York have thus far been rebuffed. Even postal contacts have been interfered with by the authorities in San'a. The only intermittent contact with the Jewish community permitted by the authorities has been by Orthodox rabbis affiliated with the anti-Zionist Natorei Karta community in Brooklyn, who have provided prayer books and other religious items.

The largest Jewish communities remaining in the Middle East, with the obvious exception of Israel, are in Iran and Turkey, neither of which is an Arab country. Until the overthrow of Shah Mohammad Reza Pahlavi in 1979 Iran followed a pragmatic, Western, and modernizing approach. It maintained informal but close relations with Israel. Iran's 75,000 to 80,000 Jews felt secure and could travel freely. All this changed drastically with the establishment of the Islamic Republic under Ayatollah Ruhollah Khomeini. Contact with Israel became a crime, and nine Jews were executed on trumped-up charges, including support for Zionism. Jews and other non-Muslims were systematically removed from governmental and university positions. They were also occasionally harassed by local committees that sought to take over property and impose Islamic standards of modesty and conduct. Economic hardships resulting from the revolutionary policies were exacerbated by the consequences of the lengthy war with Iraq, which erupted in September 1980. Jewish young men were subject to the draft, and reportedly a few became Iraqi prisoners. Some fifteen Jews in Tehran were killed in the indiscriminate Iraqi bombings of

Jews Protect One Another

Tehran and other civilian centers.

Most Jews have left Iran, either legally or by unofficial means. It is estimated that at present only some 22,500 remain, the great majority in Tehran, with smaller communities in Shiraz and Isfahan. The Jewish communal structure continues to function under its own board of management, and there is a Jewish representative in parliament. The government supervises and pays the secular costs of the Jewish schools. Jewish religious instruction is required for all Jewish children, in keeping with the Islamic Republic's constitution, which recognizes Judaism as an authorized religion. Like other state schools, the Jewish schools are now required to be open on Saturday, since most include Muslim students. Jewish students must attend but are exempt from writing on Shabbat.

The second largest Jewish community in the Middle East is in Turkey, totaling around twenty thousand. Although some 99 percent of Turkey's population is Muslim and most of Turkey is geographically in Asia Minor, there are those who question including Turkey within the Muslim countries of the region. Since its founding by Mustafa Kemal Atatürk after World War I, the modern Republic of Turkey has followed a Western, secularist orientation. In 1950 Turkey became a member of NATO, and last year it applied for full membership in the European Community. As for the Jewish community, the overwhelming majority lives in the European part of Istanbul, with smaller communities in the city's Asiatic suburbs and in Izmir and Ankara.

Turkey maintains diplomatic and commercial relations with Israel, and there are direct El Al flights from Istanbul to Israel, where the majority of Turkey's roughly 80,000 Jews settled in the early years of the Jewish state. There was additional *aliyah*, as well as emigration to the United States and Western Europe, during the turbulent 1970s when Turkey was plagued by economic difficulties, political instability, and left- and right-wing terrorism.

In contrast to the Islamic revolution in Iran the military officers who seized power in Ankara in

September 1980 reaffirmed Turkey's basic commitment to secularism and alignment with the Western world. Today Turkey is once again functioning as a parliamentary democracy, after adoption of a new constitution and new election laws, which effectively limit the influence of Islamic or radical leftist groups. The Turkish authorities, as well as the general public, expressed their outrage and sympathy to the Jewish community after two Arabic-speaking terrorists, believed to have been connected to the Abu Nidal group, brutally attacked worshipers at the Neve Shalom synagogue in Istanbul in September 1986, killing 20 of them.

As in other countries of Western Europe, recent Israeli military actions to quell the Palestinian uprising were widely condemned by Turkish parties across the political spectrum, including a unanimous resolution of the Turkish Grand National Assembly, the parliament, on March 18, 1988. However, when Islamic extremist groups, together with PLO and Saudi representatives, attempted to exploit pro-Palestinian sympathy in mass rallies that included anti-Semitic slogans, the Turkish authorities arrested demonstrators and brought charges against them. Theodore Ellenoff, president of the American Jewish Committee, had expressed a special concern over reports that at a March 20 Istanbul rally demonstrators had cried out, "The blood of the Palestinians will be on the head of the Jews" and "Turkey will be the grave of the Jews." Dr. Sükrü Elekdağ, Turkey's ambassador in Washington, responded that the perpetrators were "a small fringe group" and would be "strictly dealt with." He went on to reaffirm to the AJC the Turkish government's commitment to "tolerance and peaceful coexistence" and its "firm stand against any religious or ethnic hatred in any segment of its populace."

As both recent and historical events amply demonstrate, Jewish life in the Muslim world is precarious at best. In those countries where their rights are not in jeopardy at present, Jews of the Western world must keep continually vigilant so these rights do not deteriorate. In countries such as Syria and Yemen, we—and indeed persons of goodwill of all faiths—must be actively engaged in demanding that their human rights be restored, including the right to emigrate and join their relatives in the free world.

(This article, published in *Na'amat Woman*, updates Dr. Gruen's 1977 *KP* survey of Jewish Muslim lands, "Situation: Precarious.")

■ The Kremlin's War against the Jews ■

Jewish settlements in Russia date back to First Temple times. By the first century Russian Jews were well established as merchants and carried commerce and civilization northward. Jewish life flourished until about the fifteenth century when a strong, growing, and vigorous Judaism encountered escalating opposition from Greek Orthodoxy, an enmity encouraged by Ivan the Terrible in his sixteenth-century bid for absolute and divine rule. From then to the present, anti-Semitism has been official Russian policy.

Although thousands of Jews have escaped from Russia in recent years, and the numbers have been increasing, millions remain behind. Some Jews wish to remain there. Others seek to leave. What emigration has occurred is linked initially to massive protests by North American and Israeli Jews following years of silence. The reading that follows emphasizes how important it is to demonstrate and to lobby our governments to intercede on behalf of Soviet Jewry, and how vital it is to keep the pressure on Soviet officialdom. History shows that the Soviet government will not, on its own, let our people go. Why? New openness in the Soviet Union has worked to the advantage of Jews who wish to emigrate. Why should we, nevertheless, continue—perhaps redouble—our efforts to secure their freedom?

■ The Kremlin's War against the Jews

BY WILLIAM KOREY ■

(Ed. Note: In December 1978, when the following interview was published, the Soviet Union was a vastly different society from the one it has become during the era of *glasnost* (openness) and *perestroika* (restructuring) instituted by Soviet Premier Mikhail Gorbachev. Since his accession to power in 1986, the worst excesses of officially sanctioned anti-Semitism and anti-Zionism reported in the following pages have ceased but not the activities of such populist and openly anti-Semitic organizations as Pamyat, which first took hold during that period of state-sanctioned discrimination.

Today Soviet Jews find themselves threatened not so much by the ruling Communist party but by a broad coalition of anti-Semitic and nationalist groups vying for power in an increasingly unstable society. As Dr. William Korey predicted in 1978, the greatest danger to Jews lay not so much in party policy as in the possibility of some major social upheaval unleashing pogromlike violence. Now is such a time of political uncertainty, with indigenous groups demanding greater autonomy from Moscow, the Soviet Union's allies in Eastern Europe in flux, and the Soviet economy in near chaos. This instability, coupled with widespread threats of violence, has resulted in a mass exodus of Jews from the Soviet Union to Israel and the United States.)

The Soviet Union has been conducting a calculated anti-Semitic propaganda campaign in its controlled media. In addition, Jews are being excluded from the universities and denied jobs in security-sensitive areas. Do these policies indicate a carryover of anti-Semitism from prerevolutionary times?

Yes, it's a carryover. Anything that has an international character is immediately suspect, particularly if its root, or its largest component, is perceived to be in the "capitalist" and "imperialist" West. They are also aware of the Jewish emphasis on *mishpachah* (family), which transcends national borders. The Soviets want to untie this family knot and therefore subject Jews to special shocking blows. It is the nationalism component masquerading as communism that produces anti-Semitism. Russian xenophobia historically has been tied to anti-Semitism, and what we see is simply a continuation.

How is Soviet anti-Semitism linked with anti-Zionism?

Ever since 1967 there has emerged a virulent, day-in-day-out propaganda assault on Jewry, which is disguised as anti-Zionism. The Soviet government has resurrected variations on the notorious anti-Semitic forgery *The Protocols of the Elders of Zion* for mass consumption, on state TV and radio, in the press and in books. This happens to be the seventy-fifth anniversary of the *Protocols*, which was used by the czars and by Hitler to prove that the chosen-people concept drives Jews to aspire to world domination through diabolical schemes involving the control of the press and the banks.

On January 22, 1977, and again on March 11, a viciously anti-Semitic program entitled *Traders of Souls* was aired on prime-time Soviet television encompassing all of the *Protocols* elements. And it was in this program that Sharansky was first identified publicly as an agent of the world Zionist plot. Zionism heretofore had been linked with many different evils–murder, imperialism, capitalism, prostitution, drunkenness, and so forth. But a major theme that emerged in 1977 was the linkage of Zionism with espionage and

with the CIA. Thus the Zionist is portrayed as a spy, an advocate of war, of militarism. This plays into the Soviet public's fear of war. In World War II no Russian family escaped the impact of the war that claimed 20 million deaths.

A recent Soviet book by Lev Korneyev, a member of the Academy of Sciences, contends that the Mafia is run by Jews and is linked to Israel through Jewish underworld figure Meyer Lansky. Supposedly, Mafia money supports the Israeli secret service, which is part of a Sicilian-Mafia-Zionist plot. Korneyev also claims that, of 165 military-industrial complexes in the Western world, 158 are controlled by the Zionists. These include Lockheed, General Dynamics, General Motors, Chase Manhattan Bank, and the oil industry. It's all absolute nonsense made legitimate by a scholarly veneer complete with footnotes. This is just one in a barrage of government-supported and published anti-Semitic books circulated throughout the USSR.

You mentioned 1967 as the year in which a virulent anti-Semitic policy emerged. There must be some connection with the Six Day War?

The impact of the Six Day War upon Soviet Jews was extraordinary. They read the Soviet press and, remembering the Holocaust, feared that Israel would be destroyed. It was a gut reaction; Israel meant something to them. And when Israel not only survived but won gloriously they felt a tremendous feeling of relief. The Jewish reaction stunned the Soviet leadership. Fifty years after the revolution, fifty years of assimilation, and somehow Soviet Jews developed a love of and a devotion to Israel. The government embarked upon an anti-Zionist campaign of fear and intimidation to stifle these feelings among the Jewish population and to indicate to the public at large that such emotions are a matter of utmost concern to the state.

On February 18, 1971, *Pravda* published a major story that set down the line on Zionism. For the first time since the thirties, the epithet "enemy of the people" was used–anyone who becomes a Zionist becomes an enemy of the people. During the great Stalinist purges of the thirties millions were thus labeled, and that justified their elimination.

There seems to be a systematic exclusion of Jews from the mainstream of Soviet society.

Over the years following the revolution Jews have been deprived of religious, cultural, and political rights. In 1939, Jews constituted 15 percent of the Central Committee, the policy-making body of the Soviet Union; today there is one token Jew in the 239-member body. Jews have been excluded from the party leadership, the state leadership, and from the diplomatic corps, which once included massive numbers of Jews. Despite these limitations, Jews have done well in the arts and sciences.

Isn't that changing now as a result of stringent university quotas for Jews?

Yes. Up until 1967-68 the number of Jews in the universities was on the increase. In 1968-69 the number of Jewish students enrolled was 11,900. In 1976-77 the number was down to 6,900, a 40 percent drop due to severe quota restrictions for Jews. My own prediction is that the rate will continue to plunge. The number of Jews in scientific work, medicine, and other fields that require a university education will decline sharply, and this is a major factor in the Jewish emigration movement. In addition to university quotas, there is a special secret circular stipulating that Jews may not be hired in security-sensitive areas such as atomic weaponry, rocketry, or advanced space programs. Jews are not being fired in the main, but they are not being promoted. Until recently Soviet Jews were permitted in all occupations except foreign trade. At the present time 68 percent of all Jews are regarded as specialists in the economy and 15 percent of the Academy of Sciences are Jews. They achieved this status through the university, the passport to success in the Soviet Union. The undermining of career opportunities is the latest in the stepped-up anti-Zionist campaign. Jews are realizing that they and their children have no future in the USSR.

Is there a danger that this anti-Semitic campaign could get out of hand and lead to an uprising against the Jews?

That danger only exists if there is a war or some upheaval in the USSR. The Soviets would not like to see an uprising. Everything has to be tightly controlled. That is not to say that an individual Jew will not be beaten up or victimized by hooligans.

I suppose that a more likely scenario is that the Jews will become impoverished, not only culturally and religiously, but socially and economically.

Correct. And emigration is the only solution, not only for maintaining their heritage and identity , but for surviving on a level above a simple clerk. In this movement toward emigration you have two elements: Zionists who are drawn to Israel (about 50 percent now) and "dropouts" (*noshrim*), those who elect to settle in countries other than Israel. The "dropouts" have never felt particularly Jewish; in fact, they are running away from forces pointing to their Jewishness. They had wanted to be assimilated into Soviet society, but the inescapable fact that their passports are stamped "*Yevrei*" (Jew) and the frightening rise of official anti-Semitism have compelled them to join the exodus.

If the Soviet government finds its Jews to be potential Sharanskys and has determined to cut them out of the mainstream anyway, why not give the green light to those who want to leave and finally solve the festering problem?

The Soviets don't want anyone to leave for several reasons. First, if they permit exit to one group, how will they stop others from demanding the same right? Second, when people leave, it exposes the great Soviet myth that they have created a utopia. Either there is something wrong with these people or there is something wrong with the system. Third, there are many Jews in highly advanced technical areas such as electronics, physics, computers, and space whose work is indispensable. That is why when a person like the distinguished Soviet Jewish physicist Benjamin Levich wants to leave, the authorities come down hard on him as a warning to others. Now, if they can't trust Levich, who can they trust? To solve the problem, they will stop Jews from going to universities and at the same time they try to stop or at least to limit emigration of the highly skilled.

Can they stop the emigration movement?

They can't stop it completely because it percolates from within and there are pressures from without. The Soviets want to be regarded as a civilized state in the world community. They want to project an image of respectability among for-

eign communists and among countries concerned with human rights and with whom they can do business. They can't afford to be Stalins. That means that they are and will be responsive to world public opinion and to economic and moral pressures from the U.S. and other Western countries. In a real sense the Kremlin considers the emigration rights of its Jewish community to be a negotiable item on the agenda of its ongoing, multifaceted discussions with the West. Our responsibility, in the face of this reality, is clear: to raise our voices on behalf of our Soviet brothers and sisters in a determined and sustained manner.

▪ Are We One? ▪

Most of us feel closer to our Israeli branch of the Jewish family than to many of the others. That special relationship is a source of joy, strength, and mutual pride. It is also a source of friction. The two great Jewish communities, Israel and North America, are bound inescapably and inextricably to each other. What affects one, affects the other. In the deepest sense, we need each other. The connections may be weaker or stronger from time to time, but they are eternal. Why, then, is the relationship often tense and confrontational?

The following examines critical issues affecting how Israeli and North American Jews get along. You will consider the extent to which Diaspora and Israeli Jewry are one in the context of ideas like centrality and interdependence. Is one of the communities central to the disadvantage of the other? How is interdependence expressed? What responsibilities does each community have toward the other? How can we negotiate our disaffections? Explain how laws in Israel might affect Jews in the Diaspora.

▪ Are We One? BY ROLAND B. GITTELSOHN ▪

We are one.
The UJA says we are.
So do the prime minister of Israel and the chairman of the Jewish Agency Board of Governors, especially when demanding higher levels of American financial and political support for Israel. Yet there are disturbing and discordant rumblings from time to time that make us wonder if this proud proclamation is truth or only slogan.

Prominent Israelis question whether we who are non-Orthodox and prefer to live in the United States or Canada are Zionists, sometimes even whether we are authentic Jews. For our part, we rush to the Western Wall to witness ecstatic young Chasidim as they welcome Shabbat with dance, then ask ourselves in calmer, less emotional moments how much we really have in common with them. One of America's most prominent Jewish editors, a Zionist since childhood, is considered a renegade by the Zionist establish-ment because he frequently criticizes Israel. At the same time we who support synagogues on this continent challenge the Jewishness of the Israeli who belongs to no congregation, affirms no faith in God, and spends Shabbat on the beach.

Just what is the relationship between the Jews of the Diaspora and the Jews of Israel? Are we really one? Allies or competitors? Partners or antagonists? One people or several? To answer these questions intelligently, we must first inquire into the meaning of certain concepts.

The Meaning of Centrality

The basic charter of the Zionist movement is the Jerusalem Platform. One of its principal ten-ets, perhaps the most important, affirms the "centrality of Israel." What does centrality mean, not just for Israelis but for all Jews?

Many Israelis–perhaps most–would explain it by saying that only in Israel can Jewish life be lived fully or Jewish survival be assured. Those Jews who live elsewhere, they say, are doomed either to suffer perpetual persecution or to dis-appear as Jews through assimilation. Our value as Diaspora Jews is limited only to what we can do in the short run on behalf of Israel. Even we who persist in identifying ourselves Jewishly will inevitably find that our Judaism is so diluted by the predominant cultures in which we live that it will of necessity wear away.

The extreme opposite view of centrality is that of early Reform Judaism, which denied any role at all in a national Jewish identity. While there were always some Reform Jews who were out-standing Zionist leaders, our movement at its beginning proclaimed that we Jews have entirely outgrown the national phase of our existence, that our mission is to live scattered among the nations, teaching religious truth to all peoples.

Most Reform Jews today would reject both extremes. We affirm centrality in a qualitative, not a geographic, sense. This means that more than one country can be central to Jewish exis-tence and survival. Just as, in earlier centuries, there were vibrant, creative centers of Judaism

in both Palestine and Babylonia–each serving as counterpoint and stimulant to the other–so today both Israel and the Diaspora, especially our Jew-ish communities in the United States and Can-ada, are central to contemporary Judaism. Nei-ther can be complete without the other. We understand centrality in the sense of being essential, not exclusive. We understand it also as conditional.

What the Jewish communities of Israel and North America, for example, can mean to each other depends on what they become as well as what they have been. An American Jewish com-munity that is weakened and diminished almost to the point of disappearance can mean nothing to Israel or, for that matter, to itself. An Israel that reflects as its national nature the Orthodox extremism of Mea She'arim or Gush Emunim would certainly not be central to us American Jews. An Israel that is reduced, God forbid, to the dimension of just another narrow, petty, ingrown Levantine fiefdom like so many others in the Middle East could have little meaning, if any, for us. An Israel that approves the obscene vul-garities of those who advocate terrorism against Arabs and their expulsion from the state, far from being central, would be antithetical to everything in Judaism we hold precious.

Healthy Tension

Thinking of centrality as conditional imposes great responsibility both on Israel and on us. There must be mutual and healthy tension between us. We must help Israel become the kind of Jewish state, while Israel helps us be the kind of Diaspora Jewish community, that together make *both* central to the creative survi-val of Judaism at its best.

Perhaps an analogy will help. Israel and the Diaspora should be central to Judaism in the same way that heart and lungs are central to each of us. We cannot survive without a heart vigorously pumping blood. But even with a healthy heart survival is impossible in the absence of normally functioning lungs, infusing our blood with oxygen.

Depending upon Each Other

Is it reasonable to anticipate an active, identifiable North American Jewish center in the year 2300 without Israel? Your immediate, almost spontaneous answer may well be affirmative. Jewish life, you may say, survived throughout the world for nearly nineteen centuries in the absence of a Jewish state; why should we fear its continued existence, if necessary, under the same circumstance?

A moment's reflection will disclose that in the twenty-first century the circumstance, in fact, would not be the same. From the year 70 to 1984 there were preservative factors in and affecting Jewish life that no longer operate. One such factor was intense anti-Semitism, symbolized most vividly by the ghetto and the Holocaust. Rejected by most of the world, with only occasional brief periods of remission, Jews, wherever they lived, necessarily turned inward, cherishing and developing their heritage more deeply. While it would be foolish to pretend that anti-Semitism is a thing of the past, surely we must not predicate our Jewish future on the masochistic hope that prejudice in its crudest forms will persist.

A second positive factor increasing the probability of Jewish survival in former times was the depth of our people's religious faith. With rare exception Jews were confident that they were serving God through their suffering; that, if they were patient enough and faithful enough, God would redeem them. Very few–even among those of us who are deeply religious–harbor that kind of faith today.

A third preservative in the past was closely related to the first two. In part because they were not accepted by the larger society, in part because of their firm faith, our ancestors gave their children intense forms of Jewish education. Five and a half days a week–except on Friday, from sunrise almost to sunset–young Jews studied only Jewish subjects and sources. This, to be sure, closed them off from general culture and knowledge, but it also helped them understand and appreciate Judaism to the point where they very much wanted to continue being Jews, even in the rare instances where they had a choice. While we have no exact statistics, we know that today, outside Israel, only a minority of Jewish children receive Jewish education, and even for a substantial portion of that minority Jewish studies amount to no more than a few hours a week.

Need "Booster Shots" from Israel

In short, none of the three factors leading to Jewish survival in the past is fully operative today. In their absence it is at best questionable whether Jewish life can survive in the Diaspora without an invigorating center in Israel. In other countries Judaism can be only our secondary civilizational setting. In the United States and Canada, for example, we speak English and partake primarily of our native nation's mores and values. Israel is the only place on earth where language, history, literature, faith, lifestyle, and ideals all add up to a social and intellectual setting that is basically Jewish. It is therefore the one place where the Judaism of today can be most actively lived and the Judaism of tomorrow most hopefully and creatively encouraged. We in the Diaspora need regular "booster shots" from Israel to spur our own Jewishly creative efforts and increase our prospect for surviving as Jews.

Only in Israel? We Reform Zionists would respond no. We assert that, to ensure Jewish survival, Israel needs us perhaps as much as we need it. This is obviously true in a physical sense. Without the influences of American and Canadian Jews on their respective governments, without the massive financial and political contributions we make on Israel's behalf, it is doubtful whether Israel could survive, indeed, whether it could ever in the first instance have been established. But Israel needs us in a still more penetrating and pervasive way.

Judaism has always consisted of an inseparable synthesis between religion on the one hand, nationality or ethnicity on the other. Most Jews in Israel place excessive emphasis on nationality, to the exclusion of religion. Most Jews on this continent give extra emphasis to religion, ignoring nationality. For the integrity and authenticity of Judaism to be maintained, we and Israel must serve as correctives to each other's imbalance.

Israel's current political turmoil reflects a much deeper battle for the nation's soul. On the one hand there are those forces–sometimes almost fanatical–repudiating every evidence of modernity: science, reason, pluralism, humanitarianism, liberalism–everything distinguishing the twentieth century from the fifteenth. These factions resist peace with the Arabs even where this is possible, approve Jewish terrorism, distort our tradition to prevent integration of Jews and Arabs, and endorse the use of violence to stifle dissent. Opposed to them are those who insist that Judaism must not be trapped nostalgically in a vanished past but must use the insights and values of the past to help shape the future. They say that Israel must strive to become what the prophet envisaged for it, an *or lagoyim*, a light unto all the nations. In this crucial battle Israel needs us desperately. The outcome will determine the kind of Jewish state our children will know, the prospect for Jewish continuation throughout the world, perhaps even the survival of humanity.

A Burning Question Remains

As mutually dependent partners, do we have the right to criticize each other? Assuming each must in the last analysis make its own decisions–listening respectfully to the other but yielding to no compulsion or dictation–where is the boundary between fair criticism and carping complaint, between constructive or damaging comments?

Specifically, are Israelis entitled to argue against the trend toward assimilation and mixed marriage here? Or to insist that Jews elsewhere have a duty to make *aliyah*? The very words *aliyah*–meaning, literally, going up–for immigrating to Israel and *yeridah*–going down–for emigrating from Israel imply greater virtue on the part of Jews who live there.

We need not all agree on this matter. My opinion is that Israelis have every right to press their view, to assert that *aliyah* is good for the Jewish people as a whole and can, in some instances,

improve the quality of life for individuals. I believe they step beyond the bounds of reasonable criticism, however, in acting as if those who prefer not to make *aliyah* are second-class Zionists or Jews.

Even more crucial are objections by Diaspora Jews to certain features of Israel's society or selected policies of the Israel government. Do we on the North American continent have a right to criticize such actions as Israel's 1982 invasion of Lebanon? The rise of Jewish terrorism in response to Arab terrorism? Israeli indifference to the demands of religious pluralism for Jews? A refusal even to consider the possibility of territorial compromise in the quest for peace?

Many Israelis as well as many American Jews respond that any such public criticism jeopardizes Israel's security by giving ammunition to its enemies. Without denying the risk, American Reform Judaism has officially responded that a silent partner is not truly a partner, that we have not only a right but a responsibility to voice honest criticism. All else being equal, it would be wiser and safer for such views to be voiced privately, within the family, so to speak, rather than publicly. But experience has taught us that neither the government of Israel nor the World Zionist Organization pays much attention to advice offered quietly and privately. Unfortunately, public expression is often the only effective kind.

We are convinced that such public expression is necessary on both practical and ideal grounds. From a practical point of view whatever Israel decides or does profoundly affects us. If non-Orthodox Judaism is repudiated there, our stature and prestige are thereby diminished everywhere. No less is true ideally. If policies that subvert the highest ethical insights of Jewish tradition are pursued by the Cabinet or Knesset in Jerusalem, we as a community and Judaism generally are both damaged. Israel is a means, not an end–a means toward the survival both of the Jewish people and of Judaism at its best. We are no less responsible than the Israelis to see that means and ends are not confused, that they must always be consistent.

The best way we as Reform Jews in the Diaspora can meet our share of this responsibility is to support ARZA (The Association of Reform Zionists of America) in the United States, Kadima in Canada, and the World Union for Progressive Judaism everywhere. We shall continue to criticize Israel when necessary, always trying to express ourselves constructively and supportively, always sensitive to the fact that the Israelis themselves will benefit most from our wisdom and suffer most from our mistakes.

Conclusion

The question we began with can now be answered. Are we really one? In biology when two forms of life are mutually dependent we use the term "symbiosis." Perhaps the best way to summarize the relationship between the Jews of Israel and those of the Diaspora is to describe it as symbiotic.

There is more than one way for two components to become unified. We are not one in the sense that the boa and the mouse it has just swallowed are one. We are rather one in the way a husband and wife become one in a good marriage. Each retains individual autonomy and uniqueness, yet neither can be entirely fulfilled except together with the other.

Israel needs us to prevent its becoming a narrow, ingrown distortion of Judaism. We need Israel to keep us from degenerating into a weak, diluted, pallid facsimile of Judaism. In a deeper, more fundamental sense than most leaders of the UJA, the Jewish Agency, or the government in Jerusalem usually suppose, we are indeed one!

X

A JEW CONGREGATES
WITH OTHER JEWS

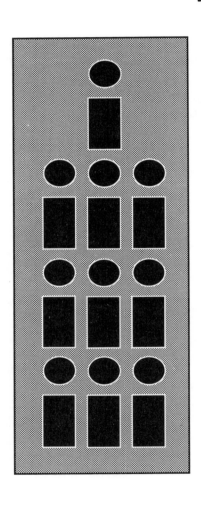

JEWS SUPPORT AND PARTICIPATE IN THE LIFE OF THE SYNAGOGUE. Scholars don't agree about the origins of the synagogue. Nevertheless, all agree that the synagogue, which the prayer book says is central to the Jewish people, is particularly suited to its Jewish purposes. At the same time, the synagogue embraces universal principles and opens its doors to all people. The synagogue thus reflects important twin aspects in Judaism: particularism and universalism. Particularism assures group identity, cohesiveness, and survival. This the synagogue has done admirably. Universalism recognizes the legitimacy of other groups and peoples, accords them respect, makes room for them, and espouses ideals that profit them and protect their humanness. As the guardian of Judaism's teachings, the synagogue has fulfilled this role exceedingly well. Ever since Abraham insisted that God was one and unique, ever since Moses conveyed God's words to the people, Judaism has trod this dual path: protecting and welcoming the stranger and the alien and enabling them to enter the faith if they wish; strengthening and preserving the Jews as a realm of priests and a holy nation. Just as the synagogue has been at the center of both tasks, its leadership and institutions stand at the center of Judaism today.

The synagogue is not an abstraction. It is a concept made actual, a real place where Jews meet to study, pray, socialize. In that place Jews take counsel with one another on the pressing concerns of the day and on perplexing issues of Jewish belief and practice. The synagogue is where Jewish religious viewpoints receive form and substance. When you enter a synagogue and observe its customs, you can tell to which denominational or movement view its members subscribe. The interior design also provides clues to its members' *minhag*, or custom, whether Sephardic, Ashkenazic, or Oriental.

In most ancient civilizations, religion was a domestic affair with periodic public displays in vast temples and arenas. Gods were private matters, worshiped according to the customs of the household. The young learned what they saw, which might be different from what their friends saw and learned in their homes. With Jews it was different. A written Scripture imposed a general uniformity; a body of law required an institution to safeguard it and to provide interpretation according to the need. Jewish schools did that; so did synagogues. The practice of Judaism was institutionalized around and in the synagogue. It was first known as *bet hamidrash*, a house of learning. In the synagogue Jews learn together through study, prayer, and practice; function together as a people. Of the synagogue the prayer book states: "[it] is the sanctuary of Israel. Born out of our longing for the living God, it has been to Israel throughout our wanderings a visible token of the presence of God in [God's] people's midst. Its beauty is the beauty of holiness; steadfast it has stood as the champion of justice, mercy, and peace. Its truths are true for all people. . . . Its God is the God of all people, as it has been said: 'My house shall be called a house of prayer for all peoples.'" (*Gates of Prayer.* New York: CCAR, 1975. p. 31)

This chapter explores the roots of the synagogue as a unique Jewish institution. You will encounter the special concerns North American Jews have about synagogue life. You will explore how the synagogue evolved to its present forms. Because the synagogue is intimately connected to the ideologies of American Jewish religious movements, the chapter will also consider the development and basic tenets of the four major Jewish religious movements in North America.

▪ Roots of the Synagogue ▪

The Bible speaks variously of holy convocations, "high places" or "*bamot,*" prayer in Solomon's Temple, prayer meetings conducted by the prophets in homes or other buildings. Might these have been the precursors of the synagogue? What of Jewish gathering places that must have served the Babylonian exiles in the absence of their Jerusalem Temple? Were these early synagogues? What's the relationship/difference between the Jerusalem Temple and synagogues? What do we know about early synagogues that might help us understand today's synagogue more fully? The synagogue was and remains the quintessential Jewish institution. In various forms it has served the Jewish people for at least two thousand years. It predates the church and the mosque, thus setting its stamp on much of modern religion and art. Uniquely Jewish, the synagogue has nevertheless had wide-ranging significance for others.

The following evokes the mystery and drama surrounding the search for synagogue origins. How does archeology enlighten and, at the same time, further complicate the search?

▪ Roots of the Synagogue   BY JOSEPH GUTMANN ▪

When the Romans destroyed the Jerusalem Temple in 70 C.E., an important phase of Judaism was extinguished. Not only did the Jewish state cease to exist, but a mode of worship that had lasted for about a thousand years came to an abrupt end.

The Jerusalem Temple, built by King Herod, had taken the place of the original Temple, built by King Solomon in the tenth century B.C.E. and destroyed by the Babylonians in 586 B.C.E. Each of these Jerusalem temples had served Judaism as its major cultic shrine. The Temple was God's house; its function was to ensure the fertility of the Land of Israel in an essentially agrarian economy. To attain that goal of fertility, intermediary hereditary priests offered the daily sacrifices prescribed in the Pentateuch, particularly in the Book of Leviticus.

Conflicting Theories

While the Temple was still standing, a new institution–the synagogue–began to emerge. There is little agreement among scholars as to why, when, and where the synagogal institution came into existence. Most traditional Jews believe the synagogue was established by Moses at Mount Sinai. The majority of scholars, however, place the synagogue's emergence in sixth-century Babylonia. They reason that the destruction of the First Temple–the Solomonic

Jews Congregate with Other Jews

Temple—left a void for the exiles of Babylonia, which they filled by the creation of this novel institution. On the other hand, some scholars feel that the origin of the synagogue must be sought in seventh-century B.C.E. Judah. At that time King Josiah instituted the "Deuteronomic Reformation" and ordered the destruction of all local shrines (called *bamot*).

The absence of these local shrines in the rural countryside demanded the creation of a new meeting place. This meeting place, these scholars assume, was the synagogue. Still other scholars contend that the synagogue's origins must be traced to third-century Egypt, since we find prayer houses (called *proseuchai*) cited in extant literary sources of that period.

Arguments of Silence

All of these theories for the early origins of the synagogue are largely based on arguments of silence, as no indisputable archeological evidence is at hand to substantiate the synagogue's existence in ancient Babylonia, Judah, or Egypt. The proof adduced by scholars for the synagogue's origin in these countries rests on the shaky and slender foundation of semantic arguments—on words and phrases found in biblical texts. However, those expressions—*mikdash me'ut* (minor sanctuary), *bet ha'am* (house of the people), and *mu'adei el* (meeting places of God)—are torn from their original biblical context and ascribed a meaning that arose only at a much later period.

The prayer houses (*proseuchai*) of ancient Egypt were not necessarily synagogues. Often prayers were uttered in connection with sacrifices offered at cultic shrines and as part of the mystery religions that flourished at that time. In any case, the problem of the purpose and function of these Egyptian prayer houses had not been solved.

It is highly likely that the origins of the synagogue are linked with rabbinic Judaism, which arose to meet the challenges and needs of Jews living in the cosmopolitan Greco-Roman world. This new Judaism used the Bible as a proof text in order to create a novel twofold legal system known as the Written and Oral Law. The Written Law referred to the Hebrew Bible and the Oral Law (which came to be called the Talmud) to the legislation and interpretations of the rabbis; both laws, it was contended, had been transmitted to Moses at Sinai.

Rabbis Replace Priests

Democratically elected scholars, later called rabbis, began to take the place of the hereditary priests, while many decentralized synagogues replaced the one centralized Temple in Jerusalem. As fitting substitutes for cultic sacrifices, there were prescribed prayers, righteous acts (called *mitzvot*), and laws (called *halachot*), as well as the reading and studying of the Torah. Emphasis was no longer laid on the fertility of the land and its people but on the individual's attainment of the salvation of the soul in the world to come and on ultimate bodily resurrection.

The synagogue is not mentioned in the Hebrew Bible. It is a Greek word denoting a place of assembly. Unlike the Temple, in which God resided, the synagogue was simply a meeting place where congregants called God into being through prayers, ceremonies, and the reading and studying of the Torah. The physical building itself had no sanctity.

The existence of the synagogue is amply attested to in first-century C.E. sources, such as the writings of the Jewish historian Josephus, and in the Christian Scriptures. However, the buildings mentioned in these sources elude concrete identification, as they probably were not distinguishable from other domestic architecture until the third century C.E. From early times the rabbis tried to demonstrate that, although the synagogue was a fitting and worthy replacement for the destroyed Temple, it was, at best, a surrogate or temporary substitute for the original Solomonic Temple, which would be rebuilt in the messianic future. Thus, worshipers were instructed to face toward the east during their prayers, as the Jerusalem Temple had been located in the east. Since the synagogue was considered a surrogate Temple, it was legitimate to observe, in the synagogue, practices that paralleled those performed in the Jerusalem Temple. Thus, fixed prayers were offered in the synagogue three times daily, in place of the sacrifices that had been offered at corresponding times in the Temple. In addition, the agricultural Temple-centered festivals were kept in the synagogue, albeit in a much transmuted form.

Many synagogues have been excavated both in the Holy Land and the Diaspora in areas formerly under Roman and Byzantine jurisdiction. However, no synagogues have been discovered in the former major centers of Judaism in Babylonia, where the Babylonian Talmud was forged, although we know many existed there.

At one time it was argued that the excavated synagogues, dating roughly from the third to the seventh centuries, could be divided chronologically into three distinct groups–the early synagogue (dating from the late second to the fourth centuries), a transitional synagogue (dating from the late third to the fifth centuries), and a later type (dating from the fifth to the seventh centuries). This division has now been abandoned, as scholars realize these excavated synagogues may simply be localized, regional types, and not representative of particular stages in the chronology of ancient synagogue development.

Aside from the problem of dating–few of these synagogues carry evidence of the time of their construction–these synagogues pose many other questions. Quite a few of them carry both symbolic representations and figural decorations in mosaic or paint. This raises the perplexing issues of the meaning of these decorations (as it is commonly conjectured that Judaism tolerated no figural images of any kind) and the nature of the Judaism that was practiced in these synagogues.

Dura-Europos

The discovery in 1932 of a small synagogue in the Roman provincial military outpost of Dura-Europos in Syria has challenged previously held theories about contemporary rabbinic Judaism, the role images played in Judaism, and the unexpected issue of whether Christian art rests on the solid foundations of an antecedent Jewish art.

The Dura synagogue is accurately dated to 244/45 C.E. and carries on its walls a large cycle of figural paintings that appear to be drawn from the Hebrew Bible. Yet close examination reveals that these biblical paintings do not seem to follow the chronologically arranged narratives of the Bible; rather, they are placed in a seemingly disorderly array on the walls. Furthermore they include narrative details not accounted for in the Bible. No other synagogue has been unearthed with a similar series of paintings. As a matter of fact, the biblical scenes in the Dura-Europos synagogue are the earliest extant and appear two hundred years before related biblical cycles are found on the walls of churches.

Since the discovery of this monumental cycle of paintings in Dura-Europos, scholars have been forced to reevalute long-held theories. The widely accepted hypothesis that only one Judaism prevailed at that time–a so-called "normative rabbinic Judaism"–is gradually disappearing as scholars realize that many expressions of Judaism must have flourished at that time, of which the Dura synagogue is but one visual example. It is also realized that the complex meanings of this extensive cycle of paintings cannot be found in the Hebrew Bible; rather, the meaning of the paintings appears to rest in contemporary liturgical practices and prayers. These new practices and prayers cull biblical stories out of context in order to convey new meanings never intended by the biblical stories. What unites these paintings, then, are not the texts of the Bible but the texts of current synagogal prayers. The extrabiblical stories found there are explainable through *agadah*–the embroidery and elaboration of the biblical stories as recounted in contemporary rabbinic sermons.

Mystery Mosaics

In addition to figural decorations in paint we also find standard symbols on synagogue mosaic floors from the fourth century on. These symbols are the *lulav* and *etrog*, the *shofar*, an incense shovel, and two three-legged seven-branched *menorot* on either side of a depiction of the synagogal Torah ark. While the *lulav* and *etrog* can be associated with the *Sukot* holiday, and the *shofar* with *Rosh Hashanah*, the incense shovel remains an enigmatic symbol, since no known synagogal ceremony is linked with it. Since the reproduction of the seven-branched *menorah* was forbidden in the Babylonian Talmud, we are not certain what it symbolized in these mosaics.

Role of Women

The role of women in the early synagogue has not been resolved. At one time it was believed the upper story of these early synagogue buildings was for the accommodation of women, a theory that has now been abandoned. However, several synagogue inscriptions do prominently mention women donors. It is clear that the role and function of women in the early synagogue needs more research.

Although many aspects of the synagogue's origins, its decorative programs in paint and mosaic, and its architectural development remain in doubt, no one questions the crucial role of the synagogue for Diaspora Judaism in the last two thousand years. The synagogue has been rightly called the spiritual mother of the church and the mosque.

▪ The American Synagogue ▪

The saga of the synagogue in North America is the story of the evolution of the Jewish community from small and precarious beginnings in 1654 to the large, prosperous, and multisynagogue communities of today. Those early houses of Jewish worship were for Sephardic gatherings. Today, that once-proud and numerous assemblage is nearly overwhelmed by the later Ashkenazim; Sephardic synagogue ritual and architecture are functioning ghosts of the past. In early days, synagogue readers were lay leaders, the *chazan* was more important than the rabbi, and the Orthodox *minhag* prevailed. Much of that has changed.

This essay traces important developments in the evolution of the American synagogue. What is your synagogue's architectural style? What's the leadership balance between synagogue professionals and lay leaders? From what countries did your founders come? What's the origin of present members? What role does your synagogue play in the general community?

▪ The American Synagogue

BY MALCOLM H. STERN ▪

In 1654 a boatload of refugees from a Dutch colony at Recife, Brazil, landed in Dutch New Amsterdam. Among them were twenty-three Jewish men, women, and children. Two weeks earlier a single Jew, Jacob Barsimson, had arrived directly from Amsterdam. Dutch Governor Peter Stuyvesant did not want the Jews or anyone else who was not from his own Dutch Reformed Church to settle in the colony. But the Jews wrote to their relatives in Amsterdam, some of whom were stockholders in the Dutch West India Company, which paid Stuyvesant's salary, and he was ordered to permit the Jews to remain. Nevertheless, they were not allowed to hold services in public. The following winter six Jewish merchants from Amsterdam joined the group in the New World. They brought with them a Sefer Torah and began meeting for worship in a private home, holding the first Jewish services in North America.

When they asked Stuyvesant's permission to buy land for a cemetery, he refused their request, probably wondering why the Jews needed a burying ground when none of them had died. But the following year, 1656, one of the Jews must have died, for a plot of land was finally granted on what the Dutch records call "a little hook of land." We don't know where it was because all trace of it has disappeared.

Life in pioneer New Amsterdam was difficult, and by 1664, when the British drove Stuyvesant out and renamed the colony New York, only one Jew was left in town, Asser Levy, a butcher by trade and undoubtedly a *shochet* (kosher slaughterer). By the time he died in 1682, the town had attracted new Jews, who began renting places for worship.

Jewish communities, even small ones, are quick to divide up into factions. Today we have Reform, Conservative, Orthodox, and Reconstructionist Jews in America. In the pioneer colonial communities all Jews were Orthodox, but those whose ancestors came from Spain and Portugal followed the Sephardic tradition, while those whose ancestors came from Germany and Poland followed the Ashkenazic tradition. The Sephardic Jews had been forced to convert to Catholicism in Spain and Portugal, and when their descendants escaped to lands where Jews could worship as they wished, they converted back to Judaism and developed a dignified form of worship, led by a *chazan* (cantor).

Having lived among the Christians and not in segregated ghettos, the Sephardic Jews looked down on the Ashkenazic Jews, whom they considered ill-mannered and poorly educated in the ways of their Christian neighbors. The Ashkenazic Jews complained that Sephardic Jews were not sufficiently observant of Jewish law and tradition. Until synagogues were built in colonial communities, Sephardic and Ashkenazic Jews often held separate *minyanim* (gatherings of at least ten males over age thirteen needed for congregational worship).

First Synagogue

By 1728 there were enough Jews in town to build a synagogue. By that date every Christian denomination had built a house of worship and the Jews felt motivated to build theirs.

To raise enough money, the leaders wrote letters to the growing, wealthy Sephardic congregations in Amsterdam and London, and to those in the Caribbean—Barbados, Curaçao, and Jamaica. (In colonial times these Caribbean islands had bigger Jewish populations than all of North America.) A reply to New York from the Curaçao congregation stated, "We understand that your congregation is full of *Tedeschi* (Portuguese for Germans). Our gift is predicated on your using the Sephardic ritual." So for all the colonial congregations, the Sephardic way of worship became the American way.

First Ashkenazic Congregation

It was not until 1795, when a tiny group of Ashkenazic immigrants started Congregation Rodeph Shalom in Philadelphia, that America had an Ashkenazic congregation, too. As more and more Jews arrived from Germany and Poland in the early decades of the nineteenth century, new Ashkenazic congregations were established, but until about 1840, as the Ashkenazic immigrants prospered, they joined the "more American"-feeling Sephardic synagogue.

The New York Jewish story was copied in each of the early American communities: Newport, Rhode Island; Savannah, Georgia; Philadelphia, Pennsylvania; Charleston, South Carolina; and, after the Revolutionary War, Richmond, Virginia.

At first lay people conducted the services, but as the communities grew, they sought trained cantors, usually from Europe. In the Orthodox tradition rabbis did not conduct services. They were supported by the entire community or by wealthy relatives so they could devote themselves to the study of Torah and Talmud, to writing books, and to teaching Jewish law to a new generation of rabbis. It was not until 1840–almost two hundred years after the arrival of those first Jews in New Amsterdam–that an ordained rabbi settled in the United States. By that time the cantors had adopted the pattern of Protestant ministers: reading services, preaching sermons, performing lifecycle ceremonies (*berit milah*, marriages, funerals), and teaching the young. . After 1840 this role was gradually taken over by the rabbis, most of whom came from Germany with university degrees as well as rabbinic ordination. They called themselves "Reverend Doctor" to distinguish themselves from the cantors.

Shochet, Bodek, and Mohel

The early American Jewish communities had other functionaries. We have already mentioned the *shochet* (ritual kosher slaughterer). He usually also had the title of *bodek* (examiner, one who determined whether meat was kosher). Then there was the *mohel*, usually a layman, who circumcised male babies. The *chazan* (cantor) often had responsibility for the education of the young. Since public schools were slow to develop in America, the synagogue often provided all of a child's education, especially for those families that could not afford private schools. Thus, most synagogues had classrooms either in the synagogue building or close to it. When public schools became prevalent, Hebrew Sabbath Schools were established to supplement the public education with Jewish subjects. It was not until the early years of this century that synagogues began having their schools on Sunday rather than Saturday.

Sermons in the synagogue began with the birth of Reform Judaism in Charleston, South Carolina, in 1824. Charleston had the largest Jewish population of any city in America. Some of these Jews were second-, third-, and even fourth-generation Americans who did not understand the services at Congregation Beth Elohim, which were conducted in Hebrew with an occasional Spanish or Portuguese prayer or hymn. A group petitioned the temple board to include prayers and hymns in English and explanations of the Torah. When the board refused, they organized the Reformed Society of Israelites and created their own services in English. At first the congregation grew and money was raised with the hope of building a synagogue. But an economic depression sent some of the leadership north to New York, and, after thirteen years, the congregation disbanded. The surviving members rejoined Congregation Beth Elohim, but in 1838 that synagogue burned down. When a new one was erected two years later, the Reformers won an acrimonious battle to have an organ installed in the building. Many Orthodox members left and started their own congregation. This pattern of congregations splitting over differences of viewpoint is still a part of congregatioal life.

Reform Takes Hold

Reform began to take hold in America during the 1840s and 50s, introducing to Judaism confirmation as a substitute for bar and bat mitzvah, prayers and hymns in English, sermons, and lectures. As the Reform congregations began to build impressive synagogues, they adopted the term "temple" for their buildings.

Until the 1850s the synagogue was also the social service center, collecting funds to help the poor and the stranger. Women banded together to form Ladies' Hebrew Benevolent Societies to take care of the sick, newborn babies, and the needy. Gradually the larger Jewish communities began creating hospitals to take care of the poor and ill; the wealthy were cared for at home.

As more congregations came into being they banded together to form charitable societies, the ancestors of today's federations. Finally, as the Jews prospered in America, they imitated their Christian neighbors by forming social clubs and community centers.

As Jews moved across America, they carried with them the seeds of these institutions, developing the American Jewish community as we know it.

■ A Short History of American Orthodoxy ■

The Jewish religion started with Abraham. Jews are heir also to God's word, which Moses taught at Sinai. The passion of the prophets informs our religion, as does the rationalism of Maimonides. For many Jews, the line of descent from Moses through Joshua through the Great Assembly and the rabbis and teachers of later days is straight and true to acknowledged leaders today. From then to now little has changed, neither Jewish belief nor adherence to immutable Jewish law. Only such modifications as can be justified within that law, *halachah*, may be considered. This is Orthodox Judaism, for which preservation of tradition is central because the tradition rests firmly on God's teaching.

The following summarizes the American journey of several varieties of Orthodox Judaism. Against what obstacles has it struggled? From where does its authority come? What unites all Orthodox Jews regardless of differences? What are some of the differences? Where do Orthodox Jews live? How do they relate to other Jews and to the Jewish community?

■ A Short History of American Orthodoxy

BY LOUIS BERNSTEIN ■

Orthodoxy, first on the American scene, has reemerged in the latter half of the twentieth century as a major component of American Jewry's religious spectrum. In the first half of this century such leaders of American Jewry as Louis Marshall predicted the impending demise of Orthodoxy. Such predictions proved to be false as new generations of American-born Orthodox Jews constructed new communities pulsating with religious activities and assumed roles of leadership in national organizations. Two Orthodox rabbis have served as chairmen of the influential Conference of Presidents of Major Jewish Organizations. The Orthodox Jew, with his distinguishing kipah or his chasidic garb, is clearly visible in all walks of American life.

The first Jews who came to the United States were Orthodox in their religious observance. Originally they followed Sephardic rites, although many began to follow Ashkenazic customs by the time of the Revolutionary War. With the arrival of German Jews from 1820 through 1860, bringing with them Reform ideology and practice, the complexion of Jewish life in the United States was altered. The second half of the nineteenth century was the era when Reform Jewry made its greatest impact. At that time traditional Jews suffered from a lack of religious texts, schools, and leadership. The first Orthodox ordained rabbis did not arrive in the United States until almost the end of the nineteenth century.

Orthodoxy Survives Hard Times

The great waves of Jewish immigration, from Eastern Europe between 1890 and 1914 and again immediately after World War I, brought some 2 million Jews from devout Orthodox backgrounds to the United States. Many drifted away from their traditions, influenced by contact with a free society that bred assimilation and acculturation.

Poverty was another factor in driving a wedge between the immigrants and Judaism. Jews, yielding to deprivation, began to work on the Sabbath, for the first time breaching the wall of observance. Yet, despite all of these adverse conditions, Orthodoxy and its adherents began to build the foundations upon which it stands today. The earliest Orthodox institution, Yeshivat Etz Chaim, later merged with the Rabbi Isaac Elchanan Theological Seminary and became the nucleus of what today is Yeshiva University. American Orthodoxy was reinforced by survivors of the Holocaust, who arrived on the scene as Orthodoxy began to indicate signs of greater vitality.

The mantle of Orthodox Jewry covers many shades of belief and observance. What Orthodox Jews have in common is the belief that the Torah was given to the Jewish people by the Almighty on Mount Sinai and its commandments and teachings are divine, permanent, and unchangeable. This authority extends to the Oral Law and the halachah, which governs every aspect of life. Study of Torah is another important common denominator. Beyond that the divisions in the Orthodox camp are many and to the untrained eye the differences may even be greater than those that separate Orthodoxy from Reform.

Orthodox Jews Disagree about Israel

Orthodox Jews disagree about Israel. Many see the State of Israel as a beginning of the Messianic Era and celebrate Yom Ha'atzmaut and Yom Yerushalayim with religious services. They are identified with the Mizrachi movement (the Religious Zionists), which plays an important role in Israeli life. Another group, centered about Agudat Yisrael, a faction represented in the Knesset, has granted Israel recognition, although grudgingly so. The most extreme anti-Zionist faction is the small but vocal Natorei Karta (Guardians of the City), who are primarily followers of the Satmar Rebbe in New York. They view Israel as the devil incarnate and refuse to recognize the state because of its secular nature. They argue that the return to Israel must not be human-made but an expression of the divine will. Despite such opposition the greatest number of American Jews settling in Israel are Orthodox in their commitment.

Disagreement about Secular Education

Orthodoxy is also divided in its attitude toward secular education. One group–represented in the Rabbinical Council of America, the Union of Orthodox Jewish Congregations, and the National Council of Young Israel–is part of the mainstream of American life. This group created a day-school movement that emphasizes a merging of Jewish and Western cultures. Its greatest achievement is Yeshiva University, and its adherents include academics, scientists, and professional people who are meticulous in their observance of mitzvot. A second group, which at one point resisted secular education and prevented yeshivah students from receiving secular educations, now permits some of its students to spend time pursuing a secular academic degree, but only if it is for the purpose of making a living. In several chasidic circles–Lubavitch, Satmar, the village of New Square–secular education is minimal. There one can find third-generation Americans whose native tongue is Yiddish, and they can at best only stutter monosyllables in English. They retain their European traditions and style of dress and are committed to the belief that the higher the wall that separates Jews from secular life and culture the better. The less contact with a secular lifestyle, the greater the guarantee that they will not fall prey to the immorality and paganism of modern life.

Relations with Non-Orthodox Groups

Orthodox Jews are unified in rejecting nonhalachic expressions of Judaism as legitimate. Most would probably regard Reform more favorably than Conservative because of the latter's pretense to be a halachic expression while basically following Reform changes. They point to the trend toward female rabbis and increased synagogue functions for females in the religious service as an expression of this conviction. They differ, however, on how to relate to the non-Orthodox religious groups. For two decades Orthodoxy was torn by a dispute stemming from a religious decision by eleven scholars barring such participation even when the agenda did not touch on religious questions. The Agudat Yisrael, for example, does not participate in any non-Orthodox umbrella organizations although it may occasionally do so on a rare and limited issue where its own interests are at stake. The less extreme Rabbinical Council of America and the Union of Orthodox Jewish Congregations cooperate with their Reform and Conservative counterparts in the Synagogue Council of America. In recent years the Orthodox right wing has developed a sophisticated and very effective political apparatus relating directly to governmental bodies, bypassing and even competing with the major establishment Jewish organizations.

Social Issues Unite Orthodox Groups

Political and social issues in the United States tend to unite Orthodox groups. For example, all of Orthodoxy views abortion as legal murder and condemns homosexuality, which is prohibited in the Bible. Almost all favor government aid to parochial schools. During the last decade the Orthodox community has become more politically conservative than the Conservative or the Reform groups. It is basically hostile to affirmative action programs because Orthodox Jews regard American Jews as an endangered minority and regard legislation giving preference to any group as contrary to the principles of democracy. They feel that politically liberal Jews have other than Jewish considerations in their political convictions and that lately liberalism has deserted Israel.

The nature of Orthodox Judaism is such that observant Jews must live together. They must be within walking distance of the synagogue, have a mikveh, a yeshivah, and stores with kosher products. . . . They have traditionally tended to congregate in large urban areas, but since World War II many have moved to suburban areas. New York is still the center of Orthodox Jewish life,

but Los Angeles and Chicago also have large Orthodox communities. Silver Spring, Maryland; Brookline, Massachusetts; Monsey, New York–all are examples of suburban Orthodox centers. Yeshivot for high school students can be found today in smaller communities such as Scranton, Pennsylvania, and Lakewood, New Jersey. Some of the day schools in the distant communities are staffed by committed young Orthodox Jews who approach their responsibilities with pioneering zeal.

No Single Leader

Orthodox Jews have no single leader. Traditionally the rabbis are the authorities in their own communities. There are almost as many leaders as there are individual groups. Scholarship and personal charisma are basic requirements for leadership. Rabbi Joseph B. Soloveitchik of Yeshiva University and fourth generation of a famous rabbinic family is the most important figure today. His lectures on Jewish law and philosophy several times a year attract thousands of people, young and old. Rabbi Moshe Feinstein, an outstanding authority, is the final authority for most of the Agudat Yisrael community. Chasidic groups turn to their own rabbis, where leadership is traditionally inherited. Lubavitch has the most adherents. Satmarer, Bobover, and Skverer are among the other groups who have successfully reestablished chasidic life in the United States.

American Orthodoxy has proved the United States is not a sterile place for Torah learning. It constantly strives for perfection to increase Torah study and to improve the observances governing the relationships between humans and G-d and among humans with one another. All Orthodox Jews agree much more remains to be done. In the words of the sage: "It is not for you to complete the task, but you must not permit yourself to remain idle."

▪ What Is Reform Judaism? ▪

Many Jews believe that a tradition of development characterizes Judaism, that from biblical days to modern times Judaism has changed to accommodate changing times and places. Reform Jews maintain that its previous dynamism left Judaism some three hundred years ago with the acceptance of the *Shulchan Aruch* as the authoritative code of Jewish practice. Jews who were unwilling to accept a Judaism frozen in time became reformers. They saw Jewish survival threatened by a petrified religion and sought ways to continue the reforming trends of Jewish history.

The following reviews the Reform movement's assumptions. Is Orthodoxy as static and Reform as dynamic as the author suggests? Explain. What were the early Reform movement's accomplishments? Did they last? Were they good for Judaism? For Jewish survival? Would Orthodoxy agree that Reform did not alter the fundamentals of Judaism? Explain.

▪ What Is Reform Judaism?

BY ABRAHAM FELDMAN ▪

When we speak of Reform Judaism, we are not speaking of a new kind of Judaism. It was only the name that was new as it came into being near the end of the eighteenth century in Germany. This name has become the label of that interpretation of Judaism that recognizes and emphasizes the dynamic character of the Jewish religion–dynamic, the opposite of arrested or static Judaism. Reform Judaism emphasizes what is inherent in all Judaism: the principle of progression in the concepts and forms of the Jewish religion. Reform has its roots in the past! It proudly acknowledges the glory, the dignity, and the validity of Jewish tradition.

Unfreeze the Tradition

The Jewish tradition always was progressive but, especially in the fifteenth through the eighteenth centuries, an effort was made to freeze it. When the ghetto disappeared and the period of emancipation began, this frozen tradition failed to hold and to satisfy those generations because of its completely unbending and, in a very real sense, unorthodox position. It was then that a group of Jews, led by lay people at first,

decided it was time to unfreeze the tradition and attempted the long-overdue and the long-dammed-up adjustments. This was the beginning of the modern Reform movement. The Reformers did not seek escape from Judaism. If they had, the road was open and a welcome awaited them elsewhere.

Freedom of Interpretation

This matter of adjustment of Judaism to contemporary needs was not anything new in our tradition. Why is it Judaism *never* had any formal creed? Why were there controversies between the schools of Hillel and Shammai? What was the meaning of the great struggle between the Sadducees and the Pharisees? What was the meaning of the conflict between Maimonides, Ibn Daud, Nachmanides, etc.? Why the conflict in the seventeenth and eighteenth centuries between the Chasidim and their opponents, the Mitnagdim? It was in all instances the insistence upon freedom of interpretation and emphasis.

Jewish Practice Codified

The code of practice that largely governs

authoritative Jewish Orthodoxy today is the *Shulchan Aruch*, a work compiled by Joseph Karo in 1555 and first printed in 1565. Karo was a Sephardic Jew (belonging to the Spanish-Portuguese Jewish tradition). Hence, his work recorded the practices of the Jewish tradition as they were known among Sephardim.

But there were variant practices of Judaism, especially among Ashkenazic Jews (Jews in Germanic countries and in Russia and Poland). These were not included in Karo's code.

When his compilation (the *Shulchan Aruch*) appeared and came to the notice of Ashkenazim, a storm of protest broke out. The reason? Many of the practices Karo represented as "authoritative" and obligatory were not current among Ashkenazim. They were unknown. And Karo did not even mention many that were "authoritative" to Central, Eastern, and Southern European Jewry.

So, in 1578, thirteen years after the first publication of Karo's code, a new edition of the *Shulchan Aruch* appeared that incorporated Ashkenazic practices. The additions were prepared by Rabbi Moses Isserles of Cracow, Poland. Both the Sephardic and Ashkenazic practices in their respective areas became, in time, authoritative, orthodox.

Keeping Judaism Forever Contemporary

Reform asserts anew the right and duty of accelerating the process of progress and change where changes seem necessary. If some customs and practices are no longer meaningful, then they are no longer useful, and to cling to them mechanically or to acknowledge them as valid while they are largely neglected is to endanger the very survival of Jews and Judaism. In the absence of an authoritative legislative body, continuing to function while waiting for the slow process of halachic change through responsa that often takes generations is to expose the patient to danger. Therefore Reform's principal contribution is the decision to keep Judaism forever contemporary and to keep it responsive to the religious needs of successive generations.

Reform insists changes be made *when* they are needed, *in* and *by* the generation needing them, rather than waiting generations or even centuries before any perceptible adjustments occur. Our generations today and the generations tomorrow have the right and duty to keep Judaism alive by keeping it contemporary and responsive to their spiritual needs. Our people can be Jewishly religious in America, for example, without being coerced into irreligion by attempting to mold American Jews into the religious pattern or forms of Warsaw or Kovno or the chief rabbis of Jerusalem.

Saving Jews for Judaism

Reform Judaism in the United States has undoubtedly saved hundreds of thousands of Jews for Judaism and for Jewish life; it has saved Jews for Judaism in America by making it possible and proper to be religious Jews without strict and undeviating conformity to the minutiae of traditional practice. To the extent that these Jews were saved for Jewish life Reform has made a vital contribution to all Jewish religious life. It stemmed the tide of assimilation away from Jewishness.

Pioneer in Organizational Survival

Moreover, Reform in America has taught both Orthodoxy and Conservatism the methodology for organizational survival in this country. Rabbi Isaac Mayer Wise, who came to this country in the middle of the nineteenth century and became the organizing genius of Reform, early realized that only through unified endeavor would there be survival of the synagogue in America, for American Jewish religious life in his day was in a state of chaos. He therefore organized the Union of American Hebrew Congregations, i.e. , the union of congregations inclined to the liberal and progressive interpretation of Judaism. It was the same Isaac Mayer Wise who realized that rabbis for American Jews would have to be American-oriented to be effective and that these individuals would have to be trained and experienced in both the general American culture and the disciplines of classical historic Judaism. Hence, two years after he founded the Union of American

Hebrew Congregations, he proceeded to found the Hebrew Union College for the training of rabbis.

As the Reform congregations grew, the women organized themselves into sisterhoods and then into a National Federation of Temple Sisterhoods. Men organized themselves into men's clubs or brotherhoods and then into the National Federation of Temple Brotherhoods. Youth groups were organized within the congregations and then these were united under the National Federation of Temple Youth. (Other major affiliates include the National Federation of Temple Educators, the National Association of Temple Administrators, the World Union for Progressive Judaism, and the American Conference of Cantors.)

Reform Imitated

Following the lead of this pattern of Reform and observing its success, Orthodoxy and Conservatism adopted similar techniques. Orthodoxy and Conservatism proceeded to organize their congregations in accordance with the method and techniques and often even the names used by the Reform movement. Thus, there are now the Union of Orthodox Jewish Congregations and the United Synagogue of America. Each in turn developed similar departments of activity including sisterhoods, brotherhoods, youth education, etc. Modeling themselves on the Central Conference of American Rabbis, the Reform group, Orthodox and Conservative rabbis also formed associations.

Reform Innovations in Synagogue

It is not only on the organizational level that Reform influenced the religious character of Jewry in America. Reform introduced the late Friday evening service and was attacked for introducing it. Today (most) Conservative synagogues have late Friday evening services, and (some) Orthodox congregations do likewise. Preaching was reintroduced as part of the service of worship by Reform. Today this is the prac-

tice prevailing throughout Orthodox and Conservative congregations. Reading of prayers in English, the vernacular of America, was introduced into the services of Reform. Today English readings during the service are customary not only in the Conservative synagogues but in many Orthodox synagogues as well. Confirmation for boys and girls on Shavuot was introduced by Reform Judaism. Today Conservative synagogues have introduced the same rite, and in many Orthodox synagogues girls are confirmed. Likewise we have, in the Conservative synagogues, men and women sitting together, a practice first introduced by Reform for which it was vehemently attacked.

Reform Influences

There have been modifications of the traditional prayer book in the Conservative synagogue. They have mixed choirs and organ music as part of the regular worship of the synagogue. They have modified their practices in the matter of dietary laws, Sabbath observance, and some of the theology of Judaism. In all these fundamental areas the Reform attitude and practice have become the dominant pattern that is accepted and followed.

Fundamentals Unchanged

Most of the changes introduced by Reform occurred largely in the area of ritual and ceremony. The Reform attitude toward these is different. In the fundamentals of Judaism, however, there is very little divergence. All religious Jews accept the traditional definitions and concepts of God, of the place of humans in the divine scheme, of the place of the people of Israel in history, of the importance, significance, and centrality of the synagogue in Jewish life. All religious Jews share the same ethics and all have the same Sabbath and holy days and festivals.

Reform is not a different kind of Judaism. *It is Judaism*, historic, classical, traditional, but eager to remain always contemporary.

▪ Conservative Judaism ▪

By the close of the nineteenth century, Reform boasted an organization of congregations, a seminary, a platform, a rabbinical seminary, and a prayer book. The movement embraced many shades of non-Orthodox Judaism from the most radical to the most conservative. It retained attachment to the Jewish people and its history while reframing Jewish law in the spirit of nineteenth-century rationalism and American freedom. Yet conservative elements were uneasy with where Reform was leading. A counterreaction produced a new rabbinical seminary. Ten years later its future was in doubt. It and the new Conservative movement were strengthened by the influx of Eastern Europeans, whose own Orthodoxy kept them away from both American Reform and American Orthodoxy.

This reading compares Conservative with Orthodox and Reform Judaism. What are the essential differences? What is the Conservative view on matters like Jewish law, Israel, women? How do you assess Conservative Judaism's future? The movement recently adopted a statement of faith describing what Conservative Jews should believe about religion and how they should practice it. How might this affect the movement's future? Explain.

▪ Conservative Judaism   BY ELLIOT N. DORFF ▪

Of the three major groups in modern Judaism (Conservative, Orthodox, Reform), Conservative Judaism is at once both the oldest and the youngest. It is the oldest in that it carries on Judaism as it always was, from the days before Moses to our own time. Its very name, "Conservative Judaism," indicates that the intention of its leaders has been to *conserve* Judaism, to maintain it in its traditional form. And yet it is the most modern of the three movements because it was the last to organize itself as a distinct group.

The Conservative movement is often characterized as being the type of Judaism you adopt when you do not want to be too religious but not too irreligious either. Such is not the case. Conservative Judaism involves a positive philosophy and program; it is *not* just a wishy-washy mix of whatever is not Reform or Orthodox.

Conservative Vs. Orthodox

In contrast to Orthodoxy, Conservative Juda-

ism uses the most rigorous intellectual methods available to study Judaism; no questions are ruled out, and no findings are suppressed or ignored. Largely as a consequence of this, Conservative Judaism recognizes that Jewish law and ideology were not set once and for all at Sinai, or in any other time or place, but have evolved and must continue to do so if Judaism is going to be historically authentic.

Because of its emphasis on "catholic Israel" (*Kelal Yisrael*, or "the whole of Israel"), the Conservative movement has been much more involved in teaching and developing civilizational aspects of Judaism–Jewish art, music, dance, and literature; teaching Hebrew in its modern as well as its classical form; and emphasizing the attachment of the Jewish people to the State of Israel. And finally–but perhaps most sensitively–the Conservative movement has a much greater respect for the individual than do certain elements of Orthodoxy. The student in Orthodox schools (either child or adult) is seen as a vessel into which the divine message is to be poured. In Conservative education the individual is asked to interact with the Jewish tradition–absorbing it, questioning it, testing it, rejecting some of it, changing some of it, and creatively adding to it together with the rest of the Jewish community. This respect for the human element in the covenant between God and Israel is in part a direct result of the historical consciousness of the Conservative movement, for Jews have interacted in that way with the Jewish tradition in almost all times and places. It is also a reflection of the commitment to "catholic Israel" because, as the rabbis of the Talmud said, "if the people Israel are not prophets, they are at least [children] of prophets." (*Pesachim* 66a)

Conservative Vs. Reform

The chief issue that distinguishes Conservative Judaism from Reform is the Conservative conviction that Jewish law is binding. Recently a number of Reform Jews have taken on some of the traditional practices such as *kashrut* and *Shabbat* observance, but these practices are viewed by Reform as a matter of individual choice. In Conservative Judaism, on the other hand, observing Jewish law is a requirement. Moreover, the content of Jewish law is determined by the community, not by individuals. If Jewish practice is to retain any cohesiveness whatsoever, it must be defined by the tradition as interpreted by the rabbis and practiced by the observant community; it cannot be "every [one] for [oneself]." The Conservative emphasis on Jewish peoplehood has meant that the Conservative movement has been somewhat less universalistic than the Reform and more actively involved in specifically Jewish affairs and culture.

Role of Women

Three issues are currently occupying the attention of significant segments of the Conservative community. One is the role of women in Jewish synagogue life. Jewish law does not permit women to act as judges or witnesses, and Jewish custom for some two thousand years has restricted most of the leadership roles in worship to men. On the other hand, women in the Conservative movement have been given the same opportunities for Jewish education as men have, and, in contrast to the Orthodox, Conservative men and women are taught the same curriculum. Equal education for women was one of the cardinal principles Solomon Schechter affirmed in his address to the founding meeting of the United Synagogue of America in 1913.

In light of women's equal level of Jewish education, they are now being allowed to function in worship roles traditionally reserved for men. Since 1985 women have been ordained as rabbis in the Conservative movement. These issues had been resolved rather easily by the Reform movement in one way and by the Orthodox in the opposite way. In the Conservative movement, with its commitment to Jewish law and its recognition that the law may be changed under the proper circumstances, this issue remains controversial.

Status in Israel

A second cluster of concerns occupying the Conservative movement regard the status of Jews and Judaism in Israel. Only some ten or fifteen percent of Israelis see themselves as Orthodox. However, because of political considerations, there is no other form of Judaism that gets government support for its schools and synagogues, and only Orthodox marriages, divorces, and conversions are recognized in Israeli law. This has hampered the activities of both the Conservative and Reform movements in Israel, and it has meant that eighty-five or ninety percent of Israel's Jews have no alternative but to see themselves as "secular." The Conservative movement is fighting for recognition in Israel by founding synagogues, schools, and camps and by taking the legal steps necessary to get the present laws on the issue changed.

The most challenging task facing the Conservative movement, and the one that will ultimately determine its viability, is the creation of a large, *observant* following. The Conservative movement has not communicated clearly and forcefully to the laity its commitment to Jewish law. As it does so it may lose members, since it will cease being all things to all people, but Conservative leaders now are willing to make that sacrifice if necessary. For only if its members observe Jewish law can the Conservative movement be the living, authentic form of Judaism its founders intended.

Two Central Concepts of Conservative Thought

Conservative Judaism did not begin as a movement but as an approach to the study of Judaism that was used in a few rabbinical schools in Germany in the 1800s. It was only in 1913 that those who advocated that method of study founded an organization of synagogues, the United Synagogue of America, whose practices grew out of that form of study.

Positive-Historical Judaism

The Conservative form of study is called "positive-historical Judaism," in which "positive" means objective, unbiased, and certain. "Historical" indicates that those who adopt this approach want to discover how Judaism existed in the past. Together the two mean we should study Judaism by being as objective as possible about its past, by determining how it actually developed.

The "positive-historical" approach requires that we apply the exact same methods to the study of Jews and Judaism that scholars use in studying other groups and cultures. In the process we may discover some rather unsettling things about the history of our religion and our people, but the first step has got to be a commitment to honesty.

If this seems obvious, it is only because we live a century and a half after Jews began to have the courage to look at Judaism in an objective way. Until that time–and in most Orthodox schools to this day–Jews used scholarly methods in their analysis of everything except their own faith. The Bible and Talmud were interpreted in the traditional manner, which ignored factual or intellectual inconsistencies. When we apply objective study methods to Judaism, we find that its ideas, values, and practices have changed considerably (while maintaining much of its original character) in response to the varied conditions in which Jews have lived. Without this change Judaism would have petrified and died.

OBSERVANCE OF JEWISH LAW

"Positive" can mean objective, but it also connotes enthusiasm and concern. We must be completely honest in our study of Judaism, but we must also love it and practice it. That requires active work in all forms of Jewish education and communal service, and it also requires observance of Jewish law.

In the Conservative view Jewish law must be understood and observed in terms of its historical development. To go back to the *Shulchan Aruch* or any other code and use it as a cookbook is to detach Jewish law from its historical setting and, in effect, to distort it. That is what Orthodoxy has done. To be historically rooted and authentic, Jewish law must remain changeable so it can respond to current needs and continue to serve as the healthy, living guide it has always been.

Catholic Israel

The other term that has characterized Conservative Judaism from its beginnings is "catholic Israel," Solomon Schechter's translation of the Hebrew *Kelal Yisrael*, or "the whole of Israel." In his strong affirmation of Jewish peoplehood Schechter rejected the classical Reform position that Jews are only devotees of a religion and not members of a people. Probably the clearest expression of Jewish peoplehood is Zionism and the State of Israel. Significant elements of both the Orthodox and Reform movements were anti-Zionist until the founding of the state in 1948, and segments of the Orthodox community carry the anti-Zionist banner to this day. The Conservative movement is the only one of the three that never had a strong anti-Zionist wing.

THE PRACTICES OF THE PEOPLE

The concept of "catholic Israel" is of central importance in understanding the Conservative approach to Jewish law, which must be viewed in the context of how it is actually practiced in the Jewish community. Every legal system is formed by an interaction between law and custom. Societies appoint legislators and judges to make the law and apply it, but ultimately if a large number of people disregard the law, then it ceases to be authoritative–as the American experience with Prohibition (the law outlawing liquor) amply demonstrated. On the other hand, if a custom becomes firmly rooted in the practices of the people, it becomes as binding as any law or judgment. Sometimes the lawmakers enact a law that makes the custom officially part of the legal system. Because for many years there has not been an organized legislature or judiciary for determining Jewish law, the power of custom in Jewish law is especially influential. Therefore, in determining the content of Jewish law, we must pay attention to the practices of "catholic Israel," at least as much as we do to legal codes and rabbinic decisions.

PROBLEMS OF NONOBSERVANCE

Most Jews who were associated with the Conservative movement in the first three decades of this century observed Jewish law, and in that setting Schechter's concept made sense. Today, however, the number of Conservative synagogue members who live according to Jewish law are in the minority. Clearly the customs of those who have chosen not to observe Jewish law cannot determine its content. Only those people who take upon themselves the responsibilities of Jewish law have that right. Robert Gordis, a leading Conservative thinker, therefore suggested in the 1940s that, for purposes of the law, "catholic Israel" be restricted to those Jews who try to observe Jewish law. That saves the concept, but the real problem the Conservative movement faces is the need to create a knowledgeable observant laity. The people Israel *should* have a major role in shaping Jewish law, but first they have to become observant. The Conservative movement has not succeeded in making clear that Jewish law is not just for the rabbis but is binding on every Jew.

Elliot N. Dorff

▪ What Is Reconstructionist Judaism? ▪

Mordecai Kaplan, though born abroad and schooled in his early years outside America, was a product of American culture and American universities. He bestrode two worlds, two cultures. He addressed the religious needs of Jews in America from a new perspective. He looked for creative, engaging ways to make being an American compatible with being Jewish. He sought to conceive of Judaism as a civilization encompassing all experiences and thoughts of American Jews. He envisioned a reconstruction of Judaism that would synthesize the most significant elements of four great entities: Reform, Conservative, and Orthodox Judaism, and Zionism.

The following defines the basic ideas of the youngest religious group, Reconstructionism. However, Kaplan did not want another organized religious movement in America. Why? Why has that happened despite Kaplan's wish? What are the integrating components of the movement? In what ways should the Jewish people be reconstructed? The Jewish religion?

▪ What Is Reconstructionist Judaism?

BY DENNIS C. SASSO ▪

Reconstructionist Judaism is the newest and smallest of the organized religious movements in American Judaism. The ideology of the movement received its primary inspiration from the teachings of Rabbi Mordecai M. Kaplan. While Kaplan has had a considerable influence upon the other major movements (Conservative, Reform, and even modern Orthodoxy), it is Reconstructionist Judaism that has attempted programatically to carry out the full implications of his insights. Yet Reconstructionism today is broader than Kaplanism. During the past several decades a number of his interpreters and critics have expanded, modified, and helped to diversify the nature of Reconstructionism. These include rabbis trained in the Reform and Conservative seminaries and the new generation of rabbis who have graduated from the Reconstructionist Rabbinical College.

Definition of Reconstructionism

Kaplan offered a definition of Judaism that is today virtually universally quoted and accepted: "Judaism is the evolving religious civilization of the Jewish people." Reconstructionists believe Judaism is more than a mere religion and argue that, for its future to be ensured, it must be lived in a fuller dimension than just at the "religious" level. Judaism encompasses the complete historical experience of the Jewish people and must take account of the fullness of its cultural unfolding or evolution. Judaism is Jewish religion with a "plus." Kaplan used the term "civilization" to refer to Judaism in its totality. This word refers to the social, economic, and political dimensions of life, as well as the religious. It includes tradition, laws, customs, language, literature, art, and every other aspect of collective life.

Reconstructionism believes there is room and need for pluralism or diversity of expression within Jewish life. It welcomes and encourages creativity and variety in worship and celebration, yet it is faithful to the elements of permanence that have unified the Jewish people over the ages.

The Jewish People

Reconstructionist philosophy rests on the centrality of the concept *Am Yisrael*-the Jewish people is the primary element in the traditional triad-"God, Torah, Israel." The Jewish people seeks God and creates Torah. Reconstructionism differs from Orthodox Judaism, which puts primary emphasis on Torah (*halachah*-Jewish law), and from Reform, which places "God" or theology at the core of its definition of Judaism. The Conservative movement even though it, too, has traditionally considered the Jewish people as the central element in its understanding of Judaism, has, in the Reconstructionist view, permitted a nostalgic traditionalism to restrain it from allowing peoplehood to work out its full and natural implications.

Leading Advocates of Zionism

In keeping with their emphasis on Jewish peoplehood, Reconstructionists have been leading advocates of Zionism, placing the Land of Israel at the center of Jewish civilization. Kaplan symbolized the relationship between the Jews of Israel and those of the Diaspora in the form of a wheel, which has become the seal of the Reconstructionist movement. Its hub is Zion, from which emerge the dynamic forces of Judaism. Religion, culture, and ethics are the spokes connecting the lives of Jewries in the Land of Israel with those of the Diaspora. The inner rim of the wheel represents the scattered Jewish communities of the world, which through the millennia have maintained contact with the Jewish civilization rooted in the Land of Israel. The exterior rim symbolizes the general community–in our case the community of America's non-Jews, with whom Jewish civilization maintains contacts.

The Seal of the Reconstructionist Movement

Kaplan maintained that the establishment of the modern State of Israel represents nothing less than the coming of age of the Jewish people, who must now take hold of the reins of their future by giving up supernatural notions of messianism and by expressing instead the conviction that Judaism is more than just a religious system. In the spirit of Ahad Ha-Am, the nineteenth-century Zionist writer, Reconstructionists have advocated the renaissance of a creative, non-Orthodox, religiocultural Jewish center in Israel.

Kaplan called upon world Jewry to reconstitute itself as a "people," because Jews, though well-organized, seem to lack a clearly defined sense of identity. Kaplan saw as the goal of Judaism the formulation of a "Religion of Ethical Nationhood." Thus, the Reconstructionist program addresses itself not merely to the "reconstruction" of Jewish religion but also of the Jewish people.

Rejects "Chosen People" Doctrine

Despite its emphasis on Jewish peoplehood, Reconstructionism has been the only Jewish movement to reject the doctrine of the "chosen people." Most Reconstructionists find the affirmation *asher bachar banu* (that God "has chosen us from among all peoples") to be an intellectually and ethically unacceptable vestige of supernatural traditionalism. As Rabbi Eugene Kohn wrote: "We are constrained to deny that any religious society or community is 'chosen,' for all are created equal–none is chosen, none is rejected." Not only Jews but all people can develop a sense of calling or a vocation. It is in working toward their spiritual self-fulfillment that people realize their fullest potential and help to bring the world closer to the messianic goal. In this connection it is worth observing that the Reconstructionist prayer book changes the word "*goel*" (Redeemer) to "*geulah*" (redemption), rejecting the belief in a personal Messiah and affirming the hope that a concerted effort on the part of all peoples would further the coming of the messianic future.

View of God

It is in the area of theology, or the understanding of God, that Reconstructionist teaching is most unique and controversial.

Reconstructionists believe God is a reality of life, that we can detect the workings and presence of the Divine in our daily lives. But the understanding of God Reconstructionism advocates is devoid of "supernaturalism," of the miraculous and of the anthropomorphic. God is not to be considered a being, but to be sensed or experienced as a "process" or "power" that makes for "salvation"–a word summarizing the various ideals, values, and virtues that represent the highest good for the individual and for the group.

God's reality is manifest in the ongoing workings of the universe, including the human sphere. We experience God as the force or power in the universe that, when mediated through humans, manifests itself as conscience and makes for goodness, justice, kindness, and truth. God is the source of creativity and responsibility impelling us to behave in keeping with the highest moral principles that have been ascribed to divinity since the time of the Hebrew prophets.

Rabbi Harold Schulweis has made a significant contribution to this nonsupernaturalist understanding of God in his writings on "Predicate Theology." He suggests we think of God not as the *subject* of a sentence but as the *predicate*, the action part of the sentence. When we say "God is just," what we really mean is "justice is godly"; when we proclaim "God is love," we mean "love is godly." By means of our attitudes and deeds we either affirm or deny God.

Rabbi Ira Eisenstein explains that this view of religion is naturalistic and humanistic in that it affirms that truth, moral responsibility, and moral courage are not handed down from above. They are built into nature and into the human condition. All of the cosmos is filled with this power for salvation, which the Jewish people has identified as God. It is our task to continually discover and implement this power, to plug into divinity, otherwise God is of little consequence.

Torah and Law

Having explained the Reconstructionist idea of the Jewish people and of God, we come now to the third part of the classical Jewish triad–Torah. To the affirmation of traditional Judaism that "God revealed the Torah to Israel," the Reconstructionist response is that "Israel in its search for God discovers (or unfolds) the Torah." Just as there is no notion of a supernatural God, there is no notion of absolute and final truth revealed by God in the Torah. Reconstructionists view the Torah as a human document and process, recording the wisdom and insights of Israel's ongoing search for God and for purposeful survival.

Reconstructionists believe we must use our modern learning in the sciences and in the humanistic disciplines to help us in our ongoing Torah discovery, while at the same time allowing the wisdom of the Torah to influence our moral choices in all our secular activities. Reconstructionists use the word "Torah" to refer to Jewish civilization in its totality and see the need for each generation to study, interpret, and apply Torah by granting the tradition a *vote* but not a *veto*. In practice most Reconstructionists have a great deal of respect for the tradition and will observe the essentials of *kashrut* as well as

uphold many other ritual practices. But Reconstructionists also feel the responsibility to adapt and change certain traditions of the past and to be innovative whenever the present calls for it.

While retaining the traditional flavor of the synagogue service, emphasizing Hebrew and communal singing, Reconstructionists have revised the prayer book in such areas as the notion of chosenness, the teachings on the Messiah, and the *Musaf* service, to reflect a contemporary spirit and outlook. Instead of praying for the renewal of sacrifices in a restored Temple, Reconstructionists turn the *Musaf* service into a call of awareness and sensitivity toward developing a sacrificial attitude in modern life by giving of ourselves and of our possessions to help those in need.

Reconstructionist services tend to be informal in spirit, and they abound in joyous celebration and singing. Modern poetry and writings are used alongside the classical prayers. Women have full participation and rights in Reconstructionist synagogue and organizational life.

Equal Rights for Women

From its inception in 1968 the Reconstructionist Rabbinical College accepted women and so far has ordained ten women rabbis. Kaplan was among the first rabbinical leaders in this country to call for a women's movement in Judaism. Reconstructionists introduced Bat Mitzvah to American life, have created the earliest covenant-naming ceremonies for girls, and most recently have developed a ritual for an egalitarian and female-initiated *get*, or Jewish divorce. These steps give expression to the movement's philosophy, which takes tradition seriously but is unwilling to be restrained by the dictates of a frozen *halachah* created hundreds of years and even millennia ago.

In the forefront of social action Reconstructionists believe religion's primary function is the improvement of society (*tikun olam*). Some Reconstructionists, such as Rabbi Arthur Gilbert, *alav hashalom*, have achieved renown in the area of interfaith relations. Most students at the Reconstructionist Rabbinical College study for their graduate degrees at university departments of religion, where they interact with students and teachers of the world's major faiths.

Reconstructionists maintain they have combined the best qualities of each of the other movements in Judaism. They accept Orthodoxy's emphasis on a full, affirmative, joyous Judaism; they uphold Conservative Judaism's classical emphasis on Jewish peoplehood; and they advocate Reform Judaism's critical, evolutionary approach to Jewish life.

▪ ABOUT THE AUTHORS ▪

Altshuler, David. Director of the Museum of Jewish Heritage, New York City.

Angel, Marc D. Rabbi of Congregation Shearith Israel, the Spanish and Portuguese Synagogue, New York City.

Bamberger, Bernard J. (ל״ז). Rabbi, scholar, teacher, author. His many works include the commentary on Leviticus in *The Torah: A Modern Commentary*, *Proselytism in the Talmudic Period*, and *The Story of Judaism*.

Bernstein, Louis. President of Religious Zionists of America. Rabbi of Young Israel of Bayside (NY). Faculty member of Yeshiva University.

Bialik, Chaim Nachman (ל״ז). Essayist, storywriter, translator, and editor. Considered the greatest Hebrew poet of modern times. The translation of the excerpt from his "City of Slaughter" is the work of Abraham M. Klein (1903).

Blumberg, Herman J. Rabbi of Temple Shir Tikvah, Wayland, MA.

Chafets, Ze'ev. Managing editor and columnist of *The Jerusalem Report*. One of Israel's leading authors and political commentators. Served as director of Israel's Government Press Office from 1977 until 1982. Author of *Double Vision; Heroes and Hustlers, Hardhats and Holymen: Inside the New Israel; Members of the Tribe; On the Road in Jewish America;* and *Devil's Night*.

Cohen, Martin A. Professor of Jewish History at Hebrew Union College–Jewish Institute of Religion, New York City.

Daum, Annette (ל״ז). Former staff director of the UAHC Committee on Cults and Missionaries, coordinator of the UAHC Department of Interreligious Affairs, and associate director of the Commission on Social Action. Author of numerous books and articles on cults and missionaries.

Dorff, Elliot N. Provost and professor of Philosophy at the University of Judaism in Los Angeles, CA.

Feldman, Abraham (ל״ז). Former rabbi emeritus of Temple Beth Israel, West Hartford, CT. His essay first appeared in a pamphlet, *Reform Judaism: A Guide for Reform Jews*© A. J. Feldman, courtesy Behrman House, Inc.

Fields, Harvey J. Rabbi of Wilshire Boulevard Temple, Los Angeles, CA. Author of *A Torah Commentary for Our Times* (UAHC Press).

Freehof, Solomon B. (ל״ז). Pioneered the introduction of responsa literature to the English-reading American Jewish public in *The Responsa Literature* (1955) and *A Treasury of Responsa* (1963). Later involved himself in the practical work of answering questions sent to him both as chairman of the CCAR Responsa Committee and in his capacity as a rabbi. Has published six volumes of Reform responsa, each with an introduction that analyzes the changing Reform view of *halachah*. The "interview" in this book, prepared by *KP* editor Aron Hirt-Manheimer, is based on the introduction of these volumes.

Gold, Manuel. Rabbi and education specialist for the Board of Jewish Education of Greater New York City.

Gittelsohn, Roland B. Rabbi emeritus of Temple Israel, Boston, MA. Author of numerous books.

Green, Arthur, and **Holtz, Barry W.** Editors and translators. This article is excerpted from *Your Word Is Fire*.

Gruen, George E. Adjunct professor of International Relations at the School of International and Public Affairs, Columbia University, and the Middle East Institute. Director of Israel and Middle East Affairs of the American Jewish Committee from 1962 to 1990.

Gutmann, Joseph. Professor of Art History at Wayne State University, Detroit, MI. Author of numerous books.

Halkin, Hillel. A free-lance writer living in Jerusalem.

Harlow, Jules. Rabbi and director of publications for the Rabbinical Assembly (the association of Conservative rabbis). Editor of the *Mahzor for Rosh Hashanah and Yom Kippur: A Prayer Book for the Days of Awe*.

Hirsch, Richard G. Rabbi and executive director of the World Union for Progressive Judaism.

Hirsh, Norman D. Spiritual leader of Temple Beth Am, Seattle, WA.

About the Authors

Hirt-Manheimer, Aron. Editor of *Reform Judaism*. Trade book editor for the UAHC Press. Editor of *Jagendorf's Foundry* (Harper Collins).

Hoffman, Lawrence A. Rabbi and professor of Liturgy at Hebrew Union College–Jewish Institute of Religion, New York. Author of *Beyond the Text* (Indiana University Press) and *The Art of Public Prayer: Not for Clergy Only* (Pastoral Press, Washington DC).

Kaplan, Allen S. Rabbi and associate director of the New York Federation of Reform Synagogues.

Kleiman, Nancy. A graduate student at Hebrew College, Brookline, MA, and a member of Temple Shalom, Newton, MA.

Korey, William. Director of International Policy Research of B'nai B'rith.

Kroloff, Charles A. Rabbi of Temple Emanu-El, Westfield, NJ.

Kurzweil, Arthur. Writer and lecturer. Editor-in-chief of the Jewish Book Club. The article is reprinted from *Gym Shoes and Irises: Personalized Tzedakah* by Danny Siegel © 1982 Town House Press.

Lipman, Eugene J. Spiritual leader of Temple Sinai, Washington, DC.

Marder, Janet. Associate director of the UAHC Pacific Southwest Council. Former rabbi of Beth Chayim Chadashim, Los Angeles, CA. The article is adapted from one that appeared originally in *The Reconstructionist*.

Mass, Ronald S. Assistant rabbi of Temple Beth El, Spring Valley, NY.

Orlinsky, Harry M. Professor of Bible at the Hebrew Union College–Jewish Institute of Religion, New York. Editor-in-chief of the 1962 translation of the Torah and an internationally noted authority on the Bible.

Patai, Raphael. Author of *The Jewish Mind, The Arab Mind*, and many other books and articles.

Petuchowski, Jakob J. Professor of Judaeo-Christian Studies, Hebrew Union College–Jewish Institute of Religion, Cincinnati, OH.

Rackman, Emanuel. Chancellor of Bar Ilan University, Tel Aviv, Israel.

Raphael, Chaim. Author of *The Walls of Jerusalem, Memoirs of a Special Case*, and *A Feast of History*.

Rossel, Seymour. Director of the Solomon Schechter Academy in Dallas, TX.

Sasso, Dennis C. Rabbi of Congregation Beth-El, Indianapolis, IN, where he serves with his wife, Rabbi Sandy Eisenberg Sasso, constituting the first husband-wife rabbinical team. Graduate of the Reconstructionist Rabbinical College (1974). Past president of the Reconstructionist Rabbinical Association.

Schauss, Amos. Former head cataloger and reference librarian at the Hebrew Union College–Jewish Institute of Religion, Cincinnati, OH.

Schindler, Alexander M. Rabbi and president of the Union of American Hebrew Congregations.

Schnur, Steven. Associate editor of *Reform Judaism*. Author of books for adults and children.

Schulweis, Harold M. Rabbi of Temple Valley Beth Shalom, Encino, CA.

Siegel, Seymour (ל"ז). Former professor of Theology and Ethics at the Jewish Theological Seminary and editor of *Conservative Judaism* and *Jewish Law*.

Spira, Eli. A doctor who visited the Beta-Israel in Ethiopia.

Stern, Chaim. Senior rabbi of Temple Beth El, Chappaqua, NY. Editor of *Gates of Prayer* and *Gates of Repentance*.

Stern, Malcolm H. Rabbi. Director emeritus of the Rabbinic Placement Commission. Genealogist-historian.

Weinberg, Joy. Managing editor of *Reform Judaism*.

Wisse, Ruth R. Professor of Yiddish literature in the Jewish Studies program at McGill University, Montreal, Canada. Author of a book about two of the Yunge (Moishe Leib Halpern and Mani Leib) titled *A Little Love in Big Manhattan*.

Zlotowitz, Bernard M. Rabbi and author of numerous books and articles. Director of the New York Federation of Reform Synagogues.

· INDEX ·